The Hex Files:
the goth bible

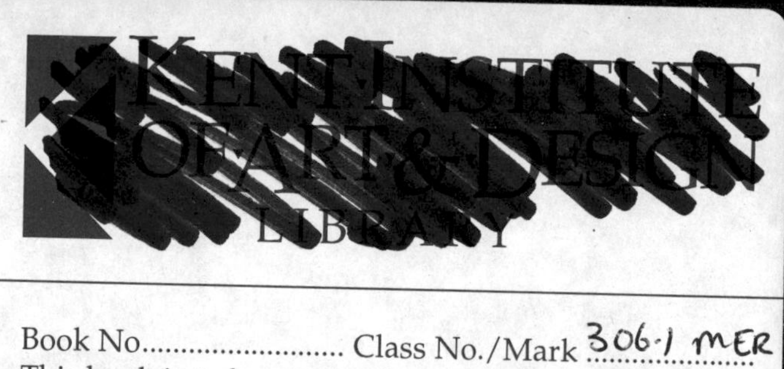

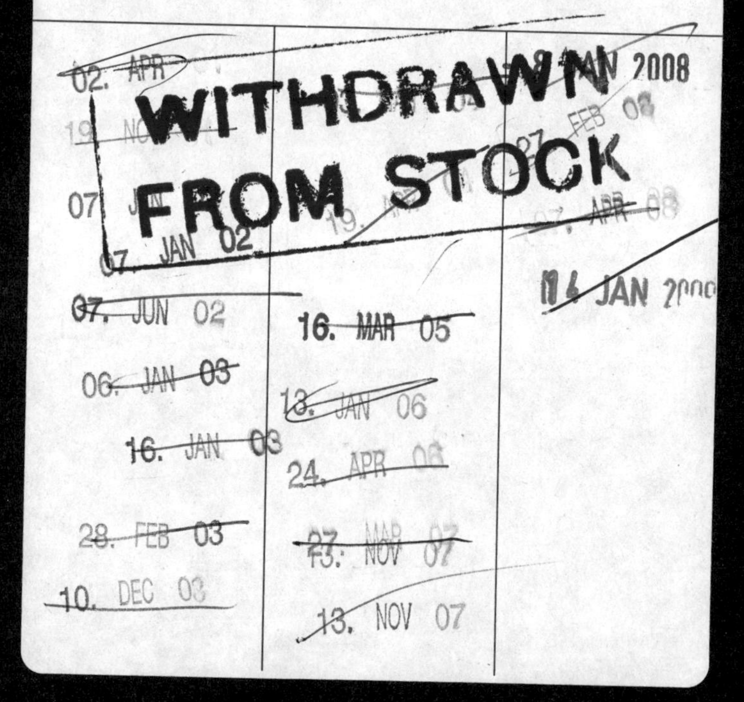

The Hex Files:
the goth bible

Mick Mercer

B T Batsford Ltd, London

First published 1996

Printed and bound by BPC Consumer Books Ltd.
a member of the British Printing Company Ltd.

for the publishers
B T Batsford Ltd
4 Fitzhardinge Street
London W1H 0AH

ISBN 0 7134 8033 5

I WOULD LIKE TO THANK THE FOLLOWING FOR THEIR ASSISTANCE AND INSPIRATION (MENTAL OR MUSICAL) IN CREATING THIS MONSTER. YOUR SECRETS ARE SAFE WITH ME.

ALIEN SEX FIEND, ARTICA, JACKIE ASKEW, ATARAXIA, AZRIEL, T. BAMFORD ESQ., SUE AND GRAHAM BENTLEY, PAUL BUCK, CAF-RIN, CAT FUD, CLAIRE (STIGMATA), NICK COLEMAN, ANDREW COLLINS, GEEZER CONISBEE, STORM CONSTANTINE, CORPUS DELICTI, *DARKWAVE OVER METROPOLIS,* KEV DEMANT, DEMIAN DORRANCE, FRANCIS & KEREN, JOAN A. GEOFFROY, GLORIA VICTIS, THE GREY SEASON, *GRIMOIRE,* INTO THE ABYSS, FRANK JARALEWSKI, BEA JOHN, MICHAEL JOHNSON, KSK, LACRIMOSA, LONDON AFTER MIDNIGHT, *LOWLIFE,* PETRA DE LUCA, TONY MCKORMACK, CHAZ MATTHEWS, ALTHEA MORIN, *NAKED TRUTH,* ALEX NOVAK, SEAN J O'FARRELL, SEAN'S MATE, PATRICK (*PROPAGANDA*), ALEXANDER POHLE, HYACINTHE L. RAVEN, ANGELA READMAN, RICHARD REYNOLDS, GRAEME ROSE, STEFANO SCIACCA, SEX BAT SIMON, SKELETON GIRLS ALICE + ALI, HANNAH STAUNTON, ANNE SUDWORTH, RENE WALZAK, PHILL WHITE, LESLEY WILKINSON, ZAHR, *ZILLO,* ZOMBA.

OUTRO GRAVEYARD SHOTS: JOAN A. GEOFFROY

COVER MODEL: SARAH (SEE ALSO PAGE 84) **COVER PHOTOGRAPHY:** ANDY CAMERON

Introduction

Good evening, ladies and gentlemen.

You're probably wondering why I called you all here. I hadn't exactly expected to be here myself, after the response to my last book. Hatred, anger and feeble death threats go with the territory on Planet Goth but the cretinous nature of the abuse I received was a genuine affront. I'm not facile enough to merely drool over everything, as there's no point. Probably none of us ever have more than a handful of bands we love, a larger group of twenty or so that we devote any real time to and, with the majority, we either ignore them or shake disapproving heads. Some we even come to loathe. And yet when I cover as much as possible in a book, obviously from a personal perspective, people react very weirdly to any criticism. That's pathetic. You don't like everything, so don't expect me to. I found this reaction last time offensive, not because so many disagreed (my writing has never been driven by ego) but for why they were so angry. It became hideous to learn how many felt wholly satisfied with their lot. All was well with the world, apparently, in 92 for the retro-goth, cosseted in their safe, static state; for the vegetative outfits across the globe, particularly Britain, mindlessly spewing out endless Nephilim or Mission impersonations was just what the good doctor ordered. If that was what people wanted, I came to snort, then so be it.

Of course, it isn't that easy to switch off. Squid also like to eat their own sick but nothing says I have to watch. Goth in one way means everything to me, as in other ways, many aspects mean nothing. We all feel that in one way or another. To me Goth hasn't happened yet. Not even now, when things are looking up. This is simply, finally, the interesting phase, where Goth is in orbit, prior to landing. We have the map, the treasure is waiting. Everyone knows that the original Goth spell came through disenchantment with Punk, but couldn't help being influenced by it - hence the Post-Punk tag. Then, through the heavy-handed involvement of major labels in the mid-80's we found ourselves lumbered with Gothic Rock, which crept back to encompass pre-Punk ethics (or lack of them). By the late 80's all the life had been bludgeoned flat, the magic chased away and all that was left were occasional rubies in a tray of diarrhoea. That wasn't Goth, that was nothing, which was why, by 91, when writing the last book I simply put the boot in. I'd had enough.

Surely to God none of you reading this want to see a return to those days? Thankfully, all I hear today is people looking for a more assertive, more healthy scene, with a wider variety of tastes, so can we please accept that the premise inflicted last time round was correct and that much of my optimism now, and a few tacit suggestions, are possibly on the right track? The only alternative is that I must be insane. A woman actually phoned Batsford (publishers of this work) from America and asked

whether there was much point sending the material I'd requested, because I wasn't "very supportive". This must explain why I've spent every last penny I had trying to gather together the information you now fondle. It appears that some people are still too stupid to realise that criticism can be genuinely useful at times. Worse, it suggests that some people may believe it likely that a publisher will rejoice and start dancing on the table the moment a disgruntled writer slopes into their office grunting, "there's this scene I find disgusting. Fancy a book?".

Obviously when I began this book in the latter months of 93 I did so with the intention of helping to kickstart something that, yes, no matter how bizarre some might find it, I actually do care about, but I was also gently amused by the notion that the advancing decay was actually perfect, a fully fitting end if Goth was to finish. Behind the melancholia there always lies more sorrow than tragedy, more truth than drama. That's why Goth is the very essence of dignity. These are the things which have enabled it to become the one movement which celebrates life by never decrying it, by never warping the basic issues. On the one hand it is the most unfashionable form of music in the world, and on the other the only type which continues to develop. (If you wish to get all hyper, it is also the only non-sexist type, the only classifiable, intelligent, wholly self-supporting genre that includes virtually every conceivable element of other musical forms which are acknowledged, harnessed, accommodated but never simply copied.) This is an international music accessible to all - who listen - because it *suggests* that its primary concerns are the past, which everyone finds safe, and the human condition, which everyone finds interesting. That isn't necessarily the case, of course, the past can simply be experience, but the notion is intrinsic.

Goth is about those moments of reflection we all have - that nostalgia borne of emotion, the soundtrack of our own failings. Just as real soul music, the non-synthetic variety, is unparalleled in its ability to portray feelings of the heart, so Goth remains the only form of music at present to put the mind under the microscope. Because it is all based on humanity, the majority of Goth bands, whether they've stopped to consider it at any length, are actually singing *about* something, about subjects, trying to unravel what things mean. If it has a detached feel that cannot be helped, but it is never clinical. I couldn't help being drawn back to the topic, whether it was on its last legs or not.

I grew up on a custom-built council estate with Heathrow Airport at the end of my road, yet just around the corner was the fourth oldest church in Britain. I spent the largest part of my childhood, when I wasn't messing around elsewhere with friends, in delightful solitude, playing in the churchyard, sitting inside yew trees observing the visitors, occasionally tumbling out of them and incurring the wrath of those present. It was a brilliant place to be, as I hope you can tell from these photos. It never occurred

to me that religion had anything to do with the place. You could stroll inside the church, enjoying the smell, stare at the commemorative tomb of the guy who caught Guy Fawkes, even clamber up into the pulpit to examine the contours of the chunky wooden eagle the bible rested on, without feeling pious or moved. You could even sneak out of the house late at night and go up there, because it was always open and pretty scary, which only made you enjoy it all the more when the resultant fears were private. You could annoy the visiting satanists simply be being there and not leaving, especially when you realised what they were up to. You could also easily outrun the vicar, generally a happy fat old prat who didn't mind me wandering around, apart from when I would take airfix soldiers up there, line them up on a tombstone and set fire to their heads. Ah, happy days... This was when I was about eight, by the way. I'm not mental! And there were bats, which was pretty cool. They were all over the place, even in my back garden, strangely attracted for some reason to the door of the outside shed, where they would try and cling on. Until you lit up a cigarette and suddenly off they'd flap.

Why am I telling you this? Read on...

This was the 60's (I'm 38). Educational standards weren't quite as thoughtful as they are now. It took my ultra-shrewd teachers quite some time to realise I was chronically short-sighted, instead of chronically stupid and for two years they simply left me at the back of the class. My mother had taught me the alphabet and the rudiments of reading because the teachers couldn't be bothered. So before I even realised the churchyard existed, with my appalling eyesight to guide me, I would stumble up to my local newsagent, who used to put large revolving metal racks of comics and magazines outside on the street. Never realising these were meant to be paid for I treated this as a library, happily taking my pick of imported American comics and horror magazines through which I gradually began to make sense of language. It's how I learnt to read, by myself. More than anything, something about the horror comics appealed to my unconscious/subconscious. And it still does to this day. Something about thieving does as well, but that's Too Much Information!

So that's why I always wanted what has eventually come in the form of Goth. What's your reason? If you think back, way back beyond the musical, you'll find out what draws you to the subject and when it happened. Why one area moves you more than others. It's always been the only scene you can come to via things other than music. That's why you never totally lose sight of it, interest or hope. I have always felt sceptical of ostensibly sensible people I've known who clearly think you graduate from Indie music to Classical somewhere during life, where the only alternative might be the purgatory of MOR. I'm assuming that through Goth its own sub-strata of classical would appear anyway, and in certain cases I think it is already happening. These things take time.

You maybe thought I was rambling earlier but not so. The reason I wanted to do a book like this was because the more people realise about what is available in the world, the more open-minded they become and the more they sense the possibilities, the excitement builds and the more successful everything becomes as a result. The saddest thing is that most Goths I talk to, or who write to me, are brilliant. The sad Neffs and Sisters obsessives aren't. They're the new cider punks of this age. They pretty much predate crusties when you think about it. The real Goths still surge with power and pride over the art, literature and the effects of the music. They want to experience everything and... there was nothing there for them. It was no good expecting the music press to cover Goth, because they are governed by common sense. If nothing's happening, why should they? Up until 95 fanzine writers in this country put the bands to shame with their enthusiasm. So this book is all about Hex-communication.

I know that all the best stuff exists outside of the UK and we're nowhere near getting our own Ataraxia, London After Midnight or Sopor Aeternus, but things began to change throughout 95, thanks mainly to Trev up at Nightbreed, with both his import sensibilities and Midnight Configuration. It wasn't just him, obviously, but in a way this was the catalyst required that helped sluice out the rotting. This doesn't mean that outside of the blighted UK things are always walking talking orgasms. Far from it. I hear a lot about the posier end of the American scene and the spurious in-fighting, perhaps best summed up by a man who calls himself The Cold, who you'll discover in the American section. He came to Goth, optimistically, via the vampire route.

"I inevitably learned some of the positive and many of the negative points across the spectrum of people that made up the genre... the most dispiriting of which was the discovery of the large numbers of arrogant, stuck-up, fashion-obsessed vermin whose sole purpose seemed to be centred on looking down upon people such as myself for not owning any Bauhaus albums, or not having over-dyed black hair. I naturally felt more comfortable in leaning towards the more dismal side of the genre and associated myself only with the cemetery-dwelling fiends, with whom I knew my amount of 'gothic knowledge' didn't matter. And, in finding the more modern, ethereal-gloom/darkwave music's a bit more suitable to my personality than the classic rock-orientated sound, I immersed myself. Being a musician, I was filled with creative drive and inspiration."

And that, young rascals, is the point, is it not? That we need the full range. These are our ghosts. We must look after them. In case you think I'm being suspiciously pleasant here, rest assured that If they're lowering standards, we must disown them.

If you become confused by my approach I don't actually care what you think. It isn't important, and I mean that literally, not smugly. It is an irrelevance why I write what I write, or how. To some of you, the added Fetish, Pagan and Vampire contents, none of which interest me, may seem like a strange mixture but these are all relevant now. A lot of people have made it quite clear they want to know more, so they're in. If you hate the idea, that's your problem. This particular book is perhaps unusual in that it is designed to be a practical aid, as well as providing as good a guide to what is out there as I have been able to track down. In doing so I was limited by time and money and there will always be a percentage of people who don't, for a variety of reasons, respond to letters. In certain cases you only have addresses to go on. Most of them will be there, ready to welcome you with open arms. Only a tiny percentage may have moved on, or been locked up.

Please excuse the screeching of chalk on this metaphorical blackboard, as I scrawl the following equation: Bands + Fanzines = Coverage. Easy. What comes next?

Coverage + Goth Participation = MC^2

You hungry bastards, this book is for you, at a time when Goth stands at an exciting, pivotal moment. It has happily reached the stage whereby it can't be stopped. It may not get massive quickly, as before, but it will infiltrate other areas, consistently reaching a wider audience, while other scenes live out their three-year life spans. For its own health and sense of development it needs your input. Make the most of this book by *using* it. That is its purpose.

See you in three years.

1

2

3

Australia

Bands

BIG ELECTRIC CAT Paul Sadler - vocals/guitar, Deborah Denton - keybds/prog./vocals, David Block - bass, Dr Ruth - drums. Formed 91, taking name from Philip K Dickhead novel. Debut release, 'Suspira' MC, comprehensively overshadowed by luxuriant 'Dreams Of A Mad King' CD. Since then (94?), things stalling somewhat. PO Box 96, Cremorne Junction, NSW 2090.

CLOWNS SMILING BACKWARDS PO Box 1064, Collingwood, Victoria 3066.

CRIMSON BOY 604 Canning St, North Carlton, Victoria 3054.

DARKNESS VISIBLE David - bass, Tina - guitar, Cat - keybds. Kristian and Ben Gardiner do other things. Formed by "five darkened beings" in July 94. Aug 94 - they don't mess around! - the song 'Darkness Visible' is released and squeezed onto the Left As Sinister compilation 'Candles And Intrigue'. Future plans are "to forge ahead". Evidently, there's a big market for facsimile skulls we know very little about. David Black, 8/4 Fiona Court, St. Kilda, Victoria 3182.

DISCORDIA Greg, James, Sade, Jim and Fee. After releasing the intense, horrible 'Living Dead' there's no stopping them as one and all rampage merrily through sewers of their own devising. According to them, however, they're Post-Industrial Neo-Techno Transcendental Mind-Fuck Music. (Fax (03) 9826 8719)

DOG MACHINE Originally just the duo of Kraig Wilson and Mark, formed late 92 and made their first recording mark with a cover of 'The Sound Of Music', after which things could only improve. Now rapidly maturing with neat usage of infernal noise, their ragged-edged sounds are rumoured to be topped off by the vocals of Sade. GPO Box 2704, Brisbane, QLD 4001.

THE EBON BINDINGS Cathy - vocals, Nick - bass, Michael - guitar, Murdoch Noise - drums, Chris - guitar. Five piece pumping psychedelic sounds. Chris Adams, 26 Lutwyche Street, Petrie Tce, QLD 4000.

EDEN Sean Bowley - guitars/vocals, Tracey Ellerton - guitars, Ewan McArthur - bass, Peter Barrett - drums. Like a big fat Deadcandance. Two albums 'Fire And Rain', 'Gateway To The Mysteries'. PO Box 683, South Yarra, Melbourne 3141.

THE HOUR PO Box 704, Ringwood, Victoria 3134.

IKON Michael Carrodus - vocals, Chris McCarter - guitar/keybds/drums, Dino Molinaro - bass. Formed Sept 91 and getting better all the time. Very Goth in its own personal viewpoint but also hauling onboard the post-Joy Div/RLYL feel. 'The Echoes Of Silence' and 'In The Shadow Of The Angel' CDs and 'In A Lonely Place' MCD. Unit 3/7 Kent Street, Ascot Vale, Victoria 3031.

IN SECT PO Box 340, Clifton Hill, Victoria 3068.

KISMET Gorazd - guitar, John Hrup - vocals, P. Kazanovski - drums and Metodi Kundevski - bass. Weird and interesting a great many right now, their debut 'Dormant Dire' CD can't hide their ambition to truly be "post-darkwave, a neo-futuristic group", influenced by Balkan/Macedonian music and early 80's British darkwave. You can't ignore a band who describe their lyrics as "alphabetical anvils". PO Box 1646, South Preston, Vic 3071.

ALAN LAMB Cricketer turned Ambient-Experimental expert? Doh! PO Box 22, Glen Waverley, Victoria 3150.

LEMON AVENUE Neven - guitar, Valerios - bass and Sloth - drums. Formed 89. 'Axeman' 7", highly

1 BIG ELECTRIC CAT 2 DARKNESS VISIBLE 3 DISCORDIA
4 DOG MACHINE 5 IKON 6 NETE

PHOTO: SARAH GRAVES

4

5

acclaimed 'Love And Necromancy' album (92) but not much since apart, from a 'Cancer Come Cancer' single. c/o Left As In Sinister.

LOVE LIES BLEEDING PO Box 390, Niddrie, Victoria 3042.

MERIDIAN Karl Zeleny - guitar/keybds, Peter Zantey - drums, David Wilkinson - vocals/keybds/prog. Formed mid-May 94. (Honestly, can't they be more precise?!) Cool post-Sisters big sound. 'Surreal Embrace' demo (Aug 94). David sings as if balancing a heavy book on his head, all from the bottom of his throat, which is a shame because it sounds too affected and ruins some rare lyrical dexterity. 'Sundown Empire' CD (May 95), re-released 96 with four extra tracks and new artwork, mainly because their European label, Germany's Nyctalopia, has collapsed. PO Box 198, Camperdown, NSW 2050. (Fax: 001161 (0) 2 556 2416)

NETE Begun in 92 as a solo project of Wayne, intending to be a guitar/Industrial thing but with the appearance of Clinton on bass it became less austere. Last I heard they were a three piece with Wayne singing and they've a meticulously depressing pop edge. PO Box 263, Melton 3337, Victoria.

ORCHESTRA INFERNALE Dark Ambient with Industrial guts. Offshoot of metal band Beastial War Lust. That should give you an idea. 108 Bernard Street, Cheltenham, Victoria 3192.

OSTIA Kylie - vocals/keybds, Anthony - bass/drum prog., Justin - guitar, Pamela - cello. 92 beginnings, under the boring name of Figurehead, this trio have bloomed to become what I would demurely label Australia's Greatest New Band. 'Ostia' and 'The Euphony Of Turmoil' demos, followed by the frisky 'R2-Detox' MCD are all the evidence you require. It's pop Jim, but not as you'd know it, unless you

6

9 10

7

8

PHOTO: JASON COUCH

want the old mixed with a giddy new horizon. PO Box 106, Ashgrove, QLD 4060 is the last address I have but these people move around a lot, forever one step ahead of grieving landlords, so if you don't get an immediate reply try them via *Dark Angel*, who love them dearly. Or be hopelessly modern. (Net - http://student.uq.edu.au/-s326134/ostia.html) (e-mail: A. Greenhill@hum.gu.edu.au)

PSYCHE-CARNI PO Box 126, Balaclava, Victoria 3183.

RECKONING "Powerful, pretty, intense and emotive," according to Azriel, which suggests the dreamier side of things. Via *Dark Angel*. (See how casually I unload responsibility? I'm wonderful.)

THE REDRESSER PO Box 126, Balaclava, Victoria 3183.

PROFESSOR RICHMAN Dark Ambient.

SCREAMWORLD Metal (sluggish riffs) Goth band who separated rather than permanently dissolved, as things currently stand. However, the two main protagonists, Stephen Harris and Debbie Mansfield, currently operate as Troll, itself the name of a 95 Screamworld demo. Stephen also saw fit to include a bit of his fetish 'artwork' which I hope he won't repeat.

SHINJUKU THIEF Described by some as a Goth Sabbath. Why? PO Box 72, Glen Waverley 3150.

SICKMAN I don't have an address for this bunch of miscreants but Paul, J and Neil have allowed Sade to front them in his own distinct way. It may even be obligatory by now.

SLAM CAM 14 Long Street, Elsternwick, Victoria 3162.

11

7 OSTIA 8 SADE 9 SCREAMWORLD 10 SUBTEFUGE 11 TROLL
12 *CROWN OF THORNS* EDITOR, DONNA

12

SLOW PULSE ORCHESTRA 604 Canning Street, North Carlton, Victoria 3054.

SPINE OF GOD "Spine Of God is one person, Sade!" states Sade, one person. "Live, Spine Of God consist of live drums, bass, guitar and vocals." Spine Of God is evidently more than one person! Bludgeoning walls of distorted debauchery, this is New Age Industrial with Fetishistic interference. There's a CD coming, 'Noir', described as "a soundtrack to a movie of my mind". (Be *very* afraid.) PO Box 383, Richmond, Victoria 3121.

SUBTEFUGE Clifford Ennis - vocals/bass/drum prog. and Rick Mullen - guitars/keybds/prog. Formed late 91. Heartland offered them a deal, resulting in the 'Darkland Awakening' CD. Another chiming, climbing talent. PO Box 18086, Collins Street East, Melbourne, Victoria 3000.

T.C.H. 3/213 Dandenong Rd, Windsor, Victoria 3181.

TREASURE 342 Gilles St, Adelaide, 5000, South Australia.

TROLL PO Box 775, Petersham, NSW 2049.

Fanzines

A.T.H. K Zeleny, PO Box 652, Newtown , NSW 2042.

THE BLOOD MOON Sarah, 7a Pinner Crt, Kingsley 6026, Perth.

BLOODSONGS Horror type stuff. PO Box 7545, St Kilda Rd, Melbourne, Victoria, 3004.

CROWN OF THORNS New fanzine by Donna Cooper, also covering electronic, Industrial and experimental sounds. Bigger in size than *Ex Cathedra*, slightly less formularised, and maybe more accessible. PO Box 600, Annerley QLD 4103.

CYBERCORE ZINE PO BOx 1082, Nth. Fitzroy, Victoria, 3068.

CYBORNETIC MASTURBATION "Keep masturbating!" orders our old chum Sade at the top of his voice. (Even in the most academic of libraries.) As strange as the man himself, this seeps, drips and stinks of life. It's full of the usual piercing, toilet 'n' toys type stuff and bands called Nailbomb. Clearly, an acquired taste, through broken teeth. PO Box 2005, East Hampton, Vic 3188.

DARK ANGEL Not just the greatest fanzine in Australia, but the best underground magazine in the world, if you'll pardon my opinion. From little acorns - hardly the best printing surface - this has developed, from a naive A5 thing, *Samhain*, into a remarkably confident, yet restless epic. Beautifully produced, shot through with spirit it is somehow reckless in its disregard for nerves. It just charges onwards... and that's what we want. Only the special deserve inclusion. Azriel - Editorex - knows what she's doing, although how she finds the time to do it all staggers me. I suspect she is altering time, bending the elements to her will. Apparently *DA* shares its home with Punctured Lung Records, *Cybornetic Masturbation* zine, the band Discordia and If? Records. It's a bit claustrophobic in this shoebox they call home but the ideas seethe around and you would have to be completely dolt-like not to get this whenever you see it. It's even been free-thinking enough to include indie. (Would that you could ever say the same for indie mags, eh?) PO Box 383, Richmond, Victoria, 3121.
(Fax: 61-3-9578-0344) (e-mail: dangel@iaccess.com.au) (WWW site: http://www.realtime.net/arc/arc.htm)

13 *DARK ANGEL* EDITORIAL TEAM
15 FALOR PATHOS AND MORELLA EASTGATE

DARKWAVE OVER METROPOLIS I sense that this is an incredible magazine in the making and I've only seen a cover, which I thank them for as it inspired the cover of this book. A quarterly A5-ish Goth/Industrial magazine, it has exceptional quality in its printing standards. It also claims to be the only pure Goth/Ind. mag with national distribution left in the country. Er...see above? The strangely named Editor - Booker! - has a background in advertising and graphic design which explains why it looks gorgeous. He is also partner in something called Dominion, a Goth/Industrial centre with provides art displays, S/M, vampire, film, poetry or manga nights and masquerades. All absolutely essential. PO Box 7014, Shenton Park, Western Australia 6008. (Fax: +61 (0)9 221 4218) (e-mail: gorgon@collective.com.au)

DARK WORLDE Includes Melbourne Horror Society Newsletter. Dreadmaster, PO Box 512, Bacchus Marsh, Vic 3340.

EX CATHEDRA Ex-*A.T.H.*, a mag with the sort of production qualities that make you sick! Covering everything, doing it well with stunning, starkly beautiful visuals. PO Box 680 Newtown, NSW 2024. (Fax: 61-2-516-2390)

FATAL VISION Horror mag. PO Box 113, Northcote, Victoria, 3070.

FLEXIBLE HEAD Strangely impressive monthly mag which is free. Mainly indie but they will cover anything which proves itself worthy. Heath, 75 Gladstone Avenue, South Perth, W.A. 6151.

FRESH BLOOD X. Christidis, 7/141 Seventh Avenue, Inglewood, WA 6052.

MORTAL THOUGHTS Small, passionate, highly detailed. They're trying hard and this could easily get up there with the best of them as they've made big steps very swiftly. PO Box 393, Whitfords, 6025, Western Australia.

NIGHTSHADES New Gothic writing anthology. Contributions welcome. PO Box 142, Kensington NSW 2033.

THE PENTACLE Sin, PO Box 9166, Manly, QLD 4179.

SKINNED ALIVE Includes serial killers/ censorship/ general nutters mag. Rod Williams, PO Box 166, Roma Street, Brisbane, QLD 4003.

T.O.A.N. (Tales Of a Nomad) Amusing might be the word if it wasn't for the Editor's insistence of including readers' jokes that show a loathsome homophobic bias. Strange, as the rest of the zine is basic but okay. PO Box 775 Petersham NSW 2049.

Other sources

AUSTRALIAN HORROR SOCIETY PO Box 7530, St Kilda Road, Melbourne, Victoria 3004.

AUSTRALIAN GENERAL WEBSITE (http://wonderland.apana.org.au/-starfish/index.html)

JOSH BAKER Journalist. 13 Moorina St, Mundingburra, Townsville, Nth QLD 4812.

BLOOD FROM STONE Gothic mail order. SPO Box 50, Erskinville, NSW 2043.

THE CARPATHIAN MAGISTRATUS SOCIETY Run by Morella Eastgate, they do an excellent monthly newsletter and organise suspiciously enjoyable events. Velvet Web, Shop 12, Level 1 Mayfair Arcade, Adelaide Street, Brisbane, QLD 4000.

16

17

18

JASON COUCH *Dark Angel* photographer. Has photographs formerly known as prints for sale. PO Box 383, Richmond, Victoria, Australia 3121.

DARK OBSESSION Renaissance and Gothic fashion. 31, Valley Plaza, Fortitude Valley.

DEMOGORGON DISTRIBUTORS Gothic and Industrial releases welcome, a useful contact for people wishing to invade Australia. Run by Heartland Records, it already has over 2,000 titles. PO Box 13047, Law Courts P.O., Melbourne, Victoria 3000. (Fax: 001161 (0) 3 9329 6163).

DUDE N DUDETTES Disgraceful t-shirts. PO Box 775, Petersham, NSW 2049.

HEARTLAND Record Shop. Paul Cook, 61 Peel Street, Melbourne West, Vic 3003. (Fax: 03 9329 6163)

HELLFIRE EMPORIUM Fetish palace. 51 Bourke St, Melbourne.

THE HUB NEWSLETTER Contact point for different traditions. Peaceful Spirit Enterprises, PO Box 85, North Richmond, NSW 2754.

IRON IN THE SOUL "Gothic & Groovy Homewares." Shop 4, Elizabeth St Arcade, Brisbane 4000.

JANNIS Berlin designer now resident in Sydney. Individually designed jewellery, as well as piercing jewellery, chastity belts, paintings, sculptures and pottery. 547 Bourke St, Surrey Hills. [(02) 361 5913]

KOLLEKTIV Label. 75 Prince Charles Rd, Frenchs Forest, NSW 2086.

LEFT AS IN SINISTER Label, which has released Lemon Avenue, Picturehouse, Bender, Fools Circus and the 'Candles & Intrigue' compilation, but moreover a distribution service, which was the first in Australia. PO Box 59, Sylvania Waters, NSW 2224.

DEBBIE MANSFIELD Shouty vocalist from Screamworld and Troll shows distinct promise with her supernatural writing. She's good. PO Box 775, Petersham, NSW 2049.

WARREN MEAD Photographer of Gothic scenes in Australia. You may have seen some of his awesome colour covers for *Dark Angel*. (Phone 03-9527-6221).

MELBOURNE HORROR SOCIETY Try contacting through *Bloodsongs* magazine. Meets at the Maori Chief Hotel first Thursday every month.

MISSING LINK Record Shop. 262 Flinders Lane, Melbourne, Vic 3000.

MOONLIGHT PUBLISHING Aspiring authors might like to contact these as they allow knowledgeable folk to write about various musical subjects. I have seen Michael Finnriorden's somewhat scrambled Punk, Goth, Industrial and Darkwave history of Melbourne. The layouts are clear, the tone concise, typos abound. Moonlight offers slim tomes (some very slim, the Australian Reggae Discography weighing in at four pages!) on most genres. PO Box 5, Golden Square 3555.

MORTISHA'S Gothic and Victoriana but fashion back as far as medieval. Shop 24 , Royal Arcade, Melbourne 3000. [(03) 654 1586].

OCHRE CLOTHING 10 Elizabeth Arcade, 99 Elizabeth Street, Brisbane 4000.

PADDLES The mag you've all (not just Amps) been waiting for, covering all manner of fetish-related

16 CARPATHIAN MAGISTRATUS VAMPYRE SOCIETY PARTY 17 DEBORAH L. MANSFIELD
18 SACRAMENT 19 VELVET WEB

activity, from spanking to flagellation, rubber, leather, cp and even - glory of glories - enemas! Clare Gordon, PO Box 524, Milsons Point, NSW 2061.

PERIL 305 Music/accessories shop. 305 Swanston Walk, Melbourne, Victoria 3000.

PHANTOM RECORDS Shop. 375 Pitt Street, Sydney, PO Box A566, Sydney South, NSW 2000.

POLYESTER RECORDS Shop. (Equally interesting bookshop at 330 Brunswick.) 387 Brunswick St, Fitzroy 3065.

POLYMORPH Body piercing at the 'Body Art Gallery' along with tattoos, fetish wear, books. 82 Enmore Rd, Newtown, NSW 2042.

PORTAL TALK Pagan stuff. PO Box 970, Dickerson, ACT602.

POSSESSION Sexy stuff, Victoriana and lesser 'vintage' (30's-50's). 321 Crown St, Surrey Hills, Sydney.

RETALIATION PO Box 379, Brunswick, Victoria, 3065.

SACRAMENT Radio show offering everything you live for. Leigh, c/o RRR, PO Box 644, Gladesville 2111.

SHADOWPLAY Pagan magazine. PO Box 343, Petersham, NSW 2049.

SYDNEY BISEXUAL PAGANS (Phone 360-9104)

VAMPIRE LEGION PO Box 4202, Melbourne Post Office, Victoria 3052.

VELVET WEB Run by designer Becky Mee this is the shop which holds her own line of clothing plus records and stuff - and from here emanates the Carpathian Magistratus thing. Her clothes cover all eras, but mainly Middle Ages, Elizabethan, Renaissance and Victorian. Weird thing is... some Goths have begun carrying whittled sticks around with crystals attached to the top - like foppish walking canes. Ostensibly this sounds okay until you realise they cost a lot and anyone half sensible would go to an auction room and pick up genuine Victorian silver topped canes or even - whisper it - swordsticks - for a fraction of the cost because they're hardly in demand from other parts of society. Starfish who runs this is also a mighty contributor to the *Dark Angel*. Room 12, Level 1, Mayfair Arcade, Adelaide St, Brisbane, Qld 4000. (e-mail: starfish@wonderland.apana.org.au)

WEB OF WYRD Something weird? PO Box A486, Sydney South, NSW 2000.

XANTHI CHRISTIDIS Poet. 7/71 Fourth Avenue, Mt Lawley, WA 6050.

Austria

AORTA Seriously interesting occult fanzine in both Austrian and English. Spartan layout, beautiful quality and always thought-provoking. (Be warned, some German occult or Pagan mags nosedive intentionally into serious Nazi excrement. Find a decent mag and ask which ones to avoid.) Petak, Postfach 778, 1011 Vienna.

ANUBIS Occult mag. Postfach 45, 1203 Vienna.

CHELSEA CHRONICLE Fanzine. Piartstengasse 1, 1080 Vienna.

KISS THE BLADE Florian Neyer - bass, Andreas Hansbacher - guitars, Paul Cuska - vocals/prog.

Fantastically bruising sound and with more than a few memorable melodic twists inside the madness. A tendency on the demos ('KTB', 'Day X') to plunder the past rather than exploring their own identity but overall this is sterling stuff. 'Walk The Knife's Edge' CD. Paul Cuska, Leopoldstr. 16, 6020 Innsbruck.

NOCTURNE This is a sweet little A5 zine dedicated solely to the Banshees for any still interested. Josef Reid, Strindbergasse 2/16/19, 1110 Vienna.

PROJECT EARTH LINK Spacy-Earthy matters. Oliver Stummer, Komodiengasse 3/24, 1020 Vienna.

STUDIO GUM Fetish clothes. Heavy. Scholgasse 11, A-1020 Vienna.

TROST Tape label. Andreas Hollering, Schonborngasse 16/6, 1080 Vienna.

UNKENRUFE Tape label/distribution service. Wolfgang Paster, Peilstein 98, A-4513.

VISCERAL EVISCERATION Band. Dominick Lirsch, Posthorngasse 3/13, 1030 Vienna.

WONDERLAND AUSTRIA This is the Austrian wing of the German label Alice In... and their Wonderland mail order service includes tons of things. Daniel Weber and Gaby Haudek, Herzgasse 57/22, 1100 Vienna.

Belgium

Bands

BLOK 57 Dirk Ivens and Guy Van Mieghem offer weird dark dancy Industrial menu. 'Blok 57' CD on Cleopatra.

THE BREATH OF LIFE Isabelle Dekeyser - vocals, Philippe Mauroy - guitar, Bonoit Sokay - bass, Giovanni Bortolin - keybds/sax. Formed 89. First release 10 track eponymously titled MC, in Sept 90, and with that off they went touring, notably Czechoslovakia, which led to the 'Live In Praha 92' album, alongside their studio debut 'Painful Insanity'. In 93 the second studio album, 'Taste Of Sorrow' earned them even more admirers after a year spent playing everywhere. Their sound, easily compared to a modern Ghost Dance crossed with some of the brighter elements of late 80's Banshees, is one of subtle power and emotionally charged confusion. By 94 they were sharing stages with the likes of Love Like Blood and The Cocteau Twins. Their third album 'Lost Children' came out in 95, although there was a 'Shining' EP between the two. Latest CD - 'Taste Of Sorrow'. They now have their own label, Magic Language Records, but are licensed to Hall Of Sermon. Info/Merchandise: Patrick Hendrix, Baty du Grand Bernard, B-1470 Baisy-Thy. (Fax: +32-67.77.37.63).

21 THE BREATH OF LIFE, SEEN HERE RUNNING THE WORLD'S LEAST SUCCESSFUL CAFE. 22 SWAN DEATH

DE VOLANGES A favourite of *Fight Amnesia*. Powerful and interesting female-led band with a strong line in melodic power and arresting atmosphere. Roxane, BP 4, B-7061 Casteau.

GOYASNADA A collective of Goth players, some of them from Brain Damage And Death (split 92) who have resurfaced now under the name of K-Oz Office. These men have been in the scene since 87 and cannot be stopped, so you'll find something to enjoy on their 'Rage Rage Rage' CD. Delvaus Floch, Av de l'Aulne 93 bte 29, 1180 Brussels.

SIN OF SINS Christian Death meets Madre Del Vizio. 'Demo' demo available. Schildersstraat 27A, 2000 Antwerp.

SWAN DEATH Heidi Kanters - synth/piano/harpsichord/organ/vocals, Paternot Gaëtan - vocals/guitar/synth/piano/strings/drums, Logick Ives - bass, Gaij M - alto and violin. Formed 89 under original name of Actuaries Table. 'Swan Death' CD (93), 'Endless...a means to an end' CD (95). 'Black Wolf, Somewhere, Something More' CD planned for 96, and a five song video available. A quixotic blend of rarified musical atmospheres. Swan Death Paternot, Av. 9 Provinces, 36, Box 17/1, 1083 Brussels.

THIS VALE OF TEARS Simons T, Willem Van Laerstraat 6, 2600.

THE TREES Stephan Fievez, Av. St Hubert 30, 7090 Hennyeres.

ZYON Merrill, Beekstraat 25, 8800 Roeselare.

Fanzines/Other sources

ARTROCK Promoter. 7 Rue de Croisons, 7750 Amougies.

BOOGIE-CD-STORE If you want your stuff distributed in Belgium this is the place to start! Retail/wholesale/mail order for Gothic-Industrial-Electro. Predikherenstraat 11, 8000 Brugge.

BOUTIQUE MINUIT Fetish fashion. 60 Galerie Du Centre, 1000 Brussels.

BREAK THE CHAIN Zine/News service. Louis Sylvie, 5 rue du Pond du Bois, 5170 Bois Villers.

CASSETTE CASSE-TETE Tapezine. Etienne Verenaeve (Le vere), Av. Jean Hermant 5, B-11 Rixensart.

CCP Label. Lessingstr. 8, 4020 Linz.

LA CHRYSALIDE DE L'ANGE Louis Sylvie's fanzine which concentrates on more Goth and Noisy stuff than the traditional Belgium love of electronics. Etienne Verenaeve (Le vere), Av. Jean Hermant 5, B-11 Rixensart.

COLD DEPRESSION Interesting item containing the themes of death, religion, suicide and such, in poetry and fiction. Vierlindenstraat 18, 8710 Wielsbeke.

DARK ENTRIES Goth zine written all in Dutch. PO Box 93, 9100 Sint-Niklaas.

DIODE ELECTROSIDE (Radio - Rivsa FM) c/o Hautot Francois, Boulevard Des Archers JS, B. 1400 Nivelles.

DROWNING MAN Fanzine. Frederic Cosme, 94 Rue du Monument, 5544 Agimont.

ESCAPE 3 TAPES Cassette label. P. Stevens, PO Box 52, 2070 Zwijndrechi.

FOOL'S PARADISE Tapezine. Robin T. Chuter,

23

Sneppenlaan 5, 3080 Tervuren.

BERNARD HEBLENNE Promoter and good contact for bands. Place Cockerill 16, 4000 Liege.

SYLVAIN HENNIN Tape compilations. 23 Cite Henri, Soyer, 7610, Rumes.

INSANE MUSIC Tape label. Alain Neffe, 2 Grand Rue, 6190 Trazegnies.

THE INVITATION Reliable gig promoter. Alain Meulebrouck, Oostrozebekestraat 140, 8760 Meulebeke.

MILLE & UNE NUITS Fetish clothes. Rue du Meridien 4 , 1030 Brussels.

NOYADE MECHANIQUE Magazine. 74/2 Av. Duceptiaux, 1060 Brussels.

PANGEA Fanzine. Wim Neefs, E. Ruelensvest 5, 3001.

RENDEZVOUS Massive S/M mag photo-based. Chaus Business, 7 rue de l'Eglise, 1060 Brussels.

RITUAL Fanzine. Marc Haleng, Rue Delsupexhe 71, 4040 Herstal.

SECRET I suppose I have to declare my particular interest in the Fetish scene here. I find it all hilarious. There, that wasn't too difficult. True, leather looks cool and rubber/latex has a visually energising dynamic all of its own but the idea people find the items in the photos more interesting than the people is all a bit too weird. Being appreciably less (means more) than Neanderthal I also realise what people see in it and recognise the quality of what exists inside it - the imagination and the dedication of those involved. *Secret* is easily one of the most beautiful magazines I have ever seen. Printed on premier glossy paper, laid out with a delightful simplicity, featuring stunning photography, it is everything anybody connected with the fetish scene could possibly want and makes *Skin Two* look tacky. Winning the Nobel Prize for Modesty, its Editor claims it's a fanzine! *Secret* is, in essence, a work of art. It's also a hoot. I can't help but laugh like a drain when I see people in rubber body suits, with all the grace of frogmen, wearing gasmasks, posing in what is supposed to be an alluring manner! *That's* comedy! In the issue I saw there was even a guy in his bath wearing a rubber floatation suit you'd use in a sea rescue. Marvellous. The sexual element is always the thing that lets these mags down because they're trying to convey the delight that their furtive world provides them with. Obviously. It's far better to have disturbing Pan-like imagery (spooky face and horns) but most mags, unlike *Secret*, prefer something like a manky early 80's rock vid. Still, you pays your money and... I don't. BP 1400, 1000 Brussels 1.

SENTIMENT MODERNE Fetish clothes. PO Box 443, 1000 Brussels 1.

SHIVER RECORDS Label. Hans De Wyngaert, Amerstraat 112, 3200 Aarschot.

SIDE-LINE Fanzine. Dolimont Seba, 86 Rue des 7 Petites, 6120 Nalinnes.

STUDIO NEBRASKA Label. Van Aelst, PB 152, 2000 Antwerpen 1.

TALONS AIGUILLES Magazine with interview with dominatrixes. Presage Parallele, BP 1635, 1000 Bruxelles 1.

TANZ DER ROSEN Goth-Industrial-Dark-Techno-Occult fanzine. G. Roelandt, Reynaertpark 204, B-9100 Sint-Niklaas.

TRAFIC INFLUENCE Goth-Electro-Art-Fashion zine. Didier Delhez, Rue Sohet 27, 4000 Liege.

3 RIO ART Fanzine. Julisandillenstraat 22, 2018 Antwerp.

UNDER THE FLAG Fanzine. Didier Delhez/UTF, 4 Rue St Veronique, 4000 Liege.

Brazil

YGGDRASIL Radio Vropeco. 105.7FM Thursdays. Stefan Panis, Vrasenestraat 11, B-9120 Beveren.

Bulgaria

PATHOLOGICAL FEAST A fanzine of sorts, I think. It's certainly an art project and Borislav is involved with tape distribution, including the local band Cloaca. Borislav Arapchev, Kometa 11, Plovdiv 4004.

Canada

ALL DRACULA'S CHILDREN Bi-monthly journal for vampires. 305 11th Avenue South, Cranbrook BC, V1C 2P7.

AMONG THE RUINS Nice fanzine, heartily recommended by Mistress McCutcheon. 1100 Bloor St. W. #50, M6H 1M8 Toronto, Ontario.

ANTONELLA Gothic craftsperson. 3380 South Millway #16, Mississauga, Ontario L5L 3L8.

THE BLADE & THE CHALICE Pagan mag. PO Box 10131, Adelaide St Stn, Toronto.

BOUDOIR NOIR Mag for weird nightlife. Box 5, Station F, Toronto, Ontario M4Y 2L4.

CABAL Artist. 9759 Avenue Peloquin, Montreal, Quebec, H2C 2JS.

FACTORIA Andrew Amy, 3139 Duchess Ave, North Vancouver, B.C. V7K3B7.

THE GOTHIC SOCIETY OF CANADA See: Siren.

LONDON LIFE LEAGUE Corsetry. PO Box 1319, Place Bonaventure, Montreal H5A 1H1.

MAGICKAL VAMPIRE COVEN R.L.Robert, The Cillei Order, PO Box 358 Succ. St Hubert, QC, Canada J3Y 5T3.

THE NINTH WAVE Fanzine. 80-689 Queen Street West, Toronto, Ontario M6J 1E6.

NORTHBOUND LEATHER 19 Saint Nicholas Street, Ontario, Ontario M4Y 1W5.

SIREN Run by Morpheus Blak and Groovella, husband and wife, this qualifies as North America's longest established Goth and Vampire shop. There's a full scale glossy catalogue for those of you who send enough postage. (Make a guess, then double it). This lively pair are co-Presidents of The Gothic Society Of Canada, an organisation founded in 93, which holds monthly meetings and runs a variety of events. Everything they do shrieks excellence. 463 Queen Street West, Toronto, Ontario, MSV 2A9.

SONGS OF THE DAYSHIFT FOREMAN Pagan mag. Box 71, Kanansis Kis, Alberta.

THRIVE Atmospheric, rather ambient, somewhat groovier Mephisto Waltz? Spider Records, PO Box 6625, Station A, Toronto, M5W 1X4.

TRANSYLVANIAN SOCIETY OF DRACULA PO Box 23240, Churchill Square P.O., St Johns, NF A1B 4J9

Chile

MUSICA MARGINAL Magazine. Guillermo Escudero B. Arrayan, 2702 Dep 305, Santiago 9.

Croatia

UNKNOWN DEATHS A radio show desperate for your tapes. God knows they could do with some fun. Dean Cakic, Unknown Deaths, Vilete 7, 52220, Labin.

Czech Republic

AZYL Label. Jana Zelivskeho 39, 3 Prague 1300.

PRIESSNITZ Sort of early 80's Goth influences but art-rock too. Concept-based band, about the area they live in! (Man and nature!) Two albums. Nerudova 1188, 790 01 Jesenik.

REACTION-ECSTASY-TRANCE (RET) 'Depression' album raved about in *Fight Amnesia* for its crazed amalgam of Goth metal and Classical. MAB Records, PO Box 17, 73306 Karvina 8-Hranice.

RADIO 1 This would appear to be a radio show. Lodecka 2, 11000 Prague 1.

Denmark

CONFLICTO "Haute Couture In Leather", says the little advert I saw, but is there something else at play? If you look at the titles of the people involved and bear in mind that their ad implores, "don't forget to donate your bones to us!" you have to

25

24

24 IN ABSENTIA 25 (ACTIVE) MEDIA DISEASE 26 DANCING GOLEM
27 NEUROACTIVE 28 TWO WITCHES

wonder. Dr Otilio Shoshan and Dr Dorrit Shoshan, Johnstrups Alle 1, st.th, 1923 Frederiksberg. (Fax: +45-31350382)

HARD RECORDS Label. C.F.Richs Vej 122, 2.th., 2000 Fredriksburg. (Fax: +45 31869187)

IN ABSENTIA Henrik Marx - prog./vocals, Sune Groule - management/lyrics(!), Tommy B-Kuhlmann -artwork/vocals/lyrics. They also breastfeed animals. Highly regarded by those in the EBM know. 'Abscence', 'Deviance' and 'Darkness' CDs recommended. On Hard Records - Denmark, Subtronic - Germany. In Focentia, Agtrupvej 54, 2.th., 6000 Kolding. (URLP:http://www.aau.dk/-geomtw/inabsentiA.html)

LEATHER STRIP Claus Larsen fronts one of Europe's leading Electro-Industrial bands. A mass of material available. 'Solitary Confinement', 'Fit For Confinement', 'Underneath The Laughter', 'Double Or Nothing', 'Serenades For The Dead'. c/o Cleopatra.

Finland

Bands

(ACTIVE) MEDIA DISEASE Caetlin C. Roeg - vocals/prog., Dim Jay - vocals/keybds, Sam Bizarre - keybds. Rated by many as the best noisy electric thing since Nine Inch Nails. 'Lost' CD recommend-ed. Cyberware, PO Box 623, Fin 3301 Tampere. (Fax: +358-(9)-31-21-31 554) (e-mail: cyberwar@sci.fi) (Net: http://www.sci.fi/-cyberwar/e.html)

DANCING GOLEM Look, if you lived in Finland you'd probably look and sound like this bunch.

26 27 28

It's cold, alcohol costs a fortune, when you can find it, and it's a got a seriously high suicide rate. To their eternal credit Dancing Golem do their damnedest to reverse that statistic. They've been going, on and off, since 91. In one of the oddest press releases I've ever received they announce, "the band got a new keyboard player in Summer 93. Half a year later they broke up because everyone got tired without any specific reason". By the way, in a post-Sisters and Banshees manner, they rock like bastards, with some attractively light vocals. Jari Poutanen, Jokiaro 3 B 11, 13210 Hameenlinna.

DECORYAH They see themselves as melange of Goth, Doom, Rock and Classical, which makes for a heady mix of murk. One of the few bands to boast the use of a grand piano. Mikko Laine, PO Box 53, SF-20781 Kaarina.

NEUROACTIVE Vesa Rainne - vocals, Ville Brusi - percussion/synth, Jarkko Tuohimaa - prog. Best-known new Finnish electro outfit. 'Phonic Trace' CD. Cyberware. (e-mail - cyberwar@sci.fi)
(Net: http://www.sci.fi/-cyberwar/e.html)

SAD PARADE Cure copyists. c/o Darklands, the label run by Jyrki of Two Witches.

SAMI VAUHKONEN Rapakivenkuja 2 E 41, 00710 Helsinki.

SHADE FACTORY Two Witches spin-off, ex keyboard? Savipajakatu 12, 28610 Pori.

TWO WITCHES Once the premier band of Finland, before tastes changed. Once full of people and now only the foundling father, Jyrki, remains. Formed 87, soon grew popular internationally with tightly wound, raw stuff. As well as regular fanzines they've released three singles - 'Cat's Eyes' (88), 'Like Christopher Lee' (89) and 'Dead Dog's Howl' (91). Various album length CDs exist, including repackaged early material - 'Agony Of The Undead Vampire' (92), 'The Vampire's Kiss' (93), 'Phaeriemagick' (93), 'Bloody Kisses' (94), 'Bites' (95) and somewhere there is a very early video of 'Cat's Eye' (89). Jyrki may do the next CD by himself, in an enclave of synths. Either way he finds himself in the position of many others. The gloom is lifting. Time to get urgent. Darklands, Box 29, 33201 Tampere.

Various

JOUKKOMURHA PRODUCTS Non-profit tape label. Jupe Luoma, Lant Pitkaka 2 D 19, 65380 Vaasa.

PLASTIC PASSION Smart fanzine. Mattila, Kataraistentie 1 A 2, 20740 Turku.

SIVULLINEN Occasional fanzine and newsletter. Waarakangas, Kaarelentie 86 B 28, 00420 Helsinki.

France

Bands

ACT OF CRUELTY Formed 91 whereafter frequent changes have kept their existence fairly fruity. Originally a four piece playing cold wave, when the new singer Michael (original guitarist) turned them gently into a classical Darkwave Goth band. Two years later Fabrice brought to the drums more power, replacing the beatbox, as a man with a past in Thrash would. Dominique P. joined on second guitar and Etienne replaced the romantically named Fred on bass. Then Dominique quits, leaving just Etienne and Michael struggling on. They've done the usual

29 30 31 32 33

29-33 BROTHERHOOD OF PAGANS 34 CORPUS DELICTI

compilation route and have at least three demos available, plus the 'Tools For Creation' CD. Mike, 3 rue Jean Bart, Apt 3, 62114 Sains en Gohelle.

A SACRIS More spooky Deadcandance. Bit weird. 'A Sacris' CD. Primary, PO Box 32313, London SW2 3QQ.

A SORDID POPPY Marco Fallacara - bass, Gilles Mislin - guitar, Christophe Marquet - drums, Vincent Fallacara - drums. One of the most important French bands, according to themselves. First LP, the dippy 'Dehiscence' (91) followed by the moodily enchanting 'The Rooms Where The Trees Dance All Night' (93). It's no coincidence that they've supported And Also The Trees a few times, being essentially willowy, intelligent and cheeky. Vincent Fallacara, 24 Rue des Petities Fermes, 67200 Strasbourg.

AVOID CATOBLEPONE Darkwave with boppy pop infusion. Demo - 'Deporte Sur Terre' available. 10 Allee du Grand Charpentier, 44600 St. Nazaire.

BELLADONNA 9CH, 86 rue Nau, 13005, Marseille.

BROTHERHOOD OF PAGANS Vox Populi - guitar, Alien - rhythm guitar/vocals, Coccs - synths, Elrik - bass, Sailor - drums. Formed March 90. Very impressive music which takes all the modernity of today's Goth scene and avoids any sterile stodge of the late 80's; all of it mixed and whisked with the passionate striving of early 80's Indie. Two demos - 'Flower Of Oblivion' and 'Inquisition Day' and CD 'Tales Of Vampires'. Highly recommended. Domingues Philippe, 6 Rue Du Marais, 60350 Trosly-Breuil.

CHERCHE LUNE Medieval style Pagan Goth, not unlike Ataraxia. 'Dan Emrys' CD. 5 Rue D'esiree, Colombe, 44100 Nantes 9.

CLAIR OBSCUR One of the true originals, formed in 81 and thought to have faded away in 92, but there should be a new CD out this year. Too much detail to include for a book this slim and anyway, it may not happen. If it does, investigate because they were always like the empathic but genuinely crazier brothers of The Virgin Prunes, with strange stage antics, utterly compelling musically, and a forerunner to so many of the modern bands. Go initially for the following CDs with a thrill in your heart - 'Rock', 'A Collection Of Isolated Tracks 82-88', 'Play' and 'In Out', as they cover the full period.

CORPUS DELICTI Sebastian - vocals/synths, Jerome - guitars, Chrys - bass, Roma - drums/prog.
Formed 91, by Chrys and Roma, and including Jerome's predecessor Franck, their influences are obvious - Bauhaus, Christian Death, Virgin Prunes - which whipped up together sort of makes sense when you encounter this dream-ridden noise. An awesome band and certainly the most interesting and beautifully realised in France, they not only do everything right, they do everything they can. I've rarely seen a band that manages to put the beauty of their work as much into the related packaging of their discs as the music itself. Everything they do works in harmony with everything else. Even their flyers are tenderly rendered. 'Twilight' CD (March 93), 'Noxious' MCD (Oct 93), 'Sylphes' CD (May 94), 'Obsessions' CD (Sept 95), and for a certain time you should still be able to obtain their video, recorded on the 'Procession' tour of America. You ignore them at your peril. Roma Propriete Andrea, 606 Chemin de la Gabelle, 06220 Golfe-Juan, or via their new label WMD, 99 Rue du Cherche-Midi, 75006, Paris. (Fax: [0033] 933 43538)

DAIONE SIDHE One man medieval project which is more than listenable and quite touching. Nazgul Prod., 34 bd C Flammarion, 13001 Marseille.

DAMAGE DONE Started Sistersy, but now guitar-

based Industrial. Westernland Corp, 6 Rue D. Casanova, 91170 Viry Chatillon.

DAZZLE AND DELIGHT Thomas Floyd, 2, Rue Centrale, 06600 Nice.

DEAD SOULS RISING Alastrelle - vocals, Fabrice - bass and Sebastien - guitar. Formed Dec 93 and produced their first demo after only a few months. There has been a new demo since, and they're slowly getting there. It's very nice, which is the hallmark of French stuff, it's often too nice, too charming at times. I think this band have more scope inside them for something important than most French bands. Their demos are available through Darkside distribution.

DESACCORD MAJEUR A band (and label!) both in the experimental/ambient world, so if you're into the more intriguing and hypnotic sonorous styles their catalogue might be worth getting. The label has been going, starting with cassettes, since 89. 56 Rue Louis Ruffel, 80080 Amiens. (Fax: +33 1 40 39 98 11)

DIABOLOS RISING Over the top dramatic Industrial vamp band who flirt with some crappy Nazi imagery. Go along and LAUGH at them. Long and loud. Then throw things. Hard and fast. P. Prod, BP 57, 62990 Beaurainville.

DIES IRAE Jerome Grousset, 9 Alle des Coquelicots, 44240 La Chapelle/Erdre.

DRAMA OF THE SPHERES Jerome AD - vocals/guitars, David O. - basses, Arnho - keybds/vocals, Oliver £ - lead guitar. Formed Feb 93. Initially it was Jerome, Arhno and David, all Alien Sex Fiend/Virgin Prunes fans and well equated and influenced in a healthy way by aspects of the past. Their first demo, 'Don't Yell So Loud' got a good response from fanzines. Other demos - 'A Dead End' and 'A Dead End 2' fared equally well. Onstage they go for a dramatic show, which adds to the live tension. During 95, while playing the 2nd International Gothic meeting in Strasbourg, they met Remy Pelleschi of Mlada Fronta/Tribal Productions who has worked with them on their debut CD, 'Usual Things' which should just have emerged. Jerome, 36 Impasse des Allemands, 57000 Metz.

ELEND Nicolas Ramaget. 12 Boulevard Du Marechal Leclerc, 21240 Talant.

ERSZEBETH Bucci, BT B2 'Les Hauts de Talagard', 13300 Salon.

EULEN SPIEGEL It's just a duo, doing what they call Electro Fiction, formed out of what was once Chris And The Christ, featuring journalist Christine Tabusso, who has played with Dazzle And Delight. In this band she joins boyfriend Jean-Pierre Bagnato, ex drummer with Mlada Fronta. They love fairy tales and works of capricious fiction so you would expect such music as these dizzy delights. Christine-Carol Tabusso, 3 Rue Marcellin Berthelot, 06400 Cannes.

EVIDENCE Weird. Group founder LSK, who attended the Nantes academy of fine arts, with a musical past involving psychedelia, an admiration for Van Der Graff Generator and the 'Theatre Of Cruelty' of Artaud, wrote his autobiography (eh?), entitled *The Life and Death of LSK*. In 89 he met S. Dephts, himself a pretty accomplished painter. Utilising other, varied musicians over the next few years they worked on their opera, 'From The Heart's Grave', which has since spawned 'St Matthew Passion' and 'A Real Host'. They claim to have somehow linked VDG, King Crimson, Legendary Pink Dots and clear 4AD ideals. It certainly sounds warm and moving enough. There is a haunting feel and a beautiful, uplifting voice which gives everything a nervous, personal intimacy to the delivery, amid classical constraints. D. Clavreul, 15 Rue A. Brizeux, 44000 Nantes.

FORGETTE MI NOTE Nicolas Richard, 74 Rue Pelleport, 75020 Paris.

THE GOTHIC MISSION Astrid de la Croix, La Boudelais, 35250 Chasne/Illet, Bretagne.

JACQUY BITCH Mad, exciting and a modern version of Sex Gang. This dramatic little man does everything on the recent eponymous CD, and there is a whole host of similarly well produced and imaginative demos. Well worth investigating. 25 Rue Denfert Rocheau, 02100 St Quentin.

LAND OF PASSION Lagartija Nick - guitar/vocals, Mister H - keybds, Pat - guitar, Jeff Stoley - bass, Federico Iovino - drums. Founded 89, current line-up stabilised early 93. French/Belgian band citing Bauhaus, Christian Death and Sisters as influences and often compared to the late 80's mould for the deeper sound. Also stir in medieval and gregorian stuff. Quote: "Land Of Passion is a way to Religion, all religions. Emotions, dreams, God and mysticism ride our lives. We are, as lots of dark and Gothic people, the last knights of the other side of life, made of purity, love and faith. We are the Batcave children who glorify the universe and the hidden things. We are Brotherhood of Darkness. We are the unknowing threshold." Four demos, each one hour long, available - 'Even Death May Die' (91), 'Darksound' (92), 'The Prayer' (93), 'Stigmata Sessions' (93/4), and the 'Nigra Opera' CD should be out now, on Appollyon. They do stir in unusual elements. They also have a sweetly brutal guitar and a singer with more than his fair share of vocal charisma. In fact he's the only person I've heard tackle a Bauhaus song and get it right by not merely copying, while at the same time empathising with the original feel of the thing. I'm shocked the French zines don't make more of this band. They deserve excess coverage. F. Iovino, 25 Rue Des Murs, 59230 St-Amand-Les Eaux.

LE SUCCUBE Renaud Ferre, 34BD Camille Flamarion, 13001 Marseille.

LBM Jerome Soudan, 29 Rue Tupin, 69002 Lyon.

L'HYADE ALEPH Francois Jambaud, Brenehuen, 56390 Grandchamp.

35 LAND OF PASSION

LONSAI MAIKOV Thierry Jolif, 42 Rue de la Fougeroille, 35760 Montgermont.

LUCIE CRIES Frederic Bertin - guitars, Marc Le Gigan - drums, Olivier Paccaud - vocals/bass. Formed 88. Their press release mentions something a lot of people do - Egypt/Ancient Rome. Or, to quote directly, "This third album is a turning-point in the life of the band, a production better than ever, a repertory more eclectic. The British post-punk soul stays deep-rooted in the music but new tendencies appear. A celtic eye, a touch of pop, guitars sometimes acid, sometimes crystalline, an omnipresent bass, tribal drums and a voice oscillating between battle-songs and litanies." These are one of the big three in France (alongside Brotherhood Of Pagans and Corpus Delicti). They openly admit that initial influences were Play Dead, Killing Joke and Joy Division. They also do their own label Alea Jact Est, which has produced five CD volumes so far of their series, 'L'Appel de la Muse' which has included work from the likes of ENDG, The Wake, Artica, Girls Under Glass etc. All three of their CDs - 'Res Non Verba', 'Semper Ad Alta' and 'Nihil ex Nihilo' - recommended. 7 Rue Henry Dunant, 60250 Mouv.

MARY (VIRGIN PRUNES) Mary has been living in France for ages and is working on new material of his own which has a reflective, secluded feel, as he digs inwards. He also has plans to make old Prunes material resurface. 198, Route de Rambouillet, 78125 St. Hilarion.

MAXENCE CYRIN One man EBM project. Paradise Movement, 10 Rue Bersot, 25000 Besancon.

MEMOIRES D'AUTOMNE Gentle Goth, sub-Cure. Becouse Herve, 59 Rue G Plasse, 42300 Roanne.

MLADA FRONTA Going under the title of Ethnorock, this is not a billion miles away from some of the K Joke hybrids Jaz Coleman has delved into, and if you like them they have a vast array of back catalogue material for you to invest in. Serious stuff. Remy Pelleschi, Tribal productions, 6 Chemin du Grand Jas, Les Glycines, 06400 Cannes.

NEUTRAL PROJECT Dark but light, positive sounding Goth. 'Secondes' MCD. Eternite Minimale, 11Bld Chateaubriand, 77000 Melun.

REGARD EXTREME 'Perspectives', 32 Rue De Carcassonne, 37100, Tours.

RENAISSANCE NOIRE Thierry Duclos - vocals/bass/keybds/photography, Olivier Picart - drums/keybds, Laurent Hardouin - guitar/bass, Kristian Dernoncourt - keybds/sampler/bass. There's been tapes from RN since 92, loads of them, but I am drawn to a fascinating little project from Thierry with his cassette, 'Im Oktober' (on Rosa Nostra). He gladly admits that it's dedicated to autumn, nostalgia and mystery, all connected to the area in which he lives, most notably the grounds inside the Royaumont Abbey and to ensure listeners appreciate this, photographs, which he insists are always a complement to his music, are included. It is weird stuff. He has an archly dramatic vocal style, quite prominent over the spacious, creepy music. Thierry Duclos 17 Rue des Hayettes, 95340 Bernes Sur Oise.

ROSA CRUX Claude Feeney - keybds, Nathalie Mequinion - double bass, Olivier Tarabo - guitars/vocals. A very odd and marvellous outfit, as artistic to behold as they are musical. Olivier came up with the name and concept while setting up a studio in a water mill, where he seemed to spending a lot of time reading books about alchemy. Their shows involve more than music with visual stimuli including dance and "plastic art installations". Naked people dance in dust and mud to tribal music. Olivier also has a weird sense of humour. Their first, illegal, performance came when he was designing an iron cage to be suspended from the vaults of St Ouen Abbey-Church. As he'd been entrusted with the key, he returned at night with a load of mates, stuck some nude bloke inside the cage and threw it twenty-two times against a huge steel plate "which served as a gong". Nowadays all these elements combine at their performances which sound like the sort of things Pina Bausch would happily die for. Musically, it's the medieval-inspired Darkwave sonority, with vocals that are based on cabalistic odes and Latin incantations. Perverse and enthralling, not to mention frequently perplexing. Discography: 'Ales Et Fles' EP (87),'Eli-Elo' single (90), 'St Ouen' single (92), 'Danse De La Terre' CD (93), 'Proficere' CD (95). Videos: 'Morituri' clip (89), 'Les Jeux De Fers' film ('92). 27 Rue de la Rose, 76000 Rouen. (Fax: 00-33-35 71 25 53)

TROUBLE FAIT Mme et M Jean-Claude Tetral, 54 Rue de Moscou, 62520 Le Touquet.

TAEDIUM VITAE Jerome G, Yannick - vocals, Jerome Pierrick - guitar. They didn't send me the details, although they did send me a blank tape, which was meant to be their debut cassette 'Sexy Death'! I cupped the sleeve against me ear and imagined. Luckily, it's *Fight Amnesia* to the rescue. Formed April 95 by two ex Dies Irae/OpusDei members. Smart tunes, accurately merging old elements of bands like Joy Division and Danse Society but given fresh 90's nuances. Diam Productions, 9 Allee des Coquelicots, 44240 La Chapelle Sur Erdre.

VIVID ATMOSPHERE Formed 91, a duo of Nathalie - bass and Jean - guitar with synth and drum machine, placed somewhere between X-Mal and RLYL. 'Ache and Grief' demo available, which includes versions of their debut 93 CD 'Hag-Ridden' (which was limited to 576 copies). Nathalie Lafontaine, 16 Avenue du Prince Noir, 33750 Camarsac.

Fanzines

ACID DRAGON Thierry Sportouche, 20 Rue Ferrandrere, 69002, Lyon.

CHARIVARI BP 67, 29267 Brest Cedex.

CONCEPT Mag including some Goth amongst its experimental, electronic coverage. Cyrile Sottile, 12 Rue de l'Ancienne Mairie, 92110 Clichy.

DARK WORLD Big, bold and very impressive. Straightforward interviews but the huge illustrated review section is its biggest strength. Erick Depalle, Allee du Chateau, 42153 Riorges.

DIANTRE Luc Santiago Rodriguez, 24 Rue de Presle, 75015, Paris.

DIOXINE Mister H, 23 C. Soyer, 7610, Rumes B.

DYADIQUE 113 Rue des Ecoles, 33760 Targon.

FORKED TONGUES Lionel Fahy, 101 Boulevard de Chatreaudun, 45000 Orleans.

FREQUENCE 15 Avenue de la Gare, 77515 Pommeuse.

GLORIA VICTIS Very well laid out and thought out magazine that embraces everything good that is occurring, particularly in Europe. Written in English. Essential. 41 Bis Place Des Capucins, Apt 2, 33000 Bordeaux.

GOTHIC Sanchez Dead Andre, 33490 St Pieree D'Aurillac.

GOTHIC CHAPTER Gael Doucet, 21 Av. Guibert, 78170 La Celle St Cloud.

GOTHIC MISSION Astrid Delacroix, Le Boudelais, 35250 Chasnet Sur Illet.

HEKATOMBE Big, varied - the emphasis is on the interesting. Laure Cornaire, 5 Rue Leredde, 75013 Paris.

KSK (KRIME SONIK) NEWS Again, absolutely essential for anyone in France. Newsletter about world-wide developments in Goth-Industrial-Electro but also has an interesting range of mail order tapes. Patrice Miossec, 12 Rue de la Dordogne, 33500 Libourne.

LACRIMA CHRISTI Amand Clerque, 1 Rue Lacroix, 69003 Lyon.

LA LEGENDE DES VOIX 21 Rue de 8 mai 1945, 37270 Montlouis.

LA RUE CLANDESTINE BP 731, 75163 Paris Cedex 04, or 34 Bd de Sebastapol, 75004 Paris.

LE SANG DE LA REVOLTE Lucie Cries fanzine. 7 Rue Henri Dunant, 60250 Mouv.

LE SUCCUBE Renaud Ferre, 2 rRe Durmont Durville, 13008 Marseille.

LES AMOREUX Du 24, BP 1115, 59012 Lille Cedex.

LES LUMIERES DU DESIR Gregory Rohart, 280 bis Rue Pierre Legrand, 59000 Lille.

MYSTIFIER Superior quality fanzine, which also has a free info service (Frankenstein Post), started 93. It's got some Gothic and a whole range of intense metal styles. No posey nonsense. Well laid out, stunning news coverage, in-depth interviews with surprisingly ugly people and a solid mass of reviews. French language. Editor Frank, who works along similar lines as the Into The Abyss chaps, reckons, "It's possible to see many conceptual and musical convergences between the Cold/Gothic scene and the underground Metal one - new ways of dark and immemorial expressions are born. They are merging into one another, elaborating silently the Ultimate Conjuration of the Sensible & Magic Lightcircle via

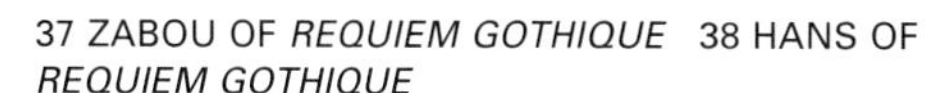
37 ZABOU OF *REQUIEM GOTHIQUE* 38 HANS OF *REQUIEM GOTHIQUE*

37 38

39

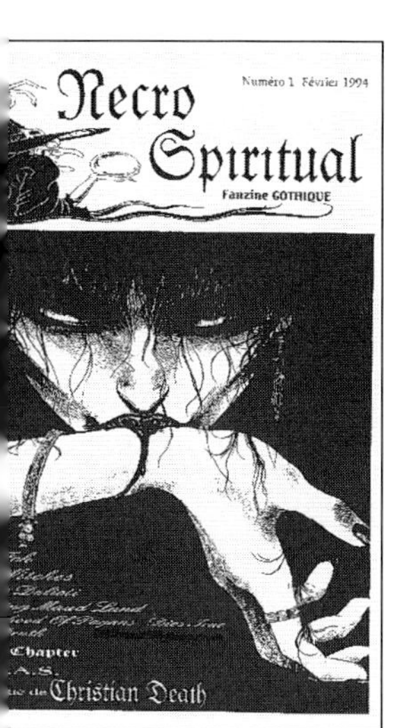

36

an Evolution/Involution of the infinite and polymorphic nature spirits." That's right. (With you as far as "it's possible") One of the writers is known as The Sperminator! Frank, 15 Rue Saint Michel, F-35000 Rennes.

NAPALM ROCK M.A., BP 252, 13608 Aix Cedex 1.

NECRO SPIRITUAL A fanzine so big you can hide inside it, covering everything, pronouncing death to racism, intolerance and violence on animals and instead supporting bodism, celtic and African culture, magic and voodoo. Another essential. Ghostvald, 2 Chemin de l' usine electrique, 06240 Beausoleil.

NOCTURNE Laure Pechmalbec Ecole J. Ferry, Rue Albert Camus, 93220 Gagny.

NOISING THERAPY Ombre Sonore, 223 Route de Colmar, 67100 Strasbourg.

NOTIONS All in French language. Plus they also do the OIW Organisation, which will appeal to people who like to question the boundaries of human perception. Small but sweet at first, it's already swelled to 52 pages. Class stuff, although cheaply produced. Costs 3 IRCs. Vincent Bondet, 5 Chemin Pierre Vincent, 13220 Chateauneuf-Les-Martigues.

NURSERY-CHRYSALIDE Free mag (IRC essential) All relevant European news but a wide reviews section and global interviews. Oliver Leonelli, 1 La Sapiniere, 57860 Montois-La-Montaigne.
NURSERY Eric Henriet, 167 Rue De Pont A Mousson, F7158, Montigny Les Metz.

OMEGA Villa Mon Refuge, 9 Allee des Lucioles, 06340 Trinite Victor.

OEIL CARNIVORE Dissidence Art Work, 26 bis Rue George Sand, 91320 Wissous.

PREMONITION 1 Square Pauklalgis, 77360 Vaires.

REMEDES ESPERES Jean-Marc Boucher & CelineGregoire, 8 Square L. Guilot, 75105 Paris.

REQUIEM GOTHIQUE Quite straightforward but jam-packed zine, very clearly laid out with a majority of Goth but a touch of Industrial in the reviews. Also encourages contributions. They're turning into an an organisation too, setting up tape compilations, so they'd like to hear from bands in any of the following categories... Goth (*all* styles), Post Punk, Electro, Industrial, Doom, Black Metal, Atmospheric and Occult. Hans Cany, 7 Rue St Georges, 35000 Rennes Breizh. Also Zabou Briere, 8 Square Du Roi Arthur, 35000 Rennes, Breizh.

SCARECROW Andre Sanchez, RN 113, 33490 St Pierre D'Aurillac.

SHADOW DEATH Thierry Collet, Place de Verdun, Arcon 42370 Renaison.

SYMPOSIUM Pascal Collobert, 4 avenue Churchill, 94220 Charenton.

SNYTHETIK Sylvia Filet, BP 103, 92120 Montrouge.

TENEBRAE 58 Bvd Marechal Foch, 38000 Grenoble.

TOURMENTS ETERNELS Pereira Julien, 7 Rue Des Raisins Blancs, 57179 Bronvaux.

ZIK-ZINE Bonnoil Marie-Pierre, 108 Avenue de Rove, 13015 Marseille.

ZINOTHEQUE PAR CORRESPONDENCE Fred Perin, 17 Rue du Marche A L'Avoine, 28230 Epernon.

Other sources

ABYSSE DIGITAL Distribution association by Valeria Cantin from Schizophrenia radio show and Les Amoreux. Du 24, BP 1115, 59102 Lille Cedex.

ADIPOCERE RECORDS Label. Christian Bivel, BP 18, 01540 Vonnas.

A.D.S. Compilation tapes. 67 Rue Anatole France, 60230 Chambly.

AL DI LA Distribution. New Waves, BP No.6, 75462 Paris Cedex 10.

ALEA JACTA EST Label/dist. 7 Rue Henri Dunant, 60250 Mouy.

ALVDALEN Distributor. 8 Rue Boyer Fonfrede, 31000 Toulouse.

BRASSICA RAPA Schmitt Christophe, 4 Rue Ste Lucie, 57190 Floranges.

DANCETERIA Label/dist. 222 Rue Solferno, 59000 Lille.

DARKLAND OF TEARS Multi-faceted organisation, including management (as yet restricted to Brotherhood Of Pagans) but also offers services concerning distribution, producing and promotion. Philippe Domingues, 6 Rue De Marais, 60350 Trosly Breuil.

DARKSIDE Mail order distribution service offering everything to do with 'darkmusic', like a tinier version of the UK's Nightbreed. Maryline Collombet, 3 Rue Louis Braille, 01000 Bours En Bresse.

DEMONIA Magazine. Societe Comedit, Demonia, 15 Cite Joly, 75011 Paris. (Fax 43 57 95 97)

DEMOTEQUE Free info service plus tape rental! BP 731, 75163 Paris Cedex 04.

DIGITAL DIFFUSION Mail order/dist. Sylvian Duc, 50 Rue Jolliot Curie BT 2B, 69005 Lyon.

ERETIC Label/dist. Van Der Linden, 1 Rue Fumouze, 93450 L'ile-Saint-Denis.

ETERNITE MINIMALE Mail order/dist. 11 Bld 103, 92120 Montrouge.

EXPREL Compilations. Cyril Adam, 63 Quai Boissy d'Anglas, 78380 Bougival.

FACADE Label. Olivier Degardin, 5 Rue d'Andilly, 95600 Eaubonne.

FOLLIOT Videos. 30 Av. de Nioyon, 42300 Mably.

FRONT DE L'EST Mailorder distributor of alternative music including Goth. Imports stuff into France also and has large list. 13 Rue Vernier Lebel, F-80000 Amiens.

THIERRY GAYRAND Fetish artist. 8 Chemin de la Bouriotte, 81430, Villefranche D'albi.

GOTH & CELT Personalised attractive stationery from the nice people behind the *Requiem Gothique* fanzine. Zabou Cany, 29 Rue Caponiere, 14000 Caen.

DENIS GRR Fetish artist. 69 Rue d'Avron, 75020, Paris.

HARMONIE Tape compilations. Jean-Marie Boucher & Celine Gregoire, 8 Square Leon Guillot, 75015 Paris.

HERETIQUE Fabrice Prost, 7c Rue de Riplay, 39000 Lons Le Saunier.

IN MY VEINS Vampire zine. Step Le Saux, 25 Rue De L'ermitage, 94100 St, Maur.

LEMPEREUR Zine distribution. Stephane, 26 Rue du Pied Moisi, 49000 Angers.

LARMONIE ETRANGE Gig organiser. L. Huster, 2 Esplanade de l'Europe, 34000 Montpelier.

LA SCENE Fetish magazine. AF75, 102 Avenue des Champs Elysees. F-75008.

LATEX SEDUCTION CLUB Speaks for itself. Imagine a queue to get in and people getting frantic. It would sound like the *Psycho* shower scene. Eee-eee-eee. Mrs D/MC Guerif, BP 651, 44018 Nantes, Cedex 01.

LE RUDE Distributor - Fetish-related fanzines. Eric Heilmann, BP 14337 59015 Lille Cedex.

LES ATELIERS DU SON Tape compilations. Rosa Nostra, Les Ateliers Du Son, BP26 F-95 Bruyeres s/ Oise.

LONDON TAVERNE 'il y a souvent des Soirees Gothiques'. 9 Rue des Bretons, 13100 Aix-en-Provence.

METAMKINE Label. 13 Rue de la Drague, 38600 Fontaine.

NEW WAVE They have the RDS label, their own New Wave magazine and the Al Di La distribution network. B. P. No 6, 75462 Paris Cedex 10.

NOUVELLES HARMONIE Jean Marc Boucher, 4 Rue Jean Moulin, 122 Fontaine aux Pintes, 91160 Long Jumeau.

ODESSA Label/organisation. Philippe Saintlos, 'Semantic', 17 Rue Gambetta, 54000 Nancy.

ODD SIZE Mail order/distribution. 24 Rue de Laghouat, 75018 Paris.

OFFRANDE A Fetish magazine, quite slim, black and white but it has that authentic feel about it that suggests involvement with a scene rather than detached observance. APMC BP No. 6, 75462 Paris CDX 10.

OIW A society! I don't know what he's on about, something about original energies relating to past societies of Indian and European culture and the human metaphysics as popularised by celtic mythology. Or something. Vincent Biondet, 5 Chemin Pierre Vincent, 13220 Chateauneuf-les-Martigues.

OMBRE SONORE Music mail order. 223 Route de Colmar, 67100 Strasbourg.

OMEGA Mail order. Actus Dei, Phillipe Olivier, Villa Mon Refuge, 9 Allee des Lucioles, 06340 Trinite-Victor.

ORCHADIA MACHINA Mail order/distribution. La Gare 18390 Savigny En Septaine.

PERSPECTIVE French association, planning zine and broadcasting their own radio show. Tape also available. 32 Rue de Carcassone, 37100 Tours.

PHILIPPE PISSIER Attempting to set up Sex Magick organisation. 23 Av. de la Premiere Armee Francaise, 95160 Montmorency.

PHYLEA French bondage stuff. Christophe Mourthe, 8 Rue Frochot, 75009, Paris.

PLASM 69 Mail order/distribution. Darnaud Christophe, 9 Rue Gervais Bassiere, 69100 Villeurbanne.

PRACS Label/dist. Poste Restante, 77100 Meaux.

PREMONITION Magazine. 1 Square Paul Algis, 77360 Vaires.

PRIKOSNOVENIE Label. La Manceliere, 85190 Venansault.

QUASIMODO Distribution. Phillipe Salle, 5 Avenue Palissey, 47400 Tonneins.

QUINQUINET Specialist Goth promoter. Bernard, 19 Rue Ampere, 38000 Grenoble.

ROSE SELAVY BP 521, 35006 Rennes Cedex.

SANCTUARY Ah, it's Franck Troussier again, once manager of Ar vag (deceased), now French manager of Italian band Artica, he also works for *Les Lumieres Du Desir* fanzine, on Radio Enghien and this!. Sanctuary is an association which declares its aims as "working on the Parisian area in order to organize some Darkwave, Gothic and Electro concerts. Our motivations are first our passion for this kind of music and the necessity to come up to the public expectations. We also wish to turn people's attention to bands which deserve to meet a wider success". They started in 84, and in 96 find themselves running a monthly event at La Locomotive, starting with a gig by The Breath Of Life. If you think you're genuinely good enough to be there get in touch, or if you want to meet them it's off to a pub with you every Tuesday called Piano Vache, 8 Rue Laplace, 75005 Paris. (Phone 46 33 75 03) This is a great meeting place to find about anything Goth-like which is happening in the area. Guillaume Michel, 7 Rue Royer-Collard, 75005 Paris. (Phone 46 34 28 52)

SCULPTURED SOUNDS Record label. 222 Rue Solferino, 59000, Lille.

SEMANTIC Underground/Goth dist. 17 Rue Gambette, 54000 Nancy.

SORTILEGE Fetish thing. CP91, 189 Rue d'Aubervilliers, 75886 Paris, Cedex 18. (Fax:+33 1 46076036)

SPOCK PRODUCTIONS Monthly info sheet and dist catalogue on all the usual and unusual stuff. Guillaume Dumoulin, 112 Rue d'Alembert, 38000 Grenoble.

VISA Label/radio. BP51, 93101 Montruil Cedex.

X-RAY EYES Goth clothes. 9 Ruelle De la Boucherie, 06300 Nice 93138919.

ZOORGANIZATION Concerts/tours. Scott & Clementine, 67 Place St-Leger, 73000 Chambery.

ZARDOZ Cultural association. Claude Dorote, 57 Rue Flegier, 13001 Marseilles.

Radio stations

DARKSIDE RADIO/BELOT LAURENT 5 Rue Pierre Corneille, 42300 Mably.

BLACK ET NOIR BP 21, 260 Rue de Lorraine, 57180 Terville.

CHRYSALIDE Radio show, from *The Nursery Chrysalide* fanzine people on RPL Radio 101.10 FM.

DOCTOR AVALANCHE Radio show on Clin D'oeil Radio 107.2 FM (Mondays). Laurent Le Fers, Residence Mediterranee B1, Chemin du Puissanton, F-06220 Vallauris.

ELEGIA A show on Frequence Mutine, every Sunday 7pm-10pm, produced by the Ora Pro Nobis organisation. Elegia newsletter also available. (Also 'Smurf In The Gulag' show, every Friday 10-11.30.) O.P.N., BP 67, 29267 Cedex.

FREQUENCE 15 Ave de la Gare, 77515 Pommeuse.

LES EXTRAORDINAIRES AVENTURES d'EDMOND LE PETIT TENEBRION By the time they've announced that the show's half over! Isabelle Rabau, 50 Rue Nauville, 3000 Bordeaux.

STIGMATA Insanely popular and highly regarded show, for Radio Sauvaigne, c/o Claire Vallecalle, 22 rue Mondon, 33100 Le Bouscat.

TRANZOPHOBIA On Radio Lajet 94.2 FM (Tuesday 20H/21H) c/o Zanetti Stephane, 10 Rue des Fabriques, 54000 Nancy.

RADIO CAMPUS Radio Campus is the University radio station of Lille. It has existed since 69. Show is run by Cyber, Krieg and Corwin who operate under the name of Au-Dela Du Reel. They specialise in five things: Concert organisation, Information, Promotion, Distribution and Parties. You are recommended to get in touch and send all relevant promo stuff. 106.6 Mhz FM Stereo 92.2fm in Renaison, Fridays 8.30-10pm. Fabrice Perex, 57 Rue Victor Hugo, Apt 27, 59160 Lomme.

ZWILLINGSHEXEN Every Saturday (15H.17H) on SOL FM 100.7 FM Also have their own label, Spiral Insana Prod. Belle Gregory, 248 Rue Cdt. Charcot, 69110 Ste Foy Les Lyons.

Germany

Bands

AGE OF HEAVEN Sisters ('Vision Thing') meets Project Pitchfork. 'Armageddon' CD. Delitzsvcherstr. PF 149/305, 04129, Leipzig.

ALMOST HUMAN Hedwigstr. 12, 5600 Wuppertal.

ALSO Alexander Schmidt - guitar/vocals, Oliver Gnaß - bass, Tine Warmhold - keybds. Formed 90, inspired by Joy Division and Bauhaus and determined to explore more imaginative areas, ending up now as a cross between Kurt Weill and Nick Cave in heaven, all sweet manners and quiet detachment. The experimental nightclub feel doesn't get in the way of their harder, bullish dance guitar fests either. Discography seems, sadly, entirely MC-based. 'Sisyphos' (90), 'Elegie' (91), 'Enter The Subway' (92), 'Georg' (92), 'Wonderful Day' (92), 'The Void Is Calling' (93), 'Heute Nacht' (93), 'Vahr' (93),

41 BURNING DOLLHOUSE

'Cold Rooms' (94), 'Vincent Price's Favourite Torture Songs' (96). Oliver Gnaß, Metzstraße 72, 24116, Kiel.

AM TAG UNTER NOLL Joy Div/Banshees. 'Endstadt' CD. Daniel Ferber, Eigeistein 29, 50668 Cologne.

ANGINA PECTORIS Joelen Mingi - vocals/keybds, Shay F. Astray - bass, Anthony Abzu - guitars, Cliff Hill - drums. Joelen Mingi has been in a lot of bands from 84 onwards, the longest lasting being this. Well respected throughout Europe and notable for their light turbulence. Debut 'Anno Domini' CD (92) followed by 'On The Burning Funeral Pyre', 'Anguish' and 'Insomnia' CDs. Nyctalopia Management - since collapsed.

ARTS AND DECAY Traditional Goth sound. 'Trail Of Tears' and 'Razor-Blade' CDs.

ATTAINMENT OF NIRVANA O. Koch, Monrepostr. 3, 7120 Bissingen.

AUTOMN T. Buchner, Flaschenhofst 11, 90402 Nurnberg.

THE AUTUMN STONE Decent alternative rock with goth twinges. 'Frog Talk' CD. c/o Dion Fortune.

AWAKE AT THE WALL Very nice duo of Dirk R. - vocals/bass/keybds/drums and Thorben S. - guitar and vocals, who have released one MC, 'The Awake' on Beton tapes. The drumming is fairly basic but the songs all shunt along nicely and there's the usual grandiose keyboard effects . Ultimately here are some cool comparisons to Danse Society, before Rawlings turned tubular. Very sweet and power-charged in the right places, with the vocal delivery clearly influenced by early Rozz Williams in the way the melody flows through it. Gorkon Recordings, Luruper Haupstr. 59, 22547 Hamburg.

BEYOND THE WALL OF SLEEP Yuc - bass, Benden - guitars, Martin Schwartzenberg - vocals. Formed 92. "Powerful and straight arrangements, conceptional contrasts, catchy melodies, melancholic and despairful moments but also the aspect of hope." That's what they say, boasting of musical tension and a "unique mysterious character." Interestingly, virtually everybody suggests a slower Sisters Of Mercy. Me, I plump for evil, twinkling nursery rhymes. There is something disarming about the arrangements, especially when they don't let the guitar dominate, and something sinister about a bass sound which could stun a hippo. Unfortunately the singer appears to be trapped inside a roll of carpet. 'Dark Elegies' demo (94 - sold out), 'Psychic Burnout' demo (95) available. S. Jugel, Elsa-Brandstrom-Str 35, 52134 Herzogenrath.

THE BLESSING IN DISGUISE Dark Pop-Goth, like a 90's Theatre Of Hate? 'Morphius' CD.

BLUEFIELD Nice TechnoGoth of the gentler persuasion. 'Struggling In Darkness' CD. Dossier label.

BURNING DOLLHOUSE Dieter Stuckert - guitar/vocals, Peter Weiß - bass, Chrissy Afolder - keybds, Frank Fickel - drums. Formed 90 as a studio project, involving computers and contributions flowing between travelling musicians the world over, it settled down over the next few years, making the live debut in 92, and the first CD two years later, 'Burning Dollhouse'. Odenwaldstraße 58, 64853 Otzberg.

CALVA Y NADA Electro Wave Goth. 'El Peste Perverso Lieva Mi Peluca' and 'Ipalpita, Corazon, Palpita!' CDs. C. Warter, Auf Den Sceffeln 27, 4630.

CANCER BARRACK Moving away from their brackish opening phase into a cooler electro pool.

42 DREADFUL SHADOWS 43 DRONNING MAUD LAND

42

Sisters/DAF. 'Leben' CD, 'Walking Through The...' album. Thorsten Cichowski, Im Grunnen Grunde 5, 22555 Hamburg.

CANTICUM FUNEBRIS Dark Goth folk! 'Endless' CD.

CASSANDRA COMPLEX Although in more of an alternative indiepop vein, clearly of appeal to some Goths. Recent 'Theomania' and 'Grenade' CDs should appeal.

CATASTROPHE BALLET American/German Dark Wave. High quality. 'Pandemonium', 'Torso' and 'Transition' CDs. Eric Burton, Postfach 102515, W 6600 Sarbrucken. Or c/o Claudia Schroer, Mainzer Str. 191B, 66121 Saarbrucken.

CHANDREEN Antje Schulz - vocals, Catrin Mallon - vocals, Axel Henniger - guitar, Dorothea Honstedt - flutes. The only tracks I've heard were awesome in a gentle way. Deeply attractive. A better, more pragmatic Deadcandance. Less sleepy. M Schwalm, Berkersheimer Weg 105, 60433 Frankfurt.

CHILDREN OF NO RETURN Lightly moody, thoughtful Goth. 'Looking Back In Anger' CD. Wienstr 4, 6300 Giesen.

THE CONVENT PO Box 1104, 27729 Hamburg.

CRADLE OF SPOIL Excellent Syntho-Goth. 'A Thousand Years' CD. Celtic Circle Productions, PO Box 7113, 47601 Geldern.

CREAM 8 It's just Boris and Sascha Lecher, operating as a project more than a group, making weirdly moody sounds with trad Goth guitar. 'The Emerald Touch' CD (94). K-M Musik & Sounds Of Delight, Postfach 21 14, 33251 Gutersich. (Fax: 0 52 41 - 3 66 19). Boris Brosowski, Im Oberen Markteld 14, 15271 Hilchenbach.

CROWN OF JESUS Frank Blumenhofen - music, Frank Michatz - vocals. Maddening, powerful stuff - like a corkscrewed DAF - and their debut CD 'Tales From The Pit' is worth checking out. These chaps have even worked recently with the awesome Diamanda Galas. 'Immaculate' MCD available. Dion Fortune, Hospelstr. 66, 50825, Cologne.

CRYPTIC FLOWERS Kuhlenstr. 40, Hornstr., 4330 Muelheim-Ruhr.

CYBER AXIS O. Muller - vocals/prog./keybds/drums, K Jaeger - prog./keybds, J Schott - vocals/prog. EBM/Electro-metal, acoustic ballads! Mental band, all classically trained of course. 'Cyber Axis' MC (93), 'Illusions' MC (94), 'The Final Sign' CD (95), 'The Way I Feel' CD (95), 'Fool Energy' CD (96). Mozartstraße 17, 58452 Witten.
(Fax: +49 (0) 2302-276673)

DANCE OR DIE Powerful Darkwave. 'Ever Spring' CD. Machinery Records.

DARK REALITY Philipp Kailer - guitar, Martin Heinzelmann - guitar, Oliver Ramacher - vocals, Alex Schiem - bass, Andres Waldura - recorders, crumhorn and vocals, Boss Dr Rhythm Dr 600 - drums. Ah, the crumhorn movement gathers pace. 'Baroque Gothic Art Metal', says their record company (Switzerland's Witchunt), but also used the words that strike terror into the hearts of the experienced. Jethro Tull! Andreas Weiss, Priorbergerstrasse 4, 72160 Horb-Dettingen.

DAS ICH Highly successful Goth-Dance-Everything crossover band formed 91 by Stefan Ackermann (vocals) and Bruno Kramm (electronics), who sold 30,000+ of their debut album 'Die Propheten'. Their recent album 'Straub', three years in the mak-

43

44

ing, only cements their widening reputation. Perfect for anyone with a taste for the maudlin and melodramatic. 'Stigma' and 'Sataniche Verse' MCDs also available. Danse Macabre, Luitpoldplatz 18, 95444 Bayreuth.

DE FACTO Postfach 1162, 3550 Marburg.

DEINE LAKAIEN Alexander Velianov - vocals, Ernst Horn - keybds/production. Respected Darkwave/Techno. 'Forest Enter Exit', 'Dark Star Tour Live' CDs and 'Mind Machine' MCD. Gymnastic Records, Dianastrasse 1, 80538 Munich.

DELIRIUM Atmospheric and dungeonesque mood music. 'Stone Tower' CD.

DEMONIX Devious dancing from Gitane Demone, Marc Ickx, of Fetish scene. Hyperium.

DERRIERE LE MIRIOR Deadcandance/Banshees. 'Deep' CD. SPV, PO Box 1124, 76276 Rheinstetten.

DESTROYKA/BLIND PASSENGERS Nik P. - keybds/backing vocals, Marc Range - prog./keybds and Rayner Schirner - vocals/machines. In existence since 91, and currently being seen as a very promising pop thing indeed, and yet their musical heart is still dark. They call it cyberpop, so it's catchy and soft, but there is a link and not merely a transitory one. I couldn't work out if the band or album were called either Destroyka or Blind Passengers as the layout just gave nothing away. They use part of the money they earn at gigs to sponsor a 44,000 sqm piece of rainforest in a South American nature reserve extension. Goths with a conscience! Half a dozen lovingly lurid t-shirts available. PO Box 0023, 15824 Blankenfelde. (Fax: 030-784 87 68)

DIARY OF DREAMS TechnoGoth/Cold Wave, similar to a psychotic Danse Society. 'Cholymelian' and 'End Off Flowers' CDs - side project of Adrian Hates from Garden Of Delight.

DIE FORM Philippe Fiochot - concept/prog./lyrics/sampling/vocals and Elaine P. - vocals/'special assistance' /live acting. Well, a weird one and no mistake with a past stretching so far back I can barely see, from initial tape experiments in 77. First vinyl in 79 and a release of some sort virtually every year from the late '80's onwards, the most recent I have details of being 'The Visionary Garden' which apparently came accompanied with a book. Cool! A unit ripe for multi-media interventions, or so they claim. Obviously based on electronic compositions, they drift hazily between the obscure and the obvious, in a delectable, winsome way. Hyperium, PO Box 910127, 90259 Nurnberg.

DREADFUL SHADOWS Well respected noxious bunch creating impact, coming on strong like Rosetta on steroids. CDs 'Estrangement' (94), 'Homeless' (95). Silvio Kohler, Schwedter Str 80, 10437 Berlin. Or K-M Musik.
(Fax: 0 52 41 - 3 66 19)

DRONNING MAUD LAND Another epic band, who do everything in fantastic style, just like Corpus Delicti. Gloomy Neffs comparisons have long since been discarded as they gyrate along without the pomposity of most uppity German bands. Heavenly, really. 'Aphorism', and 'Maelstrom' CDs, plus the 'Alteration' MCD. Glasnost.

DROWN FOR RESURRECTION Syntho Darkwave. 'Another Failed Legend' CD. Glasnost.

THE DUST OF BASEMENT Mild Darkwave. 'Regress' MCD. Glasnost.

E-CRAFT Guido Henning - vocals/drums, Mario Bernhardt - keybds/vocals and Enrico Wassilick -

keybds/sounds. Interesting Electro outfit, formed 93 as part of a school project! Hard sound with soft centre, now getting raving press, even awards no less. First CD 'Die Stahl AG' (96). Maschinenwelt Records, Postfach 12061, Berlin.

ENDLESS Andre Hager - bass, Jan Erdtel - keybds, Tom Kuchler - vocals, Erif Hoffman - guitars/bass/vocals, Swen Drechsel - drums, Jan Karlheinz Schaarschmidt - technics. Formed 91, releasing the 'No Better Day' and 'Devilhand' demos in 92. In 94 their first CD album, 'Beyond The Abyss' emerges on Spirit. After a tour in that year supporting Rozz Williams and Gitane Demone they are on a high and start work on the second album 'Fire' which should by now have come out on Spirit/East West. Lyrically the band profess to view the world through the angle of decay, being influenced by the prophecies of Nostradamus. Contact A. Hager, Am Moosbach 1, 09496 Marienberg. (Fax: +49 (0)373 63/ 4316)

ENDRAUM Pomp and classical, circumstantial Darkwave, seriously advised for salacious purposes by one Nightbreed maverick. 'Zeitenlicht' CD. R. Rutten Blank/Im trutz 17, 60322 Frankfurt.

ENGLESSTAUB GODKrist - guitar/sampling/prog./keybds, Lilith - bass/vocals, Janusz - guitar/vocals. Okay, you know these three as Madre Del Vizio. Well once upon a time there was MDV and Les Fleurs Du Mal. GODKrist wrote a few pieces at a time of discontent in both bands - and so Englesstaub was born. The EP 'Unholy' emerged in a limited edition of 333. Such was the demand it was re-released in a 500 run. More demands... to the extent that Lilith and Janusz wanted in there as well, both bands now existing as separate entities. CDs - 'Malleus Maleficarum' and 'Ignis Fatuus: Irrlichter'.

EXEDRA Interesting Darkwave mixture. 'Kingdom Of The Blind' CD. Alice In..., Wetzlarer Strasse 9, D-35630 Ehringshausen.

THE FAIR SEX Early 90's A.S.F-ish but now almost rap - two singers, rock guitar, electronics. Myk Jung, Drimbornweg 4, 45257 Essen.

FORTHCOMING FIRE Dark Electro, comparable to a modern Danse Society. 'Illumination' CD, 'Heliopolis' MCD. Hyperium.

FORTIFICATION 55 Darkwave electronics. 'Anthropology' and 'Atlantis' CDs, 'The Doll' MCD. Glasnost.

THE FROZEN AUTUMN Soft Goth Zymox-ish synthwork of the highest quality. 'Pale Awakening' CD. Wildschmidtstr. 17, 60316 Frankfurt.

FUNERAL PARTY Dirgy atmospherics in a Ghost Dance/Skeletals vein. 'Serpentine' CD. Silent Scream Records, 4181 2E 9th St, New York, NY 10009, US of Goddam A.

GARDEN OF DELIGHT Artaud, Thomas O'Connell and Adrian Hates. Already five Neffist CDs with esoteric crossover appeal to date - 'Enki's Temple', 'Epitaph', 'Sargnid', 'Necromanteion' and 'Symbol And Vision'. Two MCDs - 'Shared Creation' and 'The Seal'. A. Franzman, Questr. 16, 40227 Dusseldorf. Or Dion Fortune.

GARDEN OF PLEASURE Michael Scholz of Shadowplay is involved so it'll be interesting and good quality whatever type of music. Sudestr 59, 2398 Harrislee.

GHOSTING Sascha Tayefeh - music, Diana Rappauer - vocals. Another totally distinctive band, and quite a prolific one, with influences listed as Mahler to Jean Michel Jarre! There's a clear classical element, and with a trained soprano as your vocalist how couldn't there be? The early days were interesting. Sascha (alias Daemon Accolet) got the name around via flyers and info sheets before the band even existed. Unaware of the requirements of a gig (how had he failed to notice?) his band did their first with an acoustic, piano and him singing without a mike! Hardly any of the crowd heard a thing but Glasnost signed them at once. Eventually tensions within the band rose to such a point, specifically between Daemon and his guitarist, that he smashed all the guitars. Argument won, I'd say. Since then it's one man in charge, selecting musicians and of course his vocalist. And he has strong lyrical ideas, which you may not expect. His 'Der Staat Bin ich' album was all about the Shah Of Persia! Maybe he's just mad? MCs - 'Secret Books' (89), 'Brave New World' (89). 'Romeo & Juliet' (90), 'Black Romantic' (91), 'Enter My Crypt' (92) (released on CD, remixed - 94). 'Paranoia/Lunar' 7" (92), 'Pure Romantic' MC (92), 'Romantic Death' CD (92), 'Brilliants' MC (92), 'Songs From Fairyland' CD (93), 'Black Romantic Version 2' MC (93), 'Live At Eiskeller' official bootleg (93), 'Black Romantic revisited' remastered MC (94), 'Paint In White' official bootleg (94), 'Arabesque' CD (94), 'Lips Like Red' CD (95), 'Taste Blood' CD (95), 'Lifes' CD (96), 'Der Staat Bin Ich' CD (96). It's a hell of a lot. I get the impression that it's Glasnost issuing stuff at the same time as new label SPV. Diane Rappauer, Michaelisstr. 60, 64293 Darmstadt. (e-mail, via DOS/Windows: st001609@hrz1.hrz.th-darmstadt.de)

GIRLS UNDER GLASS Volker Zacharias - vocals/guitars, Hauke Harms - keybds, Axel Ermes - computers/guitars. Formed back in 87, out of the earlier band Calling Dead Roses, once described as a slow version of The Sisters. They have a devious blend of left field dance sensibilities slammed into uproarious power. Nothing is ever predictable, other than the unholy maturity that marks their work and its development. They're one of the few bands I'd recommend unreservedly because they appear to have some in-built quality control. 'Humus' LP/CD (88), 'Flowers' LP/CD (89), 'Ten Million Dollars' 12" (89), 'Random' 12" (90), 'Never Go/Beast' 7" (91) 'Positive' LP/CD (91), 'Live At Soundgarden' LP/CD (92), 'Darius' LP/CD (92), 'Christus' LP/CD (93), 'Down In The Park' EP/CD (94), 'Exitus' 2CD (Best Of and rarities...95), 'Crystals & Stones' LP/CD (95), 'Die Zeit' EP/CD (95).

45 GHOSTING 46 GHOSTING
47 GIRLS UNDER GLASS

PHOTO: MADJID ASGHARI

45

46

PHOTO: MADJID ASGHARI

48

Primary in the UK, or Barner Str. 53, 22765 Hamburg.

GOETHES ERBEN Formed Jan 89 by Oswald Henke and Peter Seipt, with the express intention of using the German spoken word in a style of musical theatre. Seipt left a year later after two MCs and Oswald continued in the studio. The band blossomed in 91 with the addition of Mindy Kumbalek (keybds/sax) and Conny R. (guitar), the team responsible for the debut album 'As Sterben Ist Asthetisch Bunt' in early 92. A second album, 'Der Traum An Die Erinnerung' was followed by Conny's departure and the arrival of replacement Troy. MCD, 'Die Brut' and a live CD 'Leben In Niemandsland' (93), with a third studio album in 94 entitled 'Tote Augen Sehen Leben'. This concluded what was known as the Goethes Erben trilogy. A mini album appeared in early 95, 'Der Die Das' which apparently confused everybody. The fourth album, mischievously entitled 'Goethes Erben', a much sparkier item, presumably sets their future course. Avant-garde? Well, not many bands feature underwater piano. Thankfully. The Concept: "The word is the coat in which the meaning silently waits to be undressed." Extra, Spitalgasse 8, 95444 Bayreuth.

GRASS HARP Bo - guitar, Gero - vocals, Fritz - guitar, Murgi - bass, Andy - drums. Formed 89, with original singer (now artist) McAlte. Debut album 'Mushroom Circus' (94), followed by 'Cosmodrome' EP (95). Also a split 10" EP, with the great Into The Abyss, which is limited to only 300 copies, so snap that up pronto! Zesty, intricate work, anything they produce bears serious investigation. They have a lot of tapes you may wish to enquire after. Moonbean Records, Friedrich-Wilhelm-Str. 26, 38100 Braunschweig. (Fax: +49(0)-531-24099367)

THE GUANAVANAA C. Bernsmann, Greve Str 5, Padreborn.

HALL OF SOULS Mildly synthesized Goth. 'Hope' CD. Alice in...

HALO SVEVO Manfred Chmielewski, Zur Burgmuhle 5, 4050 Munchen Gladbach.

HEAD ON FIRE Falk Lohoff - vocals/guitars, Daniel Gottert - bass/guitar and Hugh B. Forster - drums/prog. Formed 91. Fairly rocky but in an acceptably covert manner, leading to a strong early impact. Debut CD 'Nostalgia' (95) K-M Musik. (Fax: 0 52 41 - 3 66 19)

HOUSE OF USHER Formed 90, the main men were Markus Pick and Jorg Kleudgen on guitars and vocals each. In 91 they dragged in Rene Loffler and Robert Nessler (guitar/prog. and bass), and there are always guests to call upon. Jorg is an author of Gothic novels and releases the material of others through his publishers. Watch for his catalogue from Goblin Press, and his magazine *Gothic*. 'Stars Fall Down' CD is an assiduously melodic affair. Jorg Kleudgen, Henricht 1, 5400 Koblenz-Arzheim.

IN MITRA MEDUSA INRI Volker Rohde - vocals/guitar, Holger Meyer - keybds, Michael Gronau - bass. Ritual, mystic Goth trio. Check this out. "The chosen name comprises three symbols which can also be found in their music. 'Mitra' indicates a godship dominating the day and is a symbol of friendship. 'Medusa' presents the godship who protects against evil spirits and was formally found in temples and graves. 'Inri' is the symbol of the church who has a negative reputation due to its irrevocable actions. The contents of the band's songs offer more than the well known cliches of graveyards, demons and cults of the dead." 'Magia Naturalis' demo available, first CD due on Mystic soon. Hochstrasse 73, 41379 Bruggen.

IN MY ROSARY Dirk Lakomy, Stenbenstrasse 4A, 76185 Karlsrahe.

49

50

48 GOETHES ERBEN 49 GRASS HARP
50 INTO THE ABYSS

INTO THE ABYSS Janis Kalifatidis - guitar/vocals, Kostas Tzeras - bass, Jens Geller - drums, new boy Markus Wymetalik - guitar. One of the most important bands in this book. Three Greek students based in Germany get together in 87 and they're still with us now. Not only do they invest their music with the correct dosage of style and passion but they also do the amazing *Fight Amnesia* fanzine, which now includes their regular band-related newsletter *Fiery Serpent*. Lots of demos available, but it wasn't until 93 they hit CD with 'Martyrium' and in 95, 'The Feathered Snake'. These people have the proper attitude and they avoid any ruts. You should respect them totally. Their reputation is growing all round the world and that's because of the quality but also because of the way they have applied themselves to reaching out for contact, a lesson for all other bands. Collectors will need to be swift to track down the 10" 'Dragon Snake' (split with Grass Harp) and the 7", 'La Souer D'Icare'. Best of all, they aren't just 'important', they're enjoyable. Janis Kalifatidis, Heinheimer Str. 4A, 64289 Darmstadt. (Fax: +49 (0) 6151-74908)

LA FLOA MALDITA Darkwave electronics from members of Das Ich and Placebo Effect. A fine combination. 'Sorciere" CD. Codex sl Barfusserstr. 27, 35037 Marburg.

LORE OF ASMODAY R. Seibert, Wittmannstr. 28, 64285 Darmstadt.

LOVE IS COLDER THAN DEATH Susann Porter - vocals, Andy Porter - drums/prog. and Maik Hartung - keybds/prog. A wonderful thing, formed in 89 by Maik, Susann (then of the surname Heinrich), Ralf Donis (vocals) and Sven Mertens on keybds. Their first 12" emerged in 91 where Ralf's influence was strongest but with their first CDs, 'Teignmouth' and 'Mental Traveller' the influences of Maik won through. Soft and smooth.

51 LOVE IS COLDER THAN DEATH 52 MURDER AT THE REGISTRY

51

52

Miffed, Ralf (now vocalist with Think About Mutation) and Sven departed, and in came Andy Porter, formerly of Rose Of Avalanche, and he and Susann married. Following the CDs 'Oxeia' (94) and 'Spellbound' (95) there's no stopping them. Oddly, there's a Mexican compilation, 'Auter', available somewhere. Hyperium. (Fax +49 911 9337744)

LOVE LIKE BLOOD Gunnar Eysel, Joxx Schmidt, Peter Buchele and Yorck. Formed 88, recently rumoured to have split but haven't. Nor have they made it as big as they should because they're blatantly accessible Goth with a medium emphasis on rock. 'Flags Of Revolution', 'An Irony Of Fate', 'Sinister Dawn/Ecstasy' and 'Odysee' CDs. 'Demimonde', 'Stormy Visions' and 'Flood Of Love' MCDs. Early single around too, 'Doomsday'. PO Box 31, 73062 Unhingen.

MADRE DEL VIZIO Fulvio - vocals, Lilith - bass, Janusz - guitar, GODKrist - guitar/sampling/prog. Pretty obvious Christian Death comparisons. CD - 'In The Crypt' (93), 'Dio Dio Dio' (94/95). 'Feast Of Blood' MCD (95). Apollyon. (Fax: 0561-41601)

MARQUEE MOON Nigel D. - vocals, Christian Schlussel - guitar, Jorg Groening - guitar, Reiner Mewitz - bass, Matthias Hackbeil - drums. Formed mid-80's and obviously one of the better known German bands. The early years found problematical relationships with their first label, so bad the band split in 90, only reforming in 93. 'Beyond The Pale' Mini LP (85), 'Strangers In The Monkeybiz' LP (86), 'Here Today & Gone Tomorrow' 12" (86), 'Flying Rocket' 12" (87), 'Future Patrol' LP/CD (89), 'Angst & War' CD (93). Dark Entries, Kösener Str. 10, 14199 Berlin. (Fax: +49 (0) 30-825 86 27)

MERLONS OF NEHEMIAH Ethno-Goth. EFA distribution, Forsterstr. 4-5, 10999 Berlin.

MERRY THOUGHTS 'Milennium' CD, 'Second Generation' and 'The Pale Empress' MCDs obviously highlight the primetime Sisters influence, which explains their popularity. Again, they haven't split, despite the rumours. SPV Records.

MOONCHILD Susan d'Lavollo - vocals, Uwe Holler - guitars/e-bow, Toni De Santis - vocals, bass/prog. Hard, clear early 80's sounding Goth. 'Lunatic Dreams' CD. Nycatopia.

MORGUE Orchestral, gloomy, ultra-classical dance Goth mishmash. Subtronic Records.

MORTAL CONSTRAINT Darkwave par excellence. 'The Legend Of Deformation' CD. Glasnost.

MURDER AT THE REGISTRY Stefan Erhorn - drums, Holger Erhorn - guitars, Martin Krause - guitar/vocals/keybds/organ, Thomas Stach - bass/vocals. Uneasy to classify other than interesting. Formed 91 and their recent, first CD, 'Always On The Brink' features the work that made up several tape offerings, from 93 to 95, which only leaves the 'Soaked To The Skin' demos, if you ever find those anywhere. Thomas Stach, Rebenring 2, 38106, Braunschweig.

NADA Darker than Darkwave! 'Celmetra' CD. Target dist.

NIGHTINGALE All the standard influences - Mission, Sisters, Rosetta and some Metal parts. 'Breathing Shadow' CD. Black Mark Production, Luxemburgerstr. 31, 13353 Berlin.

OPERATING STRATEGIES Wilhelmblumstraße 45, 30451 Hanover.

PANIC ON THE TITANIC Highly rated doom and gloom merchants with electronic heart. 'Gold,

Clouds, Desire' CD. Glasnost.

PARALYSED AGE Bloodshot post-Sisters trio. 'Nocturne' CD, 'Bloodsucker' MCD. Glasnost.

PASSION NOIRE Ulrike Haas and Bernd Neumann. Nice, quiet, moody. 'Between Pleasure & Pain' and 'More' CDs. Dion Fortune.

PASSION PLAY Rock/metal version of Nephilim sound which is more interesting than it may first appear. Debut EP 'Licking Sadness' (95). Thomas Benz, Dahlienweg 16, 53557, Bad Honningen.

CARLOS PERON Known fancifully as Herr Peron to you! This man operates in the world of Fetish music, where you walk stiffly and glare at everybody while old upgraded 80's electro thunders about into the atmosphere.The man positively spews CDs, he's everywhere. These days his music takes a more undulating curvature but either you're into dense but accessible art-pop (which doubles as dance) or you're not. He spent a few years with Yello, so he knows how to turn a neat trick or two. A good indication of his work is the 'La Salle Blanche' (94) and 'La Salle Noire' (96) CDs. Carlos has been doing fetish compilations, including 'O' for the magazine itself, a hard spiky mixture, and 'Fetish Soundtracks' which is smoother and more interesting. Thonwerkstr. 4, 53501 Grafschaft. (Fax 02641 6 2 13) (e-mail: move@berensp.com)

PHOBIA Jorg Egger, Freiburger Str. 1, 5090 Leverkusen 1.

PLACEBO EFFECT Stark dancy darkwave. 'Galleries Of Pain' CD. Dance Macabre, Luitpoldtlatz 18, 8580 Bayreuth.

PP? Some hard techno items and some slow melodic things. Wrote their first demo in 90 on computer. They have an amazing array of tapes available. Debut 'Splendid Threat' CD followed by 'Itum Allenro' CD ('94). Mark D. Chicken, Narzissenstr. 35, 32602 Exter, or K-M Musik. (Fax: 0 52 41 - 3 66 19)

PROJECT PITCHFORK Classic, prodigious Darkwave/EBM band. 'Carrion' MCD and the following CDs - 'Dhyara', '10', 'Lambras', 'Corpses D'Amour', 'Entities'. Kai Lotze, Am Bucheberge 15, Hanover.

THE RADIANCE Thomas Bar, Worishofenerstr. 27, W-8950 Kaufbeuren 1.

REALM OF DOOM S. Thiel - voice/guitar, M. Pesola - bass/prog. Clumsy bedsit Goth but this naivete is quite charming. It's just hard to believe the firm sounding vocals as you know they're probably having to make a real effort to appear moody. Punky at times because the guitars are a bit painful. Oblivion/Gorkon.

RELIGIOUS VISION Christian Beckers, Am Kollbergring 1B, 31683, Obernkirchen.

REVENGE OF NEPTHYS Atmospheric but melodic (Laibach meets Zymox), in Nephilim-approved underwear. Torsten Thimm, Roonstr. 2, 38102 Braunschweig.

SBH M. Hornschuh, Garbbeweg 40, 21077 Hamburg.

SECRET DISCOVERY Neffs/Sisters. Average. 'Into The Void', 'Wasted Dreams' and 'Dark Line' CDs. PO Box 400 326, 4630 Bochum 1.

SEPULCHRUM MENTIS Gothish Metal, including contribution of Two Witches' Jyrki. 'Sepulchrum Mentis' MCD. Martin Kasprzak, Schloss Str. 68, 12165 Berlin.

SHADOWPLAY Michael Scholz's project, formed 84. He went ahead solo because he couldn't find the people who shared his interests. To date he has had to stick to tapes, 'Another Autumn Day' (88), 'An Ideal World' (90), 'Tears' (92). A 'Best Of' was released by Beton Tapes in 93. The word has eventually got around and Shadowplay's latest tape 'Reflections In A Broken Mirror' is bound to push it on further. This is quality stuff as you'd expect. Michael also DJs and organises Goth nights in his local town and he's involved in a project called The Whiplover, named after a 60's German fetish mag, moving in an Electro-Industrial direction. This is one cool man. Unfortunately, the photos he sent were shite. Knuthstr. 12, 24939 Flensburg.

SILKE BISCHOFF They look brilliant but that's all I know. Depeche Modey, I've been told. Apparently they were tasteless enough to name themselves after a young woman held hostage, then murdered by terrorists. Her parents are now suing the band. Good. Discordia dist.

SIRENSONG An electronic All About Eve? 'The Cruelty Of Children' MCD.

SOMBRAS DEL OLVIDO One man project, by Olaf Peters. A. Pohle, Lur.Haupstr. 59, 22547 Hamburg.

SOPOR AETERNUS (& The Ensemble Of Shadows) I don't have the faintest idea who does what, but that is part of the appeal. Began their Undead trilogy ('Blut Der Schwarzen Rose') with the MC called 'Es Reiten Die Toten So Scjhell', of which parts two and three, 'Rufus' and 'Till Times And Ties Are Done' are planned for CD. The 'Time Heals Nothing' MC was released and somewhere a video, no longer available, 'Ehjeh Ascher Ehjeh', containing "dances, rites, symbols". It's mainly the work of a man called Varney. As you can see from the photograph he's the life and soul of the party. In fact the first time I saw that image I thought it was simply an old image taken and tinted from the silent movie of *The Hunchback Of Notre Dame*, because that's what the first actor looked like. It would appear that he actually looks like this, or Howard Hughes is still with us. The idea of playing live fills him with dread, making him want to vomit. So unfamiliar with the modern world is he that he stays indoors, fingernails

53 SOPOR AETERNUS

growing ever longer. He admits to understanding why musicians don't want to form any long term working relationship, accepting that he's a bit of a pain, due to his depression. This 'setting', or immobilisation, has created what may well be the most Gothic band of all time. Seriously. The music is never barbaric but it has its frightening moments - just don't expect the standard line-up... and that voice! It's so hard to compare to anyone or thing but British readers of a certain age may remember a tv documentary in the early 70's about a haunted church, or house, or whatever. Anyway, it was haunted. A team went along to spend the night there hoping to record anything that might happen. In the final moments of the programme, they got it. It was a sigh of a soul so forlorn that the word anguish doesn't do it justice. Once heard, never forgotten. No actor on earth could have replicated it. Anyway, that ghost was Varney's dad if you ask me. It's so weird that you've got to feel sorrow, rather than sorry, for him. Eponymous CD available. Apocalyptic Vision, Alex Storm, Ahornweg 19, 64807 Dieburg. (Fax: 6071/5737.)

SOUL IN ISOLATION Love Is Colder Than Death, Deadcandance etc. 'On Stranger Tides' CD. Gymnastic Records.

STILL PATIENT? N.D. - vocals/prog., Beck - guitar, Kraniny - guitar, Kaluza - keybds. The good people at Nightbreed positively urinate with excitement at the merest mention of this name. I know nothing about them except they formed in 88. First demo 91, first CD, 'Salamand' 92, 'Cataclysm' CD (94). N.D. admits to Sisters influence, which is okay, and he's got two iguanas, which is even better. They uphold old traditions but want to smash the music at you. Schmiedgasse 27, 67550 Worms.

STILL SILENT A project of Goethes Erbens' Mindy Kumbalek, already responsible for the 'Sick World' CD, which has included contributions from musicians from Catastrophe Ballet, The Cassandra Complex, Project Pitchfork, and Girls Under Glass. Everything is here from pop to atmospherics. George Lindt, Barfuesserstr. 27, 35037 Msarburg/Lahn.(Fax: +49 (0) 6421/161809)

SUBSTANCE OF DREAM Alternative rocky Goth. 'The Fall Of Laura' MCD. Ncytolopia.

SWANS OF AVON Nephilimesque. 'Trust The Angels' CD. Dirk Sonnet, Alle Grenzstr. 259, 45663 Rechlinghausen.

SWEET WILLIAM Oliver Heuer - vocals/guitar, Ralf Bursch - drums, Frank Breuer - bass, Bjorn Godde - guitar. Formed in 86 and still alive. 'Have A Relapse' 7" EP (90), 'These Monologues' LP (91), 'The Snakes You've Drawn' 7" EP (91), 'Kind Of Strangest Dream' concept (!) CD (92), the snappily titled 'Development Through The Years 1986-1993' CD (93) and by now you've probably wrapped your ears around their 'Show' CD (96). 3CD Box 'Almost Ten Years' also planned for 96. A tough, pragmatic band with a wistful side. When you take your name from a hardy perennial herb you'd better have something to back up that tough talk and these hairy young men do. They've also got shocking handwriting. Oliver Heuer, Zum Breitmaar 21, 50170 Kerpen. (Fax: 0221 562364)

TEARS OF PASSION Gordon Rausch - vocals, Martin Hirsch - guitars/prog., Gunnar Ascheuer - keybds, Axel Schunder - vocals/prog./keybds. Another interesting band who have left behind the traditional instruments and gone for a very obvious, physical change. Harder and dancier than ever, but with hymnic ballads and lush traditional tracks. 'Desperation' and 'Experience' CDs. Mozartstr. 17, 58452 Witten.

THE HALL OF SOULS Patrick Crowley - bass/keybds, Alexander Slis - vocals/guitar. Formed' 92, not knowing what they were but with a gloomy, doomy sound soon found their music warmly welcomed by the Goth publications and scene. Strong literary influences, from Kafka, Yeats and co. 'Hope' CD (95), 'The Sea' MCD (96), 'Exiot' CD (96). Frank D'Angelo, Wetzlarer Str. 9, 35630 Ehringshausen.

TORS OF DARTMOOR Er... band members Heiko Mutert and Rudiger Frank both came from a band bizarrely named Printed At Bismarck's Death. Wolfgang Koch was spared that indignity, joining later. Formed 89, released their first CD in 91 and albums worth hunting down are 'The Obvious Darkness' and 'House Of Sounds', along with a live album from France. Hyperium.

UMBRA ET IMAGO Mozart - Vocals, Lutz Demmler - prog./bass, Alex Perin - guitar, Nail - keybds. Sex, religion and vampires, a singer called Mozart and their own label makes this highly visual band a serious promise of excitement for the next few years. Started late 91 following the dissolution of The Electric Avantgarde. The name is a translation for Ghostless Shadows. Their stage shows are meant to be quite dramatic. One mini album ('Remember Dito') and three albums to collect - 'Traume, Sex Und Tod', 'Infantile Spiele' and 'Gedanken Eines Vampirs'. Spirit Records.

VAMPIRE STATE BUILDING Horror Punk with a tasteful sense of fun, doing a limited edition box set with a staking kit! Limited to 359 copies ('Unholy Collection'). Target Dist.

WILL OF THE WISP Archangel, Postfach 1441, 51592 Morsbach.

X MARKS THE PEDWALK Weird Industrial extension more than Goth. Europe's answer to Skinny Puppy? 'The Killing Had Begun', 'Human Desolation, Four Fit' (Singles) and 'Abattoir' CDs on Cleopatra.

Fanzines/Magazines

AETERNA Impressive fanzine for Industrial-Electro-Gothic-Ritual... "simply everything that has a dark,

54 ALEXANDER POHLE

55

sombre, experimental or at least sinister sound or attitude". Chris Peller, Riesenburstr. 13, 81249 Munich.

BACK AGAIN Alexander Pohle's fanzine and as you would expect from one of the country's most organised men, a wide-ranging venture. It is absolutely massive and only concerns itself with a few interviews, concentrating instead on hundreds of detailed reviews. Essential reading for anybody with a knowledge of German. Luruper Hauptstraße 59, 22547 Hamburg.

BLACK Thomas Wacker, Elfeicher Weg 242, 64289 Darmstradt.

THE BLACK BOOK Goth guide to Berlin. Andreas Starosta, Kreuzbergstr. 72, 10965 Berlin.

COMIC TRASH Testament-Vertrieb, Fredy Engel, Arndtstr. 48, 33615 Bielefeld.

CRUCIAMENTUM Silvio Kessman, Lessingstr 21, 97990 Weikersheim.

DER GOLEM Art-based mag. P. Ochs, Schonleinstr. 47, 45147 Essen.

EB/METRONOM Electro/Industrial/Goth. Hospeltstrasse 66, 50825. Koln.

EBU'S CHARTBREAKER Carsten Olbrich, Bottenhorner, Weg 37 60489 Frankfurt.

ELECTRONIC DISEASE Oberaustr. 72a, J3179 Bonn.

EPITAPH Markus Garger, OhnstraBe 7, 35274 Kirchain-Schonbach.

ETERNITY Demo zine. Katja Kruzewitz, Goethstr. 62, 12459 Berlin.

FIGHT AMNESIA! The brilliant fanzine from Into The Abyss. Subscription details: 7 IRCs (Europe), 11 IRCs elsewhere. Absolutely unmissable. Janis Kalifatidis, Heinheimer Str. 4A, 64289 Darmstadt. (Fax: +49 (0) 6151-74908)

GOTHIC It's big and it's clever. Jorg Kleudgen, Henkericht 1, 56077, Koblenz-Arzheim.

IRRES TAPES Newsletter. Matthias Lang, Barebdellstr. 35, 6795 Kindsbach.

KLANGTANKE Michael Hinkes, Vogelsangstr 12, 5484 Gonnersdorf.

KODEX A stunning quality music magazine which has been in existence for three years, covering music, literature and the arts generally. Each issue contains a CD. Issue 5 is about Art and Insanity and they are desperate for input/info about the industrial movement, especially SPK. Well, if it helps I once saw a video with an SPK soundtrack set inside an autopsy lab where the severed head of a corpse was manouvred down to the naughty bits to give itself oral! That's all I care to know about SPK, thank you! Issue four of *Kodex* had a sixteen track CD (Clock DVA/Laibach/Leather Strip etc). There's precious little true Goth content but for the intelligentsia who love beautifully laid out magazines appreciative/instructive of esoteric scenes this is essential. The outer limits of Industrialism. Barfusser Str. 27, 3550 Marburg-Lahn. (Fax: 06421-161809)

LOLE Kolner Str 20, 45145 Essen.

MY WAY Ulrich Gernand, Finkenstr. 8, 4709 Bergkamen.

ELIZABETH NAGY Journalist with endless fanzine contacts. Bundesallee 106, 12161, Berlin.

56

NEW LIFE Alte Landstrae 4, 34212 Helsungen.

NO CONTROL TORTURE Wolfgang Scholz, Romestr. 94, 5400/56073 Koblenz.

PARANEUJA Oli Faul, Alte Ziegelei 8, 67454 HaBloch.

PROGRESSIVE ENTERTAINMENT Newsletter with all sorts. Send either 2 IRCs or 2 DM. Also has a massive mail order list available for a couple of IRCs extra, and they're heavily involved with their local scene, arranging festivals etc. Well worth supporting. Eichweier 13, 51515 Kurten.

REMAINS Limited to 666 copies. Spooky-wooky. Chris Biegert, Haupstr. 26, 73500 Waldstetten.

REVELATION Quarterly big glossy magazine which is meant to have been a newsletter. A severe case of enthusiasm overload. Pano Christodulopulos, Boelckestr. 24A, Mainz-Kastel.

SINNESLUST UND GEISTIGE BEGIERDE Scruffy, spirited little zine. Very nice, very eager. Narrische Creationen, Christian Lang, Alsbach 3, 51588 Numbrecht.

SONIC SEDUCER Fantastic mag, mainly Goth but all relevant electro offshoots and stuff. Available throughout Germany, sometimes Austria and Switzerland, and released every three months. Thomas Vogel, PO Box 301282. 50782 Koln.

SPIRIT Newsletter. e.v, Marienstr. 40, 7500 Karlsruhe 1.

SUBLINE Benno Limberg, Hochstr 19, 45894 Gelsenkirchen-Buer.

TROUBADICKS Markus Wosgien, Ostalbstr. 17, 73529, Schwabisch Gmund/Bargau.

UNSERE KLEINE WELT Andreas Busche, Beckserstr. 19, 31136 Hildesheim.

VERTIGO Nikolaus Schulz, Ausser der Schleifmuhle 22, 2800 Bremen 1.

WITCHCRAFT Stefan Lons, Maximinstr 26A, 56072 Rubenach.

ZILLO Quite simply, the best music magazine in Europe, by a mile. They also organise brilliant festivals. Zillo GmbH, Verlag & Veranstaltungen, Lachswehrallee 11, 23558 Lubeck.
(Ph: 0451 811 54) (Fax: 0451 86 10 89)

Fetish

BLACKSIN Fetish mag. Pourquoi-Pas, Ludwigstrasse 29, 66115 Saarbrucken.

BOUTIQUE BIZARRE Clothes. Reeperbauhn 35-40, 20359 Hamburg.

CRAZY FASHION Clothes. Schweiggerstr 30, 90487 Nurnberg.

FASHION CATS Shop. Vulkanstr 33, Dusseldorf.

HAUTNAH Fashion and bondage bits. Uhlandstr. 170, 1000 Berlin 15.

HIGHLIGHTS Shop. Gabelsberger Str. 68, 80333 Munich.

LES GRACIEUSES MODERNES Lovers of corsetry organisation, holding occasional grand balls in UK and Germany. Conderstrasse 30, 5440 Mayen.

LGS Shop. Bochumer StraBe 76, 45886 Gelsenkirchen.

LOMMEL Furniture. Hochstadenstr 27, 50674 Koln.

LOVE & FLASH Clothes. ZentralstraBe 13-17, 31785 Hameln.

S&M SOURCE BOOK Exactly what it says. Holstenstrasse 5, 24534 Neumunster.

SCHLAGZEILEN Magazine. Postbox 306 352 D-2000 Hamburg 36.

WALTER'S LEDER BOUTIQUE Clothes. Reichenbachstr. 40a, (Ecke Frauenhofestr) 8000 Munchen 5.

THE WITCH Videos. Filmproduktion Dietze, Department M-1E, Kirchberg 1, 94513 Schonberg.

Labels

ANACHRONISMS Bittenfelder Str. 5, 71640 Ludwigsburg.

APOCALYPTIC VISION Alex Storm, Ahornweg 19, 64807 Dieburg. (Fax: 6071/5737)

APPOLYON RECORDINGS Altenbaunaer. 27, D-34134 Kassel.

ARCHANGEL RECORDS Postfach 1441, 51592 Morsbach.

CTHULU RECORDS R Kasseckert, Im Haselbusch 56, 47447 Moers.

CONCRETE RECORDS Andreas Reissnauer, PO Box 1421, 77845 Achern

DANSE MACABRE RECORDS Luitpoldplatz 18, 95444 Bayreuth. (Fax: 49-921 12 23 0)

DRAGNET RECORDS Aureliusstr. 1-3, 52064 Achen.

DRONE RECORDS Stefan Knappe, Fasanenstr. 11, 26789 Leer.

FOUNDATION RECORDS Stephan Thiemann, Mousonstrasse 12, 60316 Frankfurt.

FUN FUND VIERZIG Haupstr. 49, 2411 Sandesneben.

GLASNOST Glockengiesserwall 17, 20095 Hamburg. (Fax 0410-7685726)

GYMNASTIC RECORDS Dianastrasse.1, 80538 Munich. (Fax: +49 (89) 29161491)

HYPERIUM PO Box 100 561, 8560 Lauf.

HYPNOBEAT PO Box 100 561, 8560 Lauf.

INZKZ Ludwigshohstrare 58, 6100, Darmstadt.

KM -MUSIK & SOUNDS OF DELIGHT Postfach 2114, 33251 Gutersloh.

MUSIC RESEARCH GMBH Norksdata Str 3, 61352 Bad Homburg.

NBU Olaf Seider, Bert-Brecht-Str. 46, 55128 Mainz.

PROGRESSIVE ENTERTAINMENT Eichweier 13, 51515 Kurten-Weiden.

SCOUT PRODUCTIONS Susterfeldstr 61, 52072 Aachen. (Fax: 0241/877473)

SPIRIT RECORDS Marienstr. 40, 76137 Karlsruhe.

STRANGEWAYS RECORDS GroBe Johannisstr. 15, 20457 Hamburg.

SUBTRONIC RECORDS WeiBenburgerstr. 8, 44135 Dortmund. (Fax: ++49 231 52 67 86)

VENDETTA Ulrichstr. 14, 7340 Geislingen-Steige.

WEISSER BERST Waldschmidstr. 17, 60316 Frankfurt. (Fax ++49-69-451418)

ZOTH OMMOG Music Research GmbH, Norsk-Data-Str. 3, 61352 Bad Homburg.

Other sources

ARBEAT-MEDIA Radio show. Headquarters, Ottic, Westerwaldstr. 35, 53489 Sinzig-Westum.

ARCHEGON Gunter Schroth, Regerstr. 6, 55127 Mainz.

ART KONKRET Excellent mailorder firm. Alexis Weimer, HaupstraBe 28, 69231 Rauenberg.

ARTWARE RECORDS Describe themselves as "suppliers of extreme cultures in music and printmedia" but it isn't that severe, as one of their recent releases is the Die Form book, *The Visionary Garden*, by Philippe Fichot, an art/photo book of images which have, admittedly, attracted the eagle eye of the police before. He uses positively bizarre - blasphemous - images of women. This book contains 99 of them. Limited edition of 1,000. Taunustr 63b, 65183 Wiesbaden. (Fax: +49 (0) 611 59654)

BETON TAPES Excellent tape distribution service from that man again, with titles already past the hundred mark. Alexander Pohle, Luruper Haupstrabe 59, 22547 Hamburg.

CELTIC CIRCLE Alfred Kaenders, Grunewaldstr. 38, 47608 Geldern.

DARK STAR Grobe Johannistr. 15, 20457 Hamburg.

DEATHWISH Ulrichgstr. 14, 7340 Geislingen/Steige.

DION FORTUNE RECORDS Mari Reimann, Feldstr. 72, 51371 Leverkusen.

DRAGNET RECORDS Collectors shop. This is what

started off Scout Productions. There's Dragnet records, the label, and Dragnet distribution. They have a quite magnificent mail order catalogue available which you should send for. Aureliusstr. 1-3, 52064 Achen.

DRAG & DROP Seen as a successor to the labels Dragnet and Elves (eh?). It's going to be Industrial, Ritual, Ambient etc. Anything goes.

EBU's MUSIC Tape label and distribution. Carsten Olbrich, Bottonhorner Weg 37, D-60489, Frankfurt.

GLASNOST Label's excellent mail order. Glockengiesserwall 17, 20095 Hamburg. (Fax 0410-7685726)

GOBLIN PRESS. German language only Gothic novels publishing company. Beautiful items available. Jorg Kleudgen, Henkericht 1, D-56077, Koblenz-Arzheim.

STEFFEN GRELLMANN A book for record collectors. Starting compiling second issue so get your wants in there now. Hellmundstr. 16, 65183 Wiesbaden. (Fax: +49 611 372613)

GORKON TAPES A far more selective outfit from Alexander Pohle, including works by Into The Abyss, The Venus Fly Trap, Die Blumen Des Bosen etc. Alexander Pohle, Luruper Hauptstraße 59, 2547 Hamburg.

INFRA ROT Smaller perhaps than Nuclear Blast, though I think this catalogue maybe offers more for the Goth fan. It's also got everything else in it, and it's set out alphabetically so you can see it all more clearly. Im Tafelmahd 38B, 87727 Babenhausen.

IRRES TAPES Matthias Lang, Barendelstr 35, D-66862 Kindsbach.

KAKTUS Mail Order, distribution and fanzine. Martin Roeder, Schiessmauestr 36, D-72810.

KM -MUSIK & SOUNDS OF DELIGHT Interesting label with catalogue worth sending for as they have cheapo vinyl and some mail-order only compilation CDs. Postfach 2114, 33251 Gutersloh.

MASCHINENWELT A label only set up in June 95 to continue the good work of giving exposure to interesting newcomers that Christian was already involved with as a gig promoter, after a lively past which involved work as a photographer, music journalist and running his agency. His first releases all tend towards the Electro direction and have been receiving press plaudits, so he has the right touch, the shrewdest knowledge. UK distributors should maybe contact him? Christian Weber, PO Box 12061 Berlin. (Fax: +49 (0) 30 7529290)

MDD Mailorder/distrib. mainly Metal but other interesting things too. Am Meelfeld 2, 38547 Calberlah.

MOONCHILD Promoter. Werk II, Kochstraße 132, 7030 Leipzig.

NEGATIVE CHOICE Braaker Muhle, 22145 Braak, Hamburg.

NEUZEITLICHE TONKONSTRUKTIONEN Tapes. Alex Frick, Podstfach 1131, 73277, Owen.

NUCLEAR BLAST Probably the biggest and the most organised mail order catalogue that I've ever seen. Lavishly printed, much in full colour, it boasts a good range but minus cassettes or fanzines. They do have t-shirts though, also picture discs, exclusive to them and a smattering of interviews, for which you'll need to read German. Haupstraße 109, 73072 Dusseldorf.

OBLIVION Martin Pesold/Simon Brunner Gbr, Johannistr. 4, 93059 Regensburg.

PRACS Promoter/band contact. Postfach 1160, 79371 Mulheim.

RADIO DREYECKLAND Radio show. Micha Frohoff, Bifonstr. 39 , 7800 Freiburg.

RADIO MARABU Radio show. PO Box 220, 342-42373 Wuppertal.

RESSURECTION Claus P. Muller, Jagerhalde 57, 70327 Stuttgart 60.

TAKE OFF MUSIC Import shop. Marienfelder Str. 52 Guetsloh.

TARGET EXPORT The successor to Dragnet distribution, making available all the Scout-related recordings but also items from other German labels. An important service. Susterfeldstr 61, 52072 Aachen. (Fax: 0241/877473)

PATRICK TAPPE This man has done a 210 page German language guide to the Sisters Of Mercy. Cost 50DM, full discography including bootlegs. Haupstr. 38, 48 607 Ochtrup.

TIMEBASE Burgerstr. 27, 40219 Dusseldorf.

TRUMMER KASSETTEN Tape label. Also distribute some vinyl and fanzines. Lutz Pruditsch, Hartenkamp 11, 26127 Oldenburg.

URBAN Distribution. Thranestr 40, 44309 Dortmund.

VAMPIREZ Froschenseestr. 10, 87629 Fussen.

WONDERLAND Mail order from the label Alice In... WetzalrerStraße 9, 35630 Ehrinshausen.

XTRA Fashion. All Goth clothes and shoes. Excellent catalogue available, which is sometimes sidesplitting, though by accident. Interesting range of masks to be had. Herdbruckerstraße 8, 89073 Ulm. (Fax 0731/6023226)

57 58 59

57 THE DROPS 58 FLOWERS OF ROMANCE
59 THE RENAISSANCE DANCE

Greece

Bands

THE DROPS Stratos Theologitis - vocals/guitar, Dimitris Stevis - drums, Panayiotis Christoforou - bass, George Komninos - guitars/keybds, Nikos Sebekopolous - guitar. Formed 90. 'Suicide In Heaven' LP (94), 'Fatal Fall' 7". Quite straightforward and very nice - medium melodic with touches of power but never harsh. Panayiotis Chridstoforou, 45 Vas. Georgiou B'Street 18534 Piraeus.

FLOWERS OF ROMANCE First demo in 86 yet they actually started in 81! Kostas Venos - guitar, Tasos Dimitriadis - bass, George Venizelos - drums and Mike Pougounas vocals kicked it off, originally influenced by punkier things like The Clash and Dead Boys. During 84, Venos and Dimitriadis go away, replaced by Lao on guitar and bassist Harry Stavrakas. Their sound turns melancholic. George then leaves, with Harry, to form a band I've never heard of, Orthodox, in England. So say hello to B.B. Romeo on drums, Teo Botinis - bass and Platon Papadimitriou - guitar. This line up releases the debut album, 'Dorian Grey' in 90, the first of its kind in Greece. They had a Greek hit with a cover of Bolan's 'Children Of The Revolution', whereupon both guitarists leave, to be replaced by Bay J. The four piece release the 'Love Means Death' EP, Botinis goes, but Harry returns. It's all getting impossibly confused as the band have also had a compilation released in Britain, credited as 'Music And Elsewhere' (88). Then B.B. Romeo has an accident and goes. Laura Ginni, one of the most famous Greek pianists meets the band and agrees to join. Bay J. leaves. 'Pleasure and Pain' album released in late 93, featuring Angelo Kakouratos - guitar and James Koukas - drums. By now they've probably all left and been replaced by somebody else as chaos clearly follows them, yet the idea surges on. PO Box 80508, 18510 Piraeus.

THE ILLUSION FADES Formed in Athens in 89. George, Thans, Nick and John have managed an eponymously titled album and a couple of singles. George Dedes, Studio A, 37 Street, Marbussi T.K. 15126 Athens.

THE RENAISSANCE DANCE Disco-Goth in parts. A refreshing change with warmly romantic, trickling guitar, like early Danse Society crossed with regrettably early Depeche Mode. Not exactly desolate but at the same time curiously empty. Also mad in places. I'm confused by the biog. It says that from XXVI until XXVIII they released three demos and a 7" under another name, all of which helped them to be considered as "one of the leading dark leftovers in Greece"! Fair enough. In XXIX (Is that 89?) two demos were recorded, 'Crucified Dreams' and 'Dying In Motion' and in XXX they produced the 'My Swan' trilogy. Their own description is fine - "the sound brings memories from the 80's dance floors and the lyrics depict the darker side of love with the gentle touch on vampirism". Pierre Bizarre, Evalkidou 23, 10444, Athens.

SPINALONGA Drablow - vocals/all instruments. There's more going on here than they've told me - and it's all interesting creepy dance-based Goth, crawling along with a sly coating of added noises chafing at the mix. More interesting still, they were doing then what most people are moving towards now. It has all the right Goth credentials and yet remains a distinct, individual beast. Their first two 12" EPs are weird. 'Bid Time Return' (93) was recorded three years earlier in America, and '13th Relation' (94) was recorded in the UK one year beforehand. There is a weird turmoil going on inside this project. "Spinalonga, or its creator, exists through constrictions," someone writes to inform me. "It is activated by misery and bears no cathartic elements whatsoever. The mortal psyche is to be pitied. Spinalonga's works will stand alone as a tragical monument of a draining yet undetermined loss. Handle with care."

62 GITANE DEMONE. 63 ROB BRAUTIGAM, EDITOR OF *INTERNATIONAL VAMPIRE*

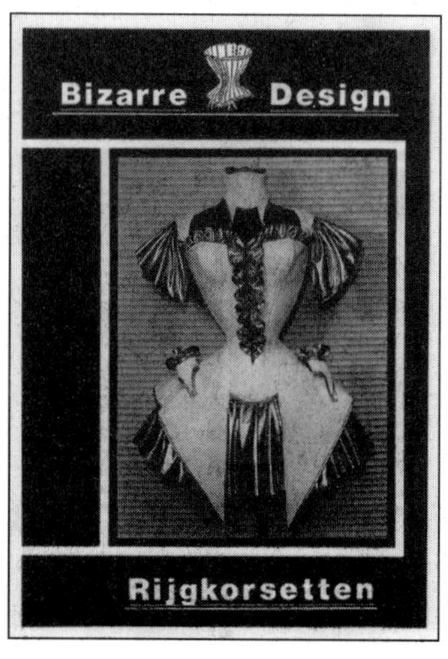

61

60

Two more releases planned for Xmas 96 - 'Imuer Ein Fur Allemal' CD and 'The Triumph Over Pride' EP, on Poeta Negra. Seriously interesting work. PO Box 10624, GR-54110 Thessaloniki.

Other sources

BEHIND THE MIRROR Fanzine. Greg Baxevandis, Grevenon Str. 6, 15234, Halandri, Athens.

THE FLOWER NATION Flowers Of Romance fanclub. Chronis Kokkinos, PO Box 80508, 18510 Piraeus.

GOTHIC Nice chunky zine written in English with a habit of putting the bands on the spot about religion and Satan! PO Box 40021, 12310 Agia Barbara, Athens.

IRO Brilliant artist. Komotinis 9, TK 11526, Ampelokipi, Athens.

METAL AGGRESSION A mainly Metal mag but open-minded enough to cover anything. Written in English. Chris Karajannis, Lindou 4, 11476, Poligono, Athens.

OPEN FORUM Fetish mag. Lianos PO Box 8343, Athenes Omonia 10010.

SPLATTERZINE Horror zine with strong Gothic feel. Lito Martinou, 9 Terpsihorsis Str., 155 62 Holargos, Athens.

STIGMATA Nice, conventional zine. Nancy Mandaltsi, 4 Mesohoriou Rd, 56123 Thessaloniki.

SUNKEN CATHEDRAL Zine for "the Dark and Goth", allegedly the largest in Greece, created by members of The Renaissance Dance. Contributions welcome. Pierre Bizarre, Evalkidou 23, 10444, Athens.

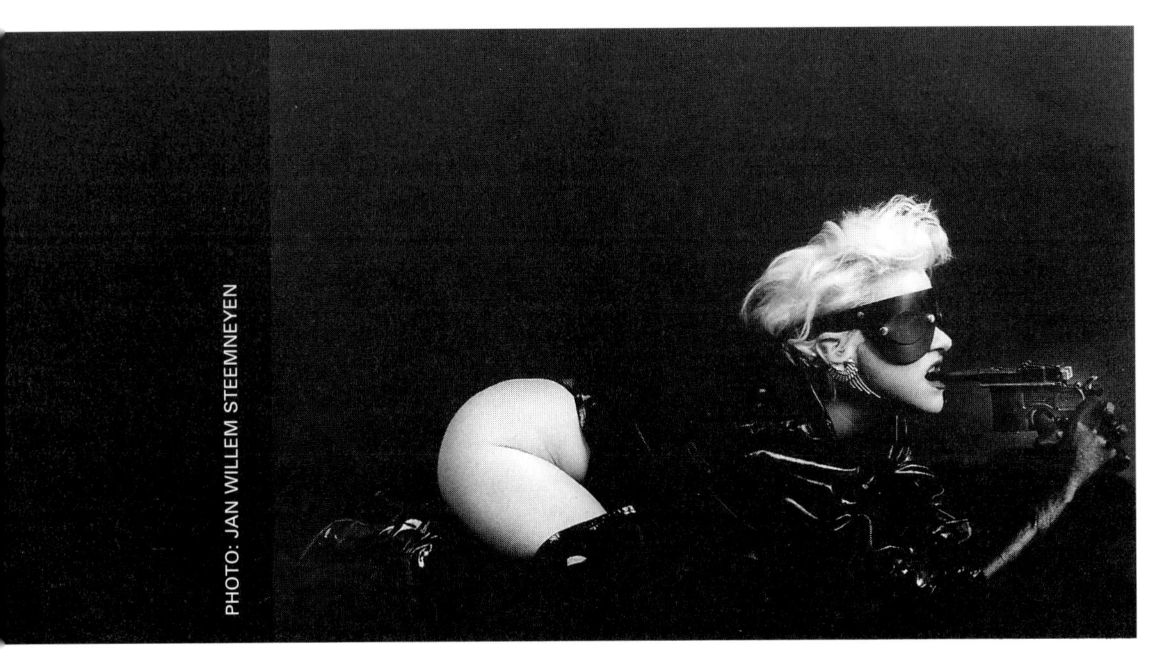

62

63

TESTAMENTUM DOMINI PRODS Distribution service run by the *Gothic* crew. Send IRC or SAE for full list. Marinos Agelopulos, Esperidon 23, 12137 Peristen, Athens.

Holland/ The Netherlands

BEN'S FASHION Fetish. PO Box 3184, 3101 ed Schiedam.

BIZARRE DESIGN Corsets, some of which are works of art and some which clearly have fetish connotations. You can have whatever you like made to order as well. The quality is quite ravishing and the attention to detail no doubt guaranteed. It makes firms like Axfords in the UK look pretty average. It's not just corsets - there's dress type things too. So it's fashion wear and naughty wear. You'll love it, unless you have no taste. Easily the best catalogue of its sort that I've seen. Marnixstraat 394a, 1017 PL Amsterdam.

BOETIEK-ATELIE 'Exclusive' rubber gear. Wagenweg 16 - 2012 ND Haarlem.

CULT EPICS Rare kitsch videos. PO Box 55670, 1007 Amsterdam.

CULT MUSIC Label. PO Box 55670, 1007 ND Amsterdam.

DEMASK European fetish fashion firm with unparalleled reputation. Zeeduk 64, 1012BA, Amsterdam.

GITANE DEMONE Gitane started with Christian Death in 83, on vocals and keybds, with which she continued until 89, leaving to pursue other activities, in Holland. Here she merged with the jazz field and experimentation, as well as moving towards music which caressed her interest in Fetish. Her earliest solo work appeared on the 'Facets Of Blue' album, and she went on to do her fetish collaboration with Marc Ickx (Split Second) with the 'Never Felt So Alive' CD coming under the name of Demonix. In 94 she was reunited with original Christian Death founder Rozz Williams and they toured. A CD, including a few shared songs, 'With Love And Dementia' appeared in 95 and they recorded a full album together, 'Dream Home Heartache' and they have toured again promoting this. At the time of writing Gitane is working on what her company Cult, call her 'debut' album, which I don't quite understand - but rest assured it will glow, like all her work. A true one-off. Cult Music PO Box 55670, 1007 ND Amsterdam.

FEAR OF LIFE Excellent heavily underground fanzine. Arco v Winden, Oude Leedeweg 39, 2641 NM Pijnacker.

GOTTERDAMMERUNG Guido - vocals/guitar/keybds, Marc - bass/guitars/prog., Almar - guitars/keybds/prog. 'A Body and a Birthmark' CD and 'Rearm' MCD. Fast guitar Goth some compare to Altered States, and many point the accusing Valor finger at the singer, but others brightly find it recalling March Violets/UK Decay. PO Box 3078, 5203 Den Bosch.

INTERNATIONAL VAMPIRE Fantastic magazine, produced in an almost classical sense, treating everything pretty seriously and everyone recommends the man in charge as being knowledgeable and trustworthy. Rob Brautigam, Galileiplantsoen 90-1, 1098NC Amsterdam.

NIZAGAMAH Newsletter. Hahamandad Foundation, Weststraat 38, 4571 HM Axel.

65

64

PHOSPHOR Distribution. Paul Bijlsma, Vilenstede 132, 1183 An Amstelveen.

ELLEN SCHIPPERS DESIGN Special rubber gear designed by dancer, so pretty smart stuff.
1e Jan streenstraat 112, 1072 NR Amsterdam.
(Fax 0031-20-675-0486)

VITAL Newsletter. Frans, Staalplaat PO Box 11 453, 1001 Gl Amsterdam. Or Opaalstraat 19, XK Nijmegen.

WICCAN REDE Bilingual Wiccan craft mag. PO Box 473 3700-AL Zeist.

WRAPPED Fetish clothes. Singel 434-1017 Av Amsterdam.

Hungary

GABRIELLA & ISTVAN KOLONICS Pagan artists and writers. The quality of the artwork is absolutely brilliant. If anybody needs great work done (which you're prepared to pay for) I suggest you get in touch! The work they have sent, and some of it is in this book somewhere, goes by three names - Kolonics, Daleth and Agrippa. 1092 Budapest, Hogyes E.U.11.

MASODIK LATAS A very chunky, professional standard fanzine, prone to covering a bit of everything. Tracz Mihaly, Budapest 1172, XIII. u. 35.
(Fax: 0-36-1-1258-0075)

ORDITO EQER Zine. PF 188, Budapest 1241.

PRINCESS SPIDER The ice maiden! The idea is you worship her and she allows you to. Or something. She's a Skeleton Girl, she does what she wants -

64 ARTIST: ISTVAN KOLONICS 65 PRINCESS SPIDER
66 ARTICA

what else is there to say? More details available in the UK Fanzine section. Merciless Predator, Heves 3360, Baross G Ut 10/A.

TROTTEL Label/distribution. PO Box 873 Budapest 1463.

VIRUS Excellent fanzine. PF 1206, 1245 Budapest.

STRAIGHT EDGE Fanzine. Vizler Tibor, Gyor, Sarkerekiu, 29. 9019.

Indonesia

STEPHEN ANTHONY Very possibly Indonesia's only Goth band. JL. BDN II/20, Cilandak - Jakarta Selatan 12430.

Italy

Bands

ADVENA AVIS Marco Carpiceci, Via Arbia, 40 - 00199 Roma.

AFOBIA Emiliano Bonafede, Via Quirino Majorana 140, 00152 Roma.

ALIEN MARTYR Heaven's Gate Prod, P. Terramare 5, 43040 Vicofertile, Parma.

ANDROMEDA COMPLEX Heaven's Gate Prod.

ARKHAM ASYLUM Marc - vocals/guitars, Roberta - keybds, Silvia - bass, Giovanni - guitar, Ricky - drums. Signed to the wonderful Energeia label. Started late 91, a hybrid of early, quality Goth sounds offset by diligent indie touches. Marco Fontolan, Via Mazzini 17, 31059 Zetro Branco (TV).

ARTICA Alberto Casti - vocals/guitar, Gabriele Serafini - guitar, Michele Mariela - bass, Massimo Bonavita - keybds, Stefano Marcon - drums. Very dramatic at times, yet in a tight, realistic manner, as though they want things dense. Formed 89, and although it took two years for their first demo to become available, people are beginning to take them very seriously. When you get a band who willingly get involved with things you know there's something right about them and they're the sort to establish links with other bands. They don't sit at home sulking and pretending that one day they will wake up as Rock Gods. "We didn't choose Dark & Gothic," they say. "We found ourselves in it, as a child in his mother's womb." They've melted together all the credible, edible elements of the past and are slowly crawling forward with dignity. 'Marea' (92) and 'Dahlia' demos (94), and the essential 'Ombra E Luce' CD (95). Alberto Casti, Via Merulana, 183, 00185 - Roma.

ATARAXIA Francesca Nicoli - vocals/drum machine, Vittorio Vandelli - acoustic, synth guitars, Giovanni Pagliari - piano, keybds. A truly beautiful band created to, "bring a moment of rare beauty in this world where nightmares are too many".

Further quotes are in order: "We are grown up listening and absorbing what the wave scene before and the dark one after offered in those faraway years. This happened 13 years ago, perhaps more, and here nothing has changed. I mean, people have changed, but the records listened to and bought are the same. It's quite possible that Italy is, like its always been, a quite conservative land where new suggestions and of course new sources of musical inspiration are not welcomed easily and this is quite astonishing.

67-69 ATARAXIA 70 BLOODING MASK 71 CAT FUD

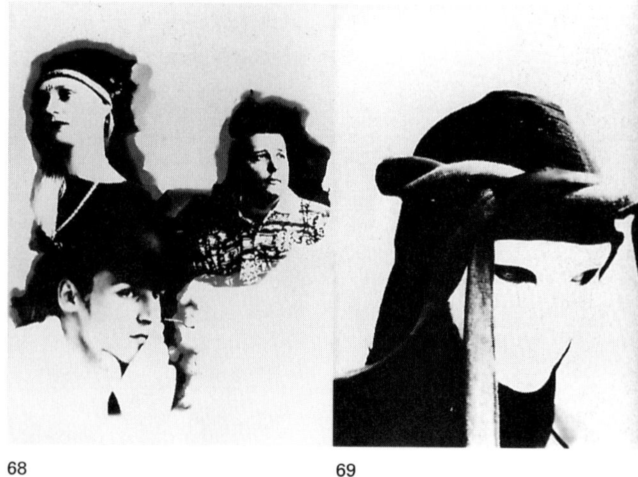

68 69

67

It's ten years we're playing and creating multimedia acts (we are involved in theatrical acts and visual performances linked to Ataraxia) and openly in the last year we saw an increasing attention towards new goth, of perhaps arcane, far off, unusual form of expressions.

"However, we go on, believing we're mediums and part of a fluxus that is born so far in time (a peculiarity of human drama) and that has dragged along the ancient civilisations of Atlantis and Mu, the Egypt linked to the celebration of death and beyond, the troubadors of the Middle Ages, the extravagant, intemperant Baroque/Rococo period and of course the symbolism, the age of Decadence and the Preraphaelite brotherhood...we are part of the same cycle and our music and visual acts are not an up to date completely XXth century defined gothic expression but a research or more often a continuous discovery of our cloudy, dim, dispirited, moody, sublime roots when goth was not a word present in the vocabulary...when vocabularies hadn't been invented."

You'll be relieved to find their recorded works as exquisite as their words, in every way. This is the most beautiful music I've encountered in years. Discography: 'Prophetia' MC (90), 'Nosce Te Ipsum' MC (91), 'Arazzi' MC (93), 'Sub Ignissima Luna' MC compilation (93) 'Ad Perpetuam Rei Memoriam' CD comp (94), 'Symphonie Sine Nomine' CD (94), 'La Malediction d'Ondine' CD (95). 'The Moon Sang On The April Chair - Red Deep Dirges Of A November Moon' (95), split 10" with Engelsstaub 'In Amoris Mortisque' limited to 1,000. Video "Would The Winged Light Climb?' (95), 'Il Fantasma dell'Opera' and 'Concerto N. 6: A Baroque Plaisanterie' CDs (96).

Final quote: "Our moods, references, figurative world is Gothic, our mother and father are History and Time."

70

71

Francesca Nicoli / Vittorio Vandelli, Via Popoli 4, 41057 Spilamberto, Modena.

THE BEL AM Alexandro Ronchini, Via Villa Glori 1, 43100 Parma.

BLACK ROSE According to *Fight Amnesia* another strictly beautiful project, heavily vocal led by Mara over the piano work of Ero Longhin, and close to Goth gospel! 'Into The Glass House' and 'The Room Inside' CDs (95). Nightbreed see them as more Cocteaus/Eves. Hyperium, PO Box 910127, D-90259, Hamburg, Germany.

BLOODING MASK Maethelyiah - vocals/keybds and Gianmarco - guitars. Formed in June 92. All songs comes from dreams and they swear that in the songs are ancient magickal formulas, in the original tongue. Voices are sometimes recorded in a trance state and lyrics in different languages. In fact they are proud to announce, "the only band singing real ancient magic formulae in their original tongue". 'All The Colors Of Death' CD released on M.B.R. (93) and 'What That Hollow Shows Through' CD on Apollyon (96). They're different again, which is no surprise as Italy, unlike any other country, produces such a wide range of equally committed acts. Very spooky, attractive stuff from the duo who prefer not to explain precisely what goes into and behind their material, rather that "every song is part of an esoteric walk." Maethelyiah and Gianmarco. V. Coolele Fiaschetta shc, 00030 S Cesareo, Roma. (Fax: 06-7183051)

BUILDING 777 Now according to them the meaning of the name is 'The Building Of Perfection' because 777 is the opposite of 666. Started between 91 and 92 after the EBM influence of bands like Frontline Assembly, Clock DVA, Front 242 etc, they reached demo stage in 93. Live performances included what I am assured involved "the disquieting presence on the stage of 'Pamela', a sexy doll which is very pleased to be raped by Unhuman (the lead vocal) and Atrox (guitar)". Oh, excellent! Melmoth and The Count are also accredited members, on all the electronic gadgetry. It's fairly stern stuff but not pushed in any bombastic manner, rather following the rhythm of the vocals as much as producing any stylistic course. There's even pop spirit purring inside the livelier parts. A decent producer would work wonders with them. Alessandro Zaupa, Via Roy, 14, 36066 Sandrigo (VI).

BURNING GATES Earlyish sound Danse Soc. to Nephilim. Michele Piccolo, Corso Grosseto 295, 10151 Torino.

CAMERATA MEDIOLANENSE Lumiitca - vocals, Pier Pezzoni - perc., Elena Previdi - keybds/harpsichord/perc., T. F. Northgate - perc./vocals/keybds, Manuel Aroldi - perc. Formed 92 and active 94, pulling together like-minded souls from the Milan underground. Aims for "a point of synthesis between absolute melodiousness and ritual percussions on the ground of the studies that we are leading for years. From the aesthetical and ethical points of view, the words are symbolic, the images metaphoric, the real communication esoterically whispered to them who listen". 'Musica Reserveta' (18.10.94) on own label, featuring Ataraxia's Francesca Nicoli on three tracks. Live debut not until 6.5.95! Manuel Aroldi, Via F. Morandi 15, 20127 Milan. (Fax +39 2 8137908)

CAT FUD Marko Resurrection - voice/guitar, Alessandra Romeo - keybds, Piero De Santis - bass. Truly cool band already responsible for the devious and delightful 'Nothing Stays The Same' demo. Bands in the UK would kill to be this obvious and graceful, for it's awesome stuff. Anyone with taste will write requesting info for their ridiculously good stuff. They were working on material for their first CD when I was finishing the book so it may be out

72

right now. Formed 92, originally with a sequencer called Larson, who Alessandra replaced. In 93, already playing the Rome scene and some squats, they brought out a 9 track demo, 'Put The Cat Out'. Bored with playing Rome to death they're now spreading out across Europe. If ever there was a band in Europe who show the ludicrous situation Goth bands can face it is Cat Fud. This band should be widely welcomed into any area of the alternative/indie scenes, as there is a rich but simple texture to their firmly inspirational sounds. It's weird the way that such a sharp bass, nimble guitar underpinned by layers of synth and a yearning voice can make you feel so good about things but this is an ultra-direct form of music because you know that nobody is trying to come over as deeply pretentious. Marko Resurrection, Via Ampio Flaviano 30, 00175 Roma.

DAWN FADES Caste - bass, Matteo - guitar/vocals, Panza - keybds/vocals, Mec - drums. 'Dawn Fades' MC (93). 'Dawn Fades' CDEP (95). Darkwave meets Joy Division, and with a Modern English cover version. Stefano Castelli, Via G. Fabbri 177, 44100 Ferrara (FE).

DEVIATE LADIES Asmodeus G. Volgar - vocals/keybds, Baby Buscher - lead guitar, Nefus - lead organ (?), harpsichord, harp and violin, Antek - bass, Dot Alexio Babmord - chorus organ, M. Auro - ghost organ, synth effects, Niki Ciddio - rhythm and lead guitars. (For Christ's sake, any more of you?) Formed by the committed A.G. Volgar in 91 from the entrails of his previous band, Eternal Punishment. They were confused initially, doing Sisters and Valor covers. By mid 92, with the crotchety 'Crown Of Darkness' demo under their belts, things were improving. "Androgynous look, sex performance, noise guitars and effects were our ingredients," A.G. insists, but he wasn't happy with his band who only wanted fame. He kept with keyboardist M. Auro, guitarist Arri and some friends, including a responsive computer and a second demo, 'Immorality's Colustrum', the translation of which I'd rather not know, and they began to settle down. This didn't get a great critical reception, because, as Asmodeus declares "we don't lick the bottom of nobody". Wise words. Their work to date strikes me as rather childish. What they term experimental appears to be half-cocked theatrical style with little power behind it. Imagine a punk band covering prime Nephilim material - it has that clumsy feel about it, usually saved by the keyboards and some sparse guitar. By 93 they got themselves saddled with a troublesome reputation for pissing onstage, and having acquired rather a large gathering of Nazi skins. When one of the main Italian metal mags went so far as to dub them as actual Nazis A.G. split up the band. After a rethink, a third line-up is born, bringing us to the final demo available, 'Diabolische Orgelwerke', which is far more assured and interesting. Deviate Ladies simply refuse to tread on safe ground because A.G. is a contentious bastard. He flirts with trouble. In fact he all but courts it. Italy being a somewhat religious country, their opening number is 'Satan's Erection'. Furthermore, if I might quote from the extensive sleeve notes, "all the effects - pissing, worms, bowels tearing - are real, not synthesized"! That's what we need, more bands capable of genuine bowel-tearing, haven't I always said? They are easy to listen to with their orchestral surrounds, but when you take away that organ on which they heavily depend, what is there? A lot more traditional rock than we'd normally expect but plenty of grit among the polish too, topped and tailed by massive wobbly vocals. Mauro Merelli, Via A. Dahlia 112, 00179 Roma.

DIATHRIBA Andrea Cavani - vocals, Davide Grimaldiu - guitar, Stefano Vignudelli - bass, Davide Borghi - drums. Formed 94 from various old bands,

73

72 FEAR OF THE STORM 73 HOLYLORE 74 PETRA DE LUCA

74

determined to do something new in the Gloom Rock variety, rather than Goth. 'Controvoglia' MC and Scomunica' MCD. D. Borghi, Via Moscadini 16, 41013, Castelfranco E.

ERMENEUMA Carlo - vocals, Atrox - guitar, Crisantemo Nemo - electro-acoustic drums, Il Conte - keybds, Tex - bass. Mad vampire band, signed to Energeia and much expected of them. 'Live At Vinile' (94) and 'Presagio' MCs. Emanuele Lago, Via Melaniga 43, 35013 Cittadella (PD).

FEAR OF THE STORM Hoax - guitars/drum prog., Valy Ash - keybds/vocals, Mad - bass, Tony Harlot - vocals/keys. In 90 Storm changed to Fear Of The Storm, producing their own 'R.I.P.' MC in 91, then signing to Energeia, which has brought forth the MCs 'The Key Of My Silence' (93) and 'So Sad To Die In Oblivion' (94) and their best-known work, the CD '1995', which digs up old ground of earlier songs. Weird band - stony vocals, deep, gloomy sound, where they purge themselves of melancholic contradictions which can then lead you into light-hearted capering outings too. Mad bastards. Antonio Olivieri, Via S. Margherita 11, 94100 Enna. Or c/o Energeia.

FROZEN AUTUMN Diego - vocals/synth/ sampler/ prog., Claudio - guitar/effects/prog./bass. Formed 93, recorded demo 'Oblivion' and after getting good reviews and some decent supports with Endraum and Lucie Cries it wasn't long before they got their deal. Lyrically they plough a familiar romantic furrow but they like to talk about what they call parallel reality in a strange time condition and the meaning of dreams. They empathise with the early 4AD period and style. 'Pale Awakening' CD available on label Weisser Herbst, in Germany, home of Endraum. There's also a six song live video 'Live In Ferrara, 94'. Diego Merletto, Via Don Bosco 106, 10144 Torino.

HOLYLORE H. Graal - 'ancient prediction' (Earth to Graal, come in Graal), H. Noxious - 'depthless guitar', H. Etienne - 'martyrdom bass/keybds', H. Cold - 'ascetic guitar', H.H. - 'holytronic machine'. Mystic Goth sound. 'Stoned To Death' MC (93). 'Sefiroth' CD (95). Hot voice, freezing synth, vitriolic guitar. Old and new, fighting it out, gloriously. Etienne Santangeli, Via G. Chiovendair 106, 00173 Roma.

LADY DOMINO Five girl band offering up their 'My Red Pornography' MC (95) for openers, which is S/M and Goth atmospheric nightmares. Psychotic Release, Via Melaniga 43, 36013 Cittadella (PD).

LE STREGHE DELL'ONIRICO Tuono - vocals, Atos Flemma - guitar, Caronte - bass, Orso - drums. 'Dura Visa' MC (93), 'La Pozione' (rarities MC), 'La Notte Delle Streghe' (live bootleg). T-shirts, posters, and an hour long live video 'Una Notte Onirica - Dracma Club' available. Formed 88, a Goth/wave thing, with a side serving of blues, rock and Spanish guitar. Singer looks like Eldritch and operates the same drowsily sly vocal style, with the music quite muted. Not too bad but lightweight. Franco Molinar, Via Fatebenefratelli 110, 10077 San Maurizio-Canavese (TO).

LIMBO Classy electro-Goth. Reminds me of 23 Skidoo put through a blender and then rubbed down with wet KLF bootlegs. Formed in the mid-80's, they've now released nine records, and although line-ups have changed it's down to one man and the German label, Discordia. The lyrical imagery and subject matter has covered Elizabeth Bathory, Thanatos, S/M, Technology, the occult, science and Fetish culture. It's gruff-voiced fun all round. GLB, Via C. Beccaria 10., 57025, Piombin (LI).

MEGAPTERA Noisy weird atmospheres. Cinematic. Target dist, Germany.

MIND DROP Andrea Bosetti - synth/drum machine, Matteo Soru - guitars, Andrea Manenti - bass/voice. Formed July 90 but took until mid-92 to record 'Rusted Eternity' MC, for Energeia. First CD, 'Side Of Mine' (96). Danse Society comparisons are nearest, but with a more conventional and beautiful keybd sound and incisive guitar input. Andrea Bosetti, Via Porro 46, 21056 Induno Olona (VA).

MONUMENTUM Doom metal goth, a slow-motion Neffs. 'In Absentia Christi' CD on Misanthropy. PO Box 9, Hadleigh, Suffolk IP7 5AU, UK.

MYSTERY PLAYS Already produced the 'Occasus' album. 80's UK influence throughout. 'Within' MC (94), 'Occasus' CD (95). Energeia, Davide Morgera, Via Manzoni 9, I-80019 Qualina (NA).

NADEZHDA Well, what can I say? There were no details with the tape ('Hope/Hence, These Tears') only photos that Petra De Luca sent about this 'band'. On first hearing, what she has done is so comprehensively different to just about anything else I've ever heard that it was strange to listen to, like an alien form. It is as different for its time as Clair Obscur were for theirs and as instinctively compelling as Christian Death's 'Only Theatre Of Pain'. It is, quite literally, astonishing. The breadth of imagination and mood contained within what are quite sternly controlled borders amaze. On the more musical moments, where very hesitant vocals intrude among chillingly simple, stark sounds, we are given a cross between cathedral opulence and musical box horror. It sounds like a child's nightmare, but then she goes into almost spoken word operations over disquieting booming, martial percussion. She takes everything from the modern avant-garde, throws it back as far as medieval minstrel styles, but if anything it ends up rooted in Napoleonic carnage. It is quite easily the most enthralling yet disturbing material you could ever wish to hear and the one work which is quite unlike anything else you will find this book. I would recommend every single fanzine get in touch with her, to spread the word about a quite extraordinary talent. It is as stunning as it is horrible. It is painful, in all the right ways, dealing with the horrors of love and behaviour in a manner which always seems proudly defiant but never rigid. You too can end up gasping for breath. Petra De Luca, Viale Del Tirreno 185, Tirrenia (Pl). There's also a temporary American address listed as 239 Avon Road, Upper Darby, PA 19882.

ORDO EQUITUM SOLIS Swirling whirly things comparable to Love Is Colder Than Death. 'Hecate' (CD) via Southern Distribution, UK.

THE PATH Davide Borghi - vocals/guitars, Elio Zambonini - keybds, Marca - bass, Lorenzo Borghi - drums. 'Gothic-Metal progressive' they call it and that's not far away. It's weird. Pushy riffs, bouncing vocals, pretty piano and punky, jousting drums. Three MCs available, 'Aura', 'Ethereality' and 'Asrai Dance'. Started in 92 and still quite healthy. Davide, Vasta 19/1, 42030 Asta (Re).

SIMON DREAMS IN VIOLET Lospellro - bass, Luigi Lar - guitar, Massimiliano Maria - vocals, Alice and Beatrice - drum machines. Formed in 92 with voice, distorted bass and drums. Band's symbol comes from a sign placed on witches graves, which is jolly. The assurance of the old sound sustained through energetic expression rather than shallow noise. Two MCs through Energeia, 'SDIV' (93), 'Dreaming The Lost' (94). c/o de Franceschi Massimiliano, Via dei Sampieri SNC. PAL.1, Int.4., 00184 - Roma. Or Rizzo Rosario, Via Del Canaraini 44, 00169 Roma.

SPIRITUAL BATS Matteo - vocals, Dario - death guitar, Joseph - tribal drums and Francesco - funeral bass. Formed in 92. Attractive positive, standard fare, marked by their 'Homonymous' LP (93) but yet to get to grips with the power required for modern times. Via Firenze. 35 - 03100 Frosinone.

THANATOS Formed 86 by Fabiano on guitar and Gianfranco on drums but there have been some changes on the other instruments. They began with a totally dark direction which encouraged little dance action. Josef appeared, to add vocals. Their earliest bassist Grazia Galassi pushed them with improvisational ideas to loosen things and was later replaced by Ruggero Folignol. In 91 they chose five of their forty songs for the first EP, following it in 92 with a single 'Crack/X Agosto', which heralded a dancier ambition. 93 saw the CD/MC that included the work of Marcelli Gallini on keyboard, but when Ruggero left, Marcelli moved to bass until former Anubi man Daniele Guerzoni joined. In 95, when they thought everything was sorted, they have more shakeups. It takes until August to finalise the lineup and in September they recorded their latest album. As with most Italian bands there is a wide range of sounds but it usually has a rich texture and a lively tone. There is a lot available - records, t-shirts and even photos. Gianfranco Righetti, Via Della Conciliazione 8, 41051 Castelnuovo Rangone, Modena.

THEATRES DES VAMPIRES New Gothic/black metal band! Psychotic Release, Via Melaniga 43, 36013 Cittadella (PD).

THEATRE OF LONELINESS Aldo Bergarnasco, Via Ferna 3, Alpignano (To).

THELEMA Massimo Mantovani - vocals./guitar, Giorgio Parmigiani - bass/keybds/drum prog. Rough but fine quality mid-80's Goth that can even appeal to a normal audience who detect Velvets comparisons in among the modern cool. It's been a weird history here. Very weird. The two men actually met back in 84 and chose a musical direction influenced by their mutual respect for Aleister Crowley, reach the debut album in 86 and split in 88. Reform 90. Split again 91. 93 marks the final reformation. Their second album comes out, at last, in 94! Discography, in chronological order: 'The Golem' and 'Rosa+Croce' demos, 'The Golem' 7" (all 85), 'Tantra' LP (86), 'The Rise Of The Snake' live video (88), 'Kubla Khan' MC (90), 'Il Cuore Cinto Dal Serpente' and 'Still Burning' MCs

75

(91), 'The Vision And The Voice' CD (94), 'My Shout' MCD (95), 'Night Of Pan' CD (96). By their standards the past eighteen months must have been exhausting. Massimo Mantovani, CP 333, 40100 Bologna Centro.

THE OTHER VOICES Sick synth band. Via Torino 17, 96100 Syracusa.

TOMBSTONE This is Emanuele Lago, alias Crisantemo Nero. Nightmarish stuff, from a band which is in fact the drummer of Ermeneuma. "We have no photos," they apologise, "and don't like them very much". They have released the frankly horrific (which is the whole idea) CD 'Gothic Land' on Death Factory, the sweetly titled offshoot of Cold Meat Industry. It's horrible. All of it...quite magnificently so. Vile is only an anagram of evil anyway, he mused, stupidly. Five other MCs available - 'A Cascade Of Tears', 'This Necrologue Of Love', 'The Terror Garden', 'Feel The Gothic Land' and 'Silva Obscura'. He has another side project going, Immortal Agony which is even noisier, even harder, even darker. (For God's sake...WHY?!) Psychotic Release, c/o Emanuele Lago, Via Melaniga 43, 35013 Gittadella (PD).

TREES Six piece formed 94 and inspired by American Indians and Wim Wenders! This makes them play a strange form of perfectly acceptable Indie Goth. Paolo d'Addio, Via Metastasio 63, 80125 Napoli.

UNDER THE ROSE Cristiano Manetti - vocals, Moi - bass/prog./keybds, David - guitars. More post Joy Div rumblings, responsible for 'The Window' ('92) and 'Is This A Way?' ('94) MCs. C. Manetti, Via G. Pavini 2, 56127, Pisa (PI).

VIDI AQUAM Nikita C. Panza, Via Venezia 10, 20093 Cologno Monzese (MI).

VOTIVA LUX Giulio Sangirardi - guitar/e-bow/noises/bass, Gabriele Bufalini - keybds, bass,prog./drum machines, Andrea Cavanai - credited with voices and, er...voices!, Stefano Pigliapoco - lead guitar, Andrea Sbaffi - drums. Their music has grace mixed with its grandeur, and a beautifully loose energy, instantly captivating. The words are weirdly mature and imaginative, the sounds ooze style. Since forming in December 88 this band, which started as a trio, has had 14 lineup changes but thankfully I'm not doing family trees. It would be an orchard. Only Giulio remains. It took a year to face an audience and wasn't until early 91 that the first demo became available but that sense of time has clearly given them a step ahead of most bands in the quality stakes because this stuff is totally striking and sumptuous. 'Visioni' MC followed two demos and established them in Italy. They have an a CD's worth of material ready to release now but no label, which is a disgrace as they are one of the best bands operating in Italy today. Giulio 'Peacock' Sangirardi, Via Turati 69, 40134, Bologna. (Fax: 00 39 51 6447237)

WASTELAND Stefano Pistone - vocals/guitar, Fabrizio Filippi - guitars, Daniele Tartaglia - bass, Vittorio Vallero - keybds, Marcio Luciano - drums.They would certainly like it known they did not take their name from the best Mission song, but formed in Turin at the end of 90. Two demos, 'Dark Age' (92) and Litanies In Time Of Plague' (94), followed by limited edition demo CD 'Days Of The Apocalypse'. Should have a new album out by now. Very well regarded all round. Strongly influenced by the original British Goth bands, they also love both the medieval period and the Romantic poets. In fact two of their songs are poems by Poe and Shelley put to music! Chirpy buggers. Stefano Pistone, Via Clemente 1, 10143 Torino.

WELTSCHMERZ Ezio Prandini - Via Catone, 21 - 20158 Milano.

Fanzines

BATTY'S TEARS Emanuela Zini, Corso Sempoione 83, 20149 Milano.

CATALEPTIC Fabio Gagliano, Viale Portogallo 8, 03100, Frosinone.

KELTIC & PRIMORDIA CISB C.P. 10944, 20124 Milano.

MARBLE MOON Formerly *Dusk Memories* and enormous, bursting at the seams with some excellent interviews, occasional retrospectives and a landslide of reviews, from those awfully nice Energeia people. All in Italian. Davide Morgera, Via Manzoni 9, 80019 Qualiano (NA). (Fax 081-8181903)

MIT LIEBE UND TOD C. so Porta Po, 147, 44100 Ferrarra.

NEO GOTHIC Born in June 93 to celebrate the

76

77

78

"decadent and dark world", this is an excellent A5 zine, which concentrates on a nice broad mix of Goth. In its way a smaller, more mainstream version of *Ver Sacrum*. Has also issued the 'Tenebrae' compilation and started organising gigs. Alessandro Fabianelli, Via Imola 1, 40128, Bologna.

SIN-ORG Newsletter/info thing by Giafranco who also does the Alternative Ocean roadshow and a tv spot where fanzines get reviewed! Giafranco Santoro, Via Adige 8, 33010 Colugna Tavagnacco (Udine).

SUFFER G. Santoro, Via Adige 8, 33010 Colugna.

THE ANGELS FALL Borelli, Via N. Provincialew n. 27, 80040 Cercola (Napoli).

UNDER THE BLACK ROSE If you live in Italy and don't buy this there is something deeply wrong with you. If you are going to support your own scene then this, *Marble Moon* and *Ver Sacrum* are your first ports of call. As *UTBR* is in English everybody else should want it too. (The other two are in Italian.) Stefano clearly covers a wide range of musical material in here but another obvious point of attraction is the beautiful look of the magazine. Recently increased to A4, it is way ahead of the European zine competition. Some of his earliest covers were breathtaking. A detailed fanzine, never stuck in a rut and building up into something momentous. He even managed to keep it going while conscripted into the army! Stefano Sciacca, Viale Marconi 10/A, 04100 Latina.

VER SACRUM Amazing, packed to the gunnels with info and arranged in an interesting stylistic manner, following "the dark and bleak path that links artists, writers, musicians... sometimes different for education and artistic style, throughout the centuries and countries". That's a pretty wide brief. Each issue centres on one central theme to analyse (various subjects - Vampires, The female image in decadent literature and art, The Plague, The Gothic in Literature, Art and Architecture.) This is how passion should be shown. Beautiful stuff, exceptionally detailed and adventurous in its tackling of weird historical areas - such as erotic carvings in church architecture! Every issue includes a Gothic short story, often previously unavailable in Italy. Naturally there's interviews and reviews galore. The team responsible for these mighty tomes also arrange concerts whenever they can, including groups from all round Europe. Marzia Bonato, Via S. Paolo 5, 56125 Pisa.

Other sources

ARAXE PROMOTIONS Run by Steph Lulini and Lesley Miglietta, whose initial DJ-ing in Turin led them to organise their own gigs, with the best Italian bands and attracting big European names to play. Well worth contacting. Via Monginevro 172/5, 10141 Torino. (Fax (0) 11/837550)

CHRISTINA SIMONELLI Otherwise known as The Black Countess. Does bizarre fetish dolls, as one-offs, called things like "Velenia, the incendiary dominatrix", painting and stitching clothes onto the doll, even using her own hair sometimes. Unusual woman. The Black Countess, Via Del Pero 102, 54038 Montignoso MS.

ENERGEIA Top label since 87. Unbeatable as the place to be. Davide Morgera, Via Manzoni 9, 80019 Qualiano NA.

HELTER SKELTER Tape label. 00162 Rome Piazzale Delle Provincie 8.

INK Radio show in the East Sicily area. Giancario

78 CHRISTINA SIMONELLI 79 CHAKO
80 WELTENBRAND 81 MARIUS KNEIPFERAVAUS

79

80

81

Curro, Cas. Post. n. 9, I-98168 Contemplazione, Messina.

'LE ALTRE VOCI' Radio show on Radio Gamma (FM 97.65, FM 101.1). Via Pecori Giraldi 15, I-38100 Trento.

LOS RANIERO Fetish type Mailart and addresses. Italian/English. Ignazio Corsaro, Via Chiaia 149, 80121 Naples.

MAZZARIOL LUCA Radio DJ. Via Buozzi, 7 31015, Conegliano, Treviso.

MUSICA MAXIMA MAGNETICA Quality label. Luciano Dari, CP 2280, 50100 Firenze. (Fax +39 571 558920)

OLD EUROPA CAFE Tape dist. Rodolfo Protti, Viale Marconi 38, 33170 Pordenone.

PSYCHOTIC RELEASE Exciting tape label, very reasonably priced. Via Melaniga 43, 36013 Cittadella (PD).

THE REPTILE HOUSE The record shop of Margaux who does *Mit Liebe Und Tod* fanzine. C.so Porta Po, 147 44100 Ferrara.

'TEDIO DOMENICALE' Broadcast on Radio Base, 92.2 FM in Faenza. Giampaolo Ricci, Via Fratelli Cervi 17, 48012 Bagnacavallo (RA).

Japan

A.Z.Z.L.O. Fetish shop. 21 Sakamachi, Shinjuku-ku, Tokyo 160. (Fax 03-3356-9810)

CHAKO Despite the Kobe earthquake interrupting her work, Chako has released a very strange CD indeed, 'Ebb & Flow'. It is always interesting if not exactly rewarding to listen to records sung in a language different to your own. Usually it is the nuances you lose that lessen the experience - but with Chako the voice may just as well be an instrument - sinewy, curving, fragmenting. She is also involved with the Jack Or Jive and Jack Or Jive Lights. Jack Or Jive CDs - 'Mujio', 'Kagura Live In Tokyo'. J-O-J Lights CDs 'A Picture Of A Dancer', 'A Solo Exhibition'. Drag & Drop/ Scout Productions, Süsterfeldstr. 61, 52072 Aachen, Germany.

Liechtenstein

WELTENBRAND Daniel H. - keybd, Rino D. - keybd, Simone S. - vocals, Corina B. - vocals, Ritchie W. - vocals, Oliver Falk - synth/vocals. Formed June 95. Darkwave fusing classical with medieval fusing, bringing to life their lyrical legends of their little known home country. 'Das Rabenland' - debut CD, on Witchunt. Oliver Falk, Ratikonstr. 18, FL-9490 Vaduz. (Fax: 075-232- 87 43).

Lithuania

BOMBA RECORDS Former promoter. Useful contact. Vytautas Juozapavicius, Zygimantu 6, Vilnius 2001.

CALMANT Fanzine. Saulius-Majauskas, Jaunimo 60-9, 4580 Alytus.

COLOURS OF FIRE Radio show which goes out on national radio. Didlaukio 20-9, Vilnius 2057.

DEATH BITE Metal-Death-Goth fanzine. Laimis

82 83

82 MANO JUODOJI SESUO 83 SIELA 84 GOTHAM NIGHTS
85 THE MORENDOES

Smergelis, Taikos 71/9, 4910 Utena.

EDGE OF TIME Swish, computer laid out mag. Stunning review section and very intelligent interviews, all in English. Masses of Metal bands, mainly, but a lot of interesting experimental acts. Giedrius Slivinskas, PO Box 982, 2300 Vilnius. (e-mail: fates@pub.of.It)

FOR YOUR SOUL Fanzine. English language. Aurius Samulenas, Taikos 20-5, 4910 Utena.

GESTANCIOS SAULES KARALYSTEJE Fanzine. Audrius Simkunas, Seliu, 24-1, 4910 Utena.

IN YOUR DREAM Band. Sarunas Zilinkas, Ausros 34c-12, 4910 Utena.

S.T. KONDRATOS Gothic writer. Vytautas Danilevicius, Taikos 217-43, Vilnius 2017.

MARIUS KNEIPFERAVAUS Artist. V. Kreves, 31.28 Kaunas 3000 .

LIBER JUSTORUM Fanzine. Tomas Vaicekauskas, Seimyniskiy 38-9, 2015 Vilnius.

MANO JUODOJI SESUO Band, formed early 92, with a few releases, notably their morose 'Reinkarnacija' album. Karalius Sarunas, PO Box 114, 3005 Kaunas.

RADIOCENTRAS Tomas, who is in charge of playing Goth music on his regular weekly show, sent me the saddest of letters. "There is one difficulty - bad economical conditions in the country. The majority of population live in poverty and music is in the background. Presently there is nothing left to do, we just 'enjoy' the fruits of some occupation. We hope our children will see the better." Suitably chastened, send him whatever you can spare and a pox on you if you don't. Tomas Vaicekauskas, Seimyniskiu 38-9, Vilnius.

REDIVIVUS Fanzine. Arentas Petroslus, Chemiku 98-32, 5000 Jonava.

SIELA Band. Formed 90 when "we felt the trembling of guitar's strings like a trembling of air over a stream of silver", which is a lot of trembling. Dark prog-folk-goth MC releases every year. Aurelius Sirgedas, Maironio 33 2 , 4910 Utena

WEJDAS Band described as both Goth and Pagan-Electronic. Impeccably peculiar, weird evocative lowing sounds, from Donatas and Darius, comprising pipes, synth, piano and bass. Total gloom. PO Box 982, 2300 Vilnius.

WOUNDED Fanzine. Minda Lapinskas, Zaibo 10-75, 2050 Vilnius.

POCCOLUS Band. Dark pagan metal. Ramunas Personis, Selie 59-8, 4910 Utena.

Malta

SCROLLS OF SORROW Fanzine. Malcolm Borg-Galea, Pope Alexander VII Junction, Balzan, BZN 06.

MALCOLM CALLUS Radio dj. 492/2 St Joseph High Rd, St. Venera HMR 18.

Mexico

ANUBIS No details about who does what, but this MC release is very distinctive and mirrors its accompanying letter, from which I must quote. "Here the life is like a cemetery - not just for the

84

85

inactivity of the people, this is because of our political system. The Government, it degrades the identity and illusions of the people, with liars and corruption. Productions like Anubis just represent the big void in the future - not as the way of the punk generation - another kind of sadness in Mexican arts, it is other kind of pain." There certainly is something "other" here, a strange mournful sense in the music. Despite having power rumbling in the background, the progress of the songs is cruelly patient. Everything trickles along with strange, almost gentle death-rattle female vocals crawling in time. Highly unusual with an occasional upsurge of noise which sounds like dinosaurs - all of which makes sense as you actually listen. It's certainly weird but more accessible than you'd imagine and strangely beautiful! US fanzines should do the world a favour and get on the case straight away! Arista 1659, See. Lidaleo, E.P.44200, Gaudalajara Val. Mexico 6148826.

CIUDAD INTERIOR Band. Ixtlahuaca 707, Col. Sanchez CP. 50040 Toluca.

CORINA Fanzine. Corina, av.iph #2126, 5C-303 Indavista, 07340 Mexico City.

DARKSIDE A bit of everything, also *Ojo Rojo* magazine and Opcion Sonica distribution. AP 21-460, Mex D.F., CP04000.

GENITAL PRODUCTIONS Label of dadaist and beyond music, with fanzine *Tabadro* to match. Juan Antonio Rotunno Espino, 10 y 11 Anaya y O. Rmz. "736, Cd Victoria, Tamaulipas 87050.

New Zealand

INTRAVENE Fanzine but no address. Sorry.

MAGICAL PENTACLE Pagan mag. Box 56-065 Dominion Rd P.O., Mount Eden, Auckland.

Norway

AGALIAREPT OCCULT BOOKS He supplies books. About the occult. Doh! Erland Salbu, Klokkarbrekka 6B, 5200 Oslo.

APOGEE The "guide des possibilities illimitees", although in Norwegian, not French, curiously. Fetish mag. Dag Haselmo, Skogstua, 1560 Larkollen.

BRISKEBY RECORDS Label. President Harbitz Gate 1, 0259 Oslo.

DUNKEL PROD Fanzine and distribution service. Moonfish Cultural Laboratory, Erik Sontum, Sagvelen 23, N-0458 Oslo.

GOTHAM NIGHTS I'm not really bothering with clubs in this book because it stands to reason that by the time you get hold of a copy clubs may well have switched venue, which happens frequently. However, this crowd have been in place since February 95 and get a regular mental, mainly Goth crowd with the inevitable "depressed dark metal geeks". This, they declare, is where "top hats and stetsons rule!" They also do gigs there from time to time, so if you fancy playing Norway? Stefan Rosell, Toftes gt. 68, 0552 Oslo. (Net: http://www/ifi.uio.no/trondh/Gotham Nights.html)

HYPERTONIA WORLD ENTERPRISES Tape label and Radio show - 'Brunt Plata' on Studentradionen (104.1-106.1-107.8 MHz. Jan R.Brunna, PO Box 4307, Nygardstangen, N-5028 Bergen.

86

87

THE MORENDOES Osten - vocals, Olsson - guitar, Jossang - guitar, Steinsto - keybds, Eie - bass and weirdest name in this book. Formed Feb 91 by Olsson and Barkved, contributing a track to a local sampler in 93, under the name of The Wake. Discovering two other bands already used this name they chose The Morendoes, a name taken from classical music terminology. Noisily quixotic, rumbling entity. Should have a new album out right now. Tommy Olsson, Alsvik, 4120 Tau.

NAERVAER Band. PO Box 7037 Vestheine, 4628 Kr.sand.

OLD MAN WILLOW Fanzine. The Hendersons, Jembanevn 71a, 3716 Skien.

RED HARVEST Cato Bekkevold - drums, Jimmy Bergsten - guitar/vocals, Thomas Brandt - bass, Ketil Eggum - guitar, Lars Sorensen - synth/samples. A booklet comes with their 'The Maztur Nation' CD, entitled, *The story of a band born to fail*. Formed 89, out of the ashes of some prog-metal (frightening!) experiment, rushing into Industrial-Goth. Within days they'd done their 'Occultica' demo, followed by another, 'Psychotica', and then straight on to what they refer to as "the aptly titled 'Nomindsland' album". 'There's Beauty In The Purity Of Sadness' followed, as they started touring abroad, notably Germany and Switzerland, where even though people call them a Swans/Nephilim hybrid they managed to end up headlining a thrash festival. A video for the track 'Wounds' off 'Beauty' got them banned on Norwegian tv. They appear down, but not out. Remixes rumoured in the next stage of their strained existence. Moonfish Cult Lab, Sagun 23, N-0458 Oslo.

RESPECT Fetish mag. PB 1089 7002 TR Helm.

SHADOW DANCERS Band. Box 3040, 1702 Sarpsborg.

TATRA Label. Box 96, 1450 Nesoddtangen.

THEATRE OF TRAGEDY Band. Hein F Hansen, Tiurv 13, 4042 H-fjord.

THE THIRD AND THE MORTAL A mournful, rockier All About Eve. 'Tears Laid In Earth' CD.

UFO NORGE UFO mag. Mentz Kaarbo, Strandgaten 221, N-5004, Bergen.

Poland

BLACK FLAMES Label, radio show and promoter. Radoslaw Kasprszak, Os Orla Bialego 53/12, 6A-25A Poznan.

CLOSTERKELLER Band turning Metal after early Banshees spell. Lustrzana 20, 01-350 Warszawa.

DARK ZONE Fanzine/label. Janusz Grzeczny, Konstytucji 3 Maja 20/4, 48-100 Glubczyce.

ELDRICH PALMER I dread to think. Krzysztof Sadza, Napoleonska 25A, o6-500 Mlawa.

ESOTERIC Zine written in English. Miroslawa Mackiewicz, UL Wybickiego 13B/5, PL-81842 Sopot.

FADING COLOURS De Coy - vocals, Tytus de Ville - guitars/keybds, Leszek Raakowski - bass, Pawel Novak - drums. Responsible for two CDs - 'Lie' and 'Black Horse'. Comparisons made between The Mission and 10,000 Maniacs had me diving for cover - unnecessarily so, because it's ravishing stuff, textured and haunting. Krzysztof Rakowski, ul. Garncarska 31/4, Boleslawiec. Or Dion Fortune, Germany. (Fax: 0221-54 28 30)

86 RED HARVEST 87 FADING COLOURS

88

IMMORTAL Magazine and mail order distribution. Arthur Wroblewski, PO Box 14, 76-200 Skupsk 1.

MORBID TRUTH Magazine. PO Box 4007, 40-749 Katowice 31.

Portugal

ANTONIO MARTINS FERREIRA Rua da Cabina n-160, S. Pedro da Cova, 4420 Gondomar.

AUDEO Records, books, t-shirts. Luis Freixo, edificio Bristol, Loja 00, Av. Boavista 1635, 4100 Porto.

BLACK AND DEATH SOCIETY Rua da Madeira 182, 4000 Porto.

CAVE CANEM Bruno Simoes - vocals, Nuno Pinheira - guitar, Pedro Pinto - bass, Sergio - synth and Ze Carlos - drums. Started late 93, with lyrical concerns dealing heavily with Goethe's romantic literature. Intense vocals, hard bass, smooth keyboards, giving a professional cinematic quality. Contact at Enochian Calls (below) if interested in 'The House Of Souls' demo.

CELLO Bubbly goth-pop a la Ghost Dance/Eves. Hyperium, PO Box 910127, 90259 Nurnberg, Germany.

ENOCHIAN CALLS All-encompassing title for the many and varied activities of one Nuno Avila, experienced dj. His fanzine, *Paranoid Angel*, represents what he regards as the best material from other (international) zines. His radio show is 'Crime No Paraiso', broadcasting every Saturday midnight to 1am on Radio Universidade de Coimbra, covering roughly what you'll find in this book. E.C. also has a few tapes, videos and zines for sale, so send for their little catalogue. Rua Dr. Jose Alberto dos Reis, No 5, R/C, 3000 Coimbra.

FAST FORWARD Label. Apt. 5204, 1706 Lisboa Codex.

KADATH Label. Nuno Loureiro, Bairro de Sta. Apolonia, Rua Bernardo Santareno, 183 1o Esq., 3020 Coimbra.

LACRIMA CHRISTI Virgilio Santos, Urb. Jardim Do Sol, Edif 13 - 100C, Arroja, 2675 Odivelas.

MARTYRIUM Lord Impirius Radamanto - vocals, Lestat - lead guitar, Gandalf - rhythm guitar, D'Aviulla - bass, Csjwthe - drums, Thanattor - keybds. Formed 94. Pretty traditional late 80's sound, brightened up live with dancers onstage. The singer sounds like McCoy having an attack of the vapours. Great spindly guitar prances throughout the songs. The voice holds an enthralling sprawling dramatic feel, lurching throughout the discipline around him. Intentional lyrical balance between vampiric themes and old stories of mystic ancestors, "making poetry dance in urns of gold" apparently. It's actually heady, powerful stuff but unfortunately the photos they sent weren't clear enough to reproduce, which may be just as well as the Lord in his top hat looked uncannily like the Penguin which surely can't have been the idea. Lestat, Rua da Picaria 97 R/C, 4050 Porto.

NIGREDO A band, of which I know nought. Paulo Maldoror, Rua Conde Nova Goa, 5, 3o Dto., 1070 Lisboa.

PERESGOTIKA This is an interesting zine. It began eight years ago, after an underground radio show, to fill the void left by the demise of the 'pirates'. First issue Dec 88. By the fourth issue they had national distribution of sorts and it now comes out quarterly.

89

Peresgotika began to develop, into a label simultaneously, beginning with the 'Bem Fundo' tape of Portugese band Caes Vadios. Their first original tape was issued in 90, featuring two bands - Daltomnics and...Ataraxia! So the tapes have progressed, with various titles - 'T. Secret Sessions', and the musical diversity increased to include indie, so that Goth would also be mixed in with rare tracks by Nova Mob or Jane's Addiction. British bands have included The Mission, Chateau Royale, Restoration II, Rosetta Stone, Dream Disciples. They also have special metal releases and naturally there is a healthy coverage of their favourite local bands. The latest issue planned at the time of writing was Issue 26, featuring a tape of four Swiss bands and Portugese outfit, Sad Cow. The editorial contents are now so broad you'll find The Deep Eynde and Midnight Configuration rubbing shoulders with Skunk Anansie, Biohazard, Young Gods and Catherine Wheel. Their activities are also supported by the radio show 'O Arco do cego', so you could always send tapes via the fanzine which may also find themselves on air. Apartado 5221, 4021 Porto Codex.

PROMOTION TAPES At a guess, tapes. Rua Do Jardim 598, 4405 Valdares, Porto.

RADIO CLUBE DO COVILHA Portugal Rebelde, c.o Marco Aurelio, Apartado 8, 6203 Covilha Codex.

RITUAL Pedro Brinca, Apartado 328, 2900 Setubal.

UNIVERSIDADE RADIO Rua do Brasil 199, RC, 3000 Coimbra.

SPH/EXTASIS Apartado 223, 2780 Oeiras.

Romania

ANTOFAGASTA Radio show, Radio Top 91, broadcast in the Suceava and Radauti areas, weekly from 11.30pm-6am. Doru also runs a fanzine from the same address which covers the same areas of gloomy music. Doru Atomel, S. Isopescu 21, BI.M, Sc.C, Ap.4, 5800 Suceava.

Russia

GORE OF DEATH Fanzine. Valery Sidorov, UI. Parkovya 18a-44, 450073 Uta.

TANGERINE WAVE Radio/tv show. PO Box 38 Moscow 113184.

Slovakia

CREWZINE Fanzine. Richard Gurtler, Druzicova 2, 82102 Bratislava.

EBM Radio show. Miro Adamov, Hlavacikova 24, SK-841 05 Bratislava.

South Africa

THE WALK Mike Adams, Carl Serfontein, Jenny Hazell and Wayne Twine constitute, by all accounts, the 'premier' South African Goth band. This seems to imply that there are others, although I have also heard that the 'best' that you tend to hear in clubs is bilge like Depeche Mode. The Walk were formed in Johannesburg in 91, when we still wouldn't have touched them with a bargepole on principle. Now we find ourselves free to give them the benefit of the doubt. PO Box 2775, Northcliff 2115.

89 ANCIENT TALES 90 *BLACK BOX* 91 GOTHIC SEX

90 91

Spain

ANCIENT TALES Manuel Casas - vocals/guitars/ drum machine, Rosa Casas - vocals/keybds, X-69 - guitar/bass. Formed 92, and released first demo 'Debris', 'Malignant Times' demo (93), 'The Ritual' 7" (94), support to The Mission during Spanish tour of 95. Debut CD should be out around now. Influenced by early UK Goth bands and in particular the 4AD feel to things, adding in elements of Middle Ages compositions and the ethnic blends of Bulgarian, Indian and Arabian music. This produces a striking, majestic sound - sort of Clannad on steroids. Rosa Casas, C/ Velazquez 27, 28001 Madrid.

ARCHIVE Wise and in-depth fanzine. Juan Fco. Camacho Conesa, C/ Porto Cristo no 4, 7 D Dcha, 28924 Alcorcon, Madrid.

BLACK BOX Beautiful quality magazine from team also organising gigs and recordings. Rocio, Apartado de Correos 214, 28922 Alcorcon Madrid. (Fax: 9-612-74-77)

COLERA DEI Interesting dark fanzine. c/Fco. M. Padilla 1, 30B 35.012 Las Palmas.

d'O FANTASY Fetish shop with all relevant literature. Apartado 128, 08950 Esplugues Liob. (Fax 340 3 473 7758)

DARK DEMONS Art zine - Death/Black/Goth. Alexis Quintana Priori, C/Paseo De Chil 79-81, 35011 Las palmas DE G.C. Las Palmas, Canary Islands.

DE SADE Fanzine. Some distribution under the name *En Negro*. Hector Noble Fernandez, c/o Augustina de Aragon 115, E-35012 Las Palmas de G.C.

ECODALIA Jose Ramon De Barrio - vocals/guitars, Cristina Muneta - vocals and everything else. Very charming, soulful but not as soothing as these directions usually turn out. 'Angel's Candour' CD (95). Gabraciones Goticas, PO Box 497, 08240 Manresa, Barcelona.

EXORCISM Fanzine. Javier Cuirias, 14 Viascon 36121 Pontevedra. Or c/o Isaac Baron 6, 1.36002 Pontevedra.

GABRACIONES GOTICAS The only Spanish label that specialises in Dark music, already running for over ten years. Manager David Prieto arranges gigs and clubs where people can also buy fanzines and CDs. PO Box 497, 08240 Manresa, Barcelona. (Fax: 34 3 8270639)

TINA GARCIA Writer and editor of own Goth books. Licenciado Vidriera 4, 40Q 18.008 Granada.

GOTHIC SEX Lady - vocals/drums, Lord - vocals/ guitar. As cool sounding as they look, formed in 89 from members of mid-80's Goth bands (Cadaveres Aterciopelados/Notre Dame), and there's been a ton of line-up changes, ending up as a central duo, with the help of additional people named Metal Storm and Dr Van Hellsing. Interestingly, the term Gothic wasn't used when they started to describe this kind of music in Spain. It was called 'Onda Siniestra' (Sinister Wave), while Europe generally opted for the term Dark Wave. Gothic Sex have clear ideas about a strongly developed image, just as they try and create music without conscious influences, although their tastes appear to include virtually everything. Live they appear pretty different too, their recent stage show finding them strewing the stage with animal innards as they and suitably dramatic extras plunged into tales of flaggelation, resurrection, sex, depravity, ultraviolence and even mutilations. They hone this down to have songs presented in certain elements through the projection of overlaid images, which can be taken from both

92

computer sequences and scanned photographs from horror, porn, and S&M. They are also involved with the magazine, *Brotherhood Of Lost Souls*. Discography: 'El Frenesi' (The Frenzy) 7" (89), 'Lord Gothic' video (92), 'Ritualis Mortis' split CD - with Los Humillados - (93), 'Divided We Fall' CD (94), 'Video Clips Of The Shadows Of Torture' video and 'Moonrise' CD (96). The true spirit of debauch, anyone? Silvestre Perez, No 15, 3o B, 50002 Zaragoza. (Fax: 34-76 496290)

LOS HUMILLADOS Artur Rios and Ester Subirana have been at it for ages, obviously, and if you'll get their 'Dark Archives 1985-1995' CD you'll appreciate why people like such a moodily delicate delight. Gabraciones Goticas PO Box 497, 08240 Manresa, Barcelona.

MUSICAS DE REGIMEN Specialist shop for 'dark sounds' and also distributor of other labels. Apdo. 497, 08240 Manresa, Barcelona.

M A MORRO Individual doing fanzine and radio show. c/v de Begona 6, 48006 Bilbao.

MESSIAH OF PAIN Nods towards Danse Soc./Xymox bounce but in a modern manner with lashings of over-zealous guitar. Jordi lladu, c/Floridablnaca 112, 3c 3a, E-08015 Barcelona.

SEKUENCIAS DE CULTO Zine and radio program from same address. c/o Apartado 4226, 35011 Las Palmas de Gran Canaria.

SONIA GARCIA Fanzine. Mas 91 1o 3o, 08904 Hospitalet Barcelona.

STURM UND DRANG Electro Goth mag on past, present and future matters and not merely music. A. Pavia and S. Garcia, Apartado 16062, 08080 Barcelona.

93 DARK SIDE COWBOYS

ZERO Nice mail order catalogue with jewellery, shoes, posters available. Calle Riewra Baixa, 12, 08001 Barcelona.

Sweden

AKASHA Fanzine. PO Box 6056, 175 06 Jarfalla.

ARABESQUE Band. M & A.

ART DIRECTE No idea. Box 31052, S-400 32 Gothenberg.

AROTOSEAL Ditto. Marksu Stenman, Oerboda 218, 905 88 Umea.

BLACK WIDOW'S WEB Fetish society. BWW, Box 11489, 404 30, Gothenburg.

BASEMENT RECORDS Label. Vaxelmyntsgatan 66, 414 83 Gothenberg.

BAY LAUREL Wild band, rapidly creating a good reputation. Noxious Records, Box 2140, 103 14 Stockholm.

BEYOND THE INFINITE? Juho Korhonen, Johannesbacksgatan 58a, 754 33 Uppsala.

CATHERINE'S CATHEDRAL Neffy-Sisters thing with weirder 70's rock input. 'Flowerdust', 'Intoxication' and 'C.C.' CDs. (Fax: 0046 8 200726)

COLD MEAT INDUSTRY A label that knows its terrain and covers it superbly. The quality of their newsletter alone - a full colour booklet - is exemplary. They have some interesting bands too, although much goes in the black metal mould there is also Raison D'etre ("Dark atmospheric ritual chants"), Penitent ("Dark majestic atmospheric Norwegian poetry"), Consono ("Ancient hymns and folk-lore Industrials"!), Mortiis ("Dark dungeon music - music for kings!"). You get the picture. PO Box 1881, 581 17 Linkoping. (Fax: +46 (0) 3 10 39 06)

DARK DIVINITY Fanzine. Lindgren, Bagevagen 128, 856 52 Sundsvall.

DARK SIDE COWBOYS Niklas Carlsson, Andre Ljunggren, Viveka Stromberg, Andreas Astrom. None have specific roles as they tend to swop instruments about. As others have noted, there are comparisons to the band House Of Usher but this is more confidently done and far more commercial. The vocals in particular would make a major label drool, like a pretty version of 'Vision Thing'-era Sisters. Formed 93, but to be weird they released, as film music, five full length demo cassettes by the title of 'Ars Moriensis'. By 94 they'd secured a deal with M&A on the strength of these and in 95 started with the sixth in the line - 'Pearls For The Swine' only available to their known fans. Nov 95, M&A release 'Pure Heart MCD. Feb 96 debut CD 'The Apochryphal'. Again this has taken the semi-soundtrack form. While I'm here...this Moriensis Productions needs clarification. It is a Producers society with full membership rules. That said, I have no idea what they mean but it also includes a fanzine, gigs and club events. 'AM III The Hall Of Pain' CD and two others available. Moriensis Productions, Skogsstigen 6, 830 70 Hammerdal. (http//:www.ing.umu.se/-dsc) (e-mail: dsc@ing.umu.se)

DAWN OF OBLIVION Neffs only rockier. Strontium records, Vastra Skansgatan 1, 413 02 Goteborg.

DECOMPOSITION Fanzine. Patrick Andersson, Utgardsgatan 48, 723 55 Vasteras.

94 95

DESOLATION THEATRE Goth society. Bjorn Kylberg, Sorgarden 113, 186 31 Vallentuna.

ENGRAVED Band. Johan Ecklund, Ondagsv 3, 906 37 Umea.

THE ESSENCE New band, giving usual Swedish sound a strangely commercial twist. M&A.

THE EQUINOX OV THE GODS Frederik Wallin - guitar/vocals, Melker Ryymin - bass, Stefan Dahlberg - guitar. Formed 90. "In our music," they coo, "there is an element of dark, romantic mysticism. It is like walking with your girlfriend in a cemetery at midnight when the full moon is shining. It is gloomy and maybe it scares you, but it is pleasant and a romantic kind of fright." Three demos - 'Songs From The Hill Of The Heartless Giant' (91), 'Watch The Shadows Dance' (93) and 'This Sombre Dreamland' (94) but all are sold out. Although certain members of the band have been through Metal and Speed phases they've never been able to keep line-ups going longer than a couple of years so while it isn't surprising that their heartier approach to the darker regions wins them instant support, development remains outside their domain. For a band not afraid to list AC/DC and Venom (!) as early influences there remains a freshness about the angry daubs of sound they wrestle over. Frederik, never one to be slow in coming forward, doesn't have much time for the fetish or vampire scene but then casually admits to drinking blood occasionally. He also collects obituaries, pictures of graveyards and recently obtained an old organ that had once been used in a morgue. Fortunately we're talking musical organ here. "It has a beautiful sound. Just like a horror movie." Marvellous, but what the Hell was it doing in a morgue? ("Have you come to view the body Inspector?","That's correct but first...we dance!") Frederik Wallin, Haggenas 3125, 830 30 Lit.

FUNHOUSE Mikael Hartle - vox/guitars, Fredrik Tack - guitars, Stefan Larsson - bass, Jonas Elmqvist - drums. Formed 86 and their easily accessible CD 'Girls' is pretty good. What's weird is that they started with an EP in 87 and it took eight years to get to an album! M&A.

GEIGERMEETER Fanzine. Smith, Alvans Vag 184, 90750 Umea.

GOBLIN AGGRO CULTURE Fanzine. Box 217, 64523 Strangnas.

GROTKAFT Band, Lajbanerna, Box 246, 833 00 Stromsund.

JOE & THE BOYS FROM ABOVE Band, possibly dead. Chaos Productions, PO Box 3812, 903 15 Umea.

LA SOLITUDE Brandy, Kaponjarsg 4b, 413 02 Goteborg.

THOMAS LOFGREN Has written definitive Sisters Of Mercy discography in book form. Norra Overby, 46170 Troillhatan.

M & A MUSICART Have done Children On Stun and Restoration II releases, as well as those of the main band Funhouse. They are negotiating with The Mission to license their future work (or not), and Medicine Rain. Andreas Larsson, Simrishamngatan 20 A, 214 33.

MAGPIE Band. Christoffer Jonsson, Storg. 1B, 903 20 Umea.

MALAISE Martin Danielsson - vocals/prog./guitars, Juno Korhonen - rhythm/lead guitars, Johan Linder - drums, Kim Boman - keybds/bass. Formed 89. Brazen rifftastic Electro-Goth. Sisters meets

94 THE EQUINOX OV THE GODS 95 FUNHOUSE 96 MALAISE

96

Frontline Assembly in sleek-cheeked duel. 'Secession' MCD (93), '52 Ways' CD (96). Odengarten 1, 36130 Emmaboda. (Fax: +46 - 471 334 23)

MEDICINE RAIN Standard late Sisters/Leather Nun sound getting a toughened 90's rock input. 'Native' CD. M&A.

MEMENTO MATERIA Label. Odengarten 1, 36130 Emmaboda.

THE MOBILE MOB FREAKSHOW Nightbreed describe the effect thus - "Imagine Carl McCoy singing with a cross between The Damned and Motorhead, but with a dash of The Cramps... and Screaming Dead". Then put those thoughts out of your head. It just isn't safe. 'Horror Freakshow' CD. Primitive Art Records, Box 4049, 300 04 Halmstad.

MONUMENT Band. Powerspot Records, Box 208, 281 22 Hasselholm.

MORIENSIS PRODUCTIONS Merchandising centre for the excellent Darkside Cowboys, offering all the releases, t-shirts etc. It also has its own newsletter, in English for the International audience and a larger version, big enough to count as a fanzine with an interesting review section, in Swedish. Moriensis Productions, Skogsstigen 6, 830 70 Hammerdal.

NEVER MIND Band. M&A.

NOCTURNAL SEA Band, not unlike Garden Of Delight. M&A.

NOVELTY Band. Bjorkman, Ginstvagen 21, 197 34 Bo.

POPOGA Fanzine. Box 68, 643 21, Vingaker.

PRIMITIVE ART RECORDS Label. Box 4049, 300 04 Halmstad.

Q-DEPARTMENT Band. J K Westerlund, Gammelv. 5, 791 41 Falun.

RELEASE Electro-Goth mag. PO Box 7144, S-402 33 Gotenberg.

S.C.U.D. Band. Franz Enmark, O Strandg 23, 903 33 Umea.

SECTOR SEX Band. PO 57, 343 21 Almhult.

SEVEN TREES Band. Henrik Karlsson, Ullavig 21A, 70357 Orebro.

SICK ODOR Fanzine. Andreas Dahlstrom Osterg, 53, 753 33 Surahammar.

SONS OF NEVERLAND Passed their degree in Neffology (Advanced) with flying colours. 'Soul keeper' CD. Primitive Art Records, Box 4049, 300 04 Halmstad.

STATION OBSCEN Band. Daniel Sundberg, Sveavagen 31C, 811 36 Sandviken.

TANELORN POST Fanzine. Kungsg @c, 520 40 Floby.

THE OTHER SIDE Fanzine. Mathias Sistonen, Ginstvagen 20, 19734 Bro.

WHISPERED IN THE WIND Slim, hilarious, delightful fanzine. Larsson, Nobelvagen 103B, 6 TR, S-21433 Malmo.

ZYNTEC Fanzine. Karin Bolin, Sjomilsg 14, 421 37 V. Frolunda.

Switzerland

AFTER DARKNESS Orlok - vocals, Harding - guitars, Knock - bass. Creepy atmospheric band, much admired in certain quarters. 'Murnau' (lovingly packaged tribute to the director of *Nosferatu*) CD on Subtronic recommended. PO Box 6204, 6000 Lucerne.

ALL SOUL'S AVENUE Fanzine/newsletter. CP 834 2000 Neuchatel.

AURAL EXCITER Mail order/dist. Dietmar Gallhammer, Albdruck AG, Herzogstasse 26 5000 Aarau.

BOUTIQUE FANC Fetish establishment. Haltinger Str 59, 4057 Basel.

DARKEN ART Designers - logos and sleeve work etc. Marco Gemmet, Dammweg 15, 3904 Naters.

DEATH NOISE Dist. Recommended by *Fight Amnesia* as the best address in Switzerland for Goth news. 3 page mail order info sheet. Jorg Zuber, Binenweg 5, 3904 Naters.

EX-ABRUPTO That's the trademark of Gothic-fetish-Avant garde clothes designer Anne Lombard, who claims to insert a design concept into her work, drawn from architectural styles, such as the Rational, Bauhaus and Deconstructivism. Her aesthetic vision is also influenced by tribal style, death art and artistic references from Surrealism, Symbolism, Pre-Raphaelism and Romanticism. These clothes, she says, are designed for Gothic-industrial parties, for fetish pleasure meetings, metropolitan tribal youth and other avant-gardeist people. Well, alrighty! Ex-Abrupto, Chemin des Aubepines 12, 1004 Lausanne.

GECKO Fanzine. Weibel, PO Box 5037, 6002 Lucerne.

GEILER GEIER Fanzine. Pille Weibel, PO Box 5037, 6002 Lucerne.

ILLUSION PERDUE Fanzine. Post Restante 1211 Geneva 8.

HALL OF SERMON The label that boasts Lacrimosa for one thing which should make you sit up and bark excitedly. Lacrimosa won the prestigious Best Alternative Band award from the ever excellent *Zillo* magazine in 95, the prize awarded by Nik Fiend. The band aim to use the money to record three bands from a competiton they've started! PO Box 749, 4310 Rheinfelden. (Fax 0041 61 8315150)

IS THIS SICKNESS? The work of Y. Teres and the sublimely named S. Kinkio. Neat, cold, dark electro-wave. Check 'Thoughts' CD (95). Conceptual Vision, 1 Rue G.-Perrenoud, 2400 Le Locle.

IT'S TIME TO... Record label, promotions dept and distributor, started by Jean-Luc Itten in 93, to cover Industrial/Electro material which naturally falls into some Goth areas. Excellent mail order catalogue - very brief but highly selective. No rubbish. Falkensteinerstr. 4, Postfach 4002 Basel. (Fax: +41 (0) 61 332 1881) (Net: http://www/worldcom.ch/Business/sMart/itt.HTLM)

LACRIMOSA Tilo Wolf - vocals/keybds/prog., Anne Nurmi - keybds/vocals, Jan Yrlund - guitar, Jan P. Genkel - bass - AC - 'Schlagzeug', or drumming. Apparently 'Lacrimosa' is the title of the last work sung, during its preparation, by Mozart before he snuffed it. Tilo Wolff, Lacrimosa's main man, is obsessed. He regards music as brilliant and beautiful, so don't expect dingy copyists ideas. A fanzine boy of the late 80's he then flogged the typewriter and bought himself a piano in the summer of 90. He also wears his black lipstick as though it were a bat, which is cute. I'll give a discography as I believe you

98

99

may want to start collecting in this case, because it really is *exceptional*. 'Clamour' (MC, 90), 'Angst' (LP, 91), 'Einsamkeit' (CD/LP 92), 'Angst' (CD, 92), 'Alles Luge' (MCD) 'Satura' (CD/LP, 93), 'Schakal' (MCD, 94), 'Inferno' (CD/2LP, 95) PO Box 749, 4310 Rheinfelden.

LUMIERE NOIRE Newsletter. 13 Rte de Veyrier, 1227 Carouge.

MALDOROR Goth-Metal band. Dark & Wild Records, 11 Rue de la Faucille, 1201 Geneva.

THE MOON LAY HIDDEN BENEATH A CLOUD Vienna-based band, formed in 92. Three CDs - 'The Moon...' (93), 'Amara Tanta Tyri' (94), 'A New Soldier Follows The Path Of A New King'. They also did the 7" single, 'Kostnice', recorded in the ossuary of Kostel Vsech Svatyc (All Saint's Church) in Bohemia, and a 10", 'Yndalonggg' containing three tracks recorded at Little Saxam Church, Suffolk! What are they up to? CDEP 'Were You Of Silver, Were You Of Gold' was due shortly after my deadline. A weird lot. Arthur's Round Table (that's the name of their label, they're not mad), PO Box 33, 9432 Walzenhauen.

MORDOR Formed by Scorh Anyroth and Dam Gomhory (formerly of Arog), Nov 90, they produced two CDs - 'Odes' and 'Csejthe' for which they were joined by Opal Ablasorh. Black Metal, doom, Goth, atmospherics and classical, crashing together. Dark Industries BP 360, 1020 Renens Vdl.

NUIT D'OCTOBRE Yves Boil - guitars, Olivier Choulet - drums, Stephanie Minne - piano/samples, Jean-Claude Cerf - bass, Pascal Choulet - vocals. Formed 84! 'Le Chant Des Disparus' 7" (87), 'Ombres d'Adieux' CDEP (90), 'Un Automne En Concert -Live' CD (91), 'Tempetes' CD (93), 'Entre Ciel Et Feu' CD (96) Excellent band. Harder indie than Goth in most ways but they have the lost, moody edge off perfectly. Strangely emotional and beautifully produced, despite being conventional they instantly suck you in. Maybe a better version of Human Drama? Quote: "Nuit d'Octobre would not be able to leave unmoved the gloomy souls of the children of spleen". I should think not. CP 14, 2925 Buix. (Fax: ++41 (0) 66 71 24 84)

1ALONE It's Jean-Luc Itten, of It's Time To... on vocals/guitar, backed up by Olivier Maumary - bass and Yvan Teres sampler/drums. Jean-Luc can't stand still, having played for In Search Of Beauty (87-90), Double Indemnity (91) and Delicatessen (92-93). The 'Alone' CD (95) reveals an accessible yet off-kilter sub-Industrial approach that could be Virgin Prunes going down with a migraine. Falkensteinerstr. 4, Postfach 4002 Basel. (Fax: ++41 (0) 61 332 1881) (Net: http://www/worldcom.ch/Business/sMart/itt.HTLM)

RADIO ZONES Operating in the Lake Geneva area, this show has been on air since 84 but is now getting more selective and seeks more Goth stuff. And seeing as the Swiss aren't noted for being short of a bob or two I'd suggest bands get involved. There's a fair-sized audience out there who'd probably buy the boots you're planning to die in. Contact Florient Mercier - excellent surname, obviously trustworthy - Decadences Underground Show, Les amis de radio Zones, 7 Boulevard carl-Vogt, 1205 Geneva.

SADNESS Steff Terry - vocals/guitar, Chiva - lead guitar, Lloyd - keybds/samples, Andy - bass, Gradel - drums/percussion. Mad and compelling band. Allow me to paraphrase what they wrote to me:

"When winter numbs our limbs and when time seems to stop, two souls, Chiva and Gradel, mad about dark chasm, met together. Steff, Terry and Erik strike up to create a single mass. Sadness was

98 NUIT D'OCTOBRE 99 SADNESS 100 SANCTUARY
101 CORINNE SPORRER: SELF-PORTRAIT

100
PHOTO: CORINNE SPORRER

born! This horde effected, eight months later their first demotape, 'Y'. 500 copies. Sold out. Erik leave, Steff Terry took his place and Sadness take a new bass player, Andy. Eight later the promotape 'Eodipus'. Sold out. 1,000 copies! 'Ames De Marbre' CD (Oct 93). 94 Lloyd joins. 'Danteferno' CD (95). Eight songs, in sad, dark and mystic way". Amen. PO Box 411, 1951 Sion.

SANCTUARY Now this is interesting. A Goth-Independent Association formed in November 95. Is this the Swiss end of the 'Sanctuary' I'd already listed in the French section? Very possibly, as its equally superb purpose is to provide info to all members about what is happening, fusing releases, parties and concerts and actively promoting some of its own, to which members naturally get in at reduced admission. They also do a good French/German/Italian newsletter. PO Box 205, 1000 Lausanne 22. (e-mail: sanctuary@worldcom.ch) (Net: http;//www.geocities.com/SunsetStrip/1680)

101

SERPENT TEARS Label/distribution, possibly still responsible for the *Sickle Moon* fanzine. CP 178, 1217 Meyrin, Switzerland. Or CP21, 1225 Chene-Bourg.

SOCORRO! Fanzine. Marcos Ortega, Santisstr 13A 8305 Dietakon.

CORINNE SPORRER Excellent photographer obviously involved with the Sanctuary scene, attracted by the character of the other participants. c/o Sanctuary.

STREIFSCHUSS Fanzine. Daniel Hainz Petri, Psarkstr 13, D-66271 Sitterswald.

WIEBEL Yes, he wobbles but he don't fall down. Compilation MCs plus *Animal Revenge Man* zine. Pille PO Box 50 37, 6002 Luzern.

102 ALIEN SEX FIEND 103 ALL LIVING FEAR

102

WITCHUNT RECORDS Excellent quality label, right down to the delicious artwork, handling Black Metal/Darkwave/Metal, offering the usual CDs but also Satanically-inclined videos! One of the funniest things in their press book is the section devoted to the band Azag-Thoth, so dangerous that they mess up churches. They wear their underpants upside down. Pure, undiluted evil. Under the category sub-heading, it lists - Inferno Black Metal Massacre. Under 'band contact' it says, simply....no contact possible. The band want no publicity. "All this filthy fanzines which are done by christians should be burned and their writers crucified". Stop wanking chaps and back in yer box! PO Box 658, 8029 Zurich.

Turkey

GURAY TOPAC Fanzine. Firin Sk. 9-1, Yenimahalle-Bakirkoy, 34720 Istanbul.

UK

Bands

ADAM'S FAMILY Jaki Florek - vocals, Bill Freeman - guitar, Ritchie Slater - drums, Ian Lees - bass. Formed in the late 80's, as a seven piece glam-punk-goth band but in 90 sensibly slimmed down to a four piece. Single 'Frustration/Timewaster' released on their own Loose Records in 94. Before this what I have listed is 'Here's Laughing At You Kid' demo (85) and 'Sometimes I Wonder' mini-LP (Nov 87). Their presence has been noticeable on the Goth scene of the past few years although Jaki's rheumatic illness have often reduced the number of gigs. They have a low key sound but with a solid sense of power moving in the background as they consistently tease melodies out, with well placed lyrics dragging the listener in. They're a lot less predictable than the majority, which you should find out on the 'Disease' album, being recorded at the time of writing. Early tracks are excellent. PO Box 67, Runcorn, Cheshire WA7 4NL.

ALIEN SEX FIEND Mr and Mrs Fiend - everything imaginable. Dave - guitar. Still one of the most disgracefully fabulous bands in the world, things should be improving now that they have escaped their old record deal, with decent re-releases available via Cleopatra. They have established their own label, 13th Moon, starting off with the 'Evolution' 12". It's the same enjoyable Fiends stretching themselves. Their decision to drag in the mad blues guitarist Dave sums them up. They know only what it can do to the sound, so the notion of judging what *type* of person is involved is not important. If you feel their longevity is likely to make them old-fashioned, you needn't worry. Their bark remains as jolly as their bite. Wolves with painted rubber teeth, they are purring through serene dance waters at times because, lest drongoes forget, ASF were already there when some technokids were (and are) still in nappies. And now, on with the discography:

SINGLES: 'Ignore The Machine' 7"/12" (83), 'Lips Can't Go' 7"/12" (83), 'R.I.P.' 7"/12" (84), 'New Christian Music' 7"/12" (84), 'Dead And Buried' 7"/12" (84), 'E.S.T.' 7"/11" (84), 'Ignore' re-lease (re-mixed) 12" (85), 'I'm Doing Time In A Maximum Security Twilight Home' 12" (85), 'I Walk The Line' 7"/12" (86), 'Smells Like' 7"/12" (86), 'Hurricane Fighter Plane' 7"/12" (87), 'The Impossible Mission' 7"/12" (87), 'Here Cum Germs' 7"/12" (87), 'Stuff The Turkey' 7"/12" (87), 'Ignore' MCD (88), 'Bun-Ho' 12" (88), 'Haunted House' 12"/MCD (89), 'Now I'm Feeling Zombified' 12"/MCD (90), 'Magic'

12"/MCD (92), 'Inferno' 12" (94), 'Inferno' MCD (95), 'Evolution' 12" (96).

ALBUMS: 'Who's Been Sleeping In My Brain' LP/CD (83), 'Acid Bath' LP/MC/CD (84), 'Liquid Head In Tokyo' (85), 'Maximum Security' LP/dblMC('It')/CD (85), 'It' LP/dblMC/CD (86), 'The Impossible Mission' MiniLP/MC - America only (87), 'Here Cum Germs' LP/MC/CD (87), 'All Our Yesterdays' MC/CD (88), 'Another Planet' LP/MC/CD (88), 'Too Much Acid?' dblLP/MC/CD (89), 'Curse' LP/MC/CD (92), 'Open Head Surgery' LP/MC/CD (92), 'Altered States Of America' LP/MC/CD (93), 'The Legendary Batcave Tapes' LP/CD (93), 'Drive My Rocket' CD (94), 'Inferno" DblLP/CD (94), 'I'm Her Frankenstein' CD (95), 'The Singles 83-95' DblCD (95). BOXED SET 'Alien Sex Fiend Box' (90).

VIDEOS: 'Purple Glistener' (83), 'Liquid Head In Tokyo' (85), 'Edit' (86) 'Overdose' (87), 'Re-Animated' (94), 'The Making Of Inferno'(94). PO Box 416, Cardiff CF1 8XU. (e-mail c/o Leon Smith. use: Issmith@glam.ac.uk) (Net: http://www.zynet-co.uk.steelwolf/ignore)

ALL LIVING FEAR Matthew North - guitar/bass/ prog./music, Andrew Racher - vocals/keybds/ lyrics. Formed Summer 92, arguably the hardest working of any of the bands in this section, they never stop touring, with as wide a variety of bands as possible, unless there are no more venues to play. Discography - 'Waiting' MC (May 93), 'Close Down' MC (Jan 94), 'Jessica' MCD (Aug 94), 'The Widows Blame' CD (Oct 95) and 'Fear Of The Road' video (Feb 96). Their music is steadily getting better (hardly easy when a duo) and they brim over with vitality. You might also care to own one of their Fucked By The Hand Of Goth t-shirts and join their info service which really keeps a flow of info coming. Matthew, Pludda House, Station Rd, Bovey Tracey, Devon TQ13 9AS. (e-mail: allfear@ mail.zynet.co.uk)

ALTERED STATES Yig Hughes - vocals/guitar, Steve Williams - bass, Des Connelly - drums. Noisy bastoid Goth with room enough for a hard pop edge to be lovingly smothered in credible rock influences, this band formed in the 80's (I'm fuzzy on detail) and then reformed in 94. 'Is Anyone Out There" (reissue - 94), 'Designer Reality' MCD (95). Primary, PO Box 3213, London SW2 3QQ. (Fax: 44 (0) 181 671 3115)

AND ALSO THE TREES They didn't like being included in the last book - because it turns out they didn't want to be in it in the first place. According to them I sounded like a Headmaster because I called them lazy. That's sweet... only soft-headed middle class boys would dream of comparing anybody to a Headmaster, but there you go. (Most would simply call me a wanker and be done with it.) I won't call them lazy anymore, because they obviously move quite contentedly at their own pace, and although everyone else sees them as Goth-y, they don't. PO Box 4, Inkberrow, Worcs WR7 4NB.

ATHAMAY It's those awfully nice *B&RV* doing electro-weirdness. See *B&RV*. (Fanzines)

ATTRITION Vague tie-ins from a band whose mentor, Martin, confesses they often get the "Goth/ Industrial tag" but they're also left of centre weird indie. They have a mass of recorded material available. Martin Bowes, 7 Radcliffe Rd, Coventry CV5 6AA.

BALAAM AND THE ANGEL Yes, they're back. I was recently told off by Matthew of All Living Fear for ridiculing this band in my last book. He maintained, accurately, that if it wasn't for Balaam there would have been no Neds, Poppies or Wonder Stuff. Hardly

104 CHATEAU ROYALE 105 CRIES OF TAMMUZ 106 DEFACTO

104

a recommendation, but I take his point. Balaam blazed a trail for rubbish to smoulder in their wake. So yes, I'll accept I was too harsh. They initially got back for some sort of reunion gig, bored with the recycled toilet paper business they have started and made a success of (no joke, it's a serious paper firm!) and had such a good time they've kept going, although it may just be a hobby. PNG/Worldwide, 10 Park Rd North, Birmingham B6 5UJ.

BARRA All About Eve meets Clannad. Nice. C. Parker, 22 Glenton Rd, London SE13 5RS.

BUS STATION LOONIES Pretty daft punk band actually - but they did let on that they are quite capable of doing an eight minute reggae version of 'Temple Of Love' when the situation demands it. Hopefully never. For address see Ruptured Ambitions. (Businesses)

THE CHAOS ENGINE Lee H - vocals/synth, Huw - guitars. Taking on the world with their classy Industria-pop. 'Conspiracy' EP available. Lee H, 100 Ashlands Rd, Cheltenham, Gloucestershire GL51 0DH.

CHATEAU ROYALE Ady/Baron - everything shared. Formed Jan 91, this duo do everything very carefully and everything turns out very nicely thank you. You'll be able to predict their approach from their photo. This is pretty much how they sound, lost in a post-vampiric swirl... melancholy, loneliness, sadness. The musician, they reckon, is the priest of the Invisible. Or, "We are the mysterious actors of the phantom cemetery of our imagination". You need locking up, mate! Two CD singles, 'Angel' and 'In Mourning'. Quite pretty. 104 Ferndale Rd, London SW4 7SE.

CHILDREN OF POWER 163 Oving Rd, Chichester, West Sussex PO20 6AG.

COUNTING THE MAD Baz - vocals/kybds, Nic - bass, Wayne - guitars, Dave - drums. Late 80's sound (Neffs/Sisters) given invigoration of a more basic variety. Primary, PO Box 3213, London SW2 3QQ.

ANGELA COSTA Former lead singer with Angel And The Drunken Gods and Presents Of Mind, both in America, Angela has relocated over here and goes out under her own name, initially with the 'Circus Beserk' MC, meant to hit CD via Planet Records, with a book, *Cock Tales*, coming soon. Her press release describes her as a writer of "transgressive Po-faction", to which we nod our heads, pleased to have found something else we can pretend we've heard about. When the press release tentatively suggests she's the illegitimate daughter of Patti Smith and Johnny Cash we can go along with that except that she doesn't show the signs of physical degradation that such a mating would have produced. (e-mail Noir69@AOL)

CRIES OF TAMMUZ Paul Nemeth - vocals, Robert Field - bass, John Currie - guitar, Steve Higgins - perc., Dan Woodard - keybds. Formed Autumn 92. Named after some Sumerian/Babylonian legend about giants, which maybe also reflects their basic Nephilim infatuation, right down to the excess of smoke and headgear. Claiming influences from goth, reggae, classical and rock, they admit to wanting to create a sound that involves power and atmosphere. The band started late 92, from the remnants of a Doors-ish band. They write about big themes rather than personal lives and I have to admit I admire their approach but they've yet to get close to the reality of their desires and all they *really* need to do is shed themselves of influences they seem to have gone out of their way to put on. I tried taking photos of them one night at a gig at the Bull & Gate and there was so much smoke, inside such a small venue that pretty soon I could hardly see the camera, let alone them. Occasionally a hat could be

105

106

made out, but that did not cheer me. Two early demos, still available - 'The Summoning' (£3.50 inc p&p), 'Alchemist' (£4 inc p&p). Paul has begun shifting his lyrical concerns away from the Western esoteric tradition to the Middle East, which should surely affect the music you'll find soon enough on the 'Dumuzi Awakens' CD (Appollyon). Paul wants it to be dark, powerful rock with an eastern taste. An intriguing venture, in which chanting will play its part. Don't look at their photo and laugh, as even Paul describes it as "a hideous picture of us, taken at Hadleigh Castle in Essex in the Summer of 95". 5 Courage Walk (off Wainright Avenue), Hutton, Brentwood, Essex CM13 2TA.

DEFACTO Music that comes halfway between Goth, Techno, *A Clockwork Orange* and some spooky cinematic wodges of sound, heavily fuelled by rampant guitars and emphatic vocals. The vocals would be ten times better if they didn't have that squashed grazed 'Goth' approach most of the time and would in fact make this a truly excellent proposition, as would a far better electro rhythm. Sounds like disco some of the time. Now this is pretty much the work of one M. Toms who used to be in old Goth band Revenant Eve ('La Premiere' EP). He fell out with singer Glenn, but not to the extent that Glenn hasn't let him strip down some older material for this debut release, 'Blue Eyes & Violins'. It's very perky but when a singer talks differently on a track to how he sings you realise he's trying to hard to portray something that isn't entirely natural and therefore not quite relaxed enough. A hugely promising start though. The mysterious maestro, who describes his work as "kind of Technorock Industrial cyberpunk sort of thing" can only get better. 65 Bridle Close, Paignton Close, S. Devon TQ4 7ST.

DEMETER FALLS David - vocals/guitar, Elsie - guitar, Hannah - flute, Simon (ex God Sister Helen) - bass, unnamed drum machine. Hmmm, a band you don't hear too much about, although they've been going since 90. David and Mark started it off, dribbled along and so there's been some demos. It's David who keeps it together and recently a violinist and trumpet player were added. Band members have come and gone, some pouring pints over him as they left. David reckons there's a PJ Harvey/4AD feel there, at the very least an influence. The fact there isn't really doesn't matter, it's the intention that counts. The man cares, thinks and will do something eventually, recognising as he does that the whole cognitive UK Goth scene has been like a dormant tumour. It's ready to start eating into the main body of music again. Two demos - 'Demeter Falls' (Jun 93), 'Jo's Songs' (Sep 94). David, 27 Calder Crescent, Whitefield, Manchester M45 6EH.

DESOLATION Previously listed in the Nightbreed catalogue, this was actually the band Trev was in before Every New Dead Ghost and what he now sees as the precursor for Midnight Configuration. Two gigs, three demos. I include this only to aggravate you all.

DIE LAUGHING Rachel Speight - vocals, John Berry - guitars, Ian Holman - guitars (everybody pitching in programming the bass and keybds - they even have backing vocals on tape!). Down from their original four, Die Laughing formed in 92 and while they haven't technically offered much that is new to the Goth scene, despite the interesting touches provided by keyboards, what they have done is matched the early 80's in terms of melodic quality. There is nothing haphazard or small-minded about Die Laughing, because like doting parents they simply want what's best for their songs. Although the easiest comparison is All About Eve (before the Hippy rot set in) they don't have the same aggression. What they do have, which virtually every other UK act lacks, is this knowledge of melody and how to twist things into delightful forms. Discog: 'Poems Of Your Life' MC (Late 92), 'Love Among The Ruins' (April 93), 'Shadows And Silhouettes' (Halloween 94), 'Nemesis' (Aug 95), 'Glamour And Suicide' CD (Sept 95), 'Heaven In Decline' (May 96). They do need some more power, to offset the overtly romantic themes, otherwise they're one of the best around, and 96 is their busiest time, with dates at various UK festivals, playing Germany and America to spread their name further. And while it is hardly rare, there seems to be something remarkably cheerful about what they do. Again, no pretentious crap going on. 29 Broxtowe Avenue, Kimberley, Nottinghamshire NG16 2HN.

DISTORSHAUS Formerly good natured Blood Sanction, formed 93, producing a punkish version of Goth with a nifty melodic attack, they have changed their name. Their business card says 'Alternative Rock' which is a great improvement on 'Goth Rock Revivalists'. Gary, 4 Agincourt St, Newport, Gwent, South Wales NP9 5JN.

DIVIDED LIVES Raj Ratan - bass, Gavin Mason - vocals, Ghost Ryder - drums. Formed 88, playing overbearingly strong power Goth. Original guitarist Sean Petherbridge left in late 92. 93/94 Raj built a little studio and in 95 recordings were made with sessionist guitar work from Pete Hughes. Raj finally switched from bass to guitar. Understandably the sound is now a bit thin which is a shame as their songs are actually good and they certainly know how to escalate power and excitement. Raj also seems unaware he has a strong voice and relies too much on constricting his throat to give it a playfully whiney edge and attendant, affected drama. If he was just himself it would really grow. Demos - 'Between Bitterness And Barbed Wire (Live)' released in two different sleeves (90), 'Different Sky (Live)' (90), 'Give Me Tomorrow' (91), 'Running With The Wind (Live)' (91), 'Twilight Years' (92), 'Dark Emotions' (95). 'Nirvana, Valhalla, Heaven, Hell' CD (96). Ray Ratan, 26 Shipley Rd, Leicester LE5 5BW.

DRAMA ASYLÙM William Asylum - vocals/samplers/prog./Teaboy, Marcus Grimm - guitars/bass/prog./Fuhrer. Of course they're demented, strangely convinced they're Industrial, yet content with live comparisons to Industrial-Thrash dance, whereas most people would say indie duo and sometimes, they claim, Gothic Industrial Pop. You might ask for their MC 'Black'. 9 Mepham Cres, Harrow Weald, Middlesex HA3 6QU.

DREAM CITY FILMCLUB No, they're not Goth but 'Pissboy' could be like a modern Bauhaus. Michael (vocals) is also the best new songwriter in the country. Imagine a commercial Nick Cave & The Bad Seeds - if Nick Cave had a voice you actually wanted to listen to, with PJ Harvey acting as a spirit guide. Then ask yourself, are you, or have you ever been, a member of the Catholic faith?

DREAM DISCIPLES Colin Lowing - vocals, Sid Bratley - guitar/keybds, Stephen McKean - bass, Mark Lundy - drums. Formed late 80's. Rocky Goth. 'Veil Of Tears' MCD (Mar 92). Worked out a deal with old Marillion man Fish, supported him constantly and released their CD 'In Amber' (94) on his label. 'In Amber' MCD (95) marked their last work for Fish as they now have their own label, Carrion, on which the new CD 'A Cure For Pain' has emerged. Another of the hardest working bands around who some, laughingly/enviously, refer to as U2! DD. PO Box 13951, Edinburgh EH 16 5ZB.

EARTH CALLING ANGELA Lively little sods Miles Fender and Paul Broome. Odd music, gently shivering rather than tempramental. Been around for almost five years and have just welcomed Ridley McIntyre on bass to flesh it out a little. Big boys now, their first CD may be out now on Germany's Alice In... label. Penystone, Camden Rd, Lingfield, Surrey RH7 6AF.

EMMA CONQUEST Started in 91 as a four piece but have since slimmed down to the regular duo of founders Ryan Swift - vocals, guitar and Simon Whitman - guitar. They even go so far as to describe themselves as dancey GothPop, opting for the faster material live, which is a good idea that quite a few

107 DIE LAUGHING 108 EMMA CONQUEST

107

108

forget. 'The Lunatic Of Substance' CD. 10 Kirby Drive, Kegworth, Derby DE74 2HI.

EN DURA Formerly AbRAXAS and while hardly Goth they agree they're dark. (AbRAXAS is the supreme Gnostic deity, fact fiends). They bring out the basics and deal with them. This is light and dark, despair and joy, signed to the Candelight label. S Pennick, 4 Verdun Tce, West Cornforth, Durham DL17 9LN.

ENDYMIONS DREAM Previously, on John McDonagh...The Machine In The Garden and This Burning Effigy. While he happily gives me as much info on possible on the others he modestly refuses to talk about his new project. Nutter. It's bound to be good - and modern. John McDonagh, 57 Kincora Drive, Clontarf, Dublin 3, Ireland. (e-mail: "endymion@iol.ie")

ENRAPTURE Anastasia Malinowska - vocals, Rob Ackerman - guitars/prog., Belle - drums, Somebody else - something else. Enrapture used to be a light-weight post-Cure pop type Goth band who then entered the twilight zone of lack of confidence and naked ambition where, misreading the signs of a strong recurrence in Goth interest, which could be exploited, they fooled themselves into thinking they're A Dance Band and the enterprising Primary Records suggest comparisons of Curve, Blondie and Nine Inch Nails. More amazing is the claim that "Enrapture have already been described as T-Rex for the 90's". Maybe they have, by mad people. 'No Heat So Cold' MCD single is not bad at all. Primary, PO Box 3213, London SW2 3QQ.

EYES OF THE NIGHTMARE JUNGLE J. Russell Webster - vocals, Colin Richardson - guitar/drums, Peter Gil Senan - bass/guitar, Guthrie Handley - vocals/keybds. Bit of a weird one. Nobody really knows much about them, possibly because of how they exist. Webster ran a studio, the ill-fated Slaughterhouse, which burnt down, we know that much. Two CDs in 'Fate' and 'Innocence', on Spectre, in Germany. A touch Sisterish, but that isn't surprising as them and The Mission came out of the Slaughterhouse aura themselves. Wayne Hussey has even contributed guest vocals on one song. Old-fashioned, in a nice, undemanding way.

FAITHFUL DAWN Sarahjane - vocals, Norman Jones - keyboards, Glenn Wilson - guitar. Formed in 91, two EPs. ('Awakened'/'Sequel') and seem to have been impressed by minor Goth flirtations with dance as a way forward for them overall. It's a new genre of dance called Darker dance. Another interesting band, with a foreign deal, so they'll be spending a healthy amount of time touring Europe. They certainly have a very confident sound and currently have 3 single/1 album deal with Paradigm. 78 Scotland Road, Penrith, Cumbria CA11 9JD. (Fax: 01931-716755) (Net: http://www.musicweb.co.uk/the_faithful_dawn/)

FAT BOB & THE CUREHEADS I don't know and I don't care. Former Nosferatu vocalist fronts Cure covers band!

GENTLE IHOR'S DEVOTION These seriously seedy looking men are Gentle Ihor - real name and vocals, Nigel Goodwin - guitars/vocals/ prog., Eddie Tempest - synth/keybds. They make intriguing, emotional music that should be of interest if and when they resurface properly. 18 Ashmore Drive, Ossett, Wakefield, W Yorkshire WF5 9SF.

GETHSEMANE Porl Morgan - vocals, Ian Palmer - guitars, Katy Helsby - bass/vocals, Bullwinckle - drums/samples/etc. They're pretty good but caught on the horns of the dilemma as to whether to flog themselves around or not. Formed 92, without Porl, the interloper. Their original bassist Simon quit,

109 THE HORATII 110 INKUBUS SUKKUBUS 111 LIBITINA

Katy took over and Porl slipped serenely in. After that it's all the usual story. You can get so far and no further unless you work constantly. Not surprisingly, many cannot. Quite heavy on the atmospherics, initially, they still appear a little steeped in the past, which is partly why it made it easy for people to be interested early on. Now, ironically, they are at their most vigorous with a blinding sense of energy coursing through the guitar sound in particular and they're probably at their least popular, despite having a better rhythmical sense than many moving into the dancier vista. Reverse that trend now for them, because this is one of the few UK bands who clearly know how to cause a genuine rumpus. You may be thinking they've been just dragging it out but they sound ten times better now. Demo Discog - 'Dark Hour' (92), 'Watch And Pray' (93), 'Here And Now' (94), 'Switch' (95), 'Demo' (95). You join their Crimpformation Service for news. 11 Winster Park, Scalehall, Lancaster, LA1 5TH.
(Fax: 01524-843443)

THE HORATII Roo - vocals, Eddie - guitar, Tim - bass, Sarah - guitar. A fancy bunch who have come on a lot since their early days.They also have a distinct style and guile about them. It's no wonder they're creating ripples already. Roo - he of the eyebrows - says, "the Goth tag feels quite comfortable because although we've never pursued the usual cliches, we maintain that the sound and the underlying values do not lose their relevance when applied to more modern or real life subjects. Musically, I find it hard to believe that so few bands ever share our excitement in the potential that Goth music has when influenced by the huge diversity of good music being made in other genres." Smart bombs, the bunch of them. Early demos - 'Annaline' (91), 'Insects' (94), 'Riposte' CD (95), enjoying a bit of a club hit with 'Darrell & Alicia' and maybe getting the sort of growing live reputation from gigs who don't recognise them as Goth! Mallory Towers, 33 Highway Rd, Evington, Leicester. (e-mail: horatii@swandom.demon.co.uk.)

INDUSTRIA Goth/Industrial/Electronic project which admits to being influenced by the likes of anything from Laibach, Danse Society and In The Nursery, right through to Ennio Morricone. 'Tablets Of Stone' tape available. Elliot Crowe, 4 Earr Rd, Newton Mearns, Glasgow G77 6LT.

INKUBUS SUKKUBUS Tony McKormack - guitar, Candia - vocals, Bob Gardener - bass. Prototype version, lurking under the name of Belas Knapp (a small mound you can actually sit inside - I've been there!), formed in 88 but the name soon changed to Incubus Succubus. They managed the single 'Beltaine' but when the initial lineup fell apart Tony and Candia, pagans both, continued as Children Of The Moon, which was well received by the Pagan crowd. Dec 91 and Bob Gardener, original drummer, rejoined and I.S. reformed, releasing all the material they'd done under Children Of The Moon as 'Beltaine'. From Sept 92 onwards they have released albums regularly, played live constantly, building up both a reputation and a loyal following. In 94 they released the 'Corn King' EP and by now were playing abroad. They have drum machinery and sequencers going like a rotting orchestra, leaving Bob to thrive on bass, his preferred instrument. (The last recording line-up included Kevin Gladwell and Jake Ridley both on bodhrans). The one thing you won't be disappointed with here is quality. The discography, goes thus: Vinyl - 'Beltaine' 7" (Spring 91), MCs - 'Beltaine' 15 track album (Autumn 91), 'Belladonna & Aconite' 11 track album (Oct 92), 'Corn King' five track EP (94), 'Wytches' 15 track album (April 94), 'Heartbeat Of The Earth' 11 track album (96). CDs - 'Belladonna & Aconite' 14 tracks (Summer 93), 'Wytches' 15 track (April 94), 'Heartbeat Of The Earth' 14 tracks (Oct 95), 'Beltaine' 15 tracks (early 96). Now off you go and

110

111

collect them! One of the main bands here. Under the pagan aegis, they have a different feel and could well be a zombie version of Fleetwood Mac at times, I kid you not, so you'd have expected a major to snap them up. Signed to Resurrection. You can never predict anything in this life, other than Tony's love for guitar antics onstage. Maybe it's psychic power spreading from their music but I have a feeling that particular aspect will never change. Pagan Fire Muzick, 18 Russell St, St. Pauls, Cheltenham, Gloucestershire GL51 OXX.

IN SENSORIUM Vocals, bass and drum machine might either seem too gloomy or not quite right but it works. Demos ('I' and 'II') prove it. Worth further investigation from those who don't demand constant noise. Pete, PO Box 214, Croydon, Surrey CR9 6HQ.

ISABEL'S SHRINE A one-man project operating under cover of some decidedly Sisters/Neffs darkness. Martin, 8 Montague Crescent, Roundhay, Leeds LS8 2RS.

KETAMINE 92 saw this much-troubled band emerge, who were down to a still functioning duo last I heard. Never overtly Goth but well in there with a sense of adventure that too small a line up cannot do justice to. Chris is a BA in Drama, "which should mean we give stunning visual performances, but I remain unconvinced". Three demos - 'Live - The Banshee' (undated), 'First Discourse' (93), 'Who's The Bastard In The Black?' (94).
Chris, 40 Markington Street, Moss Side, Manchester M14 7JB.

LEGEND You couldn't really call them a Goth-related band except for one thing which makes them slip in here. They are a self-proclaimed Pagan/Wiccan influenced rock band, which is odd enough, although there is mention of the word 'progressive', but they spared me the sight of a photograph. Hurrah! Steve Paine, Musical Director, Ceridwyn House, Percival Lane, Runcorn WA7 4UX.

LEISURE HIVE Dan - vocals/guitar, Maria - keybds/violin/vocals, Mark - bass, Warren - drums/perc. Dan and Maria formed this crew, after Proton Wedding disbanded in March 95, and produced the fairly average, clattering demo, 'The Dogs and The Blasphemy'. As a four piece they have moved on slightly to the stage where power erupts from their pores and it's a brighter sounding thing but with sluggishly doomed vocals. More life, now! They also write songs entitled 'Hound With Faster Tendrills' which is one way of paying tribute to Daisy Chainsaw. Maria and Dan also paint. Dan and Warren are art students, Mark works in a recording studio and plays in indie band The Charm, which also features Dan. Oh shut up. PO Box 552, Carshalton, Surrey SM5 2GB.

LIBITINA Darren - guitar, Jamie - bass/vocals, Peter - guitar/keybds/prog, Lady Synthia - 'percussive talents'. Formed Nov 94. Initial singer Danny left March 96. Band named themselves after an ancient Roman goddess associated with the dark and so their lyrical concerns are influenced by the trinity of love, darkness and death. First demo 'Goddess Of The Shades' (Nov 95), deemed unpopular and consigned to the scrapheap as the band have upped the bpm, attitude and direction. New tape should be out now, 'The Last Rites Of Spring', highlighting songs written as a three piece. Their favourite description of themselves is "High camp Goth Industrial guitar heroes". For reasons no other mortals can fathom they also play a cover of 'Touch Me' by Sam Fox and 'Material Girl' by Madonna. (The ultra-cool Inside Out once did a great song called 'Venereal Girl' but that's irrelevant.) They threaten to be on the road when this book comes out, so drive fast. Jamie, 99 Witham Rd, Sheffield S10 2SL. (http://greebo.globalnews.com/-jsa/libitina.html)

112 MANUSKRIPT 113 MELINDA MIEL

LILLIES AND REMAINS Born in 91, James Merryfield, Andrew McGregor and Nathan Girvan thought to themselves, our names sound pretty cool, let's do a band. They rehearsed in a turkey farm, and quote influences as diverse as Duran Duran, The Psychedelic Furs and Kafka. Thankfully they sound nothing like them. Hardly the most prolific live band they nevertheless have some good demos available. Unless they're all dead. James Merryfield, Crofton House, Wickfield, Devizes, Wiltshire SN10 5DU.

LOOK BACK IN ANGER Formerly a band during the heyday of Goth (who recorded a mini-album produced by The Cult's Billy Duffy in 84 and then "promptly split up to celebrate". Guitarist Sean J O'Farrell went on to The Fifteenth, Splashpool and Brian. Now he's back creating music with almost a sighing cinematic feel. 18a St John's Way, Archway, London N19 3RR. (See Businesses - especially if you're a new London-ish band)

MANUSKRIPT Mike - vocals, Swan - guitar, Ant - guitar, Tom - bass. Formed 90. Another band who hung on in there and are starting to get a soupcon of respect. They also have a sense of humour which helps. Their 'I Can't Believe It's Not Goth' was their best work so far, getting rhythmically more developed and harder too. It was all a bit crunched up before. Their earlier MCs may not long be available anyway but you enquire about 'Special Breed', 'The Three Card Trick' and 'Special Breed (Live)'. Recently signed to Resurrection and their debut CD should be out right now. 49 Edward Rd, West Bridgford, Nottingham. (Fax +44 (0) 115 9826962) (e-mail: skript@swandom.demon.co.uk) (Net: http://www.sys.uea.ac.uk/ - rs/swan/ skript.htm)

THE MARCH VIOLETS Simon D., they ponder. Wasn't he that thin, blonde berk? No, not quite. The big gruff 80's version led the one band in UK Goth who it can accurately be said nobody ever came closing to copying, as you'll discover on 'The Botanic Verses' compilation. Every homo sapien should have one. Furthermore there are strange rumours that after his days wilting in the rock fraternity with Batfish and D-Rok, and his new-found contentment with the freedom that computers brings, the great man is itching to get back. There is talk, albeit quiet, of a March Violets Mark II, devoid, we trust, of Cleo, who was recently spotted in an indie band reputed to be preferable to the lamentable Lovecraft - but with Craig Adams in it! That's by the by. The March Violets make sense in the 90's as they did in the 80's, by dint of being wholly original, a feat apparently achieved by Simon not listening to anyone else's stuff.

MARION I know most people think they're Indie (going on darkly commercial), but ponder their Ian Curtis fixation and wonder just what they made of all the years inbetween. Eh? Better still, listen to the guitars. Dead giveaway.

MARIONETTES Not Goth any more really. They're rock, in case you're confused. But there is an amazing range of activities coming from these chaps. They run their own studio from £125 for a 10 hour studio session, complete with engineer, to knocking up vinyl or CDs. Write for details if you're a band (c/o Kate Halford, Sales Manager). They arrange publishing, cassette duplication, tours, equipment hire, video work, photography, graphic design and some promotion. They'll even wipe your nose for you. Sonic Studios, 34B Haven Green, Ealing, London W5 2NX. (Fax: 0181 248 3481)

MATER NOSTER Mark - vocals, Vron - guitar, Splinge - keybds/samples/prog., Keech - bass, Chuck - drums. Formed 93. Melody with teeth, attitude and humour with influences from anything from The Stooges to Big Black, with the peculiar inclusion

113

of Amon Duul (warning to younger readers... do not ask questions). First Floor Flat, 40 Knowle Rd, Totterdown, Bristol B54 2ED.

MELINDA MIEL One of the best singers in the country and quite why this woman hasn't had an avalanche of attention is beyond me. Both CDs 'A Kiss On A Tear' and 'The Law Of The Dream', on Normal, are brilliant, emitting a murderous, striking sexuality and depravity. She has plenty of well-known admirers, notably Marc Almond, but very little happens. She is represented by Paul Buck, himself a well known writer and contributor to a plethora of titles. Paul Buck, Dreams & Whispers, 184 Bexley Lane, Sidcup, Kent DA14 4JH.

METHEDREAME Matthew Yexley - vocals/bass/keybds/prog., Simon Flynn - guitars. Formed Oct 89 at Matthew's college, with five different people and under another name. "Nothing much happened", he reports, breathlessly. However, Matthew decided on the current name over interest "in the paranoia and chaotic euphoria associated with met-amphetamines", and suddenly they were playing their first gig - in front of 800 people, which could imply a graduation to hallucinogens. Both chaps go to Bristol University but produce their first demo 'Dreams' in 91. 21 songs, 90 minutes. Now that's amphetamines! No more copies will ever reappear because..."the quality was shite!" *That's* amphetamines. They gigged, they studied. They produced their second album demo in 95, 'Liebe Haß and Furcht'. Only 10 tracks, 60 minutes. Plans for the third proceed, despite Simon being currently trapped in education in York and Matthew working in Bristol. It isn't as bizarre as it seems. Matthew has turned down two deals, one because the company wanted to sell a song to Cher! Bad luck has intermittently delayed their plans too, with broken limbs and studios blowing up. The second tape is available for £4, including postage. 116 Hotwell Road, Hotwells, Bristol BS8 4UB.

MIDNIGHT CONFIGURATION Trevor Bamford - vocals/guitar/prog., Lisa Ross - vocals, Nick Hopkinson - guitar. This is *the* man in UK Goth, in case you haven't realised, Trev, so level-headed you could play subbuteo on his skull. After leaving Every New Dead Ghost, he formed Nightbreed Records, a mail order service which is now the best in the country. He organised and DJ-ed at Nottingham's Visitation nightclub and the Marquis Masquerade, an entirely Fetish-based organisation. Then he forged an ugly siamese twin out of Goth and Industrial and taught it to speak. In a brutalised baritone. March 94, we have the 'Gothtec' MCD, Halloween of that year they release 'Spectral Dance' MCD. Most people talk of exorcising their personal demons with music this rough but with Trev he seems to be exercising them, on one of those long leads people take their pets out on. He pushes the things to stretching point, and then snap, in it all reels. Halloween 95 saw the album, 'The Kissing Skull', with its excellent booklet and suchlike. The album tests the patience at times, when you realise you can never escape that voice being set on remote throughout, but overall it's the barbaric polar opposite of Portishead. Seriously. As a beginning it is ridiculously strong - because regardless of my bemusement over gruff male voices, the strength of the songs is obvious, and the use of samples is unexpected and clever. As it whirls even more out of shape over time and the vocals are played with you'll be getting more and more intrigued by this strange band. It's them and Suspiria who first realised in the UK that you need to break with the past and start to take the future seriously. In the pipeline is the follow up CD, with a special edition remix CD. No title at the time of writing (apart from 'Surfing The Darkwave') but release date is 31.10.96, same as this book! Other things do exist - MCs ('Gothtec', 'Spectral Dance' and 'Remixes', which was the of the first two EPs) and 'The Carnival Of Souls' 31.10.94. Even a video,'Carnival Of Souls' - same gig. And

114, 115

114, 115 MIDNIGHT CONFIGURATION 116 NEKROMANTIK

116

there's a press book. Info service. Lisa Ross, 1 Mundela Rd, The Meadows, Nottingham.

MONICA'S LAST PRAYER An idea of Paul Broome, he of Earth Calling Angela, "stemming from a desire to write and record music with the minimal amount of fuss and technology, while at the same time creating something totally different". Demos - 'MLP' (Summer 94), 'By Night' (Winter 94), 'Distant Comforts' (96). Now this third tape, available for £3 UK (£4/$6 elsewhere) is certainly worth getting, because it has a rarified atmosphere to what is gently lowing Goth-Wave influenced music. A sense of wistful detachment pervades the whole enterprise, which is skilfully realised and the playing matches the fine quality of the singing. He labels it, "easy listening clad in a maudlin vest", I'd call it a modern day weeping equivalent to Nick Drake, except Drake was far more of a depressing case. Paul Broome, 178 Gulson Rd, Stoke, Coventry CV1 2JD.

MORBID HUNGER Caught somewhere between March Violets and Stun. Mightily melodic. 'Light And Riches' demo. 11 Pine Crescent, Brentwood, Essex CM13 1JE.

NEFILIM Quite. The Watchman, PO Box 17, Stevenage, Herts SG2 OQX.

NEKROMANTIK Martin - vocals/prog., Roi - synth/bass/prog. Formed 95. A cross between Danse Society and Nine Inch Nails, according to a *B&RV* review I saw, when they were called Deadboy Craved.They had a chap called Chris playing guitars but he fled over musical matters. The band have spiralled upwards, ditching guitars. 'Profane' demo as D.C. and now 'Someone Else's Daughter' demo. It's interesting, very impressive stuff. At the moment I would say their demos haven't quite mastered the actual sound of the rhythmic insertions - it's a bit too blatant, because the rest of it is all succulent in a bold manner and the vocals are excellent, smoothly bending to the mood. Pete Burns springs to mind. Imagine a creeping, swirling modern Dead Or Alive with some peculiar lyrics which are a touch on the right side of unnerving. Or imagine a version of late Depeche Mode that you wouldn't like to see gunned down in the street. Should become enthralling live pretty quickly. Whitey, 94 Moneybrook Way, Meole Estate, Shrewsbury SY3 9NQ.

NEVER Paul Cox is a part time researcher into paranormal activities and involved with the mag *Gothorror*. Loads of demos. Geoff, 30 Tyne Bank Rd, Winlaton, Tyne + Wear NE21 4RW.

NIGHTMOVES Jason - vocals, Zak - guitar, Rob - guitar, John - the bass, Maniac of Noise - drums. A conventional band, formed 92, who proudly admit they play a few Mission and Sisters covers. "Music is a timeless jewel which should be treated with respect," they plead in defence. Their debut CD, 'Violent Blue', should be out by now and will probably consist of much of the material from their first three demos, still available. 77 Stead Lane, Barnsley S74 OAE.

NOSFERATU Damien DeVille - guitar, Dominic La Vey - vocals, Dante Savarelle - bass. First four releases were on MC and 12" - 'Hellhound EP' (Sept 91), 'Vampyres Cry' (March 92), 'Diva' (Oct 92), 'Inside The Devil' (April 93), MC/Vinyl/CD album 'Rise' (May 93), CD/12" 'Savage Kiss' (Nov 93), 'Legend' MC/CD (Dec 93), 'The Prophecy' Vinyl/CD (Oct 94). Then they semi-split (Vlad going off to form Shadowmaker). New MCD 'The Haunting' (Nov 95), new CD 'Prince Of Darkness' (June 96). Pre-split CDs available through Cleopatra ('Rise', 'Legend', and 'Prophecy'). I never saw the excitement myself but somehow their attention to detail will certainly ensure they have a reputation for stylised, early 90's charm. Of course, it's what they do now which

counts. Having survived turbulent times I have no doubt they have a clear direction mapped out and being accessible they should prove more than capable of increasing their popularity, internationally (where it counts). Hades Records, PO Box 4741 London SE24 OXA.

NOVA STATE CONSPIRACY Sharp electro action from Alex Novak. 'Zeitgeist' CD. (See Venus Fly Trap.)

OBSESSION OF LILITH No idea, but evidently during one song they used to shout "call the ambulance" in latin, no less. Caroline Jago had been in Frantic Spiders and Toxic Shock Syndrome, but that needn't worry anyone. This lot are weird, clinky, dinky things. Nothing special, believe me, but there are plans from Caroline who was also in Dexdexter for a couple of weeks, and has only just recovered to do something in a Deadcandance/Cranes techno sort of direction. You might check her out at Holly House, High Street, Yatton Keynell, Chippenham, Wilts SN14 7BA.

OTHERWORLD Nope. I don't know either. Clare, 52 Riverbank Tower, Salford M3 7JY.

PASSION PLAY Ex Death By Crimpers member in new band caught midway between Deadcandance and The Chameleons. 38 Masons Rd, Headington, Oxford OX3 8QJ.

PERSONALITY CRISIS Jonathon and Bryn. Formed 95, Prunes meets Sex Fiend. 'Oppression' demos available in dual MC form! 201 Ransom Rd, Mapperley Park, Nottingham.

PJ HARVEY Whaddya want? "Inflammation." You won't get it. If you can't see the relevance, you're off your heads. She isn't, of course, Goth but this is the standard of excellence that others have to live up to. (And her first band even supported The Nephilim, a memory I'm sure she treasures.)

PORTISHEAD Sorry? Dance music? Dance?! You can barely walk to this stuff. No, concentrate instead on what this music *involves* and this is nothing other than perfect Modern Goth in a manner many other bands have already approached - and some have gone past. Warm, melancholic, angry or depressed it still remains fluid. (There is also the link to fellow Bristol band, Whores Of Babylon!) They're simply a few years behind some of the Darkwave operations in Europe, while fairly radical here for not being fluffy-headed in the dance market.

PRETENTIOUS MOI? Includes Tim Chandler, ex Autumn Of North and Sins Of The Flesh and Die Laughing's Rachel. Allegedly. 9 Stackpool Rd, Bristol B53 1DG.

PROPHECY Ex Restoration II + Vendemmian - Richard and Dominic respectively. Bit too rocky for my liking. I keep expecting a Zeppelin song to break out. Apparently inspired by the film *Near Dark* and what they term the "approaching triumph of chaos", The Prophecy believe it is time to turn the formula for Gothic music on its head, believing that bands have failed to balance atmospherics with real dynamics and power. They've certainly got the power. And they want to be angry which is good. Say what you like about Goth bands but attitude is usually replaced by sentiment. Richard Pyre, 78 Worthing Rd, Basin, Hampshire RG21 1TP.

QUAD PEACE Joke band, presumably.
23 Hollington Park Road, St Leonards On Sea, East Sussex TN38 0SE.

RAW NOVEMBRE Kelvyn Stanley - bass, Kevin Kelly - guitar, John Jackson - drums, Martin Kelly - vocals. 'Disturbed' CD (93), on their own Aggressive Records. 'He Is Dead' MCD (95) on Primary. PO

117 NOSFERATU 118 RETURN TO KHAF'JI

118

Box 3213, London SW2 3QQ (Fax: 0181 671 3115)

REDEMPTION Formed Jan 91. Oct 91 the line up is settled. Zef, Joss, Bob and Sam. After two years Bob and Joss skedaddled, replaced by Oli and Mike. They keep up as much activity as they can and have at least three demos available, and as many t-shirts, and *Second Face,* their fanzine. 44 Filey Rd, Manchester M146GQ.

THE REEPERBAHN '80s emergists. Spencer or Lucian, Killrton View, Rewe, Exeter, Devon.

RETURN TO KHAF'JI One of the few bands ever to emerge from Northern Ireland. Formed in 91. Guitarist/prog. Mark and bassist Steve have lost singers in their turbulently short existence (one of them to Nosferatu) but now they trust in Rod. Three early demos, all sold out. Fourth, 'Naked, Blind & Crucified' (94) outsold the lot. Signed deal with Resurrection in 95. 'From Darkest Skies' CD (95). Direct action band with nice touches. 2 Grange Close, Ballynahinch Road, Saintfield, Co Down, BT24 7NS. Or Resurrection Records (See Businesses).

REVOLUTION BY NIGHT Gary Durham-Carmichael - guitar, Nick Roberts on guitar, Byron Adamson-Woods on bass and Steve Weeks on vocals. They took this name from the title of the single they made when still called Restoration II (itself a successor to Restoration). With a bass player called Byron you'd expect them to be fairly phlegmatic about things and they are. They had quite a stodgy predictable rock element before which seems to have gone, as has the guitarist responsible. He now pursues that fiercer plan in Prophecy. Quite why Revolution By Night don't gig more escapes me. They have (had?) the potential to make quite an impact. "For the Lost," they insist, "the sky knows no limits..." which doesn't actually make sense. 1 Burbage House 1 Samuel Close, New Cross, London SE14 5RP.

ROSETTA STONE Dig in.
Sept 83? Mean anything to you? That's when Karl North (keybds) met Neil R. Garner while attending art college and formed Jam and Jerusalem. Porl King joined on guitar, responding to an ad, "freshly qualified jewellery maker required for badly named outfit". Neil leaves, embarrassed by being the only one with a girly middle initial and Porl and Karl carry on, Porl on guitar and vocals, Karl on bass. By 86 they've changed their name to Virtue, then Third Enigma, with one Ali McWatt (what, what?) on vocals and, very briefly, Andy Curtis on drums. Then...farewell. Throughout 87, Porl and Karl write. On 10.6.88 they make their live debut at Liverpool's Planet X. Fairly soon they attract the attention of some old producer who drags them off to London and material is flowing thick and fast. This is the Golden Age of Goth Guitar Rock, don't forget. Things happened fast. Their demos are made available. They sell like buggery, as they say.

89. September. A dough-faced man. Wayne Hussey. The band support The Mission, and from then on things escalate. They produce their first vinyl at the legendary Slaughterhouse studios. Soon afterwards the studios burn down, two events entirely unconnected. And so it goes on. Gigs, vinyl, virtually no press coverage. Following the release of 'Leave Me For Dead', Porl Young is forced to join the band, which is fair enough as he co-produced it. Things continue to go swimmingly with gigs and releases and no press apart from constant monitoring by Siren's Sheldon Bayley. Porl King leaves. The band sign a deal they would rather not talk about, with HTD, for the last phase of the band, which was kicked off by the 'Nothing' single. Things have not gone well. They have been scoffed at by many for their attitude. I myself bemoan their statue impersonations live. The thing is, they are simply uncompromising. They want to make it sound as good as possible, so they concentrate! They dislike much of what goes on in the bitchier element of the Goth scene so they no longer actively participate when it brings grief down upon their head. And as regards the fanzine world, they don't so much rock the boat as slip silently back to the beach, having laid mines on its hull.

People think they're po-faced bastards. I find them quite funny myself but way too pessimistic. They have faced problems - galore - but have walked too willingly into the fire. Their biog came with the line "well balanced... a chip on each shoulder".

What is weird is the way the fanzines have turned. There have been so many Goth bands who should have been hung for both sloth and lack of imagination - probably half the bands in this section are guilty of a monstrous dereliction of duty, which most have only started putting right in the past six months - yet it's Rosetta, who have at least managed to keep the releases coming, who get it in the neck! Where's the logic in that? Admittedly their dancier elements that rove beneath the rutting guitars are sometimes surprisingly clumsy, but that's hardly cause for indignation and when the furthest they have gone towards any rock area is the sort of material Terrorvision make so acceptable, there seems no crime there either. In fact the last demo I received was almost jolly! Imagine a Virtual Depeche Mode, slapped about a bit, with the best sounding guitar you'll encounter in a long time.

Furthermore, as I take some of you briefly to task, I'm going to reprint something from their "rant", previously available on the Net. They make sense here. The lack of success, as the Indie world would see it, that has been Rosetta's fate to date, is down to them being of the G persuasion. But they've never gone down the loathsome path of a Ghost Dance or Mission, whinnying, "We are not a Good band". Error. "We are not a Goth band". The bands who do that immediately fall down a great hole called Failure. Rosetta have merely been pushed into it. So those of you who have recently thought ill of this pair, think again. Or just think, period. You might like it. RANT quotes:

"Totally disillusioned with the British Music industry, and the 'Music Media' elitism, with its constant refusal to acknowledge Rosetta's indie success, and the portion of the market they represent. Rosetta have chosen to release a remix CD of 'gENDER CONFUSION'. No label, just straight from their studio, and onto compact disc. Distributed directly, via the internet. Rosetta are the first to admit there's no use protesting about anything (the conspiracy has too much control?!), but if some people believe the internet can even just dent the industries' complacency, then they wish to be part of it.

"IS THIS MEANT TO BE SERIOUS? We used to think the 'major labels' were the sharks. Small labels make their money from signing numerous bands from which the label can hope to make a very small profit (mainly back catalogue, slow but steady returns). Multiply this by the number of bands they control and those small sums of cash suddenly become enough for the label staff to live a moderately comfortable lifestyle. However, financially, on paper, the label is able to show its individual artistes the inadequate sales (slow, due to lack of immediate exposure), justifying their complacency and reluctance to invest. But...we can't gain sales to those we don't reach. And there is only so far word of mouth and reputation can take you within the confines of an underground existence.

"PAYING ATTENTION? - OR PAYING FOR ATTENTION?

"This is where the Media comes in. You will inevitably have to pay for your column inches (unless of course you drink with or fuck an established journalist), if the label is prepared to, but it may involve financial risk (gasp!), something apparently alien to most indie labels.

"IT'S A DANGEROUS THING. Enthusiasm is what makes us blind to the opportunists. The subculture ain't economically viable. But yet we still choose it, the Goth dollar. No security, no recognition, nothing.

119 ROSETTA STONE

To some it's just another media angle, to others it's the only possible course of action left to undertake. We, as songwriters, (sadly) epitomise all that we have come to define as an 'Underground Act'. Every record we have released has entered the Independent Charts. We've appeared on the ITV Chart Show twice (our last two singles) and then only because they 'had' to play it, of which one release entered the National 12" Top 40 Chart alongside Madonna and Metallica, yet the Music Media (noticeably the weeklies) refuse point blank to interview us or review our releases. We're a Goth band - and as such, we are denied the opportunities that befall most, if not all, other artists pertaining to the indie scene - of which the credible receive media attention in advance of reaching even our minimal level of success. For example, if a band came along comparable to, say, Suede, went straight into the Indie charts at 5 and appeared on the Chart Show, does anyone really believe the weeklies wouldn't pick up on it?

"If only Goth were a skin colour. Media racists? I'll settle for Bigots though, and if you're thinking, 'Yeah, well you don't *have* to be Goth' consider the implications of your conclusion. This dismissive attitude doesn't go unnoticed by the record companies. We only managed to instill confidence in our prior record labels because of our self-governed achievements. I can say without fear of exaggeration that NO other independent band has consistently charted and held the title 'leaders in their field' to our level without ever receiving even half a page feature in a weekly music publication.

"Please understand, we are not of the opinion that we are the greatest band ever to go unnoticed. To these journalists who come and go, following the mindless tradition to seek out, and take credit for, the Next Big Thing, I'd like to say, the Media has been responsible for ensuring our efforts will never be given the chance to be approved or disapproved by a wider audience. Moreover, our whole future has been put into question, simply by the influences we absorbed as aspiring musicians in our teenage years. The Media have the ability to prejudge without reason, based solely on criteria and not musical merit. Are these the same people who portray themselves as right on, encompassing sensible political ideals? Striving for ethnic and gender equality? The underprivileged? The Criminal Justice Bill? Yes, all of the above are far more important than the success or failure of one band but they could also point to a tolerance and understanding that should (if not premeditated) be applied on more general terms.

"The fact remains, that no matter how small a slice of the market we and others alike represent, the British Music Press maintains its position and strives to turn its back on a scene that grew, and still exists, right under its parasitical nose."

So there you go. It will be interesting to see whether *Melody Maker*, should it ever escape the shame of its dismal invention (not encouragement, *invention*) of Romo, has the intelligence, let alone the suss, necessary, to realise it could easily add up to ten thousand a sales a week by starting regular Goth coverage. (Probably not.)

Rosetta Discog (what they refer to as 'Stone Product'): 'Recreate and Emulate' MC (88), 'Whispers' MC (88), 'Chapter And Verse' - two diff. sleeves (88), 'Retribution' MC (89), 'And How They Rejoice' MC (89), 'Darkness And Light' 12" (90), 'Leave Me For Dead' 12"/7" (91), 'An Eye For The Main Chance' 12"/MCD (91), 'An Eye For The Main Chance' LP/MC/CD (91), 'Adrenaline' - 2 versions - 12" (92), 'The Witch' - 2 versions - 12" (92), 'On The Side Of Angels (Singles 89-92)' CD (93), 'Adrenaline' CD (93), 'Epitome' MCD (93), 'Foundation Stones' CD (93), 'Nothing - 2 versions - 12"/CD (95), 'The Tyranny Of Inaction' CD/LP (95), 'The Tyranny Of Inaction (*Revised edition 1.1*) CD (95), 'gENDER cONFUSION' CD (95).

(Rosetta e-mail: rosettastone@blakmail.demon.co.uk) (Net, WWW U.S.A. The Hiding Hole - http://www.pitt.edu/-bjpst6/rosettastone) (Net, WWW U.K. The Hiding Hole http://goth-ftp.ac.brad.ac.uk/rosettastone). wHATever listSERVEr - subscriptions to: majordomo@list.pitt.edu[inc.body <subscribe rosetta-stone>] (mail to: rosetta-stone@list.pitt.edu) 31 Ivanhoe Rd, Aigburth, Liverpool L17 8XF.

RUBICON Suspended animation? PO Box, 75 Herne Bay, Kent CT6 5WJ.

SALLY IN THE WOOD Bart Lawless - vocals, Tom Honeytongue - drums, Steve Madden - bass, Damien Smith - rhythm guitar, Andi Eade - lead guitar. "Been together roughly 4 years, haven't done a great deal of gigs cause we're all far too lazy, got all the influences you've heard before and more, sound absolutely like none of them and are much better than all of them!" That's fighting talk from Flawless Lawless who wants you to know he is incredibly beautiful, but refuses to offer photographic evidence. Demo discog: 'Sally In The Woods' ("shit!" - 92), 'Dead And Alive' ("a vast improvement" - 94), 'The Invisible Foe" ("fucking great, buy it!" - 96). Only the third tape is available, five tracks of upright, spry, charming rock with desperate vocals but a fiver seems a bit steep! Metallic guitar tendencies and an overall indication would be to dig out an old Flesh For Lulu album and spruce it up a bit, but if they could get off their arses a bit more they'd do very well. Bartchester Chronicle, 50 Victoria Rd, Trowbridge, Wiltshire BA14 7LD.

2ND COMING:SINS OF THE FLESH 2 Still around and evidently on a totally electronic voyage. Pete 268 Sharrowvale Rd, Sheffield S11 82H.

SERAPHIN TWIN Tim Riley - vocals/guitar, John Rowe - bass, Brian Terry - guitar, Gordon Young - guitar, The Machine - keybds/perc. Bright, fiddley Neph-esque guitar winking in the gloom. It's all rather exciting but when the singer clearly has such

120

120 THE STUN

121

an excellent voice the last thing you need is for him to be foolishly burying it in among everything else. 22 Bryce Avenue, Portobello, Edinburgh, ED7 6TX.

SHADOWMAKER Vlad wants to encompass dancy and techno inspiration to take things further into the future. But has he the will to continue? 138 Canterbury Rd, Harrow, Middx HA1 4PB.

SISTERS OF MERCY Don't laugh! They don't. No, what I was thinking was, how long before Eldritch and Hussey kitsch and make up? Both have careers which have stalled and the wheelclampers are moving in. They have very little chance of resurrecting individual outings, so this is the likely way out but they can't take too long or people won't know who they are, or what they were. Big tours, big press. Big bank accounts, then retire.

SKINFLICK Music that deals with "fetishism and the darker side of human nature", was started by Skinflick Productions in 92, the line-up being W.J. Lane and Jim Sin who have always worked together, compressing maddening guitar in among pounding rhythms, powerful vocals and the weird world of electronica. From their debut demo, 'Dead Girl Opened' (charming!), they have received good reviews for their work, which moves into the more experimental areas than plain Gothdom. They've done a split tape with the noise bastards Hex Minora, their own split single, 'Pretty Dead Girl', and in 95 they released another single 'Pig Sick'. What lovely titles they do choose. Currently working with Italian band Andromeda Complex on a project dealing with themes of Erotica. Probably called 'Autopsy Sandwich Gulped Down By Virgin'. Their own CD 'Harlot Eyes' will probably be available by the time you are reading this. 2 Bron-Y-De, Bangor, Gwynedd LL57 4TL.

SKIN JOB Updated Skeletal Family, or thereabouts. Allegedly.

SON OF WILLIAM It's Spencer Harrison's band, named after the half-breed spawn of a lesser fire demon and a minor djinni, genetically engineered as the Seraphim, to appear in human form. Honest, I read it in the press release, so it must be true. Pagan with guitars might be nearer. Weirdly, they formed in St. Louis. Now that is true! 'Husk' MCD, with debut album out soon. Limited edition MC of mournful 94 material, 'Knowledge & Oblivion' may still be available. Beserker, 90B High Rd, London N2 9EB.

SONS OF SELINA Describing themselves as adopted by Goths rather being Goth, although *Poison Coffin* worryingly described them as "Emerson Lake & Palmer meets The Sex Pistols". Somewhere along the line three EPs and an album exist. 16 Butterdon Rd, Rhyl, Clwyd CL18 1RF.

(CHILDREN ON) STUN Neil Ash - vocals/prog., Simon Manning - guitars, Kyle Whipp - bass. Founded 91. 'Elegance' demo (91), 'Choices' demo (92), 'Monochrome 1 and 2' demo (93), 'Hollow' 12" (93), 'The Tourniquets Of Loves Desires'; CD (94), 'Overland' CD (94). All of this work featured original guitarist Pete Finnemore, since departed due to 'personal medical commitments'. MCDs 'Celebration' and 'Celibacy & Anadin' (95), 'Style Police' (96). Should have been signed by a major label long ago, but that's Britain for you. Insanely catchy stuff sometimes, and exuding class. Carl Philsby, Fractured Cell Management (and home of the Stun *Mondo* zine), Flat 7, 12 Warrior Sq., St Leonards-on-Sea, East Sussex TN37 6BX. (Net: http://www.ics.lu.se/staff/MickeS/Stun.html) (Fax: 01424-722202)

SUSPIRIA Matthew Carl Lucian - vocals, Mark - guitars. Formed late 93, from the remains of Just Scarlet and The Heathen Chained. Originally a guitar-based four piece they've stripped it all down,

122 THE IN OVO 123 13 CANDLES

a fine example of a band who have understood that 90's UK Goth has a real fight on its hands and they reshape contemporary musical currency as and when they like it. It's their keenly explorative attitude as well as the music which is fast propelling them into the front ranks. Mind you, having blinding songs does help. So far only 95's 'Tragedy' MCD and 'Great & Secret Show' CD are with us, but by the time you have this the second CD could be out, surrounded by a mass of gigging activity. It feels good to wave goodbye to the past, no? Nightbreed, 2nd Floor, 177 Wollaton Street, Nottingham NG1 5GE.

TERMINAL POWER COMPANY PO Box 3069, Sutton Coldfield, West Midlands B76 8FX.

THE IN OVO Look at the photo - would you trust these people? Let them clean your windscreen at the traffic lights and they'll have your wipers. Just for the hell of it. More mental cases. Andy Clandillon - vocals and Richard Capener - guitar formed the band as a songwriting thing in 93. They chose the exciting name Hillbilly Shit and wrote songs with the winning titles, 'Beating Up On Elvis' and 'Go Fuck Yourself (If You Want To Buy Me Flowers)'. Quickly jaded, they hauled drummer Adrian Brownlee onboard and Stuart Fryett on bass. They were Goth, they were Pop, they were Rock. Still mad they chose another crap name, The In Ovo. Doesn't that make you think of some maudlin experimental electronic outfit from mainland Europe? Men with headcolds sitting in cafes staring dolefully at 'meaningful' books? Stupidly, the music they make is a potent racket above and beyond the call of duty, basically taking a late 80's Goth sound, but played with pace and all round vigour rather than settling placidly in place and even the guitar, which has that bright, taut sound we all know, starts to hyperventilate. Their slower material is every bit as good as the gutbusters because the vocals are of a strangely strong nature, yet with a convincing frailty too. Weird. Demos - 'Love Letter', 'Jezabel', 'Overload' and a hopeless fanzine vainly promoting themselves - *Dress Kinky For Satan*. One listen to 'Still' and you'll be impressed, caught up in the emotion of it all, pretending there's something in your eye. Of course if that was Andy singing he's gone now. Just now. Gone. Quick as that. Richard, Flat 2, 73 High St, Brentwood, Essex CM14 4RW.

THESE CRIMSON DREAMS Tamsin - vocals, Ian Ford - guitars, Pete Thomas - guitars, Juliette - drums and bass, which must be interesting live. Formed in late 92 by messrs Ford and Thomas. Very nice sounding and worthy of your support because they once lived in Bedfont, one of the most boring places imaginable. Imagine Skeletals crossed with All About Eve but a harder, more piercing guitar. They shove the sound out at you. Sadly, this means floaty vocals get lost and require more effort or power. Eponymous demo available. Expect them to hover in Die Laughing's slipstream if given the chance. Chipps Court Lodge, 2B Goring Road, Staines, Middlesex TW18 3EH..

THIS BURNING EFFIGY One of the very few Goth outfits from the Republic. Stephen Carey (guitar/keybds), Ger Egan (vocals), Brian Fallon (drums) and Mick Cowley (bass). They've been together, man and boy, since 93, when they issued the demo 'The Eternal Procession'. They appeared on the 'Dreams In The Witchouse' CD. Second guitarist John McDonagh (since departed) joined at Easter 95 and their album resulted, 'To Bestial Gods', on Grave News. 2 Garten Ave, Drumcondra, Dublin 9, Ireland. (e-mail endymion@iol.ie)

13 CANDLES Dracul - bass, Louis Holloway - vocals/guitars, Marc Hoyland - keyboards/guitars, Sex Machine - drums. Formed... er, the day before yesterday. No, no, not true. *Ages* ago. The rinky dink sound of 13 Candles early on, which has been

corrected since, obscured the fact they have ideas in their songs. They also stretched those ideas out waaaaay too long. All they need do is trim it back and boost it up, then you'll see why Nightbreed had faith in them. They've released a staggering 13 demos, or so they say, appeared in four videos (three of their own) and on five CD compilations. Most large international fanzines have covered them in some way (they have a fanclub in Australia, or so they believe!), so they're getting there. Slowly. Or leisurely. You choose. Demos still (potentially) available - 'Reflections', 'Disbelievers Remixes', 'Reflections Ltd. Edition', 'Visions Of Mortality (Live)' and 'Vamps & Tramps Ball II 96 (Live)'. Videos - '13th Hour', 'Visions Of Mortality', 'Nightbreed (Pretentious Bastards Tour 95)' and 'Vamps & Tramps II'. 'Come Out Of The Dark' CD (95) shows them developing out of the sleepy linear style they began with. They'll grow nicely. Dracul, 20 North Grove, Duckmanton, Chesterfield, Derbyshire S44 5HA.

THE TORTURED Craig Hamilton - guitar, Mike Johnston - drums/drum machine/sequencer, Ian Macintyre - vocals, Sarah - backing vocals. Formed Summer 94, with other people (including Ruaraidh Wishart who still contributes to the writing). Happily describe themselves as possessing sleaze elements unlike the general Goth band, yet also write on realistic issues. Demos - 'Visions Of This Perfect Lie' and 'Dust', with 'A Gift From Aphrodite' CD possibly out now. Info service: 18/3 Westfield Road, Edinburgh EH11 2QR. (9246331@mull.sms.ed.ac.uk)

UNCLE BRENDA This is what happened after Soul Inside (Ist EP - 'Rapture', 2nd EP - 'The Disgustingly Purple Circle EP') split and Kyle went to Children On Stun, leaving Rob alone. Brookside House, Station Road, Robertsbridge, East Sussex, TN32 5DG.

VALLECRUCIS Brian Cummins - vocals/guitars, Phil Irving - drums, Kevin Murphy - bass, Sean Rooney - guitars/vocals. This is actually a rock band but of an entirely unpredictable sound and manner because while their dark and historically mystical lyrical imagery and certain elements of the sound are similar interests to bands on the continent, they have none of the gnashing overplayed drama of their Scandinavian or German counterparts - instead they often opt for dreamier interludes which might suck them nearer the Pagan area. They quote their main influences as 20th century classical music and medieval and renaissance styles. Forty-five minute demo 'A Garden Of Verses' is recommended. Live they sound a highly promising proposition as they use theatrical sets of Celtic and medieval themes - including an interlacing portrait backdrop, shields, firestaffs and plenty of candlelight, all within lamps, billowing drapes, nets and smoke. Sean Rooney, 19 Norville Road, Broadgreen, Liverpool L14 3LU.

VAJRASATTVA SOUND STATION In their search for the missing link between technology and rock and apparently "bound for love" this 'band' is sick of the "no melody, no messages, no lyrics techno", in which case stop listening to it. Now just who is Lodro Dawa, the miscreant behind this quite mysterious outfit, apart from a member of Thee Vampire Guild? PO Box 3563, London N7 0ES.

VENDEMMIAN Dave - guitar, Mark - bass, vocals and drum machine. Formed Oct 92 and ploughing, rather than plodding, on despite several line-up fluctuations too many. Now I would imagine the duo responsible for the 'Transition' CD , after the previous 'Treacherous' CD, and 'Between Two Worlds'/'The Depth Of Innocence' MCDs (all on Resurrection) will keep it to themselves. With less likelihood of deranged vocal ablutions now, the time must be ready for them to begin to set their vision high. They have the songs, the experience and the

124 VENDEMMIAN 125 THE VOICE

name is known. Now they just need the attention. As the music is tending towards the seamless and uplifting, it shouldn't be difficult. PO Box 10164, London NW6 7WG. (Fax: +44 (0) 171 328 2146)

VENGEFUL WIDOWS I have yet to meet anyone who has seen these late 80's hermits. in fact it may all be the work of one man but there are still two charming singles and five separate demos available. Bedsit Bauhaus, sofa-bound Sisters. Gavin, Crypt Of The Necromancer (How the postman must snigger, with some justification. "I've got a parcel for the Necromancer" - "Oh, he's just having his tea"), 5 Langdale Way, Stourbridge, West Midlands DY9 7HA.

VENUS FLY TRAP Alex Novak - vocals, Gary Lennon - guitar, Andy Denton - drums and Neil Ridley - bass. Their 'Luna Tide' CD was one of the first in the world to be dedicated to astronomers everywhere. You can sort of tie them in, and out, to Goth, for lurking in among many a skittish, twisted style, VFT (around quite a while) are always evolving into something spidery and new. A couple of albums produced by The Jazz Butcher and Kevin Haskins have emerged on the French label Danceteria, as well as the odd MC or two. 'Jewel - Live In Prague' CD probably makes a good introduction. Alex Novak also does the strongly, sternly recommended fanzine *Bizarre*, and he'll be happy to inform you of what else they have available. Unlike a lot of bands you won't find any garbage in the back catalogue because he's already been through that stage with previous bands. PO Box 210, Northampton NN2 6AU.

VOICE Kieron - vocals/guitar/keybds/prog., Gary Crombie - bass, Marc Stephens - guitar, Alan Carter - keybds/'sound management', Kevin - drums. Formed Oct 91, as a side project for Kieron, from another band, Dark Force. Originally they were far from serious and called The Gothic Gurus. The members all left but Kieron worked away on a demo, drew an encouraging response from friends to the finished work and started plugging it around. It's Kieron's baby and barely toilet-trained too, taking an industrial bent and spraying it with perfume. It fits into the Goth camp with ease but they are very rarely seen. After the 'Indoors' demo and despite trouble with line-ups, a re-recorded version of the demo emerged in Nov 92 and people were still interested so he started on a second, and a vaguely reunited line-up made their debut at the George Robey, Nov 93. The new demo, 'None More Black' came out in Feb 94, as the band began to increase the live activity. As I type this the band are busy recording demos for their debut CD on Resurrection, which should see them broadening out, not restricting themselves to Goth, as the Industrial and Metal influences go unappreciated otherwise. The Voice (DFP), Bray House, Westbury Rd, Bickley, Kent BR1 2QB .

WHORES OF BABYLON Shaun Atkins - vocals, Julian Hill - guitar, Joseph White - guitar, Debora Rhodes-Grant - backing vocals/perc., Robert Vaughan (blimey!) - bass, Esther - keybds/guitar and Johnny Morris (is this some kind of a joke?) - drums. Julian and Shaun start band in 92, a year after putting together their own professional studio, 'State Of The Art'. 'Eternal' demo (April 93), followed same year by 12" remix by Portishead members Barrow and MacDonald. Also in 93 'Promo 93/94' MC. In 94 they sign, unusually, to metal label Candlelight, and CD 'Metropolis' emerges. State Of The Art Recording Studio, Unit 4, Lawnwood Rd, Easton, Bristol BS5 JEF (Fax: 0117-9541075)

THE WITCHES A nice band who make the classic mistake of saying to standoffish crowds "you can dance if you like" while playing a song you can barely sway to. An appealing edge to their work is often let down by lack of energy. May be hibernating.

22 Lutton Close, Loughton, Essex IG10 3TT.

THE WITCHING HOUR Flat 1, 180 Royal College St, London NW1 9NN.

X-13 Projected from the belching anus of Flowers Of Sacrifice, they are bloated, it says here, by excess and claim originality and plagiarism as their key! By continually staying indoors they presumably go out a lot. Phil Mears, David Gould, Pat Evans and Andy Thirteen create a mix of guitar noise thrills which allows Goth to take cover alongside other generic implants. Rough, rather than ready. Andy, The Abyss, 6 Beech Rd, Farnborough, Hants.

Book dealers/shops

ATLANTIS 49a Museum Street, London WC1A 1LY.

CADUCEUS New and secondhand - occult, magick, esoteric traditions, pagan. booksearch facility. 14 Holgate Rd, York YO2 4AB.

COLD TONNAGE BOOKS Mail order. Andy Richards, 22 Kings Lane, Windlesham, Surrey GU20 6JP.

COMPENDIUM BOOKS 234 Camden High Street, London NW1.

KEN COWLE Mail order. Trinity College, 153 Old Church Rd, Clevedon, Avon BS21 7TY.

CREATION PRESS 83 Clerkenwell Rd, London EC1.

DAYSTAR BOOKS 17 Byford Close, Stratford, London E15 4HF.

DEJA VUE & GRIMOIRE 12 High St, Glastonbury BA6 9DP.

DELECTUS BOOKS Mail order. The ultimate dealer in erotica, reprinting things like *The Petticoat Dominant, Or, Woman's Revenge*. Oh and don't forget *A Guide To The Correction Of Young Gentlemen By A Lady*, or *The Romance Of Chastisement* or *Revelations Of School And Bedroom - By An Expert*. Great t-shirts too. There are quite a few different catalogues, including serious S/M stuff, Vampires and whatever else you could probably imagine. This really is the best place to shop for rare material and for *amazing* presents! Goss has the obscene ultimate ambition of buying Portsmouth Football Club. (I've got a fiver, perhaps we could go halves?) Mike Goss, 27 Old Gloucester Street, London WC1N 3XX.

DREAMBERRY WINE What an awful name! Mike Don, 233 Maine Rd, Manchester M14 7WG.

J. EGGELING Claremont South, Burnley Rd, Todmorton, Lancashire.

ENIGMA Annual list at Xmas of ghost story books. A. Stevens, Rosemary Cottage, Dunkeswell, Honiton, Devon, EX14 ORE.

FANTASTIC LITERATURE Simon Gosden, 25 Avondale Rd, Rayleigh, Essex SS9 8NJ.

FANTASY CENTRE 157 Holloway Rd, London N7 8LX.

FRONTLINE BOOKS 1 Newton Street, Manchester 1.

GHOST STORY SOCIETY FACSIMILE REPRINTS Richard Dalby, 4 Westbourne Park, Scarborough, North Yorks YO12 4AT.

GHOST STORY PRESS BM Wound, London WC1N 3XX.

RICHARD G LEWIS Mail order. 21 Brewster Rd, London E10 6RG.

MOVIE BOULEVARD 5 Cherry Tree Walk, Leeds LS2 7EB.

MURDER ONE/ NEW WORLDS 71-73 Charing Cross Rd, London WC2H 0AA.

GM PARRY 58 Poplars Rd, Mardy, Abergvenny, Gwent NP7 6LX.

BERNARD SMITH Flintouse, 30 Clifton Rd, Worthing, Sussex BN11 4DP.

TIME FOR ENOUGH BOOKS Alan Austin. 43 Mile End Rd, Colchester, Essex CD4 5BU.

VIEVE FORWARD Egyptian books. 18 Blakeney Rd, Bristol 7.

Businesses

ALCHEMY Amazing range of goods. All manner of jewellery and metal objects in pewter or silver. Rings, pendants, bracelets, many mimicking traditional historical designs, but also brilliant things - Gothic dogtags anyone? Postcards, keyrings, egg sandtimer, drinking flasks, clocks, spoons, ashtrays (with lovely little skeletal hands at the edges to balance your cigs on!), tankards, watches, skulls. The larger items are probably hideously expensive at times but the craftsmanship deems it so. This really is awesome! You can probably find their adverts in metal mags. The last address I had is 5 Braunstone Gate, Leicester LE3 5LH.

ASCENSION RECORDS Mail order from Kenni Dodd, 45 Trafalgar Street, Greenock PA15 4ND.

BLACK TEARS DISTRIBUTION Russell Smith, 6 Elderfield Rd, Stoke Poges, Slough, Berkshire SL2 4DE.

LAURIE CAIRNS Carved panelling and brackets of exceptional quality. Probably expensive but oh so very fetching. Also individual panels and heads and stuff. Write for details if seriously interested. South Garyth Cottage, Kilham Rd, Langtoft, Nr Driffield, Humberside.

CHILDE OF THYME Tarot and crystal ball readings. Books, herbs, crystals, minerals, incenses, essential and supposedly magical oils, cards, runes, pendulums. 9 Salisbury Rd, Wood Green, London N22.

CREATURES UNLIMITED Amazing kits or sculptures available. Excellent range of Hammer-related figures, as well as Horror greats. West Lodge, 26 West Road, Clacton-on-Sea, Essex CO15 1BL.

CYPHEX COMMUNICATIONS 8 Daux Avenue, Billinghurst, West Sussex RH14 9SZ.

COUNT ORLOCK'S VIDEO EMPORIUM Funnily enough it isn't always dodgy stuff. Some of it comes with the bands' blessings. Anyway, the good Count offers everything at very reasonable rates. Paul & Alma, 18 Meadow Vale, Codnor, Derbyshire DE5 9QN.

CHRISSIE DEMANT V.A.T. Ummm, she isn't technically offering anything just yet but this woman does do amazingly good cartoon postcards from time to time. Her little vampire characters are wonderful. Badger her a bit and she may do more. Mrs Demant, 53 Hatton House, Hindmarsh Close, Cable Street, London E1 8JJ.

FOOL'S PARADISE Video/label, 20 Park Steps, St George's Fields, London W2 2YQ.

FRONTIER MODELS A sci-fi fantasy specialist, Frontier have more than just Dredd, Trek or Batman, including Japanese models and some truly unusual rubber masks. 6 Green Walk, Hailsham, East Sussex BN27 1ST.

GOTHICK CORNWALL/DEVON Etc. Guides to architecture of interest etc. Shire Publications, Cromwell House, Church Street, Princes Risborough, Buckinghamshire HP27 9AJ.

GRAVE GENERATION Various Goth-related activities. I may have this wrong, in which case try the address listed for the fanzine of the same name. Laurence, 3 Gladwyn Avenue, West Didsbury, Manchester M20 2XN.

HAMMER HORROR Trading cards, available from creative Marketing Associates, PO Box 12, Hay On Wye, Hereford HR3 5YD.

THE HOUSE OF DETENTION One of the few remaining Victorian prisons. Not mightily impressive, because only a small underground portion of it actually remains but for the first couple of minutes the sense of claustrophobic, cloying nausea you feel is probably an accurate reflection of what it was like all the time for the actual inmates so I think you should go for that. It also soon becomes sweetly amusing, especially as it boasts some of the world's worst waxworks (but *please* don't laugh, I suspect they think they're okay), and you get a cosy sub-Bob Hoskins friendly inmate's walkman travelogue of cell-to-cell activity. (It's good to die up to your neck in shite.) The upstairs prison records are a blast. Women got prison for being 'rogues and vagabonds', men get fined for 'exposing their person', and heavy fines are dished out for being in possession of flannel petticoats. Meanwhile a businessman who commits several hundred pounds worth of fraud gets bail! Plus ça change. A feeble display of torture implements is more than made up for by the woeful story of the *notorious* Jack Shepherd (i.e. we've never heard of him until the guide tells us). Jack, as a trained locksmith, was a dab hand at escaping, which was just as well because every time he committed a crime the first thing he did was get blind drunk and wander around town telling everyone at the top of his voice about his latest blag. The police could eventually lift him out of the gutter. Also genuinely disturbing are the drawings of the evil face-masks inmates wore all the time during their silent stays. This may not take long to go round but it is different and you feel relieved to get out. Open seven days a week, 10am-6pm.Clerkenwell Close, London EC1R OAS.

KICKBACK REVIEW An A-Z mail order thing, including items of interest to Goths (etc). Music-related things, plus sex, ghosts, vampires. UFOs, biorhythms, drugs, comics, heretics, videos, metaphysics - oh yeah! - sci-fi, weirdos and more. I've never seen a copy myself so I'd check they exist before paying. Kickback Publishing, Suite 1, 11 Marsh Street, Barrow, Cumbria LA14 2AE.

MICK MAGIC Mail order service - Goth, Industrial, Punk and some bands too scarey to be listened to. He has it all. 6 Farm Court, Farm Road, Frimley, Camberley, Surrey GU16 5TJ.

MILLENIUM DESIGNS Hand-painting of leather jackets. Telephone hotline 0113-266-9168.

THE MODEL ZONE Model shop whose stock includes Vampirella and Horror figures amongst usual comic book stuff. Unit K, Causeway Business Centre, Adderley Rd, Bishops Stortford, Herts CM23 2EH.

NEMESIS PROMOTIONS Michael Johnson used to do some pretty cool cartoons too but I think that is sidelined while he's one half (along with Mark Rimmell) of London's premier/regular Goth promoter, in terms of knowing what's what and putting it on. Nemesis, incidentally, is technically a word defining retribution. Vengeful justice and all that. Bit of an odd word to use, although you could imply 'Come to this gig and you'll get what you deserve'. A special night for everybody you hate could be arranged and when you get them in it turns out to be a three hour long Rozz Williams spoken word special. With Rozz inside a laundry basket. And no lights or PA. I digress. This is how Michael puts it all:

"Nemesis is a London-based gig promoter specialising in all things gothic and weird. Nemesis gigs usually take place in subterranean London clubs such as The Underworld and Borderline, where, over the last year or so the likes of London After Midnight, Inkubus Sukkubus, James Ray's Gangwar, Children

126

On Stun, Rosetta Stone and many more have all given it loads in the name of hedonism with attitude. Glamour and art and strangeness and noise, it's all there in a Nemesis moshpit. If YOU would like to be in a Nemesis moshpit, get on the free worldwide Nemesis mailing list. Uncle Nemesis himself will send you details of incoming shows under plain wrapper. Be wild, be free - and be there. Message ends."

Hmmm. Uncle Nemesis himself may well live to regret inviting half the people of the world to make him spend a fortune on postage, but I like this idea of art in the moshpit. "Mind the paintings!" PO Box 206 Twickenham TW1 3HA. (Fax: 0181 572 3679)

NIGHTBREED Run by Trev of Midnight Configuration and Mark from Suspiria. What other mail order firm does the serious Goth need? Seriously, when applying for one of their catalogues send a good quid or so of stamps to pay for it (I'm sure part of that will then be deducted from your second, when you're tapped in to their list.) This catalogue is huge and gives descriptions of what's there, which is useful. It's such an essential thing to have. It includes releases from all over the goddam world. Nightbreed also releases the occasional CD in their series 'New Alternatives'. And they have started to develop the Darkline t-shirt range which they plan to offer at very reasonable prices. It will start with bands (Suspiria, MidConfig, 13 Candles etc) but then move on to Gothic designs which should be good. Nightbreed Recordings, 2nd Floor, 177 Wollaton Street, Nottingham NG1 5GE. (Fax: 0115-955 1908)

NIGHTMOVES If you write to them, you'll find out. 349 Batemoor Rd, Sheffield S8 8FJ.

OBSCURE DELIGHT Label and zine. 58 Peel Rd, Chelmsford, Essex CM2 6AL.

SEAN J. O'FARRELL Let's face it most bands often find a problem doing any decent flyers or demo artwork. Some fanzines could do with their work laid out properly on computer and suchlike. Well Sean - who is also operating his music thing under the name of Look Back In Anger (yep, his old band), can do whatever you want, as he understands the requirements and would probably do you it all for a very decent rate. He can also do video-grab stuff for cool images, able to put music to video imagery which you can put on disk and punt round as demos, etc. As far as I know he's the only person offering this service to bands in London who may be able to actually help you with the direction you're looking for. A definite first base of call. And he won't rip you off either. 18a St John's Way, Archway, London N19 3RR.

ON THE TRAIL OF JACK THE RIPPER A guided tour of the spookily shite East End sites that were once Jack's murder spots and now play host to nothing more sinister than Kev Demant with a hangover. It's £4 for adults or £3 for students (which is a cute distinction). You meet outside Aldgate East Station at 8pm, walks take place every night! Can also be contacted at 41 Spelman Street, London E1.

ONCE & FUTURE CELT Pagan shop with various paraphernalia, 'heathen hoards' (?), goddess goods, artwork, literature, jewellery. The usual bollocks. 27 Oldbridge Rd, London SW12 8PL.

PEAKY BLINDER VIDEO PRODUCTION COMPANY By Graham Bentley. From Bauhaus to The Horatii, he's worked with them all. 21, Cotswold Avenue, Duston, Northampton NN56BT.

PHENOMENAL RECORDS Dark Wave stockists. PO Box 410, Edinburgh EH11 1BH.

RESURRECTION RECORDS An excellent shop, cover-

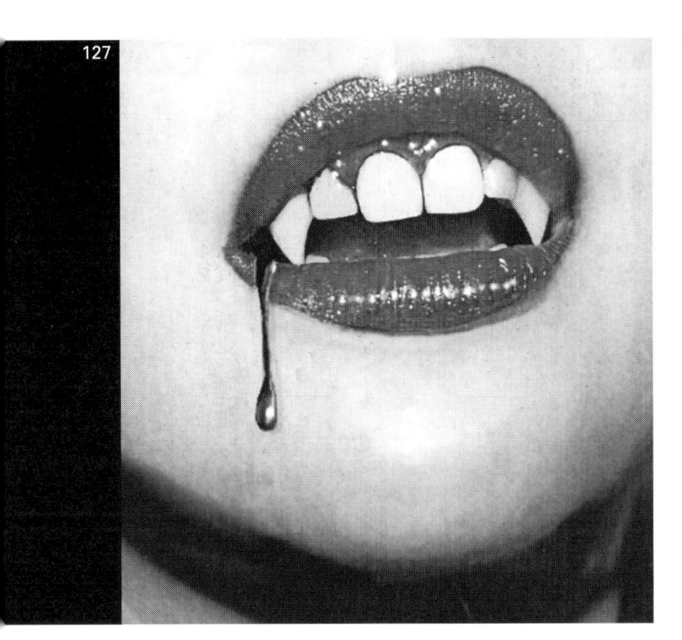

126 SERVICE WITH A SMILE, THE NIGHTBREED WAY! 127 SECOND SKIN

ing all types of music but well suited to the Goth perusal. And now...(fanfare)...a record label, already boasting Vendemmian, Return To Khaf'ji, The Voice, Inkubus Sukkubus and Manuskript. Unlike most labels they operate on a straightforward 50/50 split over profits. They export other labels' material abroad and can import work too. Excellent contacts. What Nightbreed are to the Midlands/North, Resurrection are to London and the South. Rear Basement Shop, 228 Camden High Street, London NW. (Mail Order/Correspondence, 73 Parkway, Camden Town, London NW1 7PP) (Fax: +44 (0) 171 267 5283) (Phone +44 (0) 171 813 2917)

RETRIBUTION RECORDS 2 St. Peters Rd, Manchester (or should that be Coventry?), Warks CV9 UQQ.

RUPTURED AMBITIONS Mail order firm mainly specialising in punky material, and hair dyes etc, but broadening out into Gothic jewellery, clothes and punk bondage gear. Old Forge Cottage, Rushford, Lamerton, Tavistock, Devon PL19 8RY.

SECOND SKIN Run by Mike Stringer, Ryk Milstead and Mike Bates, this is fascinating. A special F/X production house - making prosthetics, costumes, props and creature creations. Not particularly film-orientated they cater to a customer's personal needs. This is where you get your FANGS! If you don't want to pay a visit, or meet Mike at a convention you can either pay your dentist to make a cast of your teeth which you can send on, or you can make your own, utilising something a little more suitable than plasticene. Second Skin can provide you with the info you need on that. The acrylic fangs are even sculptured to your own designs and there are more than one standard type.

Even more intriguing are their 'Hybrid Events'. This is where you take the idea of a Murder Mystery Weekend and turn it into a Horror Week! It can be anywhere - a Cornish village, an island...and all with actors populating the scene, unbeknown to you, either as people or fully made up (professional standard) monsters. *Very* pricey in one way (way over a thousand pounds!), but quite an experience. I'm surprised they don't offer a weekend service which would be more popular and regular, not to mention cheaper. Blurdy amazing. Mike Stringer, High Croft, 63 Town Street, Guisely, Leeds LS20 9DT.

SPICE Distribution firm for fanzines, music, doing mail order, alternative art, poetry and fiction, fetish, whatever. Send a sae and see what's going on, or send samples. 17 Wyndmill Crescent, Charlement Farm, West Midlands B71 3RA.

SPIDER Firm handling and requesting Gothic craftwork (toys etc). 20a Trinity Rd, Tooting Bec, London SW17 7RE.

STUART SYLVAIN The man behind whatever the UK *Gothic* mag is that you may currently be reading and adoring. Was going to be called *Gothic UK* or *UK Gothic* but there turned out to be a hardware company already called that. May now be *In The Dark* but that has a strangely unconfident feel, no? c/o Rarrigini-Rosso Ltd, Priory House, Priory Gardens, Chesterton, Peterborough PG7 3UB.

LIZ TAYLOR Artist and robe-maker. Titania's Eye, 35 Culworth House, Staple Lodge Rd, Northfield, Birmingham B31 3DJ.

TWISTED CHURCH PRODUCTIONS Artwork provided for anything desired. 164 Dane Rd, Sale M33 2LQ.

THE VAULT Otherwise known as The Gothic N Rock Fans Club Shop. Run by well-known face around town, Christian, who last I heard was piecing together a weird provocative ambient influenced band. Unit B9, Kensington Market, 49-53 Kensington High Street, London W8.

V.K. RECORDS UK address for American label Deep Six - records and video. 207 Manford Way, Chigwell, Essex.

WHITBY VIDEO MEMENTO The 95, and probably the 96 too, Whitby event, captured on video. Three hours of "total crap", apparently, for the miserly sum of £7.50, but add plenty of postage depending on where you're from. Hope and pray you aren't one of the people filmed having a slash. A. Thomson, 6 Duncan Ave, Ravenshead, Nottinghamshire NG15 9BS.

WORLD SERPENT DISTRIBUTION Dark Wave stockists. Unit 717 Seager Buildings, Brookmill Road, London SE8 4HL.

Clothes/Jewellery

AARDVARK Clothes/jewellery shop. 50a Bridge Street, Northampton.

ALCHEMY Pagan/wild craft designs. Skulls a go-go. See Businesses.

INK LINK Contact club for tattos, piercing and body art enthusiasts. 21 Worle Court, Weston Super Mare, Avon BS22 9ND.

BAD Records, shoes, clothes, jewellery and accessories. New Station Street, Leeds.

BLACK HEARTS Alternative clothing. 36 Brooklyn Avenue, Worthing, Sussex BN11 SHQ.

THE CLOSET Metalwear, 'giftwear'(?), alchemy metal products, shirts, leathers, body jewellery etc. Braunstone Gate, Leicester LE3 5LH.

DARKSIDE Glasgow based shop at the Virginia Galleries, Virginia Street, Glasgow, run by Greig and Danielle of Naked Truth. Details from 39 Hamilton Drive, Flat 4, Hillhead, Glasgow G12 8DW.

DEMONE Clothes. PO Box HP8, Leeds LSA6 1XP.

DRESS TO DISTRESS Recent business. 'Alternative' clothing. S.A. Gilbert, Central Hall, Ablewell Street, Walsall WS1 2EQ. (Tel: 01922 647696)

EURASIA CRAFTS Clothes. 528 Great Western Road, Kelvinbridge, Glasgow.

GASLIGHT JEWELLERY 15 Georgina Rd, Beeston, Nottingham NG9 1GQ.

GOTHIC Clothes. 647 Great Western Rd, Kelvinbridge, Glasgow.

THE GOTHIC WARDROBE Clothes. 44 Filey Rd, Manchester M14 6GQ.

GRIM NOIR Glam, fetish, leather, body-piercing. Basement, 22 Harper Street, next to Kirkgate Market, Leeds.

GRIN Leeds Corn Exchange, usual clothes etc plus 'Stargazer' makeup range stocked.

GURU BOUTIQUE More metal and Hippy stuff than Goth but there's some okay stuff in there. Catalogue (£2) is maybe even worth getting because sometimes it is unintentionally hilarious - some of the models cannot help but appear unconvincing. They also sell Zippo lighters, Harley Davidson and Jack Daniels stuff, home things (cushions galore), joss sticks, etc. There's even metal miniatures, cast jewellery and soft leather undies! Oo-er. 24 Blackwell Gate, Darlington DL1 5HG.

JEMA DAVIES Clothes and props. 45 Shelton Street, Nottingham NG3 1DU.

JINS Clothes and accessories from goth-romantic to bizarre, fetish and re-enactment. Gothic catalogue available and dressmaking service. The Warehouse, South Place, Chesterfield. (Tel: 01742-667844)

JACKET PAINTINGS Done to your design, prices vary according to complexity. Phone Carl on 0181 645 9531.

KAOS CLOTHING 'Purveyors of finest corsetry and Alternative Apparel' no less and occupying a fairly exclusive address. Katie, 1st Floor, 177 Wollaton Street, Nottingham NG1 5GE. (Fax: 0115 912 3456)

THE MAY TREE Unit 34-36, Corn Exchange, Manchester M4.

MORGANA Goth, Punk Glam, PVC, Rubber. 11 Cheapside, Wakefield, West Yorkshire.

NO MORE TWIST Established by designer-maker Cobweb, in 94, originally doing jewellery... and then: "nobody caters properly for Goths and because we couldn't just buy the things we wanted, we ended up making them ourselves. Since then we've made just about everything from gargoyles and mirror frames, to Gigeresque breastplates and moulded rubber tops. We also produce 2-D artwork for flyers, posters, t-shirts, record covers etc, and paint/ customise leather coats/jackets. Basically if you've got an idea for something and can't get it anywhere, we can probably make it for you." 76 Bayswater Mount, Harehills, Leeds LS8 5LW.

OASIS Clothes. 35 Market Street, Manchester M1CR M1.

OSIRIS Clothes. 487 Great Western Road, Kelvinbridge, Glasgow.

PEEPSHOW Clothes. First Floor, Virginia Galleries, Virginia St (City Centre), Glasgow.

RELIGION Clothes shop. 50 Park Row, Bristol BS1 5lH.

128 NO MORE TWIST 129 SAPPHIRE OF S.A. JEWELLERY 130 RELIGION

128

PHOTO: IAN CLARIDGE. MODEL: MICHELLE

130

129

RISHKA ALTERNATIVE CLOTHING 209 Market Centre, Manchester M2.

S.A. JEWELLERY 138 Canterbury Rd, Harrow, Middlesex HA1 4PB.

SHOCK Clothes,shoes,belts, accessories. Leeds Corn Exchange.

VAMPIRA DESIGNS Rosaries, velvet chokers, ear-rings, rings and hatpins. Cheque for 50p to L. Watson. 'Vampirella', the woman who designs everything is particularly keen to link up correspondence wise with other female vamps. 93 Fortescue Rd, Colliers Wood, London SW19 2CA.

VOID 38/40 Carlton Street, Hockely, Nottingham NG1 1NN.

WATERLOO ANTIQUES Behind the Corn Exchange, Leeds. Genuine Victorian and Edwardian outfits onwards.

L. WATSON Gothic style hand-made jewellery chokers, rosaries, ear rings etc. Catalogue for 50p UK ($2 US) 237 Anlaby Park Rd South, Hull, Humberside HU4 7JD.

WAYLANDS SMITHY Pagan/Occult jewellery. Box No. A191, Link House Magazines Ltd, Dingwall Avenue, Croydon CR9 2TA.

WILDSIDE Ground Floor, Virginia Galleries, Virginia St, Glasgow.

Fanzines

AFTERLIFE Hugely impressive mag that has sprung from the steaming loins of *Lowlife*. Unfortunately this was restricted to one issue due to the death of

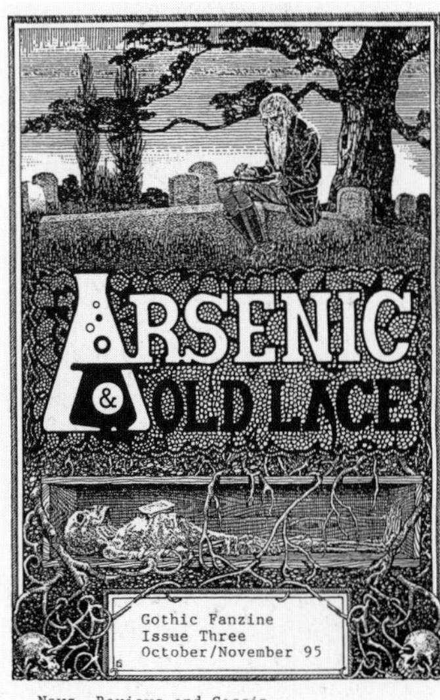

131

132

its primary editor, Phoenix, previously of *Lowlife*. Following her unexpected demise her sister Andi and fellow contributor Jason Horley decided to issue the first and only one as a tribute to her dedication. The issue they produced was like a sleeker version of what she'd been involved with before and there may well be some copies left. 3 Sandringham Rd, Rainham, Gillingham, Kent ME8 8RJ.

ARSENIC & OLD LACE A smart little item which needs to grow to explore its themes. Part, it would appear, of something called Gaslight Productions. Excellent debut issue. Contributions are always welcome - poetry, short stories, reviews etc. S.J. Smedley (aka Scooby), 15 Georgian Road, Beeston, Nottingham NG9 1GQ.

ASYLUM Quarterly mag from Primary and with good contents, for its brief size, mainly reviews but a feature or retro-piece here and there. PO Box 3213, London SW2 3QQ.

BATS & RED VELVET Coo, posh! A general Goth fanzine which followed on from the purely Vampiric *House of Dracula* (begun in 1991). It's now the longest running Goth zine in the country and it's nice to find a UK zine so actively searching for talent abroad. It interviews authors and designers and matters pertaining to the scene itself as much as just concentrating on music because its aim, same as this book, is to be of some use and encouragement. Currently quarterly but soon to go bi-monthly! Contributions welcomed, in handwriting (clear, obviously), typed or on High Density double sided 3.5 disc compatible with Microsoft Word or Microsoft Publisher PC applications. Four issue subscription is £8 UK or £12/$18/24DM/30,000 Lire - by any means necessary! Jo, Flat 1, 112 St George's Terrace, Newcastle Upon Tyne NE2 2DP.

BLACKMAIL Rosetta Stone newsletter. See Bands.

BLACK PLANET A fascinating little project that goes as far as any I've seen to do the unexpected. There is very little music, and there's a few crass pieces given too much space (a virtual idiot's guide to the Tarot for instance), but there are excellent ideas too - how to turn your house into a Gothic lair, taking it room by room, even if they failed to find any black toilet paper. They have looked at the relevance of animals in magic, they traipse around famous ghost walks, appraise peculiar haunted hotels. There's the conventional - body art, piercing, fashion and make-up, but also cemetery visits, literature, aphrodisiacs and unusual buildings of interest. Excellent stuff. By the time you read this there should also be an exclusive range of jewellery for sale, which will be have been launched at the third Whitby weekend. Rhona Burt, 12 Arthur Kennedy Close, Boughton Under Blean, Faversham, Kent ME13 9BQ.

BLUEPRINT Produced by Kevin from Raw Novembre and Aggressive Records. Eco-concerned fanzine with varied musical tastes, 60 packed A5 pages. 4 issue subscription £5 UK. Also deals with the Aggressive mail order list. 4 The Beehives, Ballindery, Mullingar, Westmeath, Ireland.

DKHRS Paul 47 Brandhill Drive, Crofton, Wakefield WF4 1PF, or in America there's Shawnee, 5629 River Bluff Drive, Suffolk, Virginia 23435. Very funny zine. Very classy and if there was room I'd tell you their Eldritch/God joke.

THE DARK IS RISING Run by Siobhan McCarthy, who is involved with everything in Liverpool. She certainly knows what's what. The fanzine naturally reflects that. 99 Van Dyke Street, Toxteth, Liverpool L8 ORS.

DEADHEADS Goth, Punk, Industrial Dark Wave, Ambient. Oh, everything. Francis & Keren, 5 Pant Glas, Pentwyn, Cardiff CF2 7EU.

133

134 JOHN TUCKER AND PHOENIX HITCH (R.I.P.) OF *LOWLIFE*

134

DEADLANDS Allied to 'The Exodus Information service'. They've several titles, many of which sell swiftly, so be quick. They even do things like a strip involving Children On Stun. R. Ahlfeld, 5 Anne Gds, Gourock PA 19 1AL.

ECLIPSE Chris, 28 Winchester Rd, Alton, Hampshire GU 34 1RX.

EDGE OF HEAVEN Formerly *The Pilgrim*, the Vendemmian zine. David Nash, 11 East Vale, Third Avenue, Off The Vale, Acton, London W3 1XX.

EXODUS The first Gothic/Avant garde comic to appear, I'm fairly sure. The first issue didn't really work, with splodges of poetry and flyers, but the idea is obviously worth pursuing. Hopefully they are. Graeme Rose, 9 Mallaig Avenue, Dundee DD2 4TW.

THE EMPTY QUARTER Although I've not seen this lately this is/was the foremost leader in beautifully presented introductions to all that is unconventional in international experimental, avant-garde and intellectually stimulating or swindling musical operations. (Most of it's probably unlistenable crap in other words). PO Box 87, Ilford, Essex IG1 3HJ.

FIENDZINE Stylish mishmash of news and worldwide press clippings of the Alien Sex Fiend menagerie and their various adventures or periods of hibernation. Blue Crumb Truck, PO Box 416, Cardiff CF1 8XU.

FIST Chunky, black and white semi-gloss outing for what editor Dean calls 'forgotten cultures'. (Dean is also in a band, Enslave.) In the issue I ploughed through you saw Swans, Coil, Death In June, some fiction - all well written - and an article about De Sade, bits and bobs, reviews galore and we get to ponder the cover question, 'Do androids dream of electric bulldogs?' Not the ones that I know, no. It's excellent quality and well laid out, with an intellectual streak kept in place by the simple desire to communicate. A bit like Re-search musical coverage, without the boring drivel. 85 St Agnes Pl., Kennington, London SE11 4BM.

GRAVE GENERATION Maybe quite conventional, with a few Pagan and industrial entries, but it's very good quality and regular. Caf-Rin, 222 Clarendon Street, Hulme, Manchester M15 5ED.

GRAVEN IMAGE Nice, open approach, taking all too brief glimpses at matters outside music ('Goth vs. Normality'), or asking 'Whatever happened to The March Violets?' and then not even pretending to attempt an answer. But it has a good feel to it and although the questions given to bands are fairly repetitive in postal interviews, they pick decent bands in the first place. All that is needed is a lot more thought before they set about their work. Stephanie Lees, 12 Ings Crescent, Guisely, Leeds LS20 8DD.

GRIMOIRE This was the Nosferatu magazine before Vlad and the guys went splitsville. Haven't heard anything about it since. 138 Canterbury Rd, Harrow, Middlesex HA1 4PB.

hELLE It's a magazine all about dolls, which presumably interests some people. Sindy dolls, that sort of thing. You can even buy photos of the dolls. I'm shaking my head even as I type. Network X, 88 Steppingley Rd, Flitwick, Beds MK 45 1AR.

LIGHT OF THE WORLD Balaam zine! ALF, Pludda House, Station Rd, Bovey Tracey, Devon TQ13 9AS.

LOWLIFE Begun in 93, this was the most authoritative UK Goth zine (music-wise) around for two years as *Naked Truth* didn't exist and *B&RV* was too irregular. John Tucker and Phoenix Hitch went their

135

136

137

separate ways before she began working on *Afterlife*. John does intend carrying on, possibly broadening the musical scope (Indie was creeping in), when he's got over the shock of it all. Maybe by now. 11 Parkwood Rd, Hastings, East Sussex TN34 2RN.

MONAS HIEROGLYPHICA Name taken from the work of 16th century alchemist Dr John Dee, of course. Jamie's a published poet, but we don't need to talk about that. He can tell you about it as you may wish to write to him about it. Jamie has an excellent attitude to things. A bit wee but a nice combination of fiction, poetry, music and occult/pagan stuff. The historical pieces give a nice feel to this and it also helps having artwork by Jason Horley to leap out of the pages at you. Jamie Spracklen, 58 Seymour Rd, Hadleigh, Benfleet, Essex SS7 2HL.

NAKED TRUTH It's enormous. Obviously, from the musical slant this is now by far and away the best UK Gothzine, not just by a mile but a marathon. (Any fanzine which shows readers how to make an Eldritch Sock Puppet gets my vote.) This fanzine erupted into life with a sleek computer printed look and a wild sense of humour as well as neatly ordered sense of passion. That was March 94. It's got glossy and its spreading, to the Darkside clothes shop and Darkside promotions, organising live events, ever since March 95. Danielle Diver and Greig Glendnning, 39 Hamilton Drive, Hillhead, Glasgow G12 8DW.

NIGHTMARES IN WAX Emma, 20 Vine Street, Lincoln LN2 5HZ.

ORGAN This is great. Both a gigantic sized fanzine as well as random free paper issues, there are as many as 20,000 copies of their newsheet distributed around town at any one time, by Sean Worrall and Marina Anthony. It isn't Goth, it's scuzzy indie of every description as a rule but by the same token there are no rules. *Organ* covers everything the team find even vaguely enjoyable. And their fingers aren't so much on the pulse as pushing right through the wristbone. And if it's Goth, so what, they have no problem with that. They also have a voracious appetite. If you want something reviewed they will not flinch. Unit 205, The Old Gramophone Works (so?), 326 Kensal Rd, London W10 5BZ. (Fax: 0181 964 5626.)

THE PENNY DREADFULL It's the best fanzine in the UK that covers more than mainly musical areas of Goth, because of its approach. It's attitude to music is actually a touch strange, as though it isn't that important and they don't seem to make too much effort to investigate. Tut, tut. However, it has the same feel in a way as *Dark Angel*, and that's the ultimate compliment. (Lack of credibility points however go to Angela sneaking into her friend Luan's fanzine to dribble frenetically over an out of body experience fondling Adam Ant's shoes.) Angela Readman, 39 Shaftesbury Grove, Heaton, Newcastle Upon Tyne NE6 5JA.

POISON COFFIN Jez, 3 Gatensbury Place, Princes Risborough, Bucks HP27 ODS.

PRINCESS SPIDER Fanzine devoted entirely to the Hungarian wild woman. Written and illustrated by admirers! Ty Fraen, The Park, Blaenavon, Gwent NP4 9AG.

RAGE ON PAGE Fanzine based on Revolution By Night but independent from the band. 1 Burbage House, Samuel Close, New Cross, London SE14 5RP.

RAZORCHILD A bit basic but bursting with spirit. She also does airily garish paintings. Worse there is a threat, "One day I'll find some like-minded odd bods

138

137 ANGELA READMAN

to turn my strange words and pretty melodies into creepy, spine-chilling monstrous song type things." Possibly. Then you'll be sorry. Sherin Hodgson-Watt, 2 North View, Shutta Road, East Looe, Cornwall PL13 1HR.

SANDS OF TIME 24 Greenway Rd, Taunton, Somerset TA2 6LB.

SKELETON GIRLS Very strange fanzine addressing the sole topic of dark goddesses, which is not crude or unbalanced. It takes the form of illustrations and poems done by people in tribute to certain individuals. It's an odd fanzine, somehow tied in with other publications - *Princess Spider*, and the more free-range *Roisin Dubh* which is meant to be poetry and artwork but goes onto music as well. All extremely interesting and unusual. Ty Fraen, The Park, Blaenavon, Gwent NP4 9AG.

THE SKY'S GONE OUT Normal Goth/Alternative zine. GJ, 62 Hendre Road, Pencoed, Mid Glamorgan, CF35 6JN.

SOWTHISTLE Regular coverage of all manner of what they perkily term 'subterranean' matters and music dedicated to Industrial, tribal, Experimental, Avant-garde, Gothic, The Occult, Art, Ancient Cultures, Animal Rights, The Environment, Philosophy, Extremities of all kind and news of the global underground. Participation is clearly welcome so write for submission guidelines. From the Son Of William office. 90b, High Road, London N2 9EB. (Fax: 0181-883-0882)

TERMINAL STATE TS Park House, Buckhold Rd, Wandsworth, London SW18 4AT.

VAGABOND HEART Highly recommended for its Goth-Glam-Sleaze cortex. 20 Leopold Street, Barnsley, South Yorkshire S70 6AN.

V.A.T. Funniest zine I've ever encountered, and flying right in the face of those frosty souls who think wit is the enemy of Goth. You need it. Kev Demant, 53 Hatton House, Hindmarsh Close, Cable Street, London E1 8JJ.

VISIONARY TONGUE COLLECTIVE A new concept in fanzines, from the minds of Storm Constantine and Eloise Coquio, of darkly sensual fiction "produced by writers drawn to the Gothic genre", including Cleo Cordell, Graham Joyce, Brian Stableford, Freda Warrington. The editors are looking for top drawer stuff - whether it be poetry (snarl!), fiction, reviews, related articles and artwork. It is a non-profit organisation so don't expect to get paid, other than by a free copy of the zine. Visionary Tongue, 6 St Leonards Avenue, Stafford ST17 4LT.

*** Now, I ask you, does that seem like a lot of fanzines for this country? I'm certain there's room for far more. As long as you think things out beforehand it is perfectly possible to produce interesting, varied zines and not lose money. Anyone planning the standard old outing, interviewing the same six bands everyone thinks of first, or sending abroad for postal interviews with utterly dull questions means nobody in their right mind will want a copy. Do it from a totally personal perspective and away you go. It's also brilliant fun. I did one for sixteen years, so I should know. ***

Fetish

ACADEMY CLUB School uniform organisation. Runs events including four day specials at an actual boarding school. PO Box 135 Hereford HR2 7PE.

ADULT LEISURE GUIDE Adult sex paper. PO Box 2639, London N8 7QJ.

AE SERVICES Domination implements. Dept DR, PO Box 94, Sandbach, Cheshire CW11 0ZD.

ARMORY Rubber fetish gear. 'Barbarellas' upstairs, specialising in lacy underwear. 10 Greyhound Street, Nottingham.

ARTSCENE Wet catalogues/videos. Artscene 20, PO Box 1597, Bath BA1 6YA.

AXFORDS Corsets and Victoriana jobbies. 82 Centurian Rd, Brighton, Sussex.

BAL DES GRACIEUSES Corsets. 40 Whaley Rd, Wokingham, Berkshire RG11 1QA.

BANNED Glamour clothing, 1920-1950. Old undies and corsetry. 2 Cross St, London N1 2B1.

BEAUTY AND THE BITCH 'Outrageous Fetish Rock Band', apparently, featuring Hayley Harlow (male to female transexual) on guitar/vocals, Izzy Smart (female to male transexual) on guitar and boring, unchanged Andy Piborough-Skinner on bass and long name. The Bitchettes, Christine, 311a Alexandra Avenue, Harrow HA2 DX4.

BELT & BUCKLE OFF Bondage and cp stuff. PO Box 593 London SW4 0HT.

BETWEEN THE SHEETS Erotic bedding - Satin, velvet, pvc, latex, silk. 18 Calne Business Centre, Harris Rd, Calne SN11 9PT.

BLACK MAGIC WOMAN Leather 'Warrior Woman' designs. 451 Roman Rd, London E3 5LX.

BODYFORM Bondage gear. 88 Macdonald Street, Birmingham B5 6TN.

BODYART MAGAZINE Dept 44, Blake House Studios, Rayne, Braintree, Essex CM7 8SH.

BODY JEWELLERY Gold and silver body jewellery. Peter on 0181 690 2872.

BOOKLINES Bookshop stocking British and American bondage mags and books, CP, rubber/leather. 11 Camden Street, Liverpool L3 8JR.

BOUND II Fetish shop. 104 Milton Rd, Weston Super Mare BS23 2UJ.

BULKCOURT LTD Fetish shop. Harmony Centre, 41 Cross Street, Manchester M2.

BV TAPES Erotic cassettes by all accounts. The name Danielle Black is involved, which I presume means something. 7 Buddleia Close, Ipswich, Suffolk IP2 OXG. (Something Barry Fuller neglected to mention, naughty boy!)

CAMPAIGN AGAINST CENSORSHIP 25 Middleton Close, Fareham PO10 1QN.

CANDID Contact group. PO Box 125, Leatherhead, Surrey AT23 4JA.

CARESS The Erotic Writer's newsletter. Flat 1, 11 Holland Rd, Hove, Sussex BN3 1JF.

CATALOG CONNECTION Fetish clothing companies worldwide. A booklet of catalogues, saving you some time. Freepost, 7 Fulham High Street, London SW6 3YZ.

CERTAINTY MAGAZINE Fetish mag. Century House, 100 George Street, Romford, Essex RM1 2EB.

CLOTHES FOR PRACTITIONERS Made to measure pvc, spandex/leather. 140c Kennington Lane, London SE11 4UZ.

COCOON Strange rubber, including gas masks. Opening shop in Birmingham too. Mackintosh House(!), Green Street, Kidderminster DY10 1JF. (Fax: 0562 66773)

NICK COLEMAN Graphic designer and graphic/ technical illustrator. 25 Monks Way, Silverdale, Nottingham NG11 7FG.

CONTACT CENTRE Worldwide contact organisation for subs and doms. Contact centre, (S/M), Irene Arsha Subiela BCM Cuddle, London WC1V 6XX.

COUNTDOWN ON SPANNER Campaign for legalisation of S/M. 37 Wharfdale Rd, London N1.

COVER GIRL Shoe shop. 44 Cross Street, London N1.

CRUELLA Fashion? Magazine? Female mistresses and male domination. Equestrian. Also do bondage and restraint gear. May include music stuff. PO Box 122, Derby DE22 4XA.

CUL D'OR Spanking mag. Omega marketing, PO Box 81, Southampton SO9 7RH.

CURSIA Fetish furniture. PO Box 2, Hoddesdon, Herts EN11 0SA.

DESIRE Fetish and tv shop. 619 Attercliffe Rd, Sheffield.

DESIRE Sex mag covering naturism to transvestism to S&M. PO Box 282, London SW4 0QQ.

DESPICABLE CLOTHING Made to measure quality clothes. 130 Wharncliffe St, Chanterlands Avenue, Hull HU5 3NA (Tel: 01482 449999)

DIVINITY Unusual and interesting multi-themed mag. Divine Press, PO Box 108, Stockport, Cheshire, SK1 4DD.

DOC ROC Fetish stuff. 59 Camden High St, London NW1.

DOMINA Dungeons/Fantasy Rooms designed and fitted. PO Box 159, Warwick, CV35 8JG.

DOMINA Magazine. 27 Old Gloucester St, London WC1R 3XX.

DOMINIQUE Relevant contact mag. 154 Bedminster Down Rd, Bristol, BS13 7AF.

E-GARBS Corsetry and jewellery. 9 Boyces Street, The Lanes, Brighton, BN1 1AN.

EAGLE LEATHERS Leather clothes. PO Box 57, Northolt, Middx, UB5 4SB.

EAST OF EDEN Wetlook and transvestite fashion. 519 Cambridge Heath Rd, London E2 9EU.

ECTOMORPH Quality rubber and leather clothes. Unit 1, 42-44 De Beauvoir Crescent, London N1 5SB.

ELAINE WILLIAMS Fetish shop. 1st Floor, 52 Church Street, Manchester.

ENHANCE Support group for lovers of gentle eroticism! (Why should they require support?) Newsletter plus advice and help. PO Box 164, Amersham, Bucks, HP8 4LZ.

EROTEAK Top quality specialist furniture. Thaney House, Denmark Rd, Lowestoft, NR32 2EN.

ETHOS TV clothes and accessories. 1102 Stockport Rd, Levenshulme, Manchester M19.

EVENTS Organising social events and Fetish gatherings. PO Box 292, Acocks Green (no-one said it would be easy), Birmingham, B27 7UD.

EXCEPTIONS Fetish shop. 75 Great Eastern Street, London EC2A 3HU.

THE FEDERATION Leather, rubber, wetlook. 33 Heathcote St, Hockley, Nottingham, NG1 3AG.

FEMININE DISCIPLINARY SOCIETY It's a women only club in one way and they do *Feminine Magic*, as below, and another magazine, *Imperial Angel* which again dives into the fake land of Romantia. It's beautifully rendered and nothing I particularly understand. Reminds me a lot of turn of the century comics by Frank Richards and it is in fact by far the most imaginative publication of any of those listed in this book, although I don't mean to imply it is particularly enjoyable. It is 'interesting'. BM Perfect, London WC1N 3XX.

FEMININE MAGIC Linked to the above, and all I have to hand is a booklet which includes notes on 'the Patriarchal octopus'. Should come in handy. It centres around a 1920s Balkan state to parallel how people saw women's position set against their potential. What do you get if you subscribe? According to them you help push civilisation towards women, but apart from that you get the feminine tape 'A Feminine Journey', free copies of the mag as well as occasional surprise publications. You are confronted by issues such as Healing, Fairies, Discovering Your Inner Child, Matriarchal History, reclaiming Femininity, Playing Games With Time, Poison And How To Expel It and all the other aspects that make it the true forerunner to *Loaded*. Your £8 fee also grants your honorary membership of The Daughters Of Enchantment. I seriously doubt there is a more interesting society in the country, and I don't even care. BM Labrys, London WC1.

FEMINISTS AGAINST CENSORSHIP Oh, don't go on about it! BM Box 207, London WC1N 3XX.

FETISH TIMES 131A Munster Rd, London SW6 6DD. Or KP Publishing, BCM Box 6883, WC1N 3XX. (Fax 071 731 5950)

HEADPRESS Religion, sex and death magazine. PO Box 160, Stockport, Cheshire SK1 4ET.

FETISH FETISH Bondage fashion. 1a Peter Street, London W1 3RR.

FETTERS Bondage gear, particularly harnesses. 40 Fitzwillliam Rd, London SW4 ODN.

FOUR D RUBBER CO LTD Heanor Gate Industrial Estate, Heanor, Derbyshire, DE75 7SJ.

CHARLES H FOX TV clothes and makeup. 22 Tavistock Rd, London WC2.

FRANS Fetish collection, leather and rubber. Unit 18, 60 Regent Place, Birmingham B1 3NJ.

FUNCTION ONE Fetish shop. 43 High St, Hull HU1 1TS.

GENDER DYSPHORIA TRUST TV/TS support, advice and counselling. BM Box 7624, London WC1N 3XX.

GET WET BCM Box 3564, London WC1N 3XX.

G. M. FASHIONS Fashion mags. Century House, 100 George Street, Romford, Essex RM21 2EB.

GOVERNESS Mag of the Alice Kerr-Sutherland Society. Domination stuff. Best produced of all journals according to Delectus. AKSS, Box 12, Hastings, East Sussex.

HAIR BY CHAIR Fetish hair specialist! 43 Anerley Rd, London SE19.

HALAWA HENNA Temporary body adornment. (061 737 9722)

THE HARMONY LEAGUE Women interested in dom and sub, run by people out of Victorian retreat. Kincasslagh House, BM Labrys, London WC1N 3XX.

HARMONY TWO Books, mags and videos covering all aspects. 180, Holdenhurst Road, Bournemouth.

HEADPRESS Cultural and behavioural excess magazine. PO Box 160, Stockport, Cheshire SK1 4ET.

SARAH HEART LTD PO Box 488, Cheadle, Stoke On Trent ST10 2QJ.

HIDEBOUND Bondage restraints, harnesses, furniture. PO Box 10, Liverpool L36 6LD.

TERENCE HIGGINS TRUST Advice and support for people with HIV and AIDS. 52-54 Grays Inn Rd, London WC1X 8JU.

HONOUR Fetish clothing. 5 Riverside, 28 Park St, London SE1 9EQ.

HOUSE OF GOTHCHILD For those all important Ice Queen Nipple Shields! Don't leave home without them. PO Box 6069, Basingstoke, Hampshire RG21 4YZ.

HOUSE OF HARLOT Rubber, leather made to measure clothes as well as their own strange designs. (Tel: 0171-06-315)

WENDY JANE Special designs to order, special sizes, mags and devices. 62a Station Rd, March, Cambridgeshire PE15 8NP.

IAN KING Designs leather and metal equipment for medieval fantasies and bondage gear. The Studios, Moors Farm, Collier Sty, Nr Marden, Kent TN12 9PR.

INTERNATIONAL MACKINTOSH SOCIETY I can't quite believe this is happening. PO Box 14, Dover, Kent CT16 1XT.

JACK THE RUBBER Rubber clothes. 58 Greek Street, London W1V 5LR.

JENSEN & MORROW Fetish furniture. 14 Ingestre Place, London W1R 3 LP.

JEZEBEL Corsetry and theatrical costumes. (Tel 0181-518-4538)

KASTLEY LTD Coloured and black and white designs in rubberwear. Unit 2, Darwen Enterprise Centre, Railway Rd, Darwen, Lancs BB3 3EN.

LADY ELIZABETH Shoes and boots. PO Box 2, Ellesmere Port, S. Wirral L65 3EA.

LADY O SOCIETY Society for submissive ladies, over 18, to discuss all matters of interest. The society was formed by Deborah Ryder (of Ryder Publishing), and men can only become associate members. There is also the Ryder Book club, specialising in all relevant publications. BCM/3406 London WC1N 3XX.

LAKELAND ELEMENTS Rubber, leather, TV. 23 Broadway, Morecombe, Lancashire LA5 5BQ.

KATE LANCASTER Fine Art Photographer of piercing, body adornment and 'body play'. Mr Hayman, Rose Cottage, Bishop Lydeard, Taunton Rd, Somerset TA4 3LR.

LANEM FASHIONS Latex and pvc clothes to size 22. 11 Parsonage Gardens, Enfield, Middlesex.

JULIAN LATORRE Hand made rubber fashions. BCM Box 8827, London WC1N 3XX.

LE PREVO LEATHERS Fetish designs. Blackfriars, Stowell Street, Newcastle Upon Tyne NE1 4XN.

LEATHERWORKS Leather shoes. 77-79 Southgate Rd, London N1 3JS.

LIBERTY Civil Liberties organisation. 21 Tabard St, London SE1 4LA.

LIBIDEX BCM Libidex, London WC1N 3XX. (0171-613 3329)

LIBIDO Fetish fashion. Also got 'Little Shoe Box' on same premises. 83 Parkway, London NW1 7PP.

LIFESTYLE Fantasy fashion, amour and underwear. PO Box 4, Holsworthy, Devon EX22 7YL.

LONDON BISEXUAL GROUP Support and counselling. BM B1, London WC1N 3XX.

LONDON PIERCING CLINIC 11 Doyle Rd, London SE25 5JN. (0181-656 7180)

LUSH Corsets, basques, corsets, jackets to shoes. Unit 310, Clerkenwell Worskhop, 31 Clerkenwell Close, London EC1.

LUST "Let's face it, if you want a bit of Miao with your pussy then *Lust*'s where it's at." Definitely. I guess some of the ads and club news maybe of use, or the reviews but the only genuinely interesting piece was some modern submissive art from Japan presented in sepia. The rest is cack. Aurora Publishing, PO Box 6556, London N13 4NY.

MAGIC SHOE COMPANY Unit 6, 88 Mile Rd, London E1 4UN.

MARQUIS Superior quality fetish mag, from former 'O' man. Not quite as stunning as *Secret* magazine but then it's going for a broader appeal - Fashion, Fetish, Fantasies. Makes *Skin Two* look like the *Radio Times*. PO Box 1426, Shepton Mallet, Somerset BA4 6HH.

MARQUIS MASQUERADE Fetish mag out of the general Nightbreed activities with their M.M. club. The mag is still quite new and finding its feet (probably tied behind its head), the club events are highly organised and special. Modern fetish gatherings which aren't rooted in daft snobbery like most fetish places. Nor are there any scum involved, which again is new! 25 Monks Way, Silverdale, Nottingham NG11 7FG.

MICHE PO Rubber, leather. Box 316, Lewes, East Sussex BN8 5DG.

MICHELLE FASHIONS Leather, rubber. 105 Epping

139

New Rd, Buckhurst Hill, Essex IG9 5TQ.

MIDNIGHT LADY Wetlook, boots, rubber, latex. 20-24 Cardigan St, Luton, Bedfordshire LU1 1RR.

MODERN ARMOUR Rubber fetish clothing housed in what once was the biggest corset factory in Britain. Strangely, I once worked there - although not in any corset capacity. Unit 82, Spirella Buildings, Bridge Rd, Letchworth Herts SG6 4HD.

MOONGLOW DINING CLUB Dining club for dom men and sub women. Service without a smile. BCM/7889, London WC1N 3XX.

M.S. CHIEF Erotic photographers. PO Box 23, Reading RG2 9HG.

MUIR REFORM ACADEMY Boarding school for enthusiasts. PO Box 135 Hereford HR2 7PE.

MURRAY & VERN 3rd Floor, 61/63 Whitworth Street, Manchester M1 3MY.

NEW AGE TRADING Restraints. BM 200 London WC1N 3XX.

93S/M DESIGNS I don't really know what to make of this rubber sheathed calendar but it propounds the word of creator Jon Lange who exclaims that they are "the world's foremost exponent of the double current". Having initially responded by saying "I am deeply offended to be connected with such loathsome abominations" (i.e. you) I gave him a sound bollocking, whereupon he came to heel and and admitted that he says things like this to provoke reactions to test people's mettle, which is exactly how I work, so I understand. His work has already attracted the attention of Genesis P Orridge. Basically there is a link between Thelema (not her out of the Likely Lads) and S&M. If that's your area you should investigate further. There is also a distinctive Tarot set available. They even offer their own very specific limited edition Black Leather Bible. PO Box 10, Derby DE19SN.

NOSTALGIA PUBLICATIONS Ancient glamour and stuff. 50's onwards. Very interesting. 5x26ps for big catalogue. 1 Victoria Street, Off Nunnery Lane, York YO2 1LZ.

OD LTD Contact group. PO Box 161, Reading, Berks RG2 OUQ.

OLYMPIA PUBLISHING (UK) LTD Self-proclaimed, and with some justification, as the leading underground S&M and bondage publishers. They produce one magazine and two novels every month. They also have a video available, which I quote, "is our own work entirely, starring Terry Wakelin as the boss (which he is) and me (Dee) as his submissive secretary, which I am". The magazine is quite bright and breezy, with a reliance on rather exaggerated black and white illustrations which are of good quality, containing a few very short stories and plenty of contact ads. However, the novels seemed more like crude wank fodder. Caxton House, Old Station Rd, Ventnor, Isle of Wight PO38 1DX.

OUTRAGEOUS Rubber, leather, pvc. Liverpool Palace, 6-10 Slater Street, Liverpool 1.

OUTSIDERS This is the society for those with social and physical disabilities who feel isolated and want a considerate way to meet partners. Here you practice socialising and it's a common-sense self-help group by the sound of it, with social events in many areas, all with wheelchair access and without strobes. Library books (also on tape) covering aspects of sexuality and disability are available, mail order. PO Box 4ZB, London W1A 4ZB.

PHOTO: IAIN S. WALLACE

140 PASSION CAGE

141

142

PAGAN METAL Fetish designs. Basement, Trocadero, Piccadilly, Circus, London W1.

PASSION CAGE Fetish club set up by Iain S. Wallace, Perdita Dia and Alex Jacob, who had all been active in the Glasgow Goth scene for at least eight years. So it creates what they clearly believe is needed. I haven't mentioned other clubs but this is new. They need your support. The club will be held on the last Sunday of every month. There will be stalls, a photographer for anyone who wants to be photographed, main dance floor, a dungeon, a changing room for those who "don't want to walk around the streets of Glasgow dressed to distress" and a dedicated crowd no doubt. Perdita Dia, Flat 3/2, 26, Hillfoot Street, Dennistoun, Glasgow G31 2LF.

GARY PERKINS Rubber clothes designer, quite dramatic stuff some of it. Obviously good at design as originally made clothes for transvestites and they don't accept rubbish. Also offers body piercing service. 83 Romsley Court, Westley Street, Dudley, West Midlands DY1 1TW.

PLEASUREWEAR PO Box 36, Leeds LS1 4TN.

THE PRIVATE CASE Jewellery, books, mags. PO Box 1632, London N15 4LG.

PUSSY KAT CLUB Fetish contacts. BCM 8922 London WC1N 3XX.

QUALITY CONTROL Disciplinary equipment. 23 Watford Rd, Cotteridge, Birmingham B30 1JB.

QUEENSGATE PRACTICE TV advice and makeup. 10 Queensgate, London SW7.

QUIM "Dykes of all sexual persuasions" magazine. BM 2182, London WC1N 3XX.

RASCALS Contact mag. PO Box 161, Reading, RG3 1PS.

RED STRIPE CP-only club (no S/M). Three parties a month in London, Manchester and Leeds. PO Box 173, Ruislip, Middlesex, HA4 6BH.

REGULATION Military, Industrial, Leather and Rubber clothing. 9-17 St Albans Place, Islington Green, London N1 9QH.

RELIGION Liz Lewitt's company Religion make beautiful quality virtually high fashion fetish gear as well as equally attractive conventional clothing. Considering how superb the gear is, the prices are also far from out of orbit. Liz is also the one of the motivating forces behind the Spank club. 50 Park Row, Bristol BS1 5LH. (01272-293754)

REMAWEAR Sherwood House, Burnley Rd, Todmorden, Lancashire OL14 7ET.

REPARTEE INTERNATIONAL TV mag. PO Box 339, Roses, Sheffield S1 3SX.

RGL Designs. Bondage gear. The perfect place for those pony bit gag & harness items you've been after, along with collars and matching cuffs, a range of blindfolds, gags and hoods and a lot of suspension items. 731 Glenfield Park, Glenfield Rd, Nelson, Lancashire BB9 8AR.

RITUAL Shop specialises in stunning high heels and thigh high boots. 29 Brewer St, London W1R 3FE. (Tel: 0171 287 3830)

ROUGH TRADE Fetish contacts. PO Box 3230 London E14 8JS.

RUBBER MASK & COSTUME CO. Theatrical fashions (Batman and Catwoman). Unit B4, Maws Croft

Workshops, Jackfield Telford TF8 7LS. (Tel 0952 883994)

THE SADIE MAISIE CLUB Only S/M disco club in the UK. BM 414, London WC1N 3XX.

SCENE ONE Fetish gear. 145 Manningham Lane, Bradford BD8 7BR.

SCENE 121 Contact club with magazine, for Dom, Sub and general fetish. PO Box 648, Dunstable LU5 5FG.

SCENE 22 Fetish gear. 22 Peston Street, Brighton, Sussex BN1 2HN.

SEALWEAR Rubber catsuits and stuff. Regent Chambers, 15 Westover Rd, Bournemouth, Dorset BH1 2BY.

SECULAR SAINTS Organisation devoted to recording pain sufferers' written secrets for posterity. You tell them what it takes to excite you and how it feels and then tremble as they lock all those details away. Sad or sensible? You decide. BM Judgement, London WC1N 3XX.

THE SENTRY BOX Rubber/leather goods. PO Box 722, London SE17 3NT.

SH Women only sex shop - corsets and chainmail. Male customers are allowed but must be chaperoned by a mere chit of a gal. 22 Coronet St, London N1.

SHADOWEN In-house den/dungeon designs. 4 Colchester Villas, Falmouth Rd, Truro, Cornwall.

SHE-AN-ME Corsets, etc. 123 Hammersmith Rd, London W4.

SHOWGRADE Women's coats and suits, shiny domina outfits, maid costumes etc. PO Box 10, Bramhall, Stockport SK7 2QF.

SIMPLY RUBBER Catalogue of rubber gear from SR Manufacturing, One Hundred Austin Fields, Kings Lynn, Norfolk PE30 1RS.

SKIN TWO The original, plus shop. Skin Two, Grand Union Canal, Kensal Rd, London W105AX.

SKYES THE LIMIT S/M bondage and cp gear. 23 Thorpe Rd, London N15.

SM GAYS Advice and support group. BM SM Gay, London WC1N 3XX.

SOME BIZARRE Mag for fetishists by fetishists. PO Box 28, Stockton-on-Tees TS21 1YR.

S&M FABRICATIONS Fetish furniture. 63 Dalford Court, Hollinswood, Shropshire TF3 2PB.

SR MANAFACTURING Rubber/leather. PO Box 336, Oxford OX3 7UP.

PAMELA STEPHENS TV dressing and makeup. 24 Beauchamp Place, London SW3 (0171 225 2755)

STORY OF O Audio cassette version, see Tentacle.

STUDIO 40 Bondage. 40 Berwick Street, London W1V 3RE.

SWITCH CLUB CP group. 94 Cheverton Court, Cranmer Street, Nottingham NG3 4GB.

TABBY Boned corsets, skirts, dresses and jackets in pvc and satin. Tabby is also a model and promotes her own gear. PO Box 916, Westcliff-On-Sea, Essex SSO 8QD.

TAFFATA Gay organisation/TV lifestyle magazine. PO Box 65 Leighton Buzzard OU7 8TJ.

TALANA GAMAH & IEISH Very good clothing styles, fantasy outfits for connoisseurs. Bit pricey. BCM Blindfold, London WC1N 3XX.

TATOU CLUB Newsletter on scene, societies and domination. BCM Tatou, London WC1N 3XX.

TEMPLE PRESS Mags. PO Box 227, Brighton, Sussex BN2 3GL.

TENTACLE Truly mad rubberwear. Skinsuits as well as fetish furniture. They have a glossy catalogue available for £10, which is refundable against your order. They also sell a 3 hour long spoken cassette of erotic classic *The Story Of O*, for £8.99, including postage, although I suppose it depends who is reading it. Not Tony Slattery. PO Box 20, Grantham, Lincolnshire NG33 5RB.

THE OTHER PONY CLUB People riding people. PO Box 135, Hereford HR2 UK.

THUNDERBOLT PUBLISHING Literature for 'bottom-sexual' fetishists. BCM Thunderbolt, London WC1N 3XX.

TIGHT SITUATION Fetish fantasy clothing. Gothic. PO Box 860, London SE12 OLL.

TOLLYBOY PRODUCTS Fetish jewellery/chastity belts. PO Box 27, Dronfield, Sheffield S18 6DN.

TORTURE GARDEN Club. The Torture Garden, London WC1N 3XX.

TOTAL CONTROL 1 Uxbridge Street, London W8 7TQ.

TRANSFORMATION LTD Fetish retailer. 50 Eversholt Rd, London NW1.

TVOD Superb printed bodies. 52 Delancy Street, London NW1 7RY.

TV/TS SUPPORT GROUP TV/TS support and counselling. 2 French Place, Shoreditch High Street, London E1.

143

UNA DEVA Lycra, latex, vinyl clothes. PO Box 1426 Shepton Mallet, Somerset BA4 6HH.

UNGAWA Mag of weird films, bondage etc. PO Box 1764, London NW6 2EQ.

UNLEASHED Magazine. PO Box HP50, Leeds LS6 1TR.

UNLIMITED Supposedly the 'ultimate' wetlook catalogue. PO Box HP 50, Leeds L56 1TR.

VILLAGE CHARITY Gay charity and support group, 25 Richmond Street, Manchester M1 3NB.

VOID 38-40 Carlton St, Hockley, Nottingham NG1 1NN.

VOLLERS 112 Kingston Rd, North End, Portsmouth, Hants PO 27 7PB.

WAY OUT PUBLISHING TV guide to London. PO Box 941, London SW5 9UT.

VICKY WATSON Rubber, leather, pvc. 140 Kennington Lane, London SE11 4UZ.

WEATHER VAIN Fetish mag - mackintosh brigade. 283 Sandycombe Rd, Kew, Surrey TW9 3LU.

KIM WEST Trendy rubber fashionwear. BCM Box 8875, London WC1N 3XX.

WILBRO Corsets. PO Box 12, Lampeter, Dyfed SA48 7XU.

WILDCAT INTERNATIONAL Fetish stuff. 16 Preston St, Brighton BN1 2HN.

WILD DESIGNS Shiny stretchy wetlook. PO Box 562, London SE22 0BP.

THE WILDFIRE CLUB Miss Fleur Harrington. Produce four magazines and more, such as discipline canes and the like, and a repro of the *The Female Disciplinary Manual (A Complete Guide To The Correction Of The Fair Sex)*, along with a number of novels by suitably stern authoresses. B.M. Elegance, London WC1 (0181-989-0281)

ROSALIND WOODS Massive underwear catalogue and school uniforms and suchlike. Unit 33, Woodgreen Rd, Rushton, Cheshire SK11 0RS.

X-RATED COMICS Weird erotic cartoon strips and occasionally high quality pastiches or genuine copies of 50's art, these comics really are as filthy as you could want. GSP Ltd, Dept MO 654, 2 Goldstone Rd, Whyteleafe, Surrey CR3 OEA.

YELLOW PAGES Adults only. S. Hancock. 55 High Street, Pembroke Rd, Dyfed, South West Wales SA 72 6PB.

YESTERDAY'S PAPER Check these dated but sweet magazine titles... *Up The Mini, Violent Vixens, Sinful Playmates, Sheer Delight, Spanking Nurse, Tip Top International, Pussies In Boots, The Nylon Jungle*. More ancient glamour and related ephemera than you can cope with. They point out they don't sell heavy bondage or sado-masochistic stuff, preferring role-playing/fantasy fashions. Their 'Naughty Nostalgia' catalogues should be of interest as they include masses of printed material, some no doubt charmingly innocuous, and some of truly historical interest, including magazines dating back to 1919! There's also lingerie catalogues from around the world, old sex mags, all manner of old fetish coverage, including classic reprints. In-depth, new stuff pours in every month. I'd say this was an essential point for any serious collector of this material. PO Box 23, Whitby YO21 3YT..

144 145 146

ZEITGEIST Intelligent femdom mag with tons of fiction and high heels, rubber, leather, plastic and t-shirts. 66 Holloway Rd, London N7 8JC.

ZIPPERSTORE Rubber/leather. 283 Camden High Street London NW1 7BX.

Individuals

ARMAND Armand has run clubs and the Radioactive radio show (Wednesday 9-11pm 101 FM if you can find it). He's the man to check out for what's going on. 19 Tamarisk Dale, Kildamanagh, Tallaght, D24 Ireland.

ASH The House That Dripped Blud, 7 Cranbourne Drive, Hoddesdon, Herts EN11 0QQ.

DARREN BENTLEY Quality photographer whose work appears in fanzines internationally, has also done *Prelude* fanzine recently, as well as his previous outings, *Dreams From Within* and the *Head In The Clouds* tapezine. Too many bands have appalling quality photos, so bands in his area should get in touch. 74 Monteith Crescent, Boston, Lincolnshire PE21 9AY.

CRYSTAL INDIANKHANA CANDY I know what you're thinking - not another transexual poet, but it's true. C-I-C concerns him/herself with Gothic/Pagan/ Fetish/Transgender things. Already has had over 150 poems printed here and in the States, so if you're looking for something a little near the knuckle, and your own fingernail won't do, you could hardly do better. Elysium, 3 Tolls Close, Whitley Bay, Northumberland NE25 9XY.

ANDREW COLLINS Very strange writer who is an active psychic researcher. If you've read his books, *The Black Alchemist* or *The Second Coming*, you'll understand. If you haven't, get them, they're highly unusual works. This man and a few trusted cronies travel across the country combatting evil and never quite finding what they exactly want, whereupon they charge down the pub. That seems to be the routine. Andrew has been writing for some time, since 82 in fact and all his work touches upon bizarre happenings, which is presented in an immediately involving manner. Andrew also runs a group called Earthquest which would be fascinating for anyone in that area as they go on all sorts of exploratory adventures and events. One of a kind is Andrew. It's even stranger that a former punk now willingly provides a photo where he looks like one of Steely Dan! His PO Box number, where £9.99 will secure you a copy of *The Black Alchemist*, is PO Box 189, Leigh-On-Sea, Essex SS9 1NF.

STORM CONSTANTINE Known to virtually everybody (well, not everybody, obviously), Storm is Britain's best known Fantasy-whatever-Goth writer. She always has a new project on the go, short stories as well as novels, and has recently been involved in the starting up of the Visionary Tongue writers collective which is being born as a fanzine (see Fanzines).

Bibble: The Enchantments Of Flesh And Spirit (Macdonald h/b 87, Futura p/b 88, TOR p/b 90), *The Bewitchments Of Love And Hate* (Macdonald h/b 88, Futura p/b 88 - TOR p/b 90), *The Fulfilments Of Fate And Desire* (Drunken Dragon Press h/b 89, Orbit p/b 89 - TOR p/b 91), *The Monstrous Regiment* (Orbit p/b 91), *Hermetech* (Orbit p/b 91 - Heyne p/b 93), *Aleph* (Orbit p/b 91), *Burying The Shadow* (Headline h/b + p/b 91 - Heyne p/b 95), *Sign For The Sacred* (Headline h/b + p/b 93), *Wraethu* (Omnibus: Enchantments/Bewitchments/ Fulfilments, TOR p/b 93), *Calenture* (Headline h/b + p/b 94), *Stalking Tender Prey* (Creed/Signet p/b 95), *Scenting Hallowed Blood* (Creed/Signet p/b 96).

147 148

144 DARREN BENTLEY 145 ANDREW COLLINS
146 CLEO CORDELL 147 STORM CONSTANTINE
148 JASON HORLEY

There is also Inception, her own information service which gives the low down on all her activities as well as showcasing her interests, as she may either be interviewed about current doings, or grilling someone of interest herself. It pops up as its own zine, with reviews, events and features, even the occasional Storm short story, all suitably intriguing and run by Steve Jeffrey and Vikki Lee France, 44 White Way, Kidlington, Oxon OX5 2XA.

CLEO CORDELL A thoroughly charming woman, to be sure, who writes the dirtiest things imaginable. I was positively shocked by an example that she sent me. As Cleo the following festivals of filth have been born: *Captive Flesh*, *Senses Bejewelled*, *Velvet Claws* and *Juliet Rising*, all on Penguin's Black Lace line. Not forgetting the later releases, *Path Of The Tiger* and *Crimson Bucaneer*. Under the name of Susan Swann she has also written *The Discipline Of Pearls* but her mainstream fantasy novels, incredibly, haven't been picked up by doltish publishers. Maybe they're out now, in which case look out for *Mooncaste* and *Soul-Speaker*. No contact address in case of prowling pervs. c/o Penguin Books/Black Lace.

MATTHEW FAULKNER Promotes in the Margate area and organises tape compilations. Write for details if band or fan. Dead By Dawn, 14 Stanley Rd, Broadstairs, Kent CT10 1DA.

PORTIA DE COSTA Not her real name but another smut peddler, indeed a trollop of the highest order. It's pretty cool actually and in this case her writing has its own Gothic twinges and tinges. So, she could do other things too.

STAN EALES Quality black and white illustrator. 43 Blakenham Road, Tooting, London SW17 8NZ.

BARRY FULLER He of the noise fest Hex Minora, who also does photographic work in the S&M realm, including the French magazine *Offrande* and America's *Scream Queens Illustrated*. Secondly, he is part of a firm called 'Bedlam Art' with his partner Carol-Ann and they organise artwork for bands and 'mail art projects' whatever they are. You may have seen his work gracing the singles of Skinflick Productions, although I doubt it. Barry recommends the work of Phillipe Pissier, which is an unfortunate name, and Trevor Brown, Masami Akita and Romaine Slocoombe and then says something strange. "Am I allowed to offer one piece of advice? Beware of filthy fashion people in the S/M scene, they corrupt. Look to France for this kind of inspiration. They know and understand the philosophies of S/M." Funnily enough, I couldn't help noticing that virtually none of the fetish contacts in this book bothered replying to the letters sent by either myself or my publisher. Less than 5% probably. That is why in the next book there will be absolutely no fetish/S&M whatsoever. They're not worth my effort. You'll be okay, you're a potential customer. 7 Buddleia Close, Ipswich, Suffolk IP2 OXG.

JO HAMPSHIRE Along with the much mentioned Trev, Jo is now the other most important person in UK Goth for her highly successful annual Whitby Goth spectacular. Pretty soon she'll have world domination on her mind the way things are going. Organises vampire weekends at Whitby too. (http://whitby.globalnews.com/index.html) 6 Clarence Rd, Monk Bretton, Barnsley, South Yorkshire S71 2Nl.

JASON HORLEY Brilliant artist/illustrator, and not just his black and whites, which have already popped up in various fanzines. His paintings are horrendously good. Not quite in the Sudworth league, but in his own way only a few steps behind her. 3 Sandringham Rd, Rainham, Gillingham, Kent MG88RJ.

149 HANNAH STAUNTON

BEA JOHN Talented illustrator whose work has already appeared in many fanzines, mainly Nephilim-based as well as some work for Storm Constantine's Inception service. However, she is underused, so you should write. 7 Cleveland Drive, Trenewydd Park, Risca, Gwent, NP1 6RD.

JOHN LIGHT A scientist, painter, poet and novelist, he asked to be included, so presumably his works fit in. Photon Press, 29 Longfield Rd, Tring, Herts HP23 4DG.

TONY LUKE Writer/artist on *Dominator* (Manga comic), former singer with The Scream and Raging Angels. Diamond geezer, happily married and leading an international crusade against crusties. No, that's wrong isn't it? A man who loves the world, except crusties. I think that's right.
(Fax 01273 325772)

SIOBHAN McCARTHY The only Goth/Industrial DJ in Liverpool, connected to Liverpool's only fetish club, Catacombs. She also runs *The Dark Is Rising*, an alternative music and scene fanzine and Mirae, an information service covering metal/industrial/rock/alternative/goth events. 99 Van Dyke Street, Toxteth, Liverpool L8 ORS.

ME Oh Lord, is it that time already? Excuse me a moment. Apart from wishing to quash two bizarre rumours that have come to light these past two years - one that I live with my parents, which is news to me (unless they're *incredibly* tiny), and the other that I make my living writing under a pseudonym for Mills & Boon (I wish!) - Anthony of Ex Cathedra observed that many people thought *Siren* magazine, while under my control, effectively shat on Goth! Cobblers, I thought. Then I remembered how I left *Siren* somewhat abruptly, during its second phase. Imagine this. You're scrolling through layout plans on the computer monitor with their designer and up onscreen pops an advert you knew nothing about, requesting applicants apply for the Editorship! Call me psychic, but I began to sense that all was not what it seemed. I quit pronto. There was indeed a snarled response on the letters page from my hapless successor, who seemed incensed that anyone should think the magazine would cover Goth. That wasn't me. I was long gone. And I didn't get paid. I went to *Indiecator* mag for six months instead. And didn't get paid. Let nobody tell you different, freelance journalism is a joy.

Anyway, I've had an idea. You know how people speak fondly of Gothic novels? I want to do one. Well, I want to do a few novels about Goths. They'd still be gothic novels of a sort, only funny. (Hopefully.) All a book has to do to be profitable is sell out its print run. A cheap paperback, done with a suitably garish cover illustration, like the classic pulp detective novels of the 50's, could surely do that, don't you think? It would have a good storyline (which I'd rip off from somewhere), sufficient enough to snag passing readers and enough reference points that only the core audience would get. A nice mix. They would also constitute a wholly new kind of book. Spike Milligan has already had a go at totally re-writing and happily abusing works that are out of copyright. I could sometimes do the same thing but with the specific aim in mind of writing it around a fairly clueless but amiable group of goths. There is nothing to stop them travelling back or forth through time, or into different genres. I will probably try out a few chapters on the Net and see how well it is received. And, providing there was enough response a publisher could be lured into bringing them out as fast as they were written. That bloke who did the crap Skinhead books did one a fortnight when relaxed. I could do one every two months. Think of the possibilities. *The Gothfather*, *Rosemary's Goth*, *Waiting For Gothot*, *The*

Thirty-Nine Goths and, my favourite, *The Goth Of The Baskervilles*.

STEVE MESSAM Top quality photographer of Goth-related subject matter. He's got some smart post-cards available. Flat 3/1, 40 Blantyre St, Yorkhill, Glasgow G3 8AR.

STEPHEN MUSGROVE Poet, with three books printed, *The Legend Of The Raven's Stone, The Autumn Rose* and *Saphirra.* Fourth book soon, *Fourth Litany*. All privately printed. 12 Somerset Rd, Springwell, Sunderland SR3 4EB.

KASANDRA O'CONNELL Bit of a knowledgeable type but won't suffer fools gladly so if you want info on something in Ireland you better give something in return. 4 Longwood Ave, Dublin 8, Eire.

DR MARIE MULVEY ROBERTS Unusual author on varied weird topics. Has also been the series editor for the books which loosely gathered together under the banner of 'Subversive Women'. These books can be found through Thoemmes Press, 85 Park Street, Bristol BS1 5PJ. More importantly she has been working on the *Handbook To Gothic Literature*. 48 Fraser Street, Windmill Hill, Bristol BS3 4LY.

DAWN RODGERS Strange woman and interesting. Was doing some form of video thesis about Goth, which may or may not be available and is a writer, of books which may or may not be published yet, mainly concerning the possible effects of genetic engineering and their effects on the population of a small town bordering on Yorkshire/Lancashire (as though the rest of us would notice!) during a future civil war. Arrunden Laithe, Cartworth Moor, Holmfirth, Huddersfield HD7 1QS.

IAN SAWICKI *Deathly Dreams*, written by Ian and illustrated by Alison Burgess (poet/*Skeleton Girls* co-editor), £1.50 + sae. 10 Hatherton Rd, Cannock, Staffs WS11 1HG.

LUCIUS SHEPARD Author of *The Golden* (Millennium 1993 £5.99), a Vampire detective story!

STEVE SHEPHERD Goth photographer at gigs. May have prints for sale. May also be prepared to contribute to fanzines. The quality of his photos is certainly good enough. 20 Deepdene Rd, Welling, Kent DA16 3QL.

THE SISTERS OF NO MERCY This is an enchanting foursome (no libels intended) of Cleo Cordell, Portia de Costa, Roxanne and Cheryl.

SIMON SMITH Artist/illustrator. 120 Exeter Rd, Exmouth, Devon EXB 1QQ.

STEVE SNEYD Poet of all sorts, frequently published. 1 Nowell Place, Almondbury, Huddersfield, West Yorkshire HD5 8PB.

JAMIE SPRACKLEN Writer and published poet, outside of his self-inflicted duties as Editor of *Monas Hieroglyphica* fanzine. 58 Seymour Rd, Hadleigh, Benfleet, Essex SS7 2HL.

BRIAN STABLEFORD Vampire Author. *The Empire Of Fear* (Simon & Schuster - 88). 113 St Peter's Rd, Reading RG6 1PG.

ME (Part II) *Goth With The Wind, The Man In The Byron Mask*. Crap? I'll get back to you.

HANNAH STAUNTON Novelist-in-waiting. Every now and then somebody sends you something which has you reeling and this here Hannah has two novels which she's actually finished, unlike most people who talk about doing it - *Aram Cruentam* and *Noster Eris*, both of which are fabulous. They need tidying

150 ANNE SUDWORTH

up and greater clarity and such dreary matters that all writers have to attend to, but here, if we stick to the essence, we have a girl who could stamp on the head of James Herbert, be the spirit guide of Stephen King, be in the same whirlwind that tosses Storm Constantine about and yet still retain her own direct style and direction. Hannah deals with modern horror. Her ideas are simple yet grandiose. She will be a major star for any publisher sensible enough to cajole her. Nobody has impressed me so much with their written work, for its dense appeal. She's had stories accepted by Storm Constantine's 'Visionary Tongue' project so you can probably contact her via them easiest, because she is prone to rove around. (The 'moving target' theory, probably.)

LINDA STEVENS (a.k.a. 'Gabrielle') Artist and designer working on 3-D compositions on board. Eh? Got a ten week course in vampire studies run at Warwick University and has done Vampire lectures! Has postcards and an exclusive tarot pack available, and has just finished writing the book to go with it. Possible exhibition of what critics call her 'gothic abstract' art for 97. She is available for commission and could probably enliven any project. Flat 1, 23 Blatchington Rd, Hove BN3 3HL.

ANNE SUDWORTH Take my word for it, Anne, whose work I cannot reproduce here, because it's all twilight scenes, in colour, is an amazing artist. She designs clothes, models and sculpts too but I have no details of those activities. Outside of the music in this book, she is *the* most talented individual here, her talent going way beyond awesome. She's done a cover for a Storm Constantine book, which you may have seen but otherwise you'll simply have to hope you get the chance to attend one of her gallery exhibitions sometime. If she does one, pop along because she does do limited runs of prints of certain paintings. The paintings can go from £400 up to several thousand but the prints are only £20 and just £12 for Goths!

PHOTO: ROBERT BLANE

151 LESLEY WILKINSON

That's the bargain of your life. Phone studio on 01744-753739.

ARACELI URIARTE Works for the BBC World Service and broadcasts Goth material whenever possible. 98 Rockingham Street, Meadow Row, 1st Floor, Elephant & Castle, London SE1 6PG.

JONATHAN VAUGHAN Provides design for The Whores Of Babylon. Jonathan is a designer who can handle photography, video, montages/collages, whatever you require. He's also working on a fanzine idea, possibly *The Chronicles Of Babylon*, a dummy of which looks excellent. 27 Whitchurch Rd, Bishopsworth, Bristol BS13 7RS.

FREDA WARRINGTON Authoress and another dirty woman. Bad enough you have to live in Leicester but when you're working in medical illustration (anyone who has seen Gray's *Anatomy* will know what I mean), little wonder you crave having a novel published. But Freda made it happen. *A Blackbird In Silver* appeared in 86, followed by three sequels. These, she says, are closer to Moorcock than anything, yet her vampire series, starting with the extraordinarily beautiful and teeth-gnashingly brilliant *A Taste Of Blood Wine* (followed by a *Dance In Blood Velvet* and *The Dark Blood Of Poppies*) is nearer her heart. Now she's off on a supernatural dark fantasy theme. Small wonder when you've moved to a small Derbyshire village surrounded by frogs, horses and bears. A sound woman, listen - "I'm fascinated by religion and why people need it; this is another pet theme of mine, but in the end it's the characters who really count". Her books can be found on NEL, Pan Macmillan and Penguin. You would be seriously missing out not to investigate further. 47 Station Street, Castle Gresley, Swadlingcote, Derbyshire DE11 9JU.

CHRIS WEBB Illustrator specialising in black and white. T-shirts, etc. 43 Lyndhurst Drive, Kidderminster, Worcs DY10 2PT.

CARMEN WILCOX A poet much feted by the Westgate Press. They praise her traditional, lyrical beauty ("something lacking in today's verse"), and apparently her books are also beautifully illustrated. Available from: Paradise Press, Westhall, Halesworth, Suffolk IP19 8RH.

LESLEY WILKINSON I didn't really know where to put Lesley. Born into a world that didn't quite suit her, her in-built fascination with the occult has seen her getting involved with virtually every activity she can. A graduate in Fine Art (formerly a designer for indie labels) she sculpts, paints and draws. Then it's breakfast. She is editor/publisher of *Occular*, the illustrated journal of Paganism and Occult, fantasy and surreal horror fiction. Then lunch. In the afternoon she's the founder of Creatrix P.A.N. (Pagan Artist Network) and also the regional co-ordinator for the Pagan Federation. Studiously avoided by all local clergy on the grounds that she has admitted to being a witch, she has certain books available as well, and has designed a new Ouija board, which you will find listed under 'Ouija Board'. She never sleeps. Too busy writing her book *Burn Witch Burn*, an investigation into what actually lies behind the hysterical media onslaught over the Satanic child abuse scares which always end up completely without foundation. The book announces 'foreword by Michael Howard' so there's a bad name to be lumbered with! Rosewood Cottage, Langtoft, Driffield, East Yorks YO25 0TQ.

RODDY WILLIAMS Another quality illustrator whose work he describes as veering between Gothic and Industrial-Gothic and has already appeared in *Dementia* and *Monas Heiroglyphics*. Flat C, 37 Stoneleigh Street, London W11 4DU.

ME (III) Got it - *Gothzilla*! (Writing under that much abused pseudonym Crystal De Canta.)

WENDY WOOTTON Another Black Lace author with Gothic links, of sorts, and not only the cool black plastic business card of which I'm deeply envious. She's into cats and computers, as is anybody of taste, Ancient Egypt, Vampires, Japan, which is all fine, and only blows it with Star Trek and Sci-Fi which...hmmm...well.... etc. "It's what's going on inside that counts," she explains and right now her spleen wants out. Interestingly, her first story was entitled *The Man In Black* but since 92 she has sold a ton of stories, writing under the names of Delaney Silver and Dorothy Starr. It's mainly smut of course, as everyone goes for that, but she's had two serious novels printed by Nexus, *Adventures in The Pleasurezone* and *Return To The Pleasurezone*. She writes as Portia de Costa (three Black Lace potboilers - *Gemini Heat, The Tutor* and *The Devil Inside*) and as Elaine Platero has a novel printed in America by Masquerade, *Lessons And Lovers*. Furthermore she is one of The Sisters Of No Mercy - offering Excellent Erotica For Discerning Deviants. (Fax 01924 281213)

ZOMBA Formerly Ash to some of you. Has jovially popped more than a few addresses my way. Was working on interesting video vampire project but it got shelved. Now self-proclaimed transgender planet slut and working for international fanzines and with a couple of bands. Knows more than a thing or two and well worth contacting. 'The House That Dripped Blud', 7 Cranbourne Drive, Hoddesdon, Herts EN11 0QQ.

Occult/Pagan

ALCHEMY Discussion site: (alchemy forum@colloqium.co.uk.)

ASSOCIATION OF HEDGEWITCHES Contact circle for witches working solo or in tandem - no membership fees or hierarchical structure of society. Geoff Wright, 67 Lewin Rd, London SW16 6JZ.

BRITISH PSYCHIC & OCCULT SOCIETY PO Box 1112, London N10 3XE.

CADUCEUS BOOKS New and second hand - Occult, Magick, Esoteric, Paganism, Alternative Health, Tarot etc. 14 Holgate Rd, York YO2 4AB.

CENTRE FOR PAGAN STUDIES Run by Ken Rees offers courses and workshops in mythology, shamanism and witchcraft. Can also put enquirers onto various pagan networks, magical groups and correspondence courses. Researcher and teacher since the 70s. Flat B, 5 Trinity Rise, Tulse Hill, London SW2 2QP.

CLOAK AND DAGGER Wooden things (wands, athanes), spell boxes, robes, altar cloths, Celtic costumes, etc. 33 Bottrill Street, Nuneaton, Warks.

DRAGON'S BREATH Occult shop. Hollybush Studio, Fore Street, Tintagel.

HEART OF ALBION PRESS More Earth Mysteries than Pagan but you may find something of interest, including Finnish poet Katima's book *23 Cantos For The Goddess*. 2 Cross Hill Close, Wymeswold, Loughborough, LE12 6UJ.

HOUSE OF THE GODDESS Working Pagan temple. 33 Oldridge Rd, London SW12 8PN.

ISAEUM MORGAN GODDESS GROUP Open group interested in all aspects of the Goddess and how she is today. Write to Kath, Flat 5, 48 Delaunays Rd, Crumpsall, M8 6RF.

ISIS NEW AGE CENTRE 4 Corn Exchange, Manchester M4.

152

JD CRAFTS Shop with essential oils, incenses, candles, ritual equipment, gods and goddesses sculptures etc. 14 Holgate Rd, York YO2 4AB.

THE LITTLE RED BOOK Ultimate wicca guide. Oakleaf Circle, PO Box 513, Bamber Bridge, Preston, Lancs PR5 6UZ.

LONDON TAROT GROUP PO Box 3719, London SW17 7RG. (They'll be expecting you.)

MANCHESTER PAGAN WHEEL Manchester Society. Box 18, 1 Newton St, Manchester M1 1HH.

MANDRAKE Leading new edge publisher. PO Box 250, Oxford OX1 1AP.

THE MAY TREE New Age and Curiosity shop with jewellery, aromatherapy, 'green' toys...(She-Hulk?). Herbs, etc. Unit 34-36, Corn Exchange, Manchester M4.

NOX L SENNIT Magick and magickal art. 15 Oxford St, Mexborough, Yorkshire SG4 9RL.

OCCULTIQUE A shop offering two services really, based around occult paraphenalia, books and objects. The book selection in their catalogue is huge and varied, as their a-z goes from Alchemy to Erotica, Magic, Martial Arts, Psychedelic Drug Culture, Sacred texts, satanism, witchraft and Yoga, with all the wibbley bits in between. More interesting is the equally varied range of products available. - herbs and spices, resins, bottles and jars, tinctures, perfume concentrates, essential oils, mortars and pestles, incense - some cool and some bollocks. How about Merlin Incense, a snip at £1.50 but is it really "created from the attributes and fabled nature of Merlin"? Very possibly not. There are anointing oils and perfumes, ritual equipment, candles, virgin sheep parchment, vellum, scales, robes, crystal balls, magick mirrors, aura goggles, runes, ouija, pendulums, reproduction occult, fantasy figures, esoteric jewellery, pentagrams, ankhs...the works...and the hand engraved Egyptian cartouches for £40 are lovely. You need this catalogue, so phone 01604-27727 or fax 01604-603860 to find out how much to send. 13 Kettering Rd, Northampton NN1 4AW.

OUIJA BOARD Interesting new design available which includes simple phrases and info to make communication easier. Board alone £5, or with book £7. Cheque payable to L. Wilkinson, Rosewood Cottage, Langtoft, Driffield, E Yorks YO25 0TQ.

OXFORD GOLDEN DAWN OCCULT SOCIETY (Net - http://www.compulink.co.uk/-mandrake/ogdos.htm) (e-mail: mandox@cix.compulink.co.uk)

THE PAGAN FEDERATION Founded in 71, this could tell you anything you want to know. Works to "make Paganism accessible to people genuinely seeking a nature-based spiritual path". It's all over the country and has links with other groups (Druid, Wiccan, Nordic, Celtic, Eco-magic and women's spirituality groups). It works for the rights of Pagans as in religious rights. You couldn't want for a better place to start. They also do the magazine *Pagan Dawn*, and as well as being good visually it really is accessible because I, as a typically crass member of the Order Of The Oaf, found it easy to digest. (Net- http://www.tardis.ed.ac.uk/-ipf/pf.html), (e-mail PaganDawn @paganfed.demon.co.uk) That e-mail will actually send you into the heart of the whole PF set-up too. BM BOX 7097, London WC1N 3XX.

PAGAN HOSPICE AND FUNERAL TRUST A registered charity, dedicated to providing rites of passage to those of the Pagan faith. Membership £5 yearly

(£2.50 for OAPs and unemployed). They have an interesting newsletter and a bit of suitably chaste merchandise. They also advertise their own funeral service and, perhaps most importantly of all, an emergency number, which will help you if you want to bring a dead family member home and the hospital refuses! BM Box 3337, London WC1N 3XX.

THE PAGAN INDEX Ultimate Pagan guide? A thousand listings, which explains why my Pagan section is short. Via House Of The Goddess, 33 Oldridge Rd, London SW12 8PN.

'PRECIOUS STONES' This is a book by Lesley Wilkinson but she offers other titles, by other authors. Books available from the same address include *Simple Spells From A Witches Spellbook, Rune Magick, High Magic's Aid, Easy Astral Projection, Crystal Magick, Making Magickal Tools & Ritual Equipment.* Send a SAE to Rosewood Cottage, Langtoft, Driffield, East Yorkshire YO25 0TQ.

KEN REES Does classes and workshops in Witchcraft, Shamanism and Magic. Flat B, 5 Trinity Rise, Tulse Hill, London SW2 2QP.

SCARAB Tarot/colour therapy. PO Box 77, London W14 0QQ.

SKOOB Occult Bookshop. 17 Sicilian Avenue, Southampton Row, London WC1A 2QH.

TOWER ARCHIVES Various occult matters. Office 6, 5a Salop Street, Wolverhampton WV3 ORX.

24 HOUR OCCULT ANSWER LINE Queries on esoteric occult shops, mags, books etc. (0202-546234)

WICCA FEDERATION BM Box 7097, London WC1N 3XX.

WICCA STUDY GROUP BM Deosil, London WC1N 3XX.

WICCA Marian Green, BCM Quest, London WC1N 3XX.

JOHN GARTH WILKINSON Celtic, Gothic, Italian and Roman calligraphy. Provides illustrations and lettering for anything - menus, certificates, poems, artwork. Torphin House, Harburn, West Lothian.

Pagan publications

ASH 2 Kent View Rd, Vange, Basildon, Essex.

ACE OF RODS Contacts mag for pagan and wiccan scene. BCM Akademia, London WC1N 3XX.

AISLING "The New Voice Of Druidry." PO Box 196, London WC1A 2DY.

ALBION Wicca mag. Pete Ricketts, 43 Rowley St, Walsall WS1 2AX.

AT THE EDGE New interpretations of past and place in archaeology, folklore and mythology. 2 Cross Hill Close, Wymeswold, Loughborough LE12 6UJ.

THE BRIDESTONE All aspects of the Old religion in the New Age. PO Box 18, Hessle, E.Yorks. HU13 0HW.

BUFORA In case you thought the Rothwell footage wasn't Andy from Creaming Jesus the morning after the night before this is the place for you. 16 Southway, Burgess Hill, Sussex RH15 9ST.

CAROLINE'S NEW AGE ADVERTISER Pagan/esoteric mag. C. Blakeley, 164 Charlton Rd, Westbury on Trym, Bristol BS10 6NN.

153

ISTVAN KOLONICS

THE CAULDRON Pagan journal of old religion, Wicca and Earth mysteries. M. Howard, Caermorgan cottage, Caemorgan Rd, Aberteifi, Cymru, SA 43 1 QU. (It is important that you do *not* write 'The Cauldron' on the envelope.)

CELTIC CONNECTIONS Journal of Celtic culture. David James, Tamarisk Farm, West Bexington, Dorchester, Dorset, DT2 9DF.

CELTIC DAWN Prebendal Prens, Trime, Oxfordshire OX9 3AD.

CEREALOGIST Crop circles? George Wingfield, Hearne House, North Wootton, near Shepton Mallet, Somerset BA4 4HW.

THE CHALICE Quarterly New Age/esoteric mag. 16 Blenheim Rd, Beechwood, Newport, Gwent, S. Wales NP9 8JL.

CHAOS "Definitive mag for Chaos magicians, anarchists, iconoclasts, situationists, ufologists, illuminati, bedsit philosophers, media manipulators, paranoids, charlatans, mad scientists, dropouts, tunnel explorers, drug fiends, spies, subversives, moles and rebels." Joel Biroco, BCM Utopia, London WC1N 3XX.

CHAOS INTERNATIONAL All about Chaos magick. The Hermitage, East Morton, Keighley, West Yorkshire BD20 5UQ.

CHEIRON NEWS Gramayre, 6 Meadow Close, Bagworth, Leicester.

CHILDREN OF THE FOX Pagan mag of ancient magic. PO Box36, Whitley Bay, Tyne & Wear NE26 1TN.

CIRCULAR Barbara Davies, Old Stables, Lescrow, Cornwall PL23 1JS.

CLAN DEOSIL Quarterly journal. BM Pentacle, London WC1N 3XX.

CREATRIX Pagan Artist Network. A fast-growing network for painters, sculptors, writers, dancers, actors, photographer, poet or craftsperson. The members benefit from mutual support, info exchange, promotion of talent, media coverage, joint projects and there is the annual chance to win something called the Creatrix Chalice. Rosewood Cottage, Langtoft, Driffield, East Yorkshire Y025 0TQ.

THE CROP WATCHER Paul Fuller, 3 Selbourne Court, Tavistock Close, Romsey, Hampshire SO51 7TY.

CRYSTAL GATE Fantasy/poetry mag of new Renaissance movement. 104 Argyle Gardens, Upminster, Essex.

DALRIADA Celtic Pagan quarterly. Dunna-Beatha, 2 Brathwic Place, Brodick, Isle Of Arran KA27 8BN.

DARK LILY (The Reality Of The Left Hand Path) BCM Box 3406, London WC1N 3XX.

DEOSIL DANCE Pagan quarterly. Pentacle Enterprises, BM Pentacle, London WC1N 3 XX.

DRAGON'S BREW Edited by Dave Rankine and Ariadne Rainbird. The house magazine of Dragons Den, supplies of Occult and pagan paraphenalia and Cylch y Neidr coven. D K Rankine, 8 Connaught Rd, Roath, Cardiff CF2 3PT.

DRAGON CHRONICLES Draconian lore.The Dragon Trust, PO Box 3369, London SW6 6JN.

DRUID'S VOICE Half yearly journal of Council Of British Druid Orders. PO Box 29, St Leonard's On Sea, E Sussex TN37 7YP.

ISTVAN KOLONICS

154

EARTHWORKS Earth magic, ley lines, sites. 145 Ketts Hill, Norwich, Norfolk NR1 4HD.

ENIGMAS Regular publication by Strange Phenomena Investigations. UFOs, poltergeists, hauntings, spiritualism, life after death, etc. Malcolm Robinson, 41 The Braes, Tullibody, Clackmannanshire FK10 2TT.

FENRIR Journal Of Satanism and the Sinister. House magazine of the Nine Angle, whatever that might be. Rigeo Press, PO Box 228, York.

FORMAOS Quarterly occult art mag dedicated to Austin Osman Spare. Sothis Publishing, c/o Technique Studio, Unit A10, Hi-Tech House, 10 Blackfriars Street, Norfolk, NR3 1SF.

FORESIGHT UFOs etc. 44 Brockhurst Rd, Hodge Hill, Birmingham B36 8JB.

FORTEAN TIMES All-time classic magazine about oddities, beautifully researched, written and presented. People who saw their "man killed by landslide while having sex with chicken" will be unlikely to ever forget it. Freepost SW6096, Frome, Somerset BA11 1YA.

GANYMEDE Boy-God mag, dedicated to mystic Ralph Nicholas Chubb, C.E.R.O.S., 63 Knatchbull Rd, Camberwell, London SE5 9QR.

GATES OF ANNWYN Contact/news mag. BM Gates Of Annwyn, London WC1N 3XX.

GIPPESWIC The Odinshof Ipswich Hearth. O. Jennings, 42 Cemetery Rd, Ipswich, Suffolk.

GLOUCESTER EARTH MYSTERIES PO Box 258, Cheltenham GL53 0HR.

GNOSIS Cthonios Books, 7 Tamarisk Steps, Hastings, Sussex.

GREEN CIRCLE PO Box 280, Maidstone, Kent.

GREENLEAF FESTIVAL New Age newsletter. 96 Church Street, Redfield, Bristol.

GREENMANTLE Flat 2, 25 Goldsmid Rd, Brighton, Sussex.

HOBLINK Gay/bisexual pagan network. PO Box 45, Ramsey, Isle Of Man.

INFERNAL TEMPLER Thee Official Newsletter Ov Psychick Youth. PO Box 687, Halfway, Sheffield S19 5UX.

INSIGHT Occult magazine. 25 Calmore Close, Bournemouth, Dorset BH8 0NN.

ISIAN NEWS Newsletter of the Fellowship Of Isis. Clonegal Castle, Clonegal, Ennisworthy, Eire.

THE KABBALIST International Order Of Kabbalists. 25 Circle Gardens, Merton Park, London SW19 3JX.

KALLISTI Discordian journal from Templum Evertendum of the IOT. PO Box 57, Norwich NR2 2RX.

LAMP OF THOTH Magick, Thelema, Paganism. 31 Kings Avenue, Leeds 6.

THE LEY HUNTER Paul Deverux, PO Box 92, Penzance, Cornwall TR18 2XL.

THE LIGHTHOUSE Religion Of The Goddess. The Lantern Press, 1619A London Rd, Leigh On Sea, Essex SS9 2SQ.

YLIASTER DALETH

155

LONDON EARTH MYSTERIES R. Stephenson, Flat 6, 136 Bravington Rd, Queens Park, London W9 3AL.

LONE WOLF 20 Cedar Rd, Lancaster LA1 5RG.

MAGONIA Mag interpreting contemporary vision and beliefs. John Rimmer, John Dee Cottage, 5 James Terrace, Mortlake Churchyard, London SW14 8HB.

MARKSTONE Readings of the sacred landscape. Journal of Lincs and East Yorks Earth Mysteries group. R&J Dickinson, Glebe Farm House, Owmby by Spital, Lincolnshire LN2 3DR.

MERCURY Quarterly newsletter from British Astrological & Psychic Society. 77 Penryn Avenue, Fishermead, Wymeswold, Loughborough LE12 6UJ.

MEYN MAMVRO Ancient stones and sites of Cornwall. 51 Carn Bosavern, St Just, Penzance, Cornwall.

MOONSTONE Old Station Yard, Settle, N. Yorks.

NEW DIMENSIONS Metaphysics, Kabbala, New Age music etc. Dept 5, 1 Austin Close, Irchester, Northants NN9 7AX.

NORTHERN EARTH Northern Earth Mysteries Group. 10 Jubilee Street, Mytholmroyd, Hebden Bridge, W Yorks HX7 5NP.

NORTHERN UFO NEWS Jenny Randles, 37 Heathbank Rd, Stockport, Cheshire SK3 OUP.

NUIT ISIS Box 250 Oxford OX1 1AP.

OCCULAR "The Journal Of Occult, Paganism and Hollistics" is actually a normal, approachable zine dealing with subjects is a light way. Includes old mag *Masque* which merged into this, from the ultra-organised Lesley Wilkinson. Fantasy, Pagan, Occult, Horror and reviews. Rosewood Cottage, Acorn Lane, Langtoff, East Yorks YO25 OTQ.

OCCULTURE PO Box 687, Halfway, Sheffield S31 5UX.

ODINISM TODAY BM Edda, London WC1N 3XX.

O FORTUNA Quarterly journal of spiritual, magical and ecological progress. Esoteric subjects, beliefs and philosophies of all kinds. Folklore, poetry, art, kids pull-out sections with games and stuff. BCM Akademia, London WC1N 3XX.

OPHIR Order Of The Lamp, PO Box 1072, Incing, Sussex.

PAGAN ANIMAL RIGHTS 23 Highfield South, Rock Ferry, Wirral, Cheshire.

PAGAN LIFE The Irish Pagan Movement, Bridge House, Clonegal, Eniiscorthy, Co. Wexford, Eire.

PAGAN NEWS Phoenix Publications, PO Box 196, London WC1A 2DY.

PAGAN PRATTLE 52 Call Street, Leeds.

PAGAN VOICE Monthly newsletter of modern 'magickulture' and Paganism. 17 Blethwin Close, Henbury, Bristol BS10 7BH.

PENDRAGON Arthurian history and mythology of Britain. Fred Stedman Jones, Smithy House, Newton By Frodsham, Cheshire, WA6 6SX.

PHILOSPHER'S STONE Humorous occult mag! 59 Masons Rd, Hemel Hempstead, HP2 4QU.

PHOENIX 25 Rose Terrace, Moorview Park, Newcastle Upon Tyne.

PHOENYX Quarterly journal of Aquarian mysteries. BM Stargate, London WC1N 3XX.

QUEST Published since 1970. Articles on magic, witchcraft, divination, ritual and all aspects of modern, practical Western occultism. BCM - SCL Quest, London WC1N 3XX.

RILKO 2 journals per year, lectures, book service. R&V Cowley, 8 The Drive, New Southgate, London N11 2DY.

ROUND MERLINS TABLE Various occult articles. Quarterly. This is also the address for 'Servants Of The Light', where you can have a fifty lesson course on the Mystical Qabalah under strict supervision. PO Box 215, St Helier, Jersey, Channel Islands.

SACRED HOOP Shamanic/N. American stuff. 28 Cowl St, Evesham, Worcs WR11 4PL.

THE SILVER BRANCH Temple Of Avalon, BCM Ravenswake, London WC1N 3XX.

THE SILVER WHEEL Journal Of Native British Tradition. Eight years old and easy reading, about relevant matters. Silver Wheel also has its own range of publications. Anna Franklin, Windrush, High Tor West, Earl Shilton, Leicestershire.

SIRIUS Magazine dedicated to Pagan deities and allied occult topics. 15 Lonnant, Mydleton Park, Denbigh, Clwyd LL16 4AZ.

SKOOB OCCULT REVIEW 17 Sicilian Avenue, Southampton Row, London WC1A 2QH.

SOLAR COURIER Newsletter of Renaissance movement. P. Page, 104 Gardens, Upminster, Essex.

SPIRAL Starcraft, spirit, nature and psychic skills. 53 Hallet Way, Bude, Cornwall EX23 8PG.

STARFIRE A must for Thelemites. BCM Starfire, London WC1N 3XX.

SUT ANUBIS This comes from the Occultique people and is an interesting but slim occult mag that's easily accessible. Nothing heavy.

TALKING STICK This is just one of the most fantastic magazines in the world. If you're a pagan or whatever, your enjoyment will be thoroughly enhanced no doubt, but as your common and garden scruffy tosser without a belief in the world, I found it brilliant and not just the humour ("daemons are a boy's best friend"). Incidentally, the little self-proclaimed minxes who run this also hold fortnightly meetings in the upstairs room of the Black Horse pub in Rathbone Place (off Oxford St, near Tott. Ct Rd tube). Doors open 7.30, carnage begins 8.30. There are also regular talks taking place all over the place. You find out about those by turning up.

Dress - if you must. PO Box 3719, London SW17 8XT. I might have misread the PO Box number, so (Fax: 0181 672 1099.) (e-mail: rebis@easynet.co.uk).

THREE I PRESS Dept PW PO Box 407, Stoke On Trent ST1 3TB.

TOUCHWOOD Not, sadly, a zine dedicated to Catweazle's brooding familiar but a quarterly magazine about the British hereditary tradition. PO Box 36, Whitely Bay, Tyne & Wear NE26 1TN.

TRADITION Keeping traditions and customs alive. PO Box 57, Hornchurch, Essex RM11 1DU.

THE UFO DEBATE Bi-monthly UFO mania. 40 Stubbings Way, Shipley, West Yorkshire BD18 2EZ.

UFOs - A Mercer Theory UFOs? Don't make me laugh. Look - human beings develop, over time, correct? Look at prehistoric man? Only the old singer from Iron Maiden still bears even the remotest resemblance. So in a similar timespan human beings will have mastered time travel, right? They'll be told all the usual bollocks about not messing around with events and all that - but what's to stop them getting a touch of nostalgia? What's to stop them having the same interests as us? Organised holidays? Nothing, you bastards. UFOs aren't special, they're archaeologists of their era(s), coming back for a look. Some of them are very, very naughty, going back BC and dropping plans for pyramids where some gormless architect stumbles across them and makes a name for himself with useless inventions that can't change time. Aliens? Aliens bollocks - they're just us, aren't they? That's what we develop into, making improvements here and there for different atmospheres on different planets. We used to be fish for Gawd's sake. And abductions - well obviously our bodies will have changed in a few millennia, so they'll be after a few illegal substances - protein for example. Who cares what they're doing. And UFOs being seen? It's probably joyriders, flipping about through space, pissed. They're buzzing some town for a laugh. UFOs are like corn circles. People in cardigans get all excited about it and then someone gets bored and admits they've been doing it for a laugh.

THE WEB OF WYRD Wicca and occultism. Box 9290, London WC1N 3XX.

WEREWOLF Kevin Lock, PO Box 77, Sunderland, Tyne & Wear SR11EB.

WHITE DRAGON Newsletter of Mercian Paganlink, lots of useful Midlands stuff. 'Paganlink Mercia' 103 Abbotswood Close, Winyates Green, Redditch, Worcestershire B98 0QF.

WICCAN GATEWAY NEWSLETTER Ferm Hollow, School Rd, Ruyton XI Towns, Shrewsbury, Salop SV4 1JT.

THE WILD PLACES Paranormal. 42 Victoria Rd, Mount Charles, St Austell, Cornwall PL25 4QD.

WISHT MAEN Devon Earth Mysteries. Condors, Extreet, North Taunton, Devon EX20 2HB.

THE WITCHES BREW Magazine of the Autumn Star Lodge: about Wicca and Paganism. 57 Colesmead Rd, Redhill, Surrey RH1 2EN.

WOOD & WATER Goddess-centred, feminist-influenced pagan quarterly. 7 Parliament Hill, London NW3 2TH.

Societies

BAT CONSERVATION TRUST The only UK society dedicated to conserving bats and their roost sites. Send £1.40 for 100 adhesive ad labels. And £10 for a standard annual membership, or £7 unemployed/student/retired rate. You receive info packs, quarterly news letters and details of events around the countryside, and *Bat News*, their little mag which includes details of loads of interesting bat-related publications. There's even slides to buy and nice badges. 10 Bedford Cottages, Gt. Brington, Northampton NN7 4JE.

E F BENSON Allen Downend, 88 Tollington Park, London N4 3RA.

BIRMINGHAM UNIVERSITY GOTHSOC Formed 93. Organises gigs, trips to gigs. Open to non-students. It's probably closed down by now but you can try. Gothsec, c/o Birmingham University, Guild Of Students, Edgbaston Park Rd, Edgbaston B15 2TT.

BRITISH FANTASY SOCIETY Horror, Annual convention, fiction booklets and newsletter. Di Wathen, 15 Stanley Rd, Morden, Surrey SM4 5DE.

BRITISH PSYCHIC AND OCCULT SOCIETY Now don't mess these people around, this is serious. An organisation that investigates all types of unexplained psychic phenomena, including 'ghosts' and reported cases of vampirism but that doesn't mean they want saddoes writing to boast 'I drink blood', accompanied by a photograph smeared with ribena. David Farrant, President, has also written a book, *Beyond The Highgate Vampire*. It's a cool book, but the society is not worth considering unless you are a calm, sensible individual. PO Box 1112, London N10 3XE.

BUFORA British UFO Research Association. The Leys, 2c Leyton Rd, Harpenden, Herts AL5 2TL.

CCCS Centre For Circle Studies, responsible for *The Circular*. SKS, 20 Paul Street, Frome, Somerset BA11 1DX.

CERES/TORRO Circles Effect Research and Tornado and Storm Research Organisations, one of which publishes *Journal Of Meteorology*. 54 Frome Road, Bradford-On-Avon, Wiltshire BA15 1LD.

157

158

157 JACKIE ASKEW 158 VAMPIRES R US

EIGHTEEN NINETIES SOCIETY Deals with all writers of period, many of them ghost story writers. Dr G Krishnamurti, 97d Brixton Rd, London SW9 6EE.

GHOST STORY SOCIETY Annual convention, newsletters and booklets of previously unprinted work. Jeff Dempsey, 2 Looe Road, Croxteth, Liverpool L11 6LJ.

THE GOTHIC APPRECIATION SOCIETY P. Hussain, Flat No. 4, 150 Trinity Street, Huddersfield HD1 HDU.

GOTHIQUE FILM SOCIETY 75 Burns Avenue, Feltham, Middx.

THE GOTHIC SOCIETY Actually changed the title of its quarterly mag (*The Goth*) so as not to be confused with the scummy likes of you, I'm afraid. You'd better pretend you're some old tosser when you apply! Very serious, high quality organisation who also provide professionally produced reprints of old works. Pricey, but you get what you pay for in this world and they don't fob you off with any old rubbish. Chatham House, Gossill Rd, Chislehurst, Kent BR7 5NS.

GOTHIC SOCIETY The old Nosferatu thing, which produced *Grimoire*. No news whether that carries on. 138 Canterbury Rd, Harrow, Middx HA1 4PB.

RIDER HAGGARD APPRECIATION SOCIETY Roger Allen, 27 Deneholm , Monkseaton, Whitely Bay, NE25 9AU.

HUNT SABOTEURS ASSOCIATION PO Box 1, Carlton, Nottingham NG4 2JY.

LONDON EARTH MYSTERIES CIRCLE Rob Stevenson, PO Box 1035, London W2 6XX.

ARTHUR MACHEN SOCIETY G Brangham, The Cottage, 14 New Market Street, Usk, Gwent NP5 1AT.

MERVYN PEAKE SOCIETY Frank Surrey, 2 Mount Park Rd, Ealing, London W5 2RP.

THE POWYS SOCIETY Covers all members of the Powys family, especially John Cowper. I admit I haven't a clue who that is, I was pathetically hoping to appear intellectual. John Batten, Keepers Cottage, Montracute, Somerset TA15 6XN.

THE TILLING SOCIETY EF Benson organisation. Cynthia Reavell, Martello Bookshop, 26 High Street, Rye, East Sussex TN31 7JJ.

Vampire

JACKIE ASKEW Author of vampire novel *SunDown ... SunRise*, a story set inside the Goth music scene. Jackie has done everything to do with this bar printing it - written, edited, advertised and distributed it, costing her everything she had. Worth getting the first edition now as they're going fast. 416 page paperback. £6.35 UK, £7.50 Europe, Elsewhere £10.50 including Airmail, or £7.50 at surface mail rate. Mail order only. 90 minute tape taster available. £1.50 UK, £2.50 Europe, £3.50 elsewhere (includes voucher for £1.50 off novel) Or send C90 tape plus return postage. Cedar Rise, Emmett Hill, Chale Green, Ventnor, Isle Of Wight.

BRAM STOKER SOCIETY Mr Albert Power, 43 Castle Court, Killiney Hill Road, Co. Dublin, Ireland.

BRAM STOKER Philosophical Society, Graduates Memorial Building, Trinity College, Dublin 2, Ireland.

THE CULT OF THE VAMPIRE Now we don't really have room for everything that Anton, the representative who contacted me, has spoken of, but if you are seriously into vampirism then this must be the one for you. And I do mean serious, not you sad white faced clowns who like to boast about being something you're not, a bit like pulling your belt tight and declaring that bondage is your middle name. This modern cult apparently goes back to something called Ordo Anno Mundi, founded in England in 1888. There are seven degrees of initiation the vampire goes through in training and the first alone can take a whole year. It'll be nip and tuck whether you achieve immortality before you're dead! But I shouldn't joke. The final outcome, I am assured, is that Mr or Mrs Vampire are able to conquer death by leaving their physical body behind and at the same time achieve control over the elemental forces which make up the universe. I take that to mean we're not dealing with what we typically regard as Vampires. No body is the key. Either way, as their early practitioners are over a hundred years old I presume you're granted an audience with them somehow as proof that what they're talking about can be had, otherwise you are simply relying on faith.

Firstly you learn Magic - evocation, spellcasting, ritual and divination, and certain key elements of the secret tradition are revealed. The second degree is Pure Invocation, the third is Transcending the Physical Body, the Fourth is the Werewolf or Animal Transformation stage. The fifth degree continues 'core tradition elements', Six admits one into the Senate and the final stage makes one eligible for the post of King or Queen. An eighth degree exists only in so much as that is what it is to be a vampire who can live on, undead. The chief temple is located in Staffordshire and apparently many of the members prefer to do their first degree by correspondence. Either way if you do have leanings in this way and haven't simply collected three Damned albums too many and completely missed the point of virtually everything in your life then write. BCM Box 6485, London WC1N 3XX.

DRACULA EXPERIENCE The Dracula Museum, no less. Currently trying to operate Whitby Dracula Society, having already started *The Demeter* magazine, not bad at £1.20 plus A4 sae. The Dracula experience is "a walk-through exhibition, excellently demonstrating the travels of Vlad Dracula from Transylvania via Whitby to London, towards the end of the 19th century. Life-like models and animation guide the visitors through an insight into the world of Vlad Dracula and his servants." Night visits can be made by special appointment which scores high on the credometer. The aims of the society are a quarterly newsletter, a database of likeminded souls to be circulated freely, to organise annual conventions and 'Vamps and Tramps' balls. It is not, they rasp, "our aim to promote vampirism, blood-lust or the occult" so those people just stay away. Be gone! Vanda, 9 Marine Parade, Whitby, North Yorks.

DRACULA SOCIETY The Membership Secretary, 213 Wulfsten St, East Acton, London W12 OAB. Or RJ Leake, 36 Elliston House, 100 Wellington St, Woolwich, London SE18 6QF.

EREBUS RISING A Vampire Association and the ambitious new project from Donna Crow, the woman who brought out *Necroscope* zine. This is to be a society focussing mainly on the idea of the vampire as a reality. It will be consulting experts in the fields of psychology, philosophy, religion, physiology etc. Highfield House, 27 Little Green Lane, Farnham, Surrey GU9 8JJ.

THE HOUSE OF DRACULA May have a few back issues of this zine available. Jo, Flat 1, 112 St George's Terrace, Newcastle Upon Tyne NE2 2DP.

SEAN MANCHESTER The man. The Legend. The address. PO Box 542, Highgate, London N6 6BG.

ANNA POWELL Lecturer in Gothic and gender studies, 30 Grange Rd, Chorlton-Cum-Hardy, Manchester M21 1NY.

DR MARIE MULVEY ROBERTS Has lectured on Anne Rice. University of the West Of England, Fishponds, Bristol. Or 48 Fraser St, Windmill Hill, Bristol BS3 4LY (See Individuals)

THEE VAMPIRE GUILD I'm not sure what service they offer other than the fantastic *Crimson* mag which is worth getting sometimes just for the cover artwork but they make things interesting and fun and they have also done two great compilations, on CD/MC of a vampire theme, involving a full international cast of bands. This will obviously run and run. Ostensibly the leader, Phill White, describes the Guild as existing for "the study and enjoyment of Vampirian lore and culture". 82 Rip Croft, Portland, Dorset DT5 2EE.

THE VAMPYRE SOCIETY I can't really tell you anything because from their lofty position they regard me with false teeth bared and suspicious eyes. It seems a shame they so eagerly debase their own beliefs and fascinations appearing on rubbish like *The James Whale Show* sitting moodily around a coffin which opens to reveal the podgy host himself. Jolly exciting. I feel sure they organise events for all those of you who take this lark seriously and I fully expect their professionalism shines through. Their zine, *The Velvet Vampire* magazine is meant to be excellent quality. PO Box 68, Keighley, W. Yorkshire BD22 6RU.

VAMPYRE SOCIETY Allen J. Gittens here actually started off the first Vampyre Society and then the above popped up, opting for the fashionable end of the market. Allen's smaller mag offers the readers quite straightforward participation and while there are hardly any 'exclusives' to be found when dealing with material of this sort, he tries to give it all quite a serious edge. Just think of the nutters Allen has to contend with. "I've had letters purporting to come from real supernatural vampires, and others from confused ladies who believe I'm one of the genuine

159

160

undead and want to share my coffin. The reality is that I'm a very mortal vegetarian who can't stand the sight of blood." It also offers members free reign to contribute articles and addresses are provided so that you can forever be writing to each other going, 'ooh, yes...I know'. 38 Westcroft, Chippenham, Wilts SN14 OLY.

V.A.T. This (Vampires Against Tories) is the funniest zine I've ever encountered. It's very rarely seen, which is a shame because Editor Kev himself is a sage, of sorts. Knows his onions. The thing is a glorious vampiristic nightmare ride of gleeful self deprecating nonsense. It bases everything around the Vampire world in general and Kev and Chrissie are right in there, but instead of just sitting back talking garbage, being self-important, they crash drunkenly around at events or gawp in admiration at the people they worship. And the fanzine is such a mess that you'll be discovering new bits day after day. A real treasure. Kev Demant, 53 Hatton House, Hindmarsh Close, Cable Street, London E1 8JJ.

USA

Bands

AND CHRIST WEPT Robert Riscassi - guitar/synth/prog., Chris Massey - vocals. Formed 92 and livening up Seattle with Techno-Industrial-EBM-Goth-Death Metal. They have a pioneering spirit which makes them throw back their heads and laugh when people compare them to Ministry, Skinny Puppy et al. Sadly, while they're laughing someone picks their pockets. This is a hard, brave world. 'Destroy Existence' CD. 1405 E. John St. #3, Seattle, WA 98112. (Fax: 02066 54090)

AURORA Patricia Nigianii and Peter Spilles (Project Pitchfork). Firmly attractive. Cleopatra, 9726 Sepulveda St. D-82, Los Angeles, CA 90045.

ANGELHOOD Now this is what I call violent disorder, duo Mykel and Kelee roping together every nightmare of sound you could possibly imagine. They're spooky as Hell. Red vinyl 7", 'Whitechapel', planned, about Jack The Ripper. Also run *Dead Eyes* fanzine, distribution and a shop. PO Box 24, Bradley, IL 60915.

ANGEL OF THE ODD Aztian Records, PO Box 5672 Buena Park, CA 90622.

APOCALYPSE THEATRE Hope - keybds/vocals. Plus others. Debut MC '13'. Often compared to Specimen meets Virgin Prunes. Kitsch and brazen. PO Box 73654, Washington DC 20056.

MICHAEL ASTON Yes, ex Gene Loves Jezebel. 'Why Me Why This Why Now' CD, opting for sleeker, noise-infested material, working alongside former punk guitarist Mick Rossi. Triple X, PO Box 862529, Los Angeles, CA 90086-2529.

ASTRO VAMPS Poppyish Goth. Formed 91 by Daniel and Eyajo, releasing 'Savage Garden' LP, then vampish 'Blood & Flowers' EP in 93. Now signed to Candlelight for three CDs. Daniel and his 'ghoulfriend' Linda also working on side project, Radio Ghost. 3823 Percy Street 1a, CA 90023.

AUTUMN Neil Mckay - guitar/prog., Julie Plante - vocals, Jeff Leyda - bass. Formed 94. Exiled in the mid-West gives an air of sadness to their work. 'A Waiting Time' demo. 2546 Portland Ave South, Minneapolis, MN 55404.

BABYLONIAN TILES PO Box 7427, Orange, CA 92613.

PHOTO: SUSAN JENNINGS

161 162

BELLES ARTES 663 Monroe Avenue #2, Elizabeth, New Jersey 07208.

BELLTOWN 77041 Melrose Avenue, Los Angeles, CA 90046.

BERLIN BLACK 16419 Ledge Trail, San Antonio, Texas 78232.

BLACK ATMOSPHERE Chris (ex Christian Death) - guitars/vocals, Brian - keybds, Kenyatta - bass and Tom - percussion. Several standard Goth demos available. PO Box 20836, Seattle, WA 98102.

BLACK DAHLIA A Gothic Doors? 'Nomad' CD. PO Box 253, Wilingboro, New Jersey 08046.

BLADE FETISH Marc Linder (ex Anvil Wind, Null And Void), Ashkelon Sain (This Ascension, Trance To The Sun) and Matt Ballesteros (This Ascension). Formed late 91. Deep, dark and lively. 'Absinthe' CD. c/o Tess Records, PO Box 206, Santa Barbara, CA 93102.

BLACK TAPE FOR A BLUE GIRL Coming out of electronic project 'Projekt Electronic America' in 86, main man Sam manipulates the collaborations of others. According to poor Sam, the band grew out of depression or, better still, "the harsh slap of loneliness". Personal, introspective music. That's why so many people can slip into the seeping wounds created by samples textured time and time again to sound like virgin, pristine music. Projekt, Box 1591 Garden Grove, CA 92642-1591.

BLEAK Darker offshoot of Lycia. 'Vane' CD. c/o Projekt.

C17H19NO3 Slow and brooding, dark and vengeful, this is one of the many projects of the multi-faceted John Bergin, showcasing his "skull-expanding soundtrack for a film by a twenty-first century Bosch". PO Box 45182, Kansas City, MO 64171.

CARCRASH INTERNATIONAL I wasn't sure they were still going, but Dave Roberts clearly will not be stopped. 'Fragments Of A Journal In Hell' MC included Matt Green, Bari-Bari, Nicky Garrett and David Glass. c/o Cleopatra.

THE CHANGELINGS Regeana Morris (ex Trio Nocturna), Nick Pagan, Paul Mercier, Chandler Rentz and Damon Young. Waltzes, fugues and suchlike in the typically enchanting post-Deadcandance manner. PO Box 5583, Atlanta, GA 31107. (e-mail : changelngs@aol.com)

CHRISTIAN DEATH Why are people still confused? Christian Death was, initially, Rozz, Valor and Gitane, with their ever-changing cast of semi-regulars. After Rozz departed Christian Death was Valor and Gitane. Now it's Valor. It's perfectly simple. The fact that old material constantly resurfaces from the original period alters nothing. After Rozz left if he'd wanted to stop Valor he would have done so, but Valor took on the role, developing a particular sound and direction according to *his* taste. Christian Death (both periods) are going to end up as one of the most important underground bands of all time. Life as Art. PO Box 486, Billerica, MA 01821-0486.

CHRISTIANA Some people say Concrete Blonde-ish, I say "if Hole were interesting". 10 Jamaica Way, Suite 12A, Boston, MA 02130.

CHRISTUS CHRISTUS PO Box 2209 Scottsdale, Arizona 85252.

CRADLE OF THORNS Tamera Slayton - vocals, Ty Elam - vocals (and the man who once released thousands of live cockroaches at a gig), Kris Kohls - drums, Dave File - guitar, Rohan - keybds,

161 BLACK TAPE FOR A BLUE GIRL 162 ROZZ WILLIAMS AND GITANE DEMONE
163 CRUCIFORM - DEMIAN DORRANCE AND STEPHANIE GENIZA 164 THE CURTAIN SOCIETY

PHOTO: SUSAN JENNINGS

163

Anon - bass. Malevolence personified according to people who slavered over their 'Feed Us' and 'Download This' CDs. Some people suggest this is a March Violets for the 90's. No, it's madder. PO Box 862529, LA, CA 90086-2529. (Fax: 213/221-2778)

CRIMSON MOON 'Into The Nocturnal Forest' demo (95) available. "Five dirges of Vampiric art as cold as the stare of the serpent." 808 N. Grandview #21, Covina, CA 91723.

CRUCIFORM Demian Dorrance - music, Stephanie Geniza - vocals. Begun by Demian as solo project in 93, it takes classical theory into the electronic realm and doubles everything up and against itself for new effect. Anything goes, as long as it makes exquisite sense. Several contributions to compilations so far. CD planned for 97. The spirit of Projekt Records taken one step further into the Goth arena I should say. PO Box 12245 El Cajon, California 92022.

THE CURTAIN SOCIETY Roger Lavallee - vocals/guitar/bits, Ron Mominee - bass, and Duncan Arsenault - drums. More stimulating examples of how Goth with its well established ethereal exponents and fledgling fetishistic implants is developing healthily. If it had all been gloom bastard rock we'd have lost interest ages ago. So, consider these chaps - who begun influenced by Gene Loves Jezebel, The Cure and Love & Rockets as many lightly twisted melodic types would, but have now gone beyond "post-shoegazing, post-Goth nocturnal guitar rock". Self produced MCs - 'One Thin Second' (88), 'Phobic' (89), 'Sunlight Gives Me A Headache' (89), 'September Scar' (90), 'Therapy' (90), 'The Curtain Society' (91), 'Where Are You' (93). 'No Answer' 7" (93), 'Chelsea' 7" (93), 'Inertia' CD (95). 17 Marcy Street, Southbridge, MA 01550. (e-mail: CurtainSoc@aol.com)

ROBBIE D 1126 Folsom Street, San Francisco, CA 94103.

165

166

DAMIEN YOUTH And here he is, the real star of the book, right at the end of it all. Edgar Allan Poe just picked up a guitar. Damien, you will be relieved to hear, can create songs that are totally 1996 - stalking through the fog of distorted electrics - and also 1669, as he strums his way into the centre of your soul. He is highly *unusual*. The Westgate Gallery, who represent him, say 'Damien weaves ballads of love and melancholy...like "a ghostwind that caresses from afar"...He is the voice of the 90's, and beyond, with the presence and depth to tap into and awaken spiritual essence of all mankind.' Blimey, you're all thinking, what a load of cobblers! Think again. Strange as it may seem, everything claimed for this man is true. I'm even prepared to believe that small children stop him in the street, if they have streets in the backwoods of Hammond, Louisiana ('the wilds of the Bayou State'!) and gasp, 'Say Mister, aren't you a chrysalis of flame?' He has a quite astonishing range of styles, although at the heart of it all is his majestically lush voice, and a winning way of teasing beautiful melodies from an acoustic guitar! Instead of being Folk (music that generally makes you want to physically attack those responsible), this is a timeless approach. It stirs an instant emotional effect, partly because of his superbly interesting lyrics, but also because while the man is totally unconventional in the way that he is doing things, there is a conventional aspect here which means he can appeal to everyone from the underground to the mainstream. You can adapt easily to whatever he is doing and lose yourself in his inventive stories. (Halfway between the Salem witch trials and the X Files, his beady eyes notice everything.) Previously involved with things called Insect Chandelier and Strychnine Temple, he now has two MCs available under his own name, 'Candleroom' and 'Festival Of Death' - $11.99 each (add some postage) from The Westgate. I've virtually glued his tapes into my walkman since I received them and you'll do the same, as both will hang you up by your ribcage on a little hook, where you can froth and writhe about in stark amazement at just what emerges. Nobody does it better, but then again, nobody does it like this. Nobody! Westgate, 5219 Magazine St, New Orleans, LA, 70115.

THE DARK THEATRE The only band in the world, I assure you, who describe themselves as Industrial Egyptian Metal Rock. (Also see Screem In The Dark - a magazine, clothes, t-shirts and more.) The classically trained Vlad formed the band in 90, and they have established quite a reputation since their debut album 'Matters Of Life And Undeath'. Vlad drinks blood but it's his wife's blood, which keeps it all in the family. The band neglect neither the dancier side or the humour. Long-faced bastards will loathe them. 'Matters Of Life And Undeath' (91) 'Le Petit Morte' (94). Screem Jams is TDT's merchandising arm. PO Box 138300, Chicago, IL 60613. (e-mail: SCREEEM@Aol)

DATA BANK A Atmospheric electronics that fit the mood, based around central figurehead Andrew Szava-Kovatz, who has been releasing things since 83, and with German label Subtronic, doing a CD a year since 92. PO Box 255, Dracut, MA 01826.

DAY DREAMS IN MAUVE PO Box 250, Oak Forest, IL 60452.

DEAD END KIDS Project involving Shane from STG, Mr John Kovak, Paris, Jeremy Meza and Dave from STG. It possibly exists only in their minds.

DECAY OF THE ANGEL Formed 93, by artist Clark Wen. With plenty of keybds it's all quite lush and inviting, deserves a place in any *X-Files* episode. 'Poena Damni' demo. Now called Ordeal By Roses. PO Box 68276, Schaumburg, IL 60194.

DECEMBER Cure-influenced gloom. PO Box 7003, New York, NY 10116-7003.

167

165 THE DARK THEATRE 166-7 THE DEEP EYNDE
168 THE EMPIRE HIDEOUS

168

PHOTO: TREYCE CILONA

DECEMBER FLOWERS PO Box 57343 Sherman Oaks, CA 91413.

THE DEEP EYNDE Fate Fatal - vocals, Oren - bass, Killjo - guitar and Cat Malonna - drums. Formed 92 by which time it had already been a long journey for main man Fate Fatal. His lifestory goes like this. Bought up religious (not even allowed to watch *Bewitched*), molested at church, mother dies early of cancer, molested again, takes drugs, now suffers anxiety attacks. His ultimate pleasure is just the norm - "to be in the body of a man somewhere in the Middle Ages, after a battle, rank with the sweat of other men. He comes home to the woman in waiting, her skin poured over her soft bones. I would become both of them in the act of love making. I suppose I would be a spirit." Well, it might happen, fingers crossed. Fate has two 'designed' scars carved in his back and he enjoys the spirituality of correctly stressed S/M. The live show has included "wearing live worms, crickets, papier mache, colour plastic wrap, body paint, duct tape, shitting, pissing, cutting, burning flesh, sticking worms up my ass". I'd be standing *right* at the back. In one past life he thinks he was guillotined. In this life he may well be.

Okay, in 90 he was only doing poetry readings. 91, involved with Undead Poets Society. 92 started Deep Eynde. 93 joins Kittens For Christian. 94 Deep Eynde born again after Kittens break up.
'The Vinegar Works' MC should still be available. 'City Lights' CD (95). This is uplifting, brightly noxious. PO Box 9805, North Hollywood, CA 91609-1809. Or Apollyon, Altenbaunaer Str. 27, 34134 Kassel, Germany.

DELTA OF VENUS Anne Anslow, Darren Allen and R. Pomeroy. Formed 91. First demo 'Dark With Fire'. PO Box 369, Syracuse, NY 13201.

DEVIL DOLL Mad genius. Renaissance, 30 N. Raymond Avenue, Suite 212, Pasadena, CA 91103.

DIMESTORE HALOES Born to be cool. Previously The Penny Dreadfuls. Previously Chaz. PO Box 391785 Cambridge, MA 02139.

DICHROIC MIRROR Eileen Bowe - vocals/keybds, Michael Gougis - guitar/bass/perc. Formed 90. First two demos 'Dichroic Mirror' (90) and 'Children Of Lir' (93) appeared in part on the 'Silence Is Foo' CD (94), where they were aided by Cecilia. Their new 'Necropolis' CD should be out now, continuing their lo-fi Sisters/C.Death voyage. A nicely nagging sound. Box 92721, Long Beach CA 90809. (e-mail ebow@aol.com)

DRAIN THE DOVES Seriously doomy. Michael Rozon 5214 Strohm Ave, North Hollywood, CA 91601.

THE DUTCH MASTERS Formed by Kent Bancroft, of Spahn Ranch. Allegedly.

ELECTRIC HELLFIRE CLUB A sort of Mondo Zodiac Mindwarp in case you didn't know. Not exactly Goth. c/o Cleopatra.

ELEMENT/ELEVENTH HOUR The man from Nosferatu Productions, with ex STG, Kommunity FK and London After Midnight members, apparently. c/o Ghastly?

ELEVEN SHADOWS Box 17283 Encino, CA 91416

THE EMPIRE HIDEOUS Myke Hideous - vocals, Eve Lestrange - bass, Mars - guitar, Joey Quest - drums, Jeff Austin - guitar. These crazy bastards have been going since 88. Everything they do has a sense of precision balanced by madness. Their visuals are superb - Clockwork Orange meets early Christian Death and introducing Sgt Fury to the House Of Hammer. If you don't like humour steer clear.

169 FAITH & DISEASE 170 FALLING JANUS 171 S. SOMA OF G.L.O.D.
172 FEAR CULT

Leader Myke could be certified at any moment. He's drank blood onstage, spat blood on, and presumably off, stage, he has even 'thrown fire' at the audience. 'Out Of Anger' MC sold out, but these three are available - 'This Evil On Earth', 'Tales Of Charade' and 'Live - NYC'. Plus 'Only Time Will Tell' CD (94). PO Box 616, Hawthorn, NJ 07507-0616. (e-mail: EmpHideous@AOL.COM)

EVA O What sort of surname is this? ("It's a girl Mrs O"?!) Eva played in early LA punk band, Speed Queens, and the early Gothlings, The Superheroines. Joined Rozz Williams in Shadow Project but now going off on her own line, she's doing creamier tunes, less hazy than you might fear. The 'Demons Fall For An Angels Kiss' collection includes Paris on keyboards and Patrick Mata for one song, along with two Human Drama men. There is also the 'Past Time' CD, featuring tracks from her three former bands. Since imploded? PO Box 96241, Las Vegas, Nevada 89193-6241.

EVIL TWIN Generic Mike, 58 Wilson Hill Rd, Binghampton, NY 13905.

EXP Weird band claiming to have recorded in tunnels beneath the ocean, with largely South American instruments. Formed by Paris during Shadow Project, "EXPerimentation without limitation" is one phrase, "Catharticism is the key to our satisfaction" another. A shuddering bloody mess is mine. Paris is an interesting man, so never expect the expected. PO Box 602, Normal, IL 61761. (Ask for Bruce E.) Or PO Box 29206 Los Angeles, CA 90029-0206.

FAITH & DISEASE Dara Rosenwasser - vocals, Eric Cooley - bass, Steven Knouse - guitars, Joaquim Tavares-Sinai - keybds, Joshua Furman - perc. Formed 91 by Eric, infuriated to find himself living in a sea of pustular grunge. He craved works of beauty and imagination, not hideous immolation. Result - isolation! Until people started hearing their music. The gorgeous 'Beauty & Bitterness' CD (93), 'Fortune His Sleep' CD (95) and two 7" singles, 'Voltair's Vallerie' (sold out - tres rare!), 'Jardeau Blue'. Pert but sleepy. Ivy Records, PO Box 2721, Seattle, WA 98111.

FAITH AND THE MUSE William Faith (Wreckage, Mephisto Waltz, Christian Death and Shadow Project) and Monica Richards (Madhouse, Strange Boutique). Started writing together in 93 while assisting on the Shadow Project tour. Classical, ethnic, dark and brooding. Celtic, Gaelic, Eastern influences crammed in tight. 'Elyria' CD. Tess Records.

FALLING JANUS Harry Koniditsiotis - vocals/guitar, Dennis Bourn - keybds/drums and Mark Taraanto - bass, with added involvement from Scott Free U - sampling/ambient sounds. If you think this lot aren't cool be warned, they come recommended by none other than Poppy Z. Brite. Formed 92. Two MCs 'The Trinity Site' (93), 'The Innocence Of Isolation' (95). Single planned for this year. If a good version of My Bloody Valentine ended up on Projekt? Spectral, yet warm and wanting. PO Box 55371 Metairie, LA 70055. (Fax (504) 895 4293) (e-mail: cyk01@www.gnofn.org)

FEAR CULT Matt Riser, Cindy Wilkins and a few machines. That's all it is. And when I say all, it's all you could need. Ostensibly a 'synthesized project' Matt's been working on since 92, it reminds me of the first few times I played Ecco The Dolphin, if that makes sense. Opalescent music. A new CD may have followed his 'A Bouquet Of Signs' MC by now, as he is stepping up the action since Cindy arrived. The music shows real promise, Matt's erratic vocals need work and there's a great spirit - the songs don't just stand up, they're rigid. 5625 E. Fairmont, Tucson AZ 85712. (e-mail: MRISER@VMS. CCIT.ZRIZONA.EDU.)

172

171

PHOTO: T.M. CALDWELL

FLESH OF MY FLESH Harper Sisters, 7818 E. Glenrosa, Scottsdale, AZ 85251.

FLOORSHOW Sisters-influenced. Ho ho. 'Numinous' demo. PO Box 1120, New York, NY 10023.

FRAGMENTED Gloomy, hypnotising compositions from the man they call Anx.scan (!), an artist and writer. He does it all. "This is where the shadows find their way back inside and the words bouncing around in your head all start to make sense. You take another cold breath and concentrate on this echo of blue light on skin." 1512 Canyon Run Road, Naperville, IL 60565.

GARDEN OF DREAMS Gene Blalock, Seraph Productions, 2242 W. School, Chicago IL 60618.

GOD LOVES OVER DOSE (G.L.O.D.) David Martin - samples/keybds/violin, S. Soma - vocals/perc, Frank 107 - vocals/'treatments', Wolfgang L. - bass/guitars. Formed 88. Ominous, textural music firmly grounded in technology, powerful but not strictly Goth. 'GLOD' CD (92) 'Gnosis' (94). Box 34025 Detroit, MI 48234. (Fax: 313.368.5432) (e-mail: glod@getcom.com)

GOD'S GIRLFRIEND PO Box 3535, Hollywood, CA 90078.

GOLDEN DAWN Suffering Clown, 208 West 29th Street, Room 307, NY, NY 10001.

A.G.GREER PO Box 250, Oak Forest, IL 60452.

THE GREY SEASON Finn - vocals/bass, Mike - guitar, Greg - percussives. Dark power trio, it seems, out of Oakland, maybe Berkeley, who so struck the P. Vampire crowd with their intensity and a guitar sound they'd never experienced before that, and I quote, "we cried, we danced, we rocked - way out there like the blackness of infinity". Well, yes, except that there appears little out of the ordinary about the guitar, other than the scritchy-scratchy parts (a la Gang Of Four), whereas Finn's voice is awesome. Vocal chords soaked in gasoline, redolent with hurt and yearning, he conveys *all* the substance of his intentions. You start to live the bloody songs while they play. They have clarity most people dream about, with lyrics that would shame a shaman ("Talk to me...you fucking waste of time"!). You really do need their CD, 'The Sensory Age'. More than a bit special, it verges on instant classic status! Of all the music I received while compiling this book, only Petra De Luca (although not technically enjoyable) is more impressive. Only London After Midnight took up residence in my walkman longer. This band should be massive. Box 3662 Santa Rose, CA 95402-3662. (Fax: 707-528-8694) (e-mail: venture@ sonic.net)

HALO 461 West 12th Street, Claremont, CA 91771.

HUMAN DRAMA Johnny Indovina - vocals/guitar...and friends. Johnny's idea of a semi-ensemble group is interesting and gives fresh life to maudlin, contemplatative rock. Started off with interest from Geffen, then a deal with RCA, then on to Triple X. 'The World Inside' CD (91) 'PinUps' CD (93). 'The World Inside' video collection is worth seeing if you get the chance, not just because these truly are fantastic videos in terms of quality and imagination, but because in between rather self-serious interview snippets, where you are slowly beginning to tire of the man, he suddenly admits that his most treasured moment, was a spectacular performance in his school's football team. Real life! c/o Triple X. (Voice mail: 1-213-368-6185)

I FOUND GOD 6565 Sunset Blvd 321, Hollywood, CA 90028.

JUDITH Christopher David, Damian James, Mark Wagner. Powerful, early Christian Death/Killing Joke with melancholic, plaintive edge and peculiar ideas. "In sound and form, the band is capable of bringing its audience back in time, to the days when Mallarme, Wilde and quite possibly Jack The Ripper were drinking absinthe at their local salon, or taking tea at a corner pub". I quite like the idea of Jack The Ripper deliberately avoiding drawing any attention to himself by taking tea at a pub. 'Fohn' CD (95). T-shirts, CD and video available. PO Box 392, Peck Slip Station, NY, NY 10272. (e-mail: AmphionMU@aol.com)

KILL SWITCH...KLICK Principally the deformed brain-child of dA Sebasstian, joined by percussionist Michael Ditmore, with a host of extras. Formed 92. Lightly demented post-Industrial music with frisky elements, already signed to Cleopatra. They them-selves use the term Muzak For The Masses. 539 Queen Anne Ave North, Box 131, Seattle, WA 98109. (Net http:/www.halcyon.com/mdf/nec/ index.html)

LAST DANCE Rick Joyce, Jeff Diehm, Peter Gorritz. Formed Aug 91. First demo 'Everyone' (91), then 'Angel' (92) and 'Tragedy' (95) CDs. Put a lot of faith in guitars rising above the rhythm section in tandem with the vocals to create something unique. PO Box 9685, Fountain Valley, CA 92728-9685. (Fax: 714-775-4421) (e-mail: TLD100@AOL.COM)

LIFE IN SODOM Gerrie Brand - vocals/keybds, Daniel Heinze - guitars, Engin Saydam - drums, S. Payton Chambers - bass. No historical details but they go back a wee bit. 'The Stains' 12" (91), 'Phantasmagoria' 12" (92), 'Charader' CD (93), 'Vampire My Love' 12" (95), 'Haunting' CD (96). It's excellent stuff, almost a weird merging of early Danse Society and a de-loused Mission. Worthy of your most scrupulous attention. Nutrix, 36 N.E. 1st Street, Suite #504, Miami, Florida 33132.

LONDON AFTER MIDNIGHT Sean Brennan - vocals, Tamlyn - keybds, Michael Areklette- bass, Douglas Avery - drums, William Skye - guitar. The ultimate example of how shite the Music Biz is. Why no major label has snapped this band is a total mystery. (Correction: I have worked for a major, so I know *exactly* why!) They aren't quite the best band in the world - as they'd clearly tie with Italy's Ataraxia - but they are the coolest. Class songs and image which would make them every video director's wet dream! Live debut 90, growing steadily since, touring the world, establishing a big reputation and invoking an alarming amount of petty jealousies elsewhere. Remember, all bands do demo MCs and when they've a few available they consider themselves mighty beings indeed if they've sold a couple of hundred. LAM sold over twenty thousand! And in a scene where decadence and pretentions abounds it's also nice to see that sometimes direct thought interlopes. Such as LAM's t-shirt, 'Fascists fuck off'/'Psychos Fuck Off!' t-shirts. They don't just have the songs, the image, the intelligence (lyrics are hardly disposable in this parish), there's humour and passion squeezed into the torment and delightful tristes.

Audience member: "I love you Sean!"
Sean: "I love me too!"

One of the major forces, anywhere. Earliest MCs all sold out. Currently available, at the time of writing - 'Selected Scenes from The End Of The World' (92), 'Psycho Magnet' (95) MCs. CDs - 'Selected Scenes', 'Kiss'. Video - 'Ruins' (94). Two first class stamps or three IRCs for newsletter. Do not order CDs from their address as that slows things down. For CDs write to Com-Four, 7 Dunham Pl, Brooklyn, NY 11211. In Europe write to Apocalyptic Vision, Ahomweg 19, D-64807, Dieburg, Germany. Some merchandise available only in Europe obtainable from Infa-Rot, Lindenberg 1, D-87727, Babenhausen, Germany. $1 for catalogue. (Fax +49 8333 93114). American address for merchandise and band contact - PO Box 1377, Hollywood, CA 90078.

LOVESLIESCRUSHING Scott Cortez - guitars/vocals/loops, Isabel Arpin - vocals. Formed Dec 92. Moody, floaty, beautiful stuff. c/o Projekt.

174 MEPHISTO WALTZ 175 THE NEW CREATURES

LOVE SPIRALS DOWNWARDS c/o Projekt.

LUX SOLEMNIS "Dark ambient and Gothic overtones" by John Navroth. If the 'Lovers And Other Nightmares' MC is anything to go by, it is quite beautiful at its most turbulent... and plain seductive at its gentler pace. 13415 115th Ave. NE, Kirkland, WA 98034-2168. (e-mail: jmn@rocket.com)

LYCIA Peter Steele of the dreaded Type O Negative once saw fit to eulogise about Lycia thusly; "It is dark, ambient music. I would like our next album to sound something like this. It is the most depressing thing I've ever heard in my life. If I put it on in the morning when I get up...I am useless for the rest of the day." Keep playing it Peter, please. 'The Burning Circle and Then Dust', prompted Lycia's Mike to admit charges of musical hypnotism but believes that themes of escape predominate. 'Contentment which never forgets chaos and darkness.' He calls this rebirth. I found it calming. He is joined by David Galas - electronics and bass and Tara Van Flower - vocals. When Mike formed Lycia in 88 it was after a spell in Goth bands in the Phoenix area, although he doesn't regard Lycia as G-affiliated. You should really try and collect the CD set, all available on Projekt - 'Wake', 'Iona', 'A Day In The Stark Corner' and 'Live'. Box 41135, Mesa, AZ 85274-1135.

MARIA EX COMMUNIKATA Apocryphle Arts, 151 Hudson St, 3rd Floor, New York, NY 10013.

MASTER/SLAVE RELATIONSHIP PO Box 191211, San Francisco, CA 94119.

THE MAUVE SIDESHOW A bizarre one. Highly rated by the expert UK's 'Organ' crew, this band, a duo, advertise themselves as "Gothadelic/ambient/progressive...with adventurous female vox". Angelic vocals over a glowing drone. Four CDs, which come in handpainted sleeves... but with glitter on the CDs themselves? PO Box 19523, Seattle, WA 98109.

MEPHISTO WALTZ Cleopatra big band. Formed 86 by ex Christian Deathoids, Bari-Bari and Johann Schuman after the CD/LP 'Atrocities'. The opening phase was in Germany, then straight back to LA. Also includes David Glass and Johann Schuman of Christian Death and singer Christianna. 'Mephisto Waltz' EP (86), 'Crocsomania' LP/CD (91), 'As Apostles Forget' MCD (92), 'Terra Regina' CD (93), 'The Eternal Deep' CD (94), 'Thalia' CD (94). All excellent. PO Box 55601, Los Angeles, CA 31733. (Fax: 415 474 4211)

THE MIDNIGHT DREARY Kynann Dread - vocals, Jeff Beckstrom - drums, Tony Sandoval - bass, Jace Murphy - guitar and Jeremiah Smith - keybds. "I would like to think of us as 20th Century decadents," Kynann raves, "having more in common with Gautremont than The Sisters Of Mercy, making music that creates an atmosphere of darkness and decay instead of trying to achieve the standard Gothic Sound." 612 So. 500 E, SLC, UT. 84102.

MISSED IN DIARY Eerily aggressive band. 'Wonders Why' 7" (Jan 92), 'Remember When' 7" (June 93), 'Dissolve' CD EP (95) to bring them back. Could be contenders. PO Box 20401, Detroit, MI 48220. (Fax: (810) 541-8786)

MORPHINE ANGEL Johnny Lee - chaos, Paul Frederic - darkness, Deros Mesmeronicus - guitar, Brad Jay - signals and Alice - throbbing. Bit of Industrial, Punk and early Goth, a la Bauhaus and Christian Death. Formed 93 with a view towards "poetic terrorism and ontological anarchy". Influences range from Killing Joke and 45 Grave to Sisters and the sin in Sinatra. First demo, Sept 94, second Feb 95 and all cobbled together on first CD, 'Project Isa' (95) on Black Pepper. This is described

175

by themselves quite accurately as a mechanoid screeching guitar onslaught but that is also too harsh. This lovenest/murderfest will run and run. BP, PO Box 81854, Lincoln NE 68501.

PATRICIA MORRISON Last known contact for the woman who'd gone a bit rocky and wasn't getting particularly good reviews of her occasional gigs is the record company SPV who released her 'Reflect On This' CD (94). PO Box 1147, 30531, Hanover.

MY SUICIDE Influences: Bauhaus, Smiths, Stooges. Hendrix, Doors, Jane's Addiction. Formed 92. 'When The Water' album available. Bubbling, modern sound. PO Box 7427, Orange, CA 92613.

NATIONAL RAZOR This Ascension meets Christian Death? 'Stem Of Thorns' CD. Silent Scream.

NETHERWORLD Denis Stroup - drums, Eric Meadows - guitar, H. Ellison - bass, Patrick Cleman - vocals/guitar/piano. Crafty alternative rock. (Birthday Party meets The Stooges, only less frantic.) 1423 Ardmor Avenue, Modesto, CA 95350.

NEW CREATURES Mark S. Walsh - vocals/bass, Brett Levitt - guitars, K. Tiger Koehn - drums, John Mooney - keybds, Susan Mitchell - violin, Julia Kent - cello. Formed 89. Joy Div, Bauhaus, Doors - their own comparisons. It certainly shakes its hips in an outrageous fashion. Flaunt that power! They play it big and brash with razored guitars yet warm swathes of moodiness at the back, some of the best vocals around and superb lyrics. Everything jumps out majestically and you'd have thought labels would be queuing. Current MCs available - 'The First 1,095 Days' (a compilation of all their earliest 'hits'), 'Seven' (moody bastard stuff), 'Earache' (fourteen versions of one song?). The 96 CD I can't tell you about but this band just deserve to be so huge it's disgusting. PO Box, 220249, Brooklyn, NY 11222.0005. (Fax: (718) 389-3011)

NOISE END RAPTURE A combination of Darron Kilsunn and The Cold from Tears Ov Blood. Soundtrack of a tortured mind. 194 Central Street, Appt. 218A, Gardner MA 01440.

NOCTURNAL EMISSIONS Staalplaat, PO Box 83296, Portland, Oregon, 97283.

OCHOTILLO "A meditative Gothic experience." 'Vague' demo. Patrick Denney, 1237 East Main Street, Rochester, NY 14609.

ONE OF US Weird Goth industrial fetish outfit. 460 Albany Street, Boston, MA 02118.

ORDEAL BY ROSES Okay shoot me, I'm just a big softie but there's something blissful about this. Clark Wen changed the name from Decay of the Angel under which title he announced an avowed intent to be one at ease with the pain of loss. Oh yes, Clark is house composer for Boneyard Press on their movie escapades and when you consider he started classical training on guitar and piano at the age of nine, when he announces that the first Ordeal single is, "a piece for female voice and classical" guitar you know 'Joy' is like a little slice of heaven. Reverie breath you take, etc. It's hazily gorgeous, whereas the b-side is "a collage piece based on Yukio Mishima's treatise on death and art, *Sun and Steel*", that bobbles by as a daydream, more incidental than is required. So that's what you're in for here, transfixion and delay. Get it without. Anathema Records, PO Box 68276, Schaumburg, IL 60194. (Fax: 847 358 7471) (e-mail: despair@mcs.com)

THE ORDER OF THE NCs Lightly woven offshoot from Requiem In White. 'The Musical Works Of The NCs' CD. Sacrum Torch. Ltd, PO Box 278, Prince Street Station, New York, NY 10012-0005.

176

177 178

OUT OF ANGER Side project of Myke from The Empire Hideous.

P. VAMPIRE Mark Smith - guitars/vocals, Dianna Davis - bass/vocals, Zachary Ellis - drumology 101, Sarine Voltage - keybds/vocals. Strange name (Pinochio Vampire) for a strange band, started as a duo by Mark and Dianna, the couple behind the brainchild that is Venture Beyond Records (see Labels). Already responsible for three CDs, 'Veer & Twinge', '...Just Touching It...', '...After Dark...', like crushing Mr Bungle and early Christian Death into a blender and forgetting to keep the lid on. Box 3662 Santa Rose, CA 95402-3662. (Fax: 707-528-8694) (e-mail: venture@sonic.net)

PENAL COLONY D Madden - vocals/computers, Andy Shaw - guitar, Chris Shinkus - bass, Jason Hubbard - sampling. Dredging around somewhere in that death-industrial-mordant energy vein you've got to like their attitude - and I quote, "If you haven't read Kafka you don't get it. You don't get us, you don't get life, you're homophobic, piss off, have a nice day." 'Put Your Hands Down' and '5 Man Job' CDs. C/o Cleopatra.

PINEAL VENTANA Mitchell Foy - drums/vocals, Clara Clamp - vocals/drums, Kim Chee - guitar/drums, Shane Pringle - sax, Travis Kotler - guitar, Brian Cook - bass. That's a lot of drums but they make a fierce racket in a flagrantly diabolical manner. 'Philosopher Stone' EP, singles 'Umbilical Operator' and 'Stagnancy Is Revolting', 'Living Soil' CD (95). Praise the Heavens that none of you are vocalist Clara who Mitchell has urinated on, onstage. PO Box 55138, Atlanta GA 30308-0138.

PRAISE OF FOLLY 'Music from the Dark Side at its best' (Propaganda.) Thomas McFarlan, 15900 Crenshaw Boulevard, Suite 1-333, Gardena, CA 90249.

PRESENTS OF MIND Costa - vocals, Lamar - guitar, Murphy - bass, Stoll - drums. Punky Gothy girl band. 'Dog' single is worth nabbing. Moodswing Records, 40 Harrison St 14D, New York, NY 10013.

PROPHECY OF THE HATED Alain Harris - bass/guitar/vocals, Devin Fleenor - prog./keybds, Michael Calahan - extra vocals. Wild, noisy bastards. PO Box 913, Glendale, AZ 85311.

THE PROPHETESS Mark Hawks - vocals/keybds/guitar, Rick Joyce - bass, Tom Coyne -drums, Tony Tullai - guitars. Born Oct 88. Like a friskier, less arch Mission. With this directness comes more charm and therefore more appeal. There's no lack of power and the deft touches are always charming. It's a good mixture. On Cleopatra, licensing their own Beltane label. 'Avalon' video single (90), 'Prophetess' MC (90), 'Between The Worlds' MC (91), 'Embrace My Love' 7" (92), 'Prophetess' CD/MC (93), 'Dichotomy' CD (96). PO Box 9893, Fountain Valley, CA 92728-9893.

RAVENSONG Attractive, haunting, electronic music. PO Box 14452, Long Beach, CA 90814. (CORVUS23@AOL.COM)

REQUIEM IN WHITE Lisa Hammer - vocals, Eric Hammer - guitar, Christopher Walsh guitar/bass, Anon - drums. Demos - 'Pride's Unhappy End' , 'Of The Want Infinite'. They don't court publicity, strangely. PO Box 245, Prince St Station, New York, NY 10012

ROSEWATERELIZABETH 4-Ad-ish and fun. 24 Hour Service Station, 13821 37th St. North, Tampa, FL 33613.

SANITY ASSASSINS Eyeball - guitar/vocals, Mike - drums, Keith - grave. Formerly The Dispossessed, who some Goths respected, this is a weird indie

176 P. VAMPIRE 177 THE PROPHETESS 178 SECOND SKIN
179 THE SHROUD 180 SILENT ORDER

179
PHOTO: REBECCA M. CARAVEO

180
PHOTO: MICHELE ALEXANDER

punky band who write really imaginative melodic leftfield stuff with plenty of hidden power and hooks. They've got over twenty vinyl, cassette or CD releases in the States and the UK. If you fancy something a little more upbeat and punky than usual this could be the place to try. PO Box 380152, East Hartford, CT 06138-0152.

SATIVA LUV BOX Patrick Mata, along with Gerard and M. Segal, back in action and worth catching. Patrick - the man who made Kommunity FK glow - is always worthy of your consideration. M. Segal looks like the sort of chap you wouldn't want to meet down a dark alley... or anywhere else for that matter. 10965 Fruitland Drive No. 206, Studio City, CA 91604.

SAVIOR MACHINE Metal Goth according to *Fight Amnesia*. PO Box 28450, Santa Ana, CA 92799.

SCREAMS FOR TINA Warren Mansfield - vocals, Kent Bancroft - guitar, Billy Budd - bass, Tom Wenzel - drums. On the more accessible side of things, there is a goth heart to the bare-boned energetic mush of it all but to anyone else they're simply pretty hypnotic. Sound fairly crazed a lot of the time. Warren Mansfield, 3615 Clark #8, Burbank, CA 91505.

SECOND SKIN Singer Arron regards them as the perfect doom and gloom band. Hard working bunch who have their avowed aims. Strong stuff. 7342 E. Glenbrosa No. 3, Scottsdale, AZ 95251.

SERPENTINE Pagan influenced Swans-ish band. Box 1735, Cathedral Station, NYC 10025.

SHADOW LIGHT John E. Clough and friends. Formerly the man behind Prayers For The Raven, John admits to Pink Floyd, Bowie and NIN influences. Rumoured to be relocating to Czechoslovakia, he clearly thought better for it, or maybe he couldn't actually recognise Seattle? (Stumbling up to grunge diehards, guidebook in hand, asking politely for directions to the cake shop.) Asked to contribute a Joy Division song to a tribute album, he pulled together members of Sky Cries Mary, Faith & Disease and Rose Luna. He took the idea one step further and did a complete CD, on Ivy. Onstage he doesn't just have props and dancers, he uses actors! 'Within The Shadow Light' CD. 4739 University Way NE #1440, Seattle WA 98105. (e-mail: Shadir@eworld.com)

SHAMEFACE Noiseville Records, PO Box 93, Yonkers, NY 10704.

THE SHROUD Lydia - vocals, Rodney Walker - guitar, Iyan - bass, Hendrik - keybds, Eric - drums. Formed 91 and fittingly unveiled on Halloween of that year. Inspired by "the passion of medieval mysticism and the symbolism of Jungian archetypes." Blimey! Okay, I admit they're one of my favourites, although some people rear up on their hind legs and splutter at the very thought. It isn't just that Lydia is a class singer, it's that their music is so sweetly done without being wispy. And it is no surprise that this band have sent me some of the finest photographs I've received. Photographers don't often get in a lather about the music but are drawn to people who give off that certain something. They can detect intrinsic qualities and The Shroud have them by the ton. Debut MC 'Drowning Dreams' (92) still available. Debut CD also out now, 'Long Ago And Far Away' on Omnidisk and your collection isn't complete without it. PO Box 25112, Fresno, CA 93729.

SILENT ORDER The 'one man band-in-a-box-with-a-guitar' that is Todd Clegg. It has emotional torment gnashing inside the pretty borders of what are actually imaginative compositions. He could be a version of the Pet Shop Boys on the one hand - if he's not

PHOTO: FADI KHEIR

182

181

PHOTO: KEVIN KELLY

careful - or he could be writing some of the most stirring film music, if we're lucky. But most of all he needs to boost those vocals a bit and he'd find himself unwittingly out-energising many a mainline angst Goth guitar band. Strange man, big talent, he sits there in a studio, juggling hurricanes. Highly recommended - 'Agonist' MC (95). PO Box 190, Carlsbad, CA 92008. (e-mail: agonist@ix.netcom.com)

SKY CRIES MARY Roderick W. Romero - vocals, Anisa - vocals. That's all I know other than this married couple change costumes a lot during their dramatic show. 'Exit At The Axis' (91), 'A Return To The Inner Experience' (93) and 'This Timeless Turning' (95) CDs. No address. Bugger!

SLEEP CHAMBER Fifteen years on and the determined John Zewizz shows no sign in slowing down his Noir soundtrack to life. A prime, primal, S&M/general fetish master with occult ideas (i.e. sex magick), he has released a torrent of CDs. I see him as the modern, logical successor to people like Throbbing Gristle, but making listenable music instead of quasi-intellectual drivel. The man makes pumping noise for sleazehounds to grind to, while fondling taboos, because that is the frontier on which he stands guard. His live shows can be branded as filth (certainly few CD covers I've ever seen include pictures of women being willingly penetrated by whip handles), his post is checked, his phone tapped, his eyeballs are probably bugged. The CIA may have infiltrated his backing band. It could be anything but the irony is that *he* is out to get you. PO Box 1060, Allston, MA 02134 or try Funfundvierzig, Schmiedetwiete 6, 23898 Labenz, Germany. (Fax (0) 4536/87 99).

SLOW BURN Wayne Boyd - vocals/keybds/guitars, Vance Stanton Allen - bass/drum prog., Adam Wm. Becvar - guitars, Mark Paluzzi - guitars. Formerly

181 SLEEP CHAMBER 182 SOFIA RUN 183 STONE 588

183

The Wake RSV, when formed in 88. Changed name and began functioning with 'Candy From A Stranger' in 93. Often compared to Gene Loves Jezebel. Shadow Play Records, 101N Wacher Dr., Suite CM170, Chicago, Illinois 60606.

SOFIA RUN Denny - vocals, Joe - drums/violin (weird!), Richie - keybds Chris - bass. Formed April 92. Another contender for the future. Fresh approach to the genre - apt for a band who like music with a "psychedelic Gothic frenzy" - and likely to appeal to people to all sorts. Cute, crouched and beset by an inner craving, they have a lovely feel and everybody notices the insistence of the vocals, be they male or female. 'Dignity Of Folly' (95) and 'Intimacy' (96) CDs. Magnifique. Dark Frenzy Records, PO Box 656625, Fresh Meadows, NY 11365.

SOMA PO Box 19531, Philadelphia, PA 19124.

SOUL WHIRLING SOMEWHERE c/o Projekt.

SPAHN RANCH Athan Maroulis - vocals, Rob Morton - keybds, Matt Green - other stuff. Founded 92, but first thought of by all three in 84! What? Rob and Matt started the band then dragged the elusive one in to complete it. Okay, a bit Industrial, but so what? There's a bit of it all. Grimey techno? Sort of. Athan used to be in tres trendy Executive Slacks (a band, not a fashion disaster) but, more importantly, Farenheit 451, what he now refers to as virtually a Bauhaus cover band. Their material may resurface on Cleopatra soon. 'Spahn Ranch' CDEP (92), 'Collateral Damage' CD (94) 'Blackmail Starters Kit' CD (93), 'The Coiled One' CD (95). All available from Cleopatra except that first EP. Athan Maroulis, Verdugo, PO Box 46662, LA, CA 90046.

SRI LANKA PO Box 311, Devon, PA 19333.

STATIC GREY Matt Batchelor - vocals/keybds/guitar/drums/fire-breathing, Kam Dvoracek - bass/vocals/percussion, Tim Kietii - guitar/vocals. Slamming and twisting itself in and out of shape what we have here is a sleaze-driven rock thing which glistens with health. Matt and Tim used to be in Morticia, a band who are passing into legendary status; although they had their attractive side they also had some distinctly metal touches which dragged their ambition down. Static Grey however sounds like a cross between Colourbox, who you won't remember, and Sigue Sigue Sputnik, if they'd ever had an understanding of power rather than a PA running on one half-used battery. A further clue to their flame-brained evil - Tim's favourite guitar players include Jimi Hendrix and Ace Frehley. There are big, boosted vocals, a rattling sense of urgency about their work and humour in the placement of samples. One listen to the eponymous MC will smack some sense into you. Morticia material is also available from their address. PO Box 6741, Mpls, MN 55406.

STG Shane Talada - vocals, David Skott - bass, Chad Bishop - drummer, Allan King - drums Punky-Industrial-Goth. Formed in the late 16th century. Then again in Bavaria, 1945, leading forces against Hitler's werewolves. Finally born in 1989. First album took as long as 94. A difficult birth. 'No Longer Human'. PO Box 4208, Burbank, CA 91503-4208, or Shane Talada, 10071 Imperial Ave, Garden Grove, CA 92642.

STONE 588 Terri Kennedy - vocals, Dave Rhine - guitar, Toby S. - bass, Glenn Daughterty - drums. Formed 92, admitting a K. Joke/Banshees sense of direction, it's all firm, stroppy stuff. They're named after some druidic business in Southern Ireland, as though you didn't know. Early MCs ('Eyes Of A Statue', 'Catharsis', 'Eden Lost') were available in their own Ipso Facto mail order catalogue, as is debut CD, 'Door In The Dragon's Throat'. PO Box

184 PHOTO: JAMES ANDREWS

736, Fullerton, CA 92632-0736.

STRANGE BOUTIQUE Compared to This Ascension. c/o Beddazled Records.

STRANGE DESIRE David Holusha - songwriting/keybds, Mimi T.E.H. - writing/pre-production, W. Wright - computer prog./sound engineering. It's an electronic "soundscape" moving between the Gothic and Ambient worlds. Pretty, conventional and auspiciously perky. 87 Ellison Avenue, Westbury, New York, 11590. (Fax: 212-474-3700 room 3830 - whatever that means) (e-mail: dholusha@nycO2.cravath.com)

SUBVERSION 'Metamorphosis' and 'Damaged Gods' MC. Winsome John also appears in the Propaganda video, 'Ritual'. PO Box 242, Glendale, CA91209.

SUNSHINE BLIND Caroline Blind - vocals, CWHK - guitars, Cousin Al - Bass. Formed 91. Another smart American band who push melodies to the fore and don't bother stirring any pretentious elements in. Tour like buggery given the chance. Goth and poppy. 'Love The Sky To Death' CD . PO Box 4745, Clifton, NJ 07015.

SWITCHBLADE SYMPHONY Tina Root - vocals, Susan Wallace - keybds, Robin Jacobs - guitar. Bent. Exploratory sounds of an attractive hue. 'Serpentine Gallery' CD. PO Box 170443, San Francisco, CA 94117.

TEAR CEREMONY 741 Saint Louis, Baton Rouge, Louisiana 70802.

TEARS OV BLOOD The Cold - vocals and everything I guess. He is Mr Moody. Big sounds, very swish, maudlin and creepy. Three MCs right now, 'Infinite Winter', 'Distant Screams In Fading Dreams', 'The Return To The Gates'. Mood music from a man who lists Projekt bands, Clannad, Rozz-C. Death, London After Midnight etc as influences. A freshly molten mind you should take notice of. PO Box 179, Baldwinville , MA 01436.

TEXAS VAMPS PO Box 515, Corona, CA 91718-0515.

13 KNOTS 248 San Gabriel Ct., Sierra Madra, CA 91024.

THANATOS Padraic Ogl - vocals/guitar/bass, Sam Rosenthal - electronics, Rena - vocals. This is Total Art! Also Dark Folk Goth to some. Utterly gorgeous. 'This Endless Night Inside' CD and 'An Embassy To Gaius' CDs on Projekt. PO Box 146636, Chicago IL 60614.

THE MACHINE IN THE GARDEN Roger Frace - guitars/vocals, Eartha Harris - vocals/keybds/bass. Formed 90, in Nashville, home of the Grand Ole Gothic-Industrial Crossover. (Since relocated.) Another must-investigate band who strangely describe themselves as a Gothic-industrial crossover project, when it's all far too comely for that. Industrial has such stomping overtones! Anyway, old Roger, it transpires, is a graduate student studying Electronic Arts and his thesis 'performance' will be a multimedia stage production entitled 'Prometheus and Io', an excerpt from Prometheus Bound by Aeschylus. Eartha is a student studying multimedia and 'multidisciplinary arts'. Their former guitarist John McDonagh, who happily admits they are his favourite band of all time, reports that some of their newer material includes beautiful classical pieces, and points out that they can easily do delirious rave remixes at will. He is not alone in being baffled that nobody has dived to sign them. They *are* the complete entity! 'Veils And Shadows' EP (93), 'V&S Remixes' (95). Set for 96 is 'Prometheus And Io (original score)' and 'Deus Ex Machina', all available

185

184 TEARS OV BLOOD 185 THE MACHINE IN THE GARDEN

from Industrial Isolation Music, 1320 South Third Street, Louisville, KY 40208. Band contact - PO Box 967, Brentwood, TN 37024-0967. (e-mail: fracer@rpi.edu) (http://www/rpi.edu/-fracer) Or John McDonagh, 57 Kincora Drive, Clontarf, Dublin, Ireland.

THINE EYES Curiously enough this band has also been raved about by John McDonagh and he has obviously has good taste. So, investigate. Laird Sheldahl, PO Box 30041, Eugene, OR 97403.

THIS ASCENSION Dru - vocals, Matt Ballesteros - drums, Timothy Tuttle - keybds, Cynthia Coulter or Charles Dennis - bass, Kevin Serra - guitar. Already two CDs old, this quintet was formed in 88 by Matt Ballesteros (Blade Fetish) and vocalist Dru. They have the quiet, morose edge. 'Light And Shade' CD. Their second, 'Walk Softly, a Dream Lies Here', was produced by ex-Christian Death man, William Faith (Faith and the Muse). Vinyl debut, 'Tears In Rain', very rare. c/o Tess.

TRANCE TO THE SUN Another duo, and signed to high quality operatives, Tess, this is Zoe (er...Alexandra) Wakefield and Ashkelain Sain. Debut CD 'Ghost Forest', second CD 'Bloom Flowers, Bloom'. "Call it modern New Age, call it new Gothic," the press release trills, "we are afraid, they actually give a damn." Ashkelain goes further, refusing to use keyboards or samples - "I am sure I can create much better sounds with my guitar".

TRIO NOCTURNA Thomas Dodd - harp (seriously!), Daniel Brown - violin, Jennifer Hartshorn - vocals, Christopher Case - keybds. Medieval Goth? PO Box 52580, Atlanta, GA 30355

TRUST OBEY Yet another interesting Bergin project. A solo one, signed to the Trent Reznor label, Nothing. Contactable at PO Box 45182, Kansas City, MO 641171.

ULTRACHERRY VIOLET c/o Bedazzled Records.

UNIVERSAL BLACK The sole property of one Sarine Re Voltage who not only convinced the P. Vampire crew to release her material, of which I have no details, but she also joined their band. They describe her work as "excellent songs". They are quite accurate. Box 3662 Santa Rose, CA 95402-3662. (Fax: 707-528-8694.) (e-mail: venture@sonic.net)

USHERHOUSE Industrial-stroke-Goth, who ended up being produced by Steve Albini. 'Molting' CD (Cleopatra) drew rave reviews. 'Flux' CD also available.

VAMPIRE RODENTS PO Box 36988 Phoenix, Arizona 85067.

VAMPYR LEAGUE 8702 East Columbus, Scottsdale, Arizona 85251.

VEIL OF THORNS Peter Williams, Jarret Laitinen - guitar, Christopher McClain - bass. "Take that, wench!" screamed Peter's note to me, in a shamefully winning way. He's an artist, dammit - he actually is - a multi-faceted jaqueline of all trades. He plays guitar and cello, Christopher McClain is on bass and they now have the well named Ruddy Bitch on drums. Being an odd sort, Peter considers the band his visual side and his painting and drawing his musical side. I'm notifying the police. Fascinated by quantum mechanics (oh, not another one), when asked about his persona he furrows mighty brows and sternly barks, "I'm just a fluffy little fella." The only minus point occur when he says he was impressed by Crowley's imagery which is a bit like involving Flock Of Seagulls in an argument about smouldering sexuality. (Crowley was so brilliant a

PHOTO: ELLEN THOMPSON

186

187

man, able to bend strange forces - and people - to his will that he died a broken, pathetic pauper.) Peter on the artistic hand has used his third eye to get heavily involved with Goth and occult mags/zines for years - *Ghastly, Esoterra, Isolation, Virgin Meat*. You have probably already licked some of his work. V-O-T's 'Lust Beyond Flesh' 7" available. And some demos - 'Void', 'Study In Decay' and 'Legemet og Stemmen'. Peter E. Williams, 58 Selkirk Rd #2, Brookline, MA 02146.

VENUS WALK Andrea DiNapoli - keybds/guitar/bass/drum prog./vocals, David Winn - keybds/drum prog./vocals. Electro-Goth with gleaming Industrial elements. MC 'Nocturnal Sound Disorders', CD 'Side Effect'. Excellent vocals, mass musical variety. PO Box 282073, San Francisco, CA 94128.

VON LMO Sixties psychedelic madman still going after nearly twenty five years experimenting with the avant garde side of things. Pretty rocky in parts, the fact one of his earliest bands was called Funeral Of Art shows his heart's in the right place. Where his brain is, nobody can guess. One former band member described him as "the Salvador Dali of the music scene". Check out the CDs 'Cosmic Interception' (94) and 'Red Resistor' (96) if you dare, both on Variant records. Peter Crowley, 61 E. 8th Street #223, New York, NY 10003.

THE WAKE Troy Payne, Richard Witherspoon, James Tramel, Daniel C., Robert Brothers. Ohio's most famous Goth band, allegedly. Oft compared to the Sisters for the vocal similarities. Pretty smart item. 'Masked' CD and 'Christine' CDEP on Cleopatra. PO Box 10503 Columbus, Ohio 4321.

DAVID E WILLIAMS *Enzyme* fanzine said Richard Butler, over music of a Nick Cave meets Phillip Glass conjunction. *Dark Angel* raved too. PO Box 2422 Philadelphia, PA 19147.

ROZZ WILLIAMS Rozz is of course one of the all-time greats. Never does what you expect. A wide ranging sense of style, a not too cleverly administered sense of quality control. From the original Christian Death he has also gone dreamier in the Goth vein with Shadow Project, who have acoustic releases planned, the more howling madness ethic of Premature Ejaculation, the wayward and strange Heltir (freeform improv. - be warned!) and the punkier Daucus Karota. Now he has recently reunited with Gitane Demone on their "late-night cabaret" album, like a mutant brother to early Marc Almond maturity. PO Box 862062, LA, CA 90086-2062.

WILLOW WISP Trash band with psycho Goth image, I have been told, by someone who knows. 7225 Hollywood Blvd. 321, Hollywood CA 90046.

WRECKAGE One project of Tony Lestat, who also stars in Ghost Train (and The Sorcerors Of Caffeine Revelation, who I have a sneaking suspicion we needn't bother with). He is also listed in the poetry department, as he's done, among many things, the *Nightsongs* book. Intriguingly, Wreckage, originally Like Wreckage, formed in 88 and included Kent Bancroft (Screams For Tina/Spahn Ranch) and Billy Budd (Screams For Tina). They lasted a year. Kent and Billy headed off for SFT while Tony linked up with bassist Bill E. Bones (i.e. William Faith of Shadow Project/Faith And The Muse) and guitarist Killjo. These people have gone, but Tony remains, standing proud, joined by Dusty Jones (ex Human Drama/Reverence) on guitar and Everett Thompson on bass. Killjo and drummer Zambo are meant to be returning and maybe Shayde Taladaye. 'Subway's End' 7" (89), 'Phoenix Rising' MC (89), 'Crawling From The wreckage' CD (94), 'The Good, The Bad, The Ugly And The Dead', a Wreckage/Like Wreckage' CD comp (96). There could be a

186 WRECKAGE 187 THE CHAZ! 188-89 ATROCITIES

189

PHOTO: CURSE

188

PHOTO: CURSE

3 Cleopatra boxed set by now. 638 West Knoll Drive 4, Hollywood CA 90069. Or Jevan Records, PO Box 29519, Parma, Ohio 44129.

Clothing/Jewellery

AMAZON DRYGOODS Victorian goods. Clothes, fans, hats, toys, dolls, books and jewellery. Also Medieval/Edwardian style clothing. Dept H-12, 2218 East 11th Street, Davenport, IA 52803-3760.

ATROCITIES Shirts, dresses, cloaks, pillows, 'Ghoul Pops' (handmade, mint-flavoured), funereal veils, batwing overdresses and sorceror's bags. I'm not sure I like the term sorceror's bags somehow. Makes me feel quite ill. With a distinct link to *Spectre* magazine, I expect you'll be hurling your money at them regularly from now on. The 'proprietors' are called Curse and Kambriel (parents!). Catalogue for equivalent of $4 from C. Williams, PO Box 8282 Colorado Springs, CO 80933.

BABY DOLL 8744 Delvista, St Louis, MO 63126.

BEATNIX Vintage clothing. 3436 North Halsted, Chicago, IL 60657.

BERLIN WALL Footwear. 319 3rd Avenue, Chula Vista, CA 92010.

BLACKENED ANGELS Beautiful Goth gown specialist. PO Box 8136, La Crescenta CA 91224.

BLACK OUT FASHIONS Footwear and fashion. PO Box 8433, Grand Rapids, Michigan 49518.

CUPID'S TREASURES A veritable centre of naughtiness. 3519 North Halsted, Chicago, IL 60657.

DALEEPS Clothes/accessories. 1216 Polk Street,

190

191

San Francisco, CA 94109.

DARK GARDEN "Unique corsetry." Asphalt, 551 Hayes Street, San Francisco. [(415) 626-6264]

THE DARK IS RISING Gothic mail order. 298 5th Avenue, Suite 295-k, New York, NY 10001.

DOLL FACTORY PO Box 310174, Newington, Connecticut 06131.

DRAGONCRAFT Gothic and Sacred clothing. GPO Box 022213, Brooklyn, New York, 11202-0047.

EMPIRE OF THE DAMNED Bizarre catalogue. PO Box 20360, New York, NY 10009 .

FLASHY TRASH Vintage clothing. 3524 North Halsted, Chicago, IL 60657.

FUNERAL Occult supplies and jewellery. PO Box 3094, Hollywood, CA 90078.

JEWELLERY Goth/Vampire. Lisa Baglini, 35 Hazel Street, Salem MA 01970.

IPSO FACTO Terri Kennedy, singer of Stone 588 has been running this store for six years and carries what she calls pervy fetish fashion, clubwear and gothicwear. Shoes include skull and square buckle pointed 'witch' boots, and there's a body piercing service which I trust is optional. The shop also offers gallery space for things like performances from The Undead Poets Society and bands like Lycia and Shadow Project, which must have been a squeeze. Excellent catalogue. 517 North Harbour Blvd., Fullerton, CA 92632. (Fax: 714-525-503)

GOTHIC Astonishing quality and range, from velvet and cotton capes, men's ruffled shirts, chainmail, jewellery, reproduction gargoyles and velvet leggings. They work with certain artists and craftsmen exclusively to guarantee top quality and what might seem pricey to some will appear well worth it by those who know. 298 Fifth Avenue, 295 New York, NY 10001-4592.

GYPSY JOKER Handmade jewellery. 7661 1/2 Melrose Avenue, LA, CA 90046.

ARCHIE McPHEE Kitsch goods specialists! PO Box 30852, Seattle, WA 98103.

MEDUSA'S CIRCLE 1491 Washington Ave, Miami Beach, FL 33139.

MISTRESS INC Original and custom made jewellery in Chicago. (e-mail: mistress@csd.uwm.edu)

NECROMANCE Handmade bone jewellery! 7162 Melrose Avenue, LA, CA 90046.

NECROPOLIS Clothing/accessories. 372 Monterey Rd, #17, South Pasadena, CA 91030.

NETHERWORLD Clothes, jewellery for vampires, occult supplies, and statues! 701 N. MacQuesten Pkwy, Crypt 122, Mt Vernon, NY 10552.

99th FLOOR Vintage clothing. 3406 North Halstead, Chicago, IL 60657.

NOSFERATU'S NURSERY 128 Oakland, Pittsburgh, Pennsylvania, 15213.

PLEASURABLE PIERCINGS Concentrates on body piercing. 417 Lafayette Ave, Hawthorne, NJ 07506. (e-mail Needleboy@aol.com)

QUASI-GLAM A great place to get Macabre From The Crypt skull candelabra. 7661 1/2 Melrose Avenue, LA. CA 90046.

190 GOTHIC
193 CLINT CATALYST

192

193

PHOTO: DANA NEELY

ST. MICHAEL'S EMPORIUM A quite phenomenal catalogue is available from this shop which announces itself as a purveyor of "Gothic-Renaissance attire for the New Dark Ages". The fact that you can order made-to-measure suits of armour isn't the dominating shock here. That is reserved for the actual range on what is on offer, far more than the usual jewellery, wristbands, leggings, shirts etc. There are incredible masks, wrist and arm bracers based on any period from Agincourt or Samurai on, make-up, belts, bags, gargoyles, holsters, bras, shoulder pieces, harnesses, corsets... even facsimile weapons of the middle ages variety. In fact everything the modern civil servant might require. Stunning. 156 East Second Street, Suite One, New York, NY 10009. (e-mail: stmichemp@aol.com)

SILVER MOON Vintage clothing. 3337 North Clark, Chicago, IL 60657.

SKIN CRAWL "Want to see something really scary?" they trill. "Your necromantic sanctuary...from the erotic to the macabre". 436 E. 9th St, New York. (Phone: 212-477-2129)

SYREN 5 Custom clothes for stage, video, life. Pleasant Circle, Canton, MA 02021.

TARA GRAFIX "The dark side of t-shirt dom!" 5311 Woodlawn Drive, Harrisburg, PA 17109.

TEXAS BODY HANGINGS Cloaks and whatnot. 1719 E. Main, Nacogdoches, TX 75961 or 835 Decatur St., New Orleans, LA 70116.

TRASH and VAUDEVILLE 4 Saint Mark's Place, New York, NY 10003.

VILLAINS Clothing and accessories, 1682 Haight Street, SF, CA 94117.

Fanzines

ANEMIC BILLFORD MAGAZINE Kevin Dymond, PO Box 35, Arcata, CA 95521.

ARC OF DESCENT Humorous zine and all you could need and less, considering it wants to "suck the intestines out of your ass through a crazy straw" as though this weren't an everyday occurrence anyway. 118320 Kittridge #23, N. Hollywood, CA 91606.

AS IF The genius of little Clint Catalyst. He's like one of The Waltons who came home and created a rumpus by revealing pierced nipples. ("Grandma, get in here!") Excellent magazine in terms of its international content, the artwork and contributions. Normally poetry-based things can cause your spleen to explode with fury at wasted space but Clint knows who means what. Some of his writers are quite exceptional. You should collect each and every issue because it's important stuff. Clint Catalyst, 4104 24th St #254, San Francisco, CA 04114.

AYX OBSCURA PO Box 5554, Atlanta GA 31107.

THE AZRAEL PROJECT NEWSLETTER A weird thing that comes from the much mentioned Westgate Gallery. It recommends a few things and also reveals details of limited edition things available from them alone - like art portfolios and tarot decks. It also announces events to be held at the Gallery such as live performances/exhibitions. As to that name, Azrael. The Angel Of Death, no less! *APN* exists to "put forth His word. To conquer fear through understanding, to make people appreciate the essential nature of Death and to help humankind see their universe through His eyes." Er...good. The letters about "encounters with death" are certainly fascinating. You can also join their regular forum (The Net) and be listed, with your interests. Interesting reviews open up even more avenues for

you to explore! Westgate, 5219 Magazine Street, New Orleans, LA 70115.

BATHORY PALACE Lara, 1610 SW 3rd, Topeka, Kansas 66606-1215.

BELIEF OF STRANGERS PO Box 70521, Riverside, CA 92513-0521.

BEN IS DEAD PO Box 3166, Hollywood CA 90028.

BLACK FLAME Satanic horribleness. Box 499, Radio City Station, New York, NY 10101-0499.

BLACK LOTUS "The magazine of the beautiful and the strange", is actually a "poetry market", and is described as "an irregularly published journal in the tradition of Symbolist/Decadent literature which flourished in late 1800s' France and England and was characterised by a revolt against industrialisation and realism. Contemporized mythology, exotic sensualism, macabre erotica and aestheticism were recurrent themes among the fin de siecle writers. Contemporary treatment of this genre is encouraged. Additional subjects considered in *Black Lotus* are: Gothic Horror and eroticism, Surrealism, nocturnal melancholia, isolationism, and the alternative psycho/sexual treatment of the vampire mythos. No science fiction". It's only poetry they're really after - no short stories, although 'Prose Vignettes' may be accepted providing they contain the same poetic imagery as verse. And how does it read? God knows, I hate poetry...but it looks good and has that authentic dreaminess about it. John Navroth (he's everywhere!), 13415 115th Av NE, Kirkland, WA 98034-2168.

BLACK MOON Music and Horror combined. 1385 Route 35, Suite 169, Middletown, NJ 07748.

BLEEDING SHEEP Weird. John Bertolino, 734 N La Salle Street, Suite 1159, Chicago IL 60610.

BLOODLINES Danis The Dark Productions, 305 Hahani St #296, Kailua HI, 96734.

BLUE BLOOD By Amelia G. and Forrest Black. I've kept this aside from the Fetish section because this high quality glossy rude mag has a variety of contents. Peculiar nudey photo spreads involving Goths, plus plenty of opinionated music reviews, great photos, very strange adverts indeed and a shrewd eye on the world of different subcultures and the perversity of the human spirit. These are the good guys (and girls, naturally) who like to be bad. Mondo Totally Bizarro, Vampires, Fetish, Comics, etc. And great guidelines. The two people responsible are strange. Forrest was born in a house with thirteen black cats. He is working on a source book for something called Mage. Amelia was, and I quote, "raised bouncing from one place to another". And the authorities did *nothing*?! She wrote her honors thesis on "vampire legends as a paradigm for human sexuality". Incidentally they also do the tiny *BLT*, where nobody's driving the train! You'll love that too. CyberJunk BLT, 2625 Piedmont Rd, Suite 56-332, Atlanta, GA 30324. (Fax: 404 365-0664)

BONEYARD Another cool oddity. PO Box 742, Charlottesville, VA 22902-0742.

B-SIDE A magazine. One of the big ones with real spirit, making it less predictable than Alternative Press. PO Box 15921, Philadelphia PA 19103.

CARNAGE HALL "Victorian Sampler." PO Box 7, Lsopus, New York 12429.

CARPE NOCTEM A gallery in your hands. Amazing. PO Box 590, Cupertino, CA 95015-0590.

CATACOMB Darkside mag, clearly perverse. "Sink your teeth into us and we might just bite back!" Hush now, mother might be reading.

194

Debbie Sweeney, 1925 St. Elizabeth Street, Wilmington, Delaware, 19805.

CEMETERY DANCE PO Box 858, Edgewood, ML 21040.

CEMETERY GATES 4336 Bayesville Boulevard, Dayton, Ohio 45431.

CHILDREN OF CAIN Multi-style zine. Bill Connolly, 36 Victory Street, Bridgeport CT 06606.

CODEX OF SHADOWS 5495 Main Street #121, Williamsville, New York 14221.

COMMUNION 16419 Ledge Trail, San Antonio, Texas 78232.

CROW'S CORNER Goth penpal zine. 6324 Locust N.E. Albq, NM 87113.

DANGEROUS MUSIC PO Box 31441, Cincinatti, OH 45231. (Net: dscott@iac.net)

DANSE MACABRE 2929 Harper Street, Berkeley, CA 94703.

DARKSIDE Editor - Bryan Laborde, Co-Editor (and respected DJ) - Patrick Cusack, Art Director - Sean Barrow, Reviews Editor - Max Roy. A mag with attitude, Bryan doesn't hold with all this Vampire and Fetish stuff. "This is a no-nonsense magazine," he rumbles. "There's too many aspects of Goth that are surfacing today that truly doesn't belong. Our motto is, we would not accept garbage and the likes of Nephilim and Sisters rip-offs. If you don't care enough to be original, we don't care about you." You tell 'em! A stylish, in-depth magazine already enjoying massive development from its first issue. PO Box 1344 Madison Square Station, New York, NY 10010.

DBN PO Box 3547 Lantana, Florida 33465.

DEAD AND BURIED 22470 Foothill Boulevard, #25 Hayward, CA 99541.

DEATHREALM Horror/fiction zine. 2210 Wilcox Dr, Greensboro, NC 27405.

DEATH TO THE WORLD 824 Chestnut Street, Chico, California, 95928.

DELIRIUM Ah, pretty special, and up around the 4,000 mark on their fourth issue. Started out looking at the traditional elements - Goth, Vampire and Industrial but expanding to Doom, Ambient and Darkwave, fiction, roleplaying and as much coverage of Vampirella material as they can. Fizzy cross between *As If* and *Permission*. Sophie Diamantis, 779 Riverside Drive A-11, New York, NY 10032 .

DEPREKATION 274 Washington, Cambridge, Massachusettes 02139.

DESCENT Anji & Justin, PO Box 14432, Long Beach, CA 90803.

DE VERMIS MYSTERIS 2140 Shattuck Avenue, Drawer 2479, Berkeley CA 94704.

DIAMOND HITCHIKFR COBWEBS Box 162 Hampshire College, Amherst, MA 01002.

DIPSAS An annual zine dedicated to death and romanticized poetry. Chunky feel, presented roughly but very nicely on alternating red and green paper, with the poems illustrated. Easily worth the $3. Azyre, PO Box 5604, Dearborn Heights, MI 48128.

DISTORTED VISIONS 830 1/4 Las Palmas, LA, CA 90038.

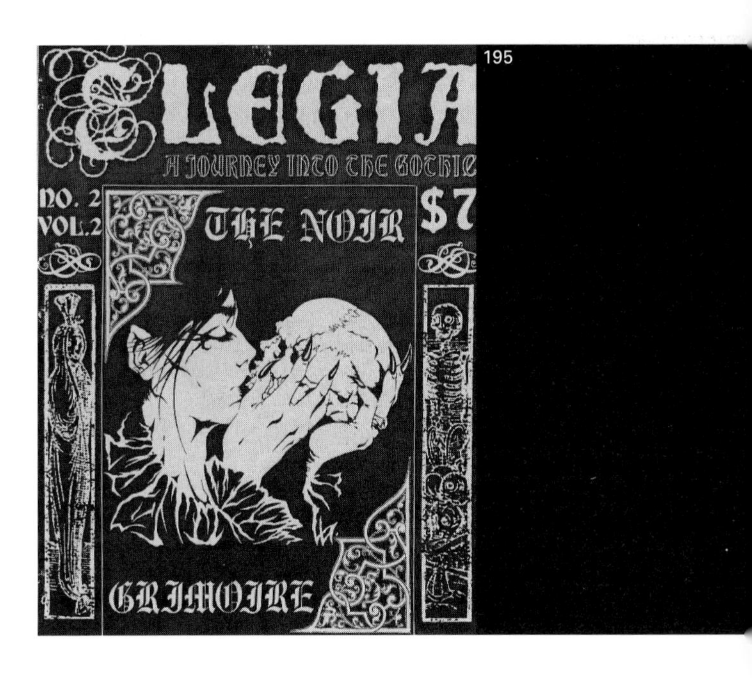

DUMAR'S REVIEWS Poetry, occult etc. Denise Dumars, Box 83, Manhattan Beach, CA 90266.

DYSMETRIA 1262 Mulberry Avenue, Atwater, CA 95301.

THE ECHO ROOM 341 Liberty Blvd, Phillipsburg, New Jersey 08865.

EEK! Networking zine. Art, music, fashion etc with a high percentage of Goth and Industrial stuff. Emory T Suchan n583808, Gulf Correctional Institution, P O Drawer 130, Wewahitchka, FL 32465.

ESKHATOS PO Box 961, Portland, OR 97297 (e-mail: eskhatos@ix.netcom.com)

ELEGIA Superb stuff. "*Elegia* is an irregularly published independent magazine which focuses specifically on the neo-Gothic genre in all of its macabre aspects: gloom, dark fantasy, vampire erotica, the occult, decadence and death - for those who are fascinated with the necro-sensual elegance and beauty of funereal terror. We feature short fiction, poetry, b/w artwork and photography, relevant non-fiction articles, interviews and book/film reviews of Gothic flavour." Incredibly detailed, provocative stuff. Beautiful cover art. Its lack of music coverage makes it all the more desirable. Marie Buckner, PO Box 2096, Ventura, CA 93002.

ENCHANTED REALM Gothic and Pagan Zine. 1800 Riviera Pkwy, Point, Pleasant. NI 08742.

ENZYME Straightforward, good reviews, enjoyable interviews. PO Box 20401, Detroit MI 48220.

ESOTERRA Chad is a writer and poet as well as a perverse character. This highlights that very well. A nervy ride. 630 South Carrollton Avenue, #110, New Orleans, LA 70018.

EVRONYMOUS 12a Elizabeth St, Atlanta, GA 30307.

LEVITY 6904 S. 12th St #1705, Tacoma, WA 98465-1705.

FIFTH PATH PO Box 1632 Charmichael, CA 35609.

FISHNET J Frede, 4211 Mesa Grande, SE #10, Albuquerque, NM 87108.

G.E.A.R. PO Box 592, Orangevale, CA 95662-0592

GARGOYLE SMILE PO Box 250, Oak Forest, IL 60452

THE GASHLYCRUMB The London After Midnight newsletter. 2 IRC's. PO Box 1377, Hollywood, CA 90078-1377.

THE GATE Pen-pal zine, ostensibly with artwork, poetry, photos, short stories. With handcrafted covers this is a work of art. Worth starting a collection. PO Box 19532, Amarillo, TX 79114.

GATEKEEPER PO Box 1341 Tempe, Arizona, 85280.

GATHERING DARKNESS Horror writings. 43 W 427, US Hway 20, Hampshire, IL 60140.

GHASTLY MAGAZINE One of the biggest and slickest in America, it reads okay and looks great, while hardly being up to the minute on musical developments - which doesn't surprise me. A lot of the older Goth fanzines appear to have rested on their laurels so long that strange patterns are embedded in their arse. Big t-shirts range. PO Box 3535 Hollywood, CA 90078.

GNASHING TEETH Shane Archer, 1 Creek Rd, Camp Hill, PA 17011.

196

GODSEND Todd Zachritz, 1401 Fuquay Rd, Evansville, Indiana 47715.

GOLGOTHA Mercy, PO Box 18150, Fountain Hills, AZ 85269.

GOTHAM Carlos Enriquez, 282 4th Street, Jersey City, NJ07302.

GOTHICA S M Jenssen, 96 Union Street, Suite 4, Brewer, ME 04412.

GRACELESS PASSION 9 Audrey Rd, Latham, New York, 12110.

HAPPY CHILDHOOD 500 Atascadero #C8, Morro Bay, CA 93442.

INDEPENDENT UNDERGROUND John Ridge, 6611 Milligan Rd, Cass City, MI 48726.

INDUSTRIAL NATION Editor: Paul Valerio. This includes plenty of Goth amongst its claustrophobically dense pages although Industrial, not surprisingly, wins out. It's incredible and does for these scenes what *MRR* did for Punk (before stagnating). *I.N.* is stuffed full of things, including torrential reviews, far flung scene reports from around the world and average-to-good interviews. A magnificent magazine. 614 Belmont, Chicago, IL 60657-4529. (Fax. 312-665-9116) (e-mail: IN@ripco.com) (Net: http://mozart.fin.depaul.edu/IndustrialnatioN)

IN RAVENS' EYES One of many throbbing titles done by the wonderful Hyacinthe, mainly concerning death-ridden poetry based around the corruption of innocence or ideals, but in *Raven* there is music too. This woman is a **major** talent. There are new items trotting along at regular intervals. Make sure you send for her catalogue. Hyacinthe L. Raven, Via Dolorosa Press, 701 East Schaaf Road, Cleveland, Ohio 44131-1227. (Net: hg191@cleveland, freenet.edu)

IN REMEMBRANCE Jenny Soup's delightful little zine with moody photos, a batch of poetry and some reviews. Very slim and thoughtful. Jenny also has a similarly smart poetry collection, *Sorrow's Velvet Garden*. PO Box 1168-584 Studio City, CA 91604. (Fax: 818 352 6293)

ISOLATION 5411 N. Grantland, Fresno, CA 93722.

JAQUORANDA Unusual. Basically a positive Indie zine, it still manages Faith & Disease on the cover and a frightening Robert Smith drawing inside, among some of the most pertinent, non-drooling, reviews of Britpop bands I've seen in American zines. It fuses all styles together without prejudice and comes up with interesting views all the time. It also looks fantastic. Quite why fanzines in Britain never look so good continues to bewilder me. *Jaquoranda* is one of the most stylish independent magazines in the world, regardless of what scene you're into. Victoria Sprung, PO Box 24332, Federal Way, Washington, 98093-1332.

KITTEN WITH A WHIP "A delightful morsel." Vamp 69, 13413 NW 5th Pl., Plantation, FL 33325.

KIRA BAT Box 942, Benicia, CA 94510.

LEVITY 6904 S.12th #1705, Tacoma, WA 98465-1705.

LA NOIRE D'IMMORTALITY Pagan influence. 912 Bidwell Street, Folsom, CA 95630.

LISA CARVER ROLLERDERBY Wild punk girl mag by Lisa Carver of Suckdog fame! A two issue subscription gets you $5 of "weird stuff". Life as experience. Filthy frolics from the woman who writes cat-based

197

PHOTO: SCOTT R. MCSORLEY

197 CHRISTIANA, EDITOR OF *MACHINE GUN ETIQUETTE*
198 MISTRESS MCCUTCHAN

operas, and the suchlike. Nobody ever seems to have heard of her but Lisa is the best writer in America, bar none. PO Box 18054, Denver, CO 80218.

MACHINE GUN ETIQUETTE The jury is still out on any new address.

MALEDICTION 688 Halifax Drive, Lexington, Kentucky, 40503.

THE MENTOR 408 N. Nanticoke Ave, Endicott, NY 13760-4139.

MO' BETTER GOTH Sarcasm zine - as required. PO Box 690816, San Antonio, Texas 782690816.

MOONLIFE PO Box 3266, South Pasadena, CA 01301.

MORBID OUTLOOK Look at her photo. Stare into the eyes of the woman with the world's best initials. That same dedicated sparkle blesses her pages. Four years and lengthening, this has gone from cut out and paste to PowerMac and it's divine. A smidgeon of music but mainly poetry, images, fiction and photography, plus some sort of network/underground source contact newsletter, *KVD*. Lovely. Mistress McCutchan, Loeb Hall, 135 East 12th St. #82, New York, NY 10003.

MURDER CAN BE FUN Mayhem nostalgia, as man's inhumanity to everything comes under the microscope, as well as tragic accidents. Weirdzine par excellence. Also available - the diary of the year - The MCBF datebook, with 365 morbid events to celebrate throughout the year. Headline of the year in 'Faster Mormon Kill Kill'. PO Box 640111, San Francisco, CA 94109.

NECRO Goth/Horrorzine, buzzing with life. PO Box 88, Royal Oak, MI 48068.

NECROPOLIS PO Box 69, Kirkville, NY 13082.

NETHERWORLD Glenn 'Diablo' Miceli, 20228 Walnut Drive, Walnut, CA 91789.

NIGHTSHADE 5528 Eagle Lake Drive. Palm Beach Gardens, Florida, 33418.

NOCTURNAL IMAGES 326 West 16th Street, Crowley, Louisiana, 70526.

NOIR Piss-take Goth zine. 1780 Wrightstown Rd, Newton, PA 18940.

NOT EXACTLY HUMAN Fanzine about the vampire characters of Wendy Snow-Laing. PO Box 5010, Suite 115, Salem, MA 01970.

NOT DEAD BUT DROWNING Beautiful drawings and poetry. Lara Haynes, PO Box 442572, Lawrence, Kansas, 66044.

NOX Loretta M. Accardo, PO Box 2467, Grand Central Station, NY 10163-2467.

THE PAIN SCRIPTURES Apocalypse Theatre. PO Box 73654 Washington DC 20056.

PARTS 451 Moody St, Waltham, Ma 02154.

PASSION & ECSTASY Caryn Cook, 9 Audrey Rd, Latham, New York, NY 12110.

PERMISSION Cool magazine. Taut layout, sharp opinions, quality writing and photography, wide scope. 1800 Market #777, San Francisco, CA 94102. (e-mail: innocent@sirius.com) (www.pacifier.com/coldwave/permission/aether.html)

PHANTASMOGORIA PO Box 1305 Flagstaff AZ 86002.

Exit

Morbid Outlook
through bitten tongues
Issue #8

PHENGOPHOBIA That means fear of daylight. Rough but interesting, a lot is promised by this as there is a strong personal perspective at its heart, from The Cold (Tears Ov Blood). Somewhat crudely put together, the actual look is fine and the variety nice. Illustrations, photos, cemetery art, articles about his own projects and those he feels a particular empathy with - and naturally the interviews draw out what you would wish to know, rather than being sedate or random questions. I'd follow the development of this if I were you. The Cold, PO Box 179, Baldwinville, MA 01436.

PRIMAL CHAOS Strange. I loathed this. 1072 Folsom #388, San Francisco, CA 94103.

PROPAGANDA Funnily enough, for all its reputation this clearly *isn't* the best Goth mag in America. What it is...is the most *unusual* Goth mag, which is even better, and/or the best realised. The music coverage has increasingly taken the backseat behind the visual ideas as they merge fiction into pictoral surrounds, and of course they've done their own acted videos. They are about exploring the elements of what makes up Goth, from their collective perspective and if some music fits in well, fine. They won't deny it. So it's odd, utterly fantastic to look at and it's only a shame it isn't more regular. PO Box 296, New Hyde Park, New York 11040.

QRM Net/CybernetD Christopher K. Derrick, 706 Brookside Lane, Frankport, IL 60423-1204.

RED ROSE OF LOVE & DEATH 2324-A E. 43 Street-13, Erie, PA 16510.

REPTILES OF THE MIND A fanzine apparently devoted to reptiles and thereby dubbed the coolest zine in America, unless there's also one on newts somewhere in which case this can fuck right off! Box 10087, Knoxville, TN 37939-0087.

REQUIEM 19 Mt Vernon Terrace, Waynesboro, PA 17268.

RITUAL SLAYINGS Andy Erikson, 7 Central St, Ilahant, MA 01908.

SCREEM Done by those awfully nice TDT people. Very stylish - glossy, lusciously laid out, chaotic yet orderly. Fiction, illustrations, funny guides to what's out there to buy and interviews with interesting creators in the horror genre (artists or designers). PO Box 138300, Chicago, IL 60613.

SANCTUARY Janet, PO Box 868, Wofford Heights, CA 93285.

SHADOWDANCE A small but exquisitely done magazine. A pinch of everything, adorable to behold. Michelle Belanger, PO Box 474, Hinckley OH 44233.

SHADOWS Gothic/Wiccan. Box 2355, Huntington, CT 06484.

SHELTERED LIFE Beautiful, albeit slim, fanzine. PO Box 71247, Shorewood, WI 53211.

SINS OF COFFEE "Upbeat Noir." PO Box 26197, San Francisco, CA 94126-6127.

SIXTH FORM 2020 Terry Avenue #718, Seattle, Washington, 98121.

SLICE OF LIFE PO Box 445 Richmond, Indiana, 47375.

SMASHLIGHT PO Box 10637, Westburn, NY 11590.

SOUL MANIFEST 540 Henry Street #1, Brooklyn, New York 11231.

SPECTRE "Post Mortem, Lunar apparitions, Dark Liquidtrance Bloodscapes, Writhing Vampyric Chasms, Cemeterial Moonlit Gloom, Shadowy Macabre, Gateway To The Gothic." And that's all got to fit on their business card? If I was being basic, almost Spartan, I'd say this was just like *Ghastly* magazine. Then I would wait for Editorex Jennifer Chen to howl like a demented beast...and I would add...with the essential added ingredient of personality. Oh, and taste. Have I left anything out? Class? Warmth? The sense that she really cares about what she's talking about? Exactly. This is the genuine article, a labour of love, not a business. She could do with reducing the type size though to get more in. Apart from that it's one of the main zines any seriously alert Goth should regard as *ultra*-desirable. PO Box 474, Lexington, KY 40585-0474.

SPLATTERLISP Bi-monthly compendium, whatever that means. PO Box 7326, Erie, PA 16510.

SPOONFUL OF DISTORTION Rt 1 Box 152, Lamkin Rd, Harlem, GA 30814.

SRI LANKA Box 311, Devon, PA 19333.

STRANGE DESIRE David P. Holusha, 87 Ellison Avenue, Westbury, NY 11590.

SUBNORMAL Another must-have for any serious American Goth, and for anybody else for that matter. Wide-ranging, spot-on, an utter disgrace. They also run *Bi-Monthly Bondage* (see Fetish). PO Box 602, Normal IL 61761

SUBSTITUTION 664 12th Street, San Pedro, CA 90731.

SUCKERS 1404 Leader Drive, Killeen, TX 76542.

TALES Any fanzine cool enough to rip of Cerebus art for a cover (issue 4?) is okay by me, or if its an accident they're geniuses anyway. Bitty Goth coverage but this should prove interesting. Soil (Soil?!), 1845 Hancock St, San Diego, CA 619-698-8276.

TEAR DOWN THE SKY 84 Seaview Avenue, Marblehead, Massachusetts 01945.

TEKELI-LI 106 Hanover Avenue, Pawtucket,

PHOTO: BRIAN WYNN

200

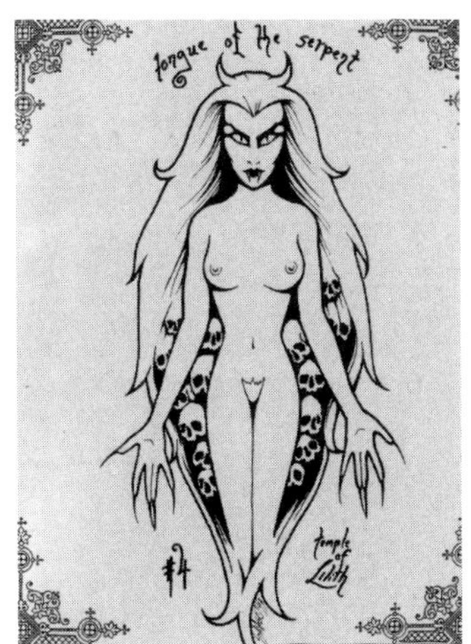

201

200 JENNIFER CHEN OF *SPECTRE*

Rhode Island 02861.

TENEMENT OF CLAY Jeannine DeSalme, 4511 Leiper Street, Philadelphia, PA 19124

TERRA X 4159 Gem Cir., N Ridgeville, Ohio 44039.

THE DEAD ARE SUSPENDED Done by artist Sorrel Smith. 1645 Furlong Rd, Sebastopol, CA 95472.

THEATRE OF THE NIGHT Lake, Box 162, Hampshire Col. Amherst, Mass 01002-5001.

3rd NAIL Varied zine, offering sage advice about anything they adore. Much raved over by *Spectre*, so that's good enough for me. PO Box 42273, Pittsburgh, PA 15203.

THISTLE Chelsea and Thaylor, PO Box 50094, Minneapolis, MN 55405.

TONGUE OF THE SERPENT The fanzine of Temple Of Lilith, lovingly presided over by the brilliant Althea Morin, it's a visual and mental aphrodisiac. And while there are usually several detailed articles about their main concern it's not entirely devoted to Lilith (and I confess I understand none of that sort of stuff) so there's other bits to admire, particularly the illustrations and especially the work of one Dawne Martin Garvin, one of the finest freelance artists I've ever seen in a fanzine. Basic beliefs: "We oppose censorship, concepts of morality, ignorance. We believe in independence and individuality, in the pursuit of True Will, in pleasure in hedonism, in the fundamental right to create, in the natural force of chaos. We are the snakes in the grass, and our tongues shall not be silenced." Precisely. Box 1483, New York, NYC 10009-1484.

ULTIMATUM It's actually Metal of the Death variety but is recommended by Westgate for quality - and it does include interviews with people like comic writers, horror comic cover artists, etc. Box 1003, Long Beach, NY 11561.

UNDERGROUND ZINE SCENE John Ridge, 6611 Milligan Rd, Cass City, MI 48726.

VEIL Poetry, art and dreams more than music. PO Box 752, Royal Oak, Michigan, 48068-0752.

VERBAL ABUSE 315 Park Avenue South, RM 1611, New York, NY 10010.

VIRGIN MEAT Small but nice with fiction, poetry and a few reviews or infosnatches. 2325 W Avenue k-15, Lancasrer, CA 93536.

VIRTUE ET MORTE PO Box 63113, Philadelphia, PA 19114-1813.

WAKE THE DEAD RT 13, Box 802, Lake City, Fl 32055.

WAMPIOR PRESS Info, ads, art, poetry. 507 Helina Dr, Sandusky, Ohio 44870.

THE WILD RAG Huge zine, mainly Death Metal but other bits too: demos, t-shirts, videos, CDs, everything. 2207 W. Whittier Blvd, Box 3302, Montbello, CA 90640.

ZINE X Apocalypse Theatre zine. PO Box 420476, San Francisco, CA 94142-0476.

Fetish

ADAM & EVE Adult mail order. Apple Court, PO Box 800, Carrboro, NC 27510.

ATTITUDE TFN Female domination mag by "The Goddess Diana Vesta, world's most beautiful

203 MISS MARTHA (NOIR LEATHER)

202

mistress" who actually looks like any old bimbo from a Whitesnake video. 13730 State Rd 84, Suite 213, Ft Lauderdale, FL 33325.

B. LEATHER Low priced, high quality S/M equipment and leather gear. 3217 Wilmington Pk 19, Kettering, Ohio 45429.

BACKSEAT BETTY "Bad things for bad girls." 1780 Haight Street, San Francisco, California 94117.

BI-MONTHLY BONDAGE A slim, provocative thing. More real, less crass than most. PO Box 602, Normal, IL 61761.

BODY PLAY & MODERN PRIMITIVES QUARTERLY PO Box 2757, Menlo Park, CA 94026-2575.

BONEYARD PRESS "The most notorious comics in print." Dept BB, 17175 Simonds St, Granada Hills, CA 91344.

BOOMERANG Leather and docs. 1128 Decatur, New Orleans, Louisiana 70116.

BOX BB-1 Mail order service advertising thousands of different zines covering every conceivable subject. 1226-A Calle de Commercio Santa Fe, NM 87505.

SUSIE BRIGHT Lesbian poet and writer of erotica. 3309 1/2 Mission Street. #143, San Francisco, CA 94110.

CHERRY COMICS Fetish humour. PO Box 4662, Santa Rosa, CA 95402.

DARKWELL LTD Bondage. PO Box 1304, Chicago, IL 60690.

DOMINATRIX CROSSROADS Bondage mag. PO Box 17070, Las Vegas, NV 89114.

DREAM DRESSER High quality fetish wear. PO Box 16158, Beverley Hills, CA 90209-2158.

DUNGEON WEAR Handmade chainwear. 7661 1/2 Melrose Avenue, Los Angeles, CA 90046.

EIDOS The mag for "sexual commandoes everywhere". POB 96, Boston MA 02137-0096.

EXPECTATIONS Fetish/bondage. 236A West 3rd Street, Suite 440, New York, NY 11011.

FANTASY FASHION DIGEST Fantasy fashion and couture. PO Box 9500, Palm Springs, CA 92263.

FANTASY FASHIONS Fetish clothing. PO Box 910, Westmont Illinois, 60559

FUTURE SEX Nicely unusual mag. 1095 Market Street, Suite 809, San Francisco, CA 94103.

GOOD VIBRATIONS Mail order - everything.1210 Valencia St, San Francisco, CA 94110.

HUBBA HUBBA Bondage/fetish store. 932 Mass Avenue, Cambridge, MA 02139.

THE HUMANE RESTRAINT CO. INC. Allegedly has a catalogue of the best selection available anywhere of medical/reform restraints. Nothing typically S/M in there just, er...everything for the amateur kidnapper by the sound of it! PO Box 16, Madison, WI 53701.

LACUNAE Wild stories. 2076 S Pleasant Valley Rd, Rm 111, Winchester, VA 22601.

LION'S MARK INDUSTRIES Hand-crafted high quality medical grade stainless steel piercing jewellery. PO Box 1753, Iowa City, IA 52240.

LUMINART Mag offering "perspectives beyond the

PHOTO: J. LYNN KOSTER

PHOTO: EUGENE SHERRILL

205

204-05 NOIR LEATHER (HELLBOUND)
206 MICHAEL AND JEANETTE (NOIR LEATHER)

roleplaying paradigm". 162 Viking Ct #4, Athens, GA 30605.

MAN RAY Interesting club, heartily recommended by the good folk of *Phengophobia* zine, open to all "left-of-center" people. 21 Brookline Street, Cambridge, MA. (617 864-0400)

N.E.S.S. The society for those who "love to spank". 14 Russell Street, Waltham, MA 02154.

NIGHTCRY An illustrated mag of impeccable artwork, combined with "terrifying, brutal stories of modern decadence". CFD Productions, 360-A W. Merrick Rd, Suite 350, Valley Stream NY 11580.

NOCTURNE "A place where every whim can be accommodated within the laws of physics." Smart custom bondage furniture and 'dungeon toys' company, already working with Noir on their 'Hellbound' spectaculars in clubs, they offer things like stocks, spanking benches, dance cages, 'tumbling racks', and loads of things people whack each other with. Shawn L. Stephenson, 640 Wordsworth, Ferndale, MI 48220.,

NOIR LEATHER Leather/bondage goods from a superb outlet. Noir Leather started in Dec 83 when Keith Howarth had a tiny shop offering Bondage/S&M gear but catering mainly for Goths and Punks. He hasn't forgotten his original customers, rather he has constantly upgraded everything and increased the variety, now including general fetish wear, clubwear and vintage clothing. Vintage Noir now offers punk and goth styles, while Faith Glamour is another shop offering club things. Noir carries more than just its own products, importing recommended items into America. They also produce stage productions for shows, with Nocturne, opening for the likes of Alien Sex Fiend, Sex Gang Children, right up to a spot on the

PHOTO: EUGENE SHERRILL

206

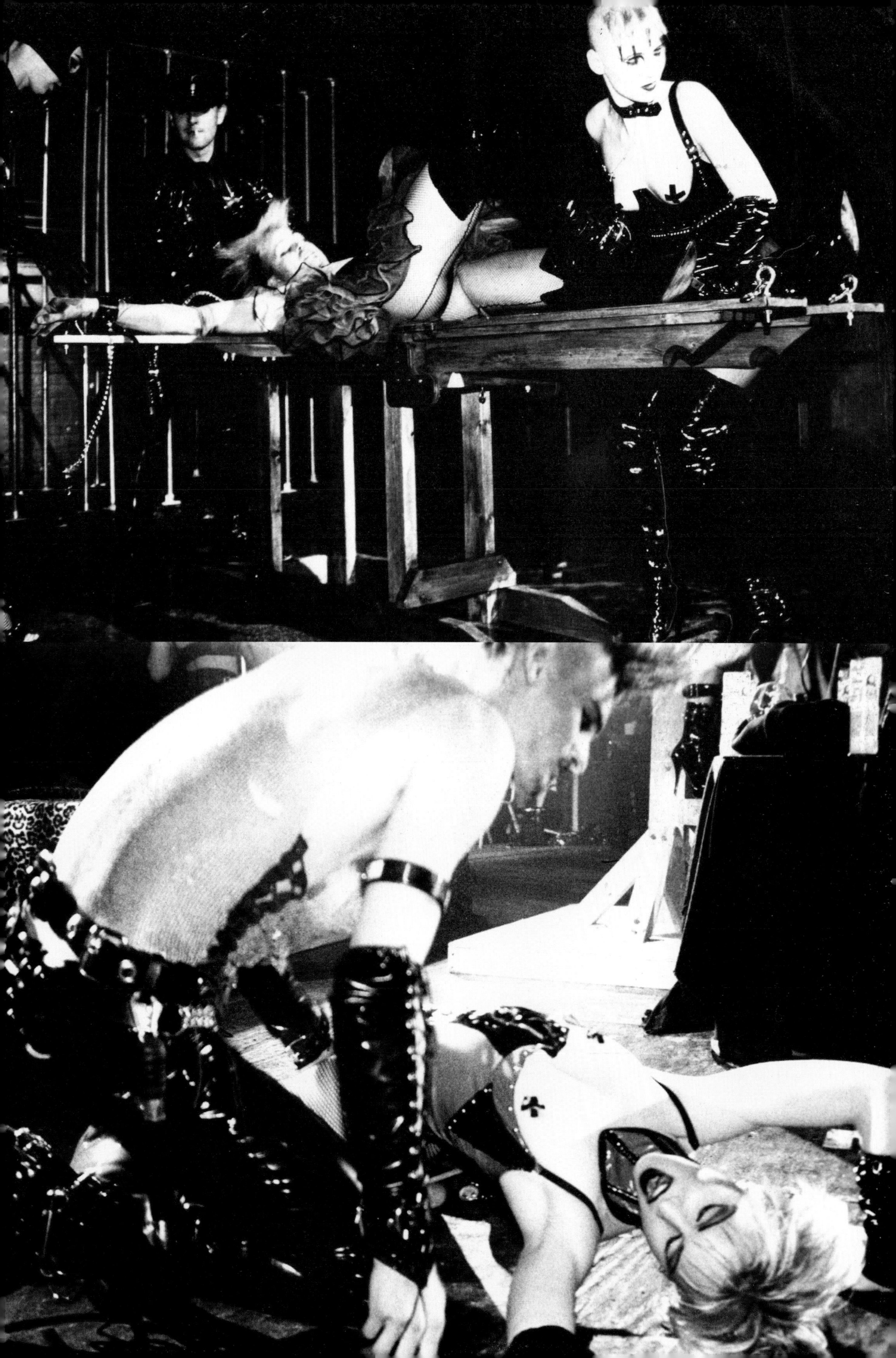

PHOTO: LEWIS DENNISON

207 NOIR LEATHER 208 TIM TV (NOIR LEATHER)
209 HELLBOUND/NOIR LEATHER

209
PHOTO: BRETT CARSON

208 PHOTO: DANIEL F. KELL

Lolapalooza tour. Their excellent catalogue shows the styles and quality of the goods. $7, extra for international postage. It lists Body Accoutrements, Bondage, Boot Tips, Bootstraps, Bracelets, Braces, Collars, Cybergear, Earrings, Necklaces, Paddles, Pewter Bracelets/ Necklaces, Real Skulls (coyote/ muskrat), Rings, Rosarys, Spurs, Studs, T-shirts, Trouser Chains, Whips and Crops and Wristbands. They also have a range of their own organised videos. 'Almighty Lumberjacks Of Death' is probably an acquired taste. Shop address - 415 South Main Street, Royal Oak, Michigan 48067. Mail order/wholesale/catalogue address - 317 S. Center Street, Royal Oak, MI 48067.

THE NOOSE Clothes, 261 West 19th Street, New York, NY 10011.

ON OUR BACKS "Entertainment for the adventurous lesbian." 526 Castro St, San Francisco, CA 94110.

PANASEWICZ Gothic erotic art/lithographs. PO Box 15991, The Strip Station, Las Vegas, Nevada 89114.

PARAMOUR Erotic fiction mag. PO Box 949, Cambridge MA 02140-0008.

DIANE PEERLESS S/M ("tickle tormenting"?) videos. 1624 W 6th St, #246, LA, CA 90017.

PLEASURE CHEST Fetish shop. 7733 Santa Monica Boulevard, West Hollywood, CA 90046.

RUBBER REBEL Magazine. Box 66306 Los Angeles, CA 90066.

SANDMUTOPIA GUARDIAN "Serious S/M news." PO Box 410390, San Francisco, CA 94113.

SARAH SEDUCTION SOCIETY Allegedly a world famous femme fatale. The mag is apparently as

)IR LEATHER 211 POPPY Z. BRITE

210 PHOTO: J. LYNN KOSTER

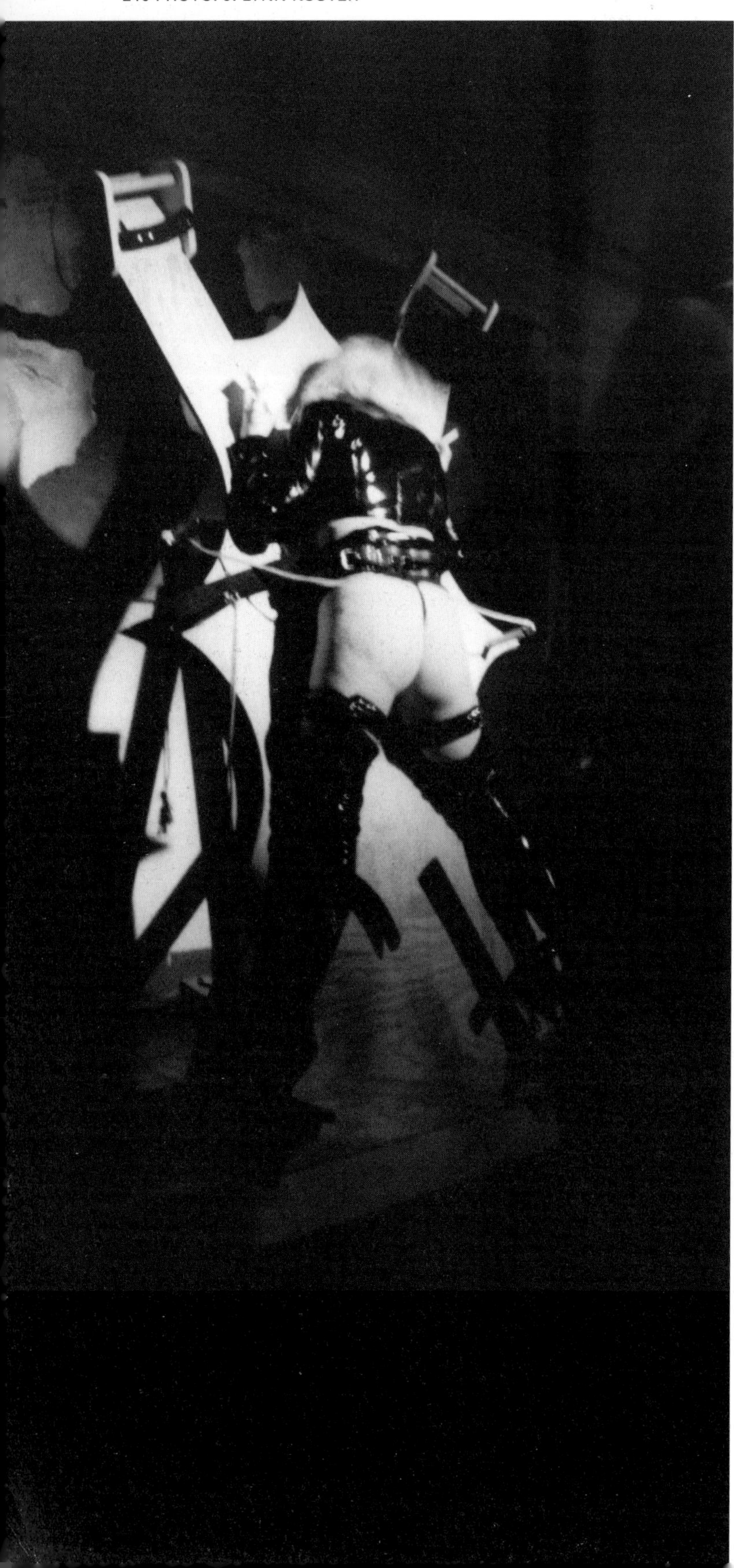

"packed as her halter tops" which is good news. You may even take part in "Sarah contests" to win one of her g-strings. How lovely. SFC, 5002 N. Royal Atlanta Dr., Suite H, Trucker, GA 30084.

SECOND SKIN Bondage, leather, latex, 512 Saint Philip Street, New Orleans, LA 70116.

STORMY LEATHER S/M equipment. 1158 Howard Street, San Francisco, CA 94103.

TASTE OF LATEX Gay fetish zine. PO Box 460122, San Francisco, CA 94146.

D.B. VELVEEDA Fetish artist. PO Box 281, Astor Station, Boston, MA 02123-0218.

VOYAGES All manner of fetish things. Stunning quality. PO Box 78550, Dept 902, San Francisco, CA 94107-8550.

WICKED WAYS Fetish and 'play' attire. PO Box 16752, Alexandria, VA 22302.

ZARA WHITE Erotic writer, with film *The Pleasure Chest* available from The Stamford Collection, Depot XN-36/PO Box 11670, L.I.C. NY 11101.

Individuals

PAUL ANGELOSANTO Author of 'The Season Passage' - an epic poem illustrated with stylish graveyard imagery. 3 Walsh Ave, Stoneham, MA 02180.

JOHN BERGIN A one man army of ideas. Apart from his projects Trust Obey and C17H19NO3, he has this Grinder organisation offering comic collaborations, including *From Inside*, the 224 page softback of James O'Barr's *The Crow*. A catalogue is advised. PO Box 45182, Kansas City, MO 64171.

JENNIFER BLOWDRYER Authoress of the novella *Wrong Wrong Wrong*, which is just plain weird. Fury, not filth from a woman who describes herself as a hack erotica writer but also does a column for *MRR* to save her soul. Zeitgeist Press, 4368 Piedmont Avenue, Oakland, CA 94611.

POPPY Z. BRITE Poppy deserves a very special mention not just because she has a Z for a middle initial and because her press release ends so brilliantly ("Poppy Z. Brite lives in New Orleans with two cats and two boyfriends"). She has also worked as a "gourmet candy maker", which looks good on anyone's c.v. I always say. (Quite what "a mouse caretaker" involved we may never know.) When erotic becomes eerie Brite seems believable where Rice doesn't. She does similar things in reality. I see from my notes she appeared in *John Five*, a short erotic film, alongside two eighteen year old boys. Probably helping them with their homework, or making paper planes. I believe that's what you young people like to do. Contact via Penguin Books.

211
PHOTO: MATTHEW GRASSE

CLINT CATALYST Author, wildman, jailbait. Clint does the devastating *As If...* zine but has also done the book, *Caresses Soft As Sandpaper*, on November-March productions out of Albany, NY. In his spare time he is a performance artist. Intriguing guy.

CLOVIS IV Excellent photographer who works for fanzines and magazines and does much of Tess Records' photographic work. PO Box 981, Santa Barbara, CA 93102. (Fax (805) 966 9076)

SHAWN COLON Artist behind *Post Modern Vampir*. PO Box 57133, Sherman Oaks, CA 91413.

BRIAN DEMSKI Custom skull and skeleton furniture, candelabrae etc. Incredible work (seen in *Batman* and *Addam's Family*). 1842 N Cherokee Avenue 306, Hollywood, CA 90028.

DEMIAN DORRANCE Now here's a chap, putting the "Oh!" back into Omen. He only took up keyboards in 88, because his brain glowed with technology, starting off in an Industrial outfit, The Torture Garden. Now he operates with vocalist Stephanie Geniza as Cruciform, and a few songs have popped out. He's a mad collector of Goth/Ethereal/DarkWave/Industrial and already has over 1300 CDs! Originally he was dj-ing on college radio, painfully aware that hardly anybody ever heard the show but also realising he had no choice but to carry on. Sometimes this music *is* you. October 17, 90, he opened SubNation Club with a friend Tom Feeney. Three months later Tom died. Demian immediately closed the club - "the decision was a very easy one to make, being the last person to see him alive and having parted on a sour note....closing was the only respectful thing to do". He was surprised by the reactions people then expressed to him about how much of a void the club had actually filled. Co-erced into doing one more night, twice as many people turned up as usual. Since those days Demian has been involved with other clubs but, most notably, Mass, since 7.7.92, with Tim Hall. Their rules are worth noting.

1: Expose Great Music - they expected feedback and would quiz their audience. They always displayed the name of the song and artist they were playing on video monitors, so people were kept informed, informally - to help shy people know what they were enjoying! 2: Play requests. Simple but rare.
3: Expand, do not repeat. Not playing the same music week after week. Mood mixing, they call it.
4: Don't pass judgement on those around you.
5: The "customer" doesn't exist, we are all friends here.

I reprint this info for you because he's sparing you mistakes if you plan something similar. Outside of club activities other events occur, including road trips (Goths ice-skating!) and film premieres. There is also the SubNation studio, which still operates today and in 95 the SubNation record label. Mr Dorrance I take my hat off to you...and I actually have a hat, so it is genuinely meant. PO Box 12245, El Cajon, CA 92022. (Fax: 619-595-1555)

STEVE ENG Archivist of Gothic/Occult literature. Box 60072, Nashville, TN 37206.

DAWNE MARTIN GARVIN Stunning artist. Box 227, Monponsett, MA 02350.

MICHELLE GLASS Michelle sent photographs of herself but didn't explain what she does, other than slinking around in metal underthings. 11541 W, 32nd St apt. #C, Mpls, MN 55408.

LAUREN GOODLAD It's the craziest Assistant Professor of Victorian Literature & Cultural Studies in the West! Madly engaging type who has lectured in Scotland about Gothic novel-related matters, works in the University of Washington and spends a

212 HYACINTHE L. RAVEN   213 ZAHR

212

regular amount of her free time contributing to serious or semi-serious Net debate and is well worth an electric visit. English Dept, Box 354330, Seattle, Washington 98195-4330. (Fax: 206-685-2672) (e-mail: Igoodlad@u.washington.edu)

JONATHAN GREY Druidic bodyguard and babysitter! Working on graphic novel comic to tie in with a gaming system. Victoria Gwaed at same address is a dancer, dominatrix and seamstress. Just your typical American household. 1505 Kirkwood Ave Apt. A, Nashville, TN 37212.

JUDY HARRIS "Underworld artist serving the dark ones." (Everyone needs a hobby.) 107 Howard St, Pittsfield, MA 01201.

DR. JOHN KURLUCK Tarot, psychic counselling. 6212 Holabird Ave #F, Baltimore, MD 21224.

J. MARTIRE Gothic vocalist/Occultist/Circle High Priestess. 1755 Potomac Avenue, Pittsburgh, PA 15216.

MAX PHOTOGRAPHY PO Box 14620. Chicago, IL 60614 0620.

ALTHEA MORIN *Tongue Of the Serpent*/Temple Of Lilith woman, Althea sports some fairly exuberant tattoos on her back, which may be reprinted here, and writes some very dirty fiction for magazines, which will most certainly not be! Box 1483, New York, NY 10009-1484.

PAULA O'KEEFE Formerly behind Nephilm zine *KIA*, she's a witch, and is into shamanism and the Mexican-American Brujeria, which is a new one on me. PO Box 1065, Washington.

PRIESTESS MUSLIMA 'Voodoo Crossroads' mag. 1308 N. Gayoso St, New Orleans, LA 70119.

HYACINTHE L RAVEN A pocket-sized genius, and for her age surely the most gifted American in this book. Tell that to her face and you'd be watching a beetroot, magically sprouting arms and flailing away madly into the distance. Ablaze with modesty, this woman has already done some poetry so immense that even a profligate poem-hater like myself has reeled in astonishment. Some of this she puts into attractively zeroxed zine form. She does fiction and her *Raven's Eye* zine on music. She has so much talent that she simply isn't aware of it. A star in the ascendant. Send for her catalogue *now*. She's working in a mortuary you know, but doesn't believe in taking her work home with her. Via Dolora Press, 701 East Schaaf Rd, Cleveland, Ohio 44131-127.

TIMOTHY RENNER "Aspects of death" illustrator. Box 9, Upperco, MD 21155.

JESSIE RITCHIE Tarot, psychic counselling. 8201 Pittman Ave, Pensacola, FL 32534.

STEVE ROBICHAUD Interesting, quality photographer. Nice graveyard shots. Also involved with the experimental music of Vanish Hall. 186 Chapel Street, Gardner, MA 01440.

JENNY SOUP Recommended writer. Bands could certainly regard her as a good contact, along with the other immortals in this section. 11684 Ventura Blvd #584, Studio City, CA 91604.

HEATHER SPEAR The woman behind *Convergence* and *The Gate*. One of the most important people there, I'd say. Certainly one of the most passionate and devoted. Drop her a line, for specifics or just for the Hell of it. (See Fanzines/Societies.)

KIMBERLEY TRAUB Pagan/Goth/Horror illustrator. 7012 Upper York Rd, #A, New Hope, PA 18938.

PHOTO: DAVID H

PAUL URIAZ Jr. Ghost photographer. 524 N. Island Ave, Wilmington, CA 90744.

RENE WALCZAK Journalist who gets everywhere in the US, and also contributes to Australia's *Dark Angel* and the UK's *Bats & Red Velvet*. If any band wants coverage in the US this is one of the main people to contact. 821 West Cornelia Ave #115, Chicago, Illinois, 60657.

ZAHR Okay, now if you're serious you write to Zahr, be you band or record company person, this woman can point you in the right direction and she seems to write for virtually everything under the sun. Another reliable contact. She's also a poet, photographer and model, although you probably won't need to ask about that, unless you're particularly nosey. 2 Flagstone, #821 Irvine, CA 92714.

Labels

AIDA HOUSE RECORDS PO Box 520053, Salt Lake City, UT 84152-00537.

ANUBIS PO Box 470666, San Francisco, CA 94147. (e-mail: anubis@cyberden.com)

ARTS INDUSTRIA SOUND PO Box 4142, South Bend, IN 46634-4142.

BEDAZZLED RECORDS PO Box 39195, Washington, DC 20016.

BLACK SAMVARA PRODUCTIONS Video label. PO Box 151244, San Diego, CA 92175.

BROKEN DISHES Drucilla Blood, BDP Post Office Box 250, Oak Forest, IL 60452.

C'EST LA MORT PO Box 91, Baker, LA 70714.

CHANNEL 83 900 W. Grandview, Roseville, MN 55113.

CLEOPATRA Hand on heart, what do I think of Cleopatra? Well, I think they, as with many other labels, tend to use too many tracks that are easily available on their compilations but, apart from that, I'd say they're the best independent label in the world - not necessarily for some of the taste displayed in their signings, or re-releases - as that's always a subjective matter - but for the quality of what they do, the regularity of releases and the *effect* they have. If you disagree, think what it would be like without them. 9726 Sepulveda St. D-82, Los Angeles, CA 90045. (http://www.cyberdencom/Cleopatra.html)

CONCISE NOISE FRACTIONALE LTD Constantly increasing range of Ethereal, Industrial, Goth etc. PO Box 1245, Gardner MA 01440.

CYKXINCORP New label, covering everything from Electronic, Goth and Instrumentals. PO Box 299, Lenox Hill Station, New York NY 10021.

DUTCH EAST INDIA TRADING Distributor. PO Box 800, Rockville Centre, NY 11571-10800.

ETHERHAUS Distribution. Box 206, Santa Barbara, CA 93102. (805-568-1603)

GOTHIC INDUSTRY RECORDS PO Box 913, Glendale, Arizona 85311.

GPC PROUDCTIONS PO Box 1515, Alientown, PA 19105-1515.

HYDE RECORDINGS Dark Folk. PO Box 831, Reisterstowne, Maryland, 21136-0831.

IVY RECORDS PO Box 2721, Seattle,

WA 98111-2721.

JEVAN RECORDS PO Box 29519, Parma, Ohio 44129.

MALAISE MUSIC 1511 Sawtelle Bl. Ste #332, LA, CA 90025

MOON MYSTIQUE Distributor 114 1/2 E. College Street, Iowa City, LA 52240-4005.

NO VISIBLE SCARS Looking for bands for compilation CDs. 36 Victory Street, Bridgeport CT 06606.

PROJEKT: DARKWAVE Their little ads state quite simply, "Ethereal, Gothic and Darkambient", but this is the truly modern 4AD if you wish. Sam Rosenthal runs it, starting very inauspiciously by organising a tape compilation of Fort Lauderdale new romantic bands in 83! He's got the Darkwave distribution thing, which handles Tess, Hyperium, Cold Meat and Dorobo. PO Box 1591, Garden Grove, CA 92642. (http:/charlotte.acns.nwu.edu/arielry/projekt/projekt.html)

PULSE SONIQ Distribution - a division of Silent Records. Andrea Parra, one of their buyers seems like an excellent contact. They deal with plenty of Goth/Industrial acts and labels, importing them into America or generally distributing home talent within the country, reaching 500 stores in the States. They also export some American things to the UK, Japan and Mexico. 101 Townsend Street, Suite 206, San Francisco, CA 94107. (Fax: 415.957.0779)

RAGE RECORDS 148-09 Northern Blvd, Apt 1K, Flushing, NY 11354.

RECONSTRUCTION/CARGO Tape label and distributor. 4901-906 Morena Blvd, San Diego, CA 92117-3432.

REALIZATION RECORDINGS 9452 Telephone Rd, No. 116, Ventura, CA 93004.

ROTTEN PO Box 2157, Montclair, CA 91763.

SCREAM RECORDS Richard Mann, 36 River Street, Rochester, NH 03867. (Fax: 603-330-0632) (e-mail: rmann77@aol.com.)

SUBTERRANEAN RECORDS PO Box 2530, Berkeley, CA 94702.

TESS RECORDS "This," Tess announce, "is a label defined by its music, its art. The only existing boundaries are those we choose to create. The sublime expression of each artist forms an integral part of our growth; another brush stroke in our mural of worlds, ranging from eloquent rage to bohemian wanderings, with much more to come. It is our wish that you experiment with our different textures and flavours, giving yourself over to this feast of the senses. We feel that our group of artists form the new aesthetic; an avant garde collection of our newest talent, offering you a myriad of moods and thoughts. We hope that you enjoy our music as much as we do. " PO Box 206, Santa Barbara, CA 93102. (Fax 1-805-2681604) (e-mail: TESSINTL@AOL,COMUS)

TRIPLE X Highly dependable label. A new sub-label, Hollow Hills should be in existence by now, devoted entirely to Goth. PO Box 862529, Los Angeles, CA 90086-2529. (Fax: 213 221 2778)

VALMONT 1534 N. Homboldt Ave #33, Milwaukee WI 53202.

VARIANT RECORDS PO Box 3852, Redwood City, CA 94064-3852.

VENTURE BEYOND RECORDS Run by Mark Smith and home to the house band, Pinochio Vampire, The Netherworld, four other American and six Russian bands. Weird, or what? They even have their own studio and CD/graphics manafacturing facilities. Mark Smith and Dianna Davis started P. Vampire in 90. They're quite, quite mad. A writer suggested they contact the owner of Russia's biggest rock mag, *NSK*. Together they hatched business plans and VBR moved into their own studio setup at the Railroad Engineers Institute in Russia. During the day they record wild bands, while at night they explode onstage. They play vast underground clubs (literally, two floors below street level), or big discos, even an 8,000 strong Asian festival in Siberia. They do this for a few weeks, head home to America and a year later do the same thing, and so it goes on, with them releasing the best bits, and the best Russian bands. A totally individual approach. Box 3662 Santa Rose, CA 95402-3662. (Fax: 707-528-8694) (e-mail: venture@sonic.net)

V.K. RECORDS 1545 Selma Drive, W. Hollywood, CA 90046.

WE NEVER SLEEP Label, plus distributor for music and literature of all sorts. PO Box 92, Denver, CO 80201.

Magic(k)

ABYSS Magick supplies. PO Box 1022, Easthampton, MA 01027.

ACHERON Satanic Metal band who deliberately, playfully, enrage Christians wherever they go. Their biggest sin, however, is to willingly cover Pink Floyd. Verily, this is Hell on Earth. "The Satanic Millennium approaches!" they snicker triumphantly. "Acheron will unleash their diabolical creations to hasten the climax of Armageddon! The world is ours for the taking - seize it and drain its life blood to the very dregs! Hail Satan!" I predict they'll all end up with Alzheimers thirty years hence, sitting on a piss-stained porch nodding along to a Bing Crosby compilation. PO Box 272929, Tampa, FL 33688.

THE AMERICAN COLLEGE OF ORGONOMY PO Box 490, Princeton, NJ 08542.

DARK REFLECTIONS Bi-monthly fanzine for the

intellectual Satanist. Jeffrey Deboo, 1442-A Walnut Street #64, Berkeley, CA 94709.

DASO Magick supplies. PO Box 123, Pomfret, Connecticut, 60258

KAOS MAGIC The Covenant Of The Ancient Ones. 1800 21st Street, #202, Sacramento, CA 85814-6812.

KHEPERU EM INU Temple of the Dark Goddess of Manifestations. Box 13025, Chicago, IL 60613.

MAGICKAL CHILDE Occult catalogue. 35 West 19th St, New York, NY 10011.

MANSABATH Ceremonial Magick. Box 13431, Reading, PA 19612.

MOON Magazine. 110278 Village Rd, Chaska, MN 55318.

MOONDOG MOUNTAIN PUBLISHING "Esoteric" titles. Box 337, Shermans Dale, PA 17090.

OCCULT EMPORIUM 102 North 9th Street, Alientown, Pennsylvania 18103.

ORDER OF THE EVIL EYE Satanist zine. Wolf Age PO Box 272929, Tampa, FL 33688.

ORGONE BIOPHYSICAL RESEARCH LABORATORY James deMeo PH.d., PO Box 1395, El Cerrito, CA 94530.
SERPENTINE Satanic mag. PO Box 512, Westwood, New Jersey, 87675.

VOODOO SPIRITUAL TEMPLE 716 North Rampart St., New Orleans, LA 70116

WILHELM REICH MUSEUM For Orgonomy fans everywhere. PO Box 687, Rangeley, Maine, 04970.

Outlets

ANCIENT FUTURES "Macabre Decor" just doesn't quite sum up what this fantastic organisation has to offer. As well as offering work on a band's image, in terms of coverage and presentation, this firm have the intention of popularising certain aspects of Horror and Fantasy Art they felt were sorely neglected or old-fashioned, making available the sort of stuff you only generally see in films. You get sculptures, like the 'Mistress Of The Sacred Text' bookends, crucified witches on trees (well, each to their own), Vamparonique merchandising, newsletters, business cards, stationery. The sculptures are the best. Skulls and candleholders are good enough, but the skulls are amazing, the Vampire's head and the gargoyles all wonderful beyond compare. A lifesize Ram's Horn Skull for $40? That's not expensive. The Undead Warrior and Werewolf Skulls would look nice on any wall. PO Box 84, Shoreham, NY 11786. (e-mail: slimaf@aol.com)
(Net: http://home.aol.com/afworld)

ARCHAIC MANUSCRIPTS Specialises in designing macabre stationary, cards, postcards, writing materials and gifts, mail order or stocked through retail stores. Ghost-shaped notepad, fuzzy bat stickers, ridiculously good value. Beautiful boxed sets of notelettes, sealing wax sets, with handmade seal, the variety of designs available for your own letter-headed stationary is fantastic. Weird little wall plaques, old victorian style mirrors and rather horrific 18th century style bookends! The catalogue is essential. PO Box 13084, Torrance, California CA 90503.

ARMAGEDDON USED CDs Highly regarded Goth-ish store. This place holds the Glossolalia poet meetings of Heather Spear and friends. 711 W. Belmont, Chicago, IL 60657.

BDG MAIL ORDER Excellent variety of musical stuff,

215 HELLBOUND/NOIR LEATHER - MS MALONE AND THE KIDD (PHOTO: BRETT CARSON)

including a wide variety of good quality "live rarities". PO Box 16184, Newport Beach, CA 92659-6184.

CABAL ASYLUM Little horror mag, beautifully done, tied with wax chord from which is suspended a tiny skull! PO Box 868, Greenbelt, MD 20768

CATALOGUE OF CARNAGE Featuring the amazing creations of Brian Demski and others. 327 W. Laguna Drive, Tempe, AZ 85282.

COENOBIUM Clive Barker zine. 455 Crescent Ave #7, Sunnyvale, CA 94087.

COFFINS The genuine article. Interior colours available - blood red, virgin white, basic black - from your original Olde English Pauper Coffin ($249), the classic metal coffin ($495) draped coffin ($675) and the Gothic Cloth 'Covered' Coffin ($395). Death Inc, 3315 Sacramento Street, #226, San Francisco, CA 94118.

DARK DELICACIES "If Hell had a gift shop..." 3725 W. Magnolia Blvd., Burbank, CA 91505.

THE DARK HOUR "Black/Death Metal" tv show. Boundaries might blur enough for you to get on? Been running nearly three years. Paul Bragelman, 7357 France Ave N., Brooklyn Park, MN 55443.

THE DARK SIDE OF THE WEB http://ted.ele.madison.tec.wi.us/dead.html

DEAD AND BURIED Mail order firm popularising magazines, music and anything you are involved with. PO Box 420441, San Francisco, CA 94142.

DRAKE ENTERPRISES Great junk aplenty. Everything from motorized monsters to gargoyles, skeletons, smoke and fog machines. PO Box 122 Middlesex, NJ 08846-0122.

DREAM SCENE MAGAZINE A mag about "nocturnal brain emissions" which kind of robs it of all magic! 38 Rossi Ave, Suite #1, San Francisco, CA 94118-4218.

EMPIRE OF THE DAMNED Bats wings, skulls, ribs, teeth, books etc. PO Box 20360, New York, NY 1009.

EPITAPES Shop/service offering odd music like tapes of music played on human bones. Box 458, Sunderland, MA 01375.

THE EVIDENCE FOR SPIRIT PHOTOGRAPHY This is a weird videotaped lecture about spirit photography from 1991. PO Box 205, Oak Lawn, IL 60454-0205.

F & F CO. Spiritual church supply. Oils, waters, candles, talismans, incense, roots, herbs, sprays, statues, they have it all. 801 N. Broad Ave, New Orleans, LA 70119.

THE FANG Horror videos. PO Box 1012, Floral Park, NY 11002.

FUNERAL A magazine-cum-catalogue ($5), which includes vintage erotica, bondage, early porn and grindhouse strippers (que?), as well as music, jewellery, occult supplies, videos. PO 3094, Hollywood, CA 90078.

GALLERY NOCTURNE 7661 1/2 Melrose Ave, Hollywood, CA 90046.

GARGOYLES Gargoyles, of course. 4550 University Way NE, Seattle, WA 98105.

GAUNTLET Piercings. 8720 Santa Monica Boulevard, LA, CA 90046.

HR GIGER/MORPHEUS INT'NTL PO Box 7246, Beverley Hills, CA 90212-7426

GOTHIC Fashion and gargoyles! 245 8th Ave Ste 395, New York, NY 10011.

GOTHIC TALES http://www.cascade.net/gothic.html

HALLOWEEN RECIPES http://www2.islandnet.com/-bedford/h-food.html

HIGHAM'S HOUSE OF HORRORS Necromantic sculptures, jewellery. PO Box 180-204, Brooklyn, New York, NY 11218.

KFR USA Radio show. PO Box 23952, San Jose CA 95153.

LAST GASP Catalogue of everything. 2180 Bryant Street, San Francisco, CA 94110.

LONELY WHISTLE Cassette label. PO Box 23952, San Jose, CA 95153.

MASTER/SLAVE RELATIONSHIP Weirdness. PO Box 191211, San Francisco, CA 94119-1211.

MASQUERADE BOOKS 801 2nd Av New York, NY 10017.

MEDIEVAL MINIS Gothic/gargoyle j decor. 3722 Greatiot Avenue, Flint

MIDDLE PILLAR Musical esoterica. "Dark, experimental, electronic, ambient". PO Box 555, NY, NY 10009. (e-mail: mpillar@panix.com)

MIND BURGER Surreal fiction. PO Box 2099, Decatur, GA 30031-2099.

MONSTERS IN MOTION Amazing models of horror and fantasy related figures as well as masks and movie props for sale. 330 E. Orangethorpe Ave. Unit H, Placentia, CA 92670.

MOON MYSTIQUE An incredible catalogue of recommended fanzines, books covering everything from anarchism to crime, crystals, graphology, all New Age stuff, every kind of Magic imaginable, ancient religions, Tarot, UFOs, Vampires etc. Plus music, badges, t-shirts. 114 1/2 E. College St, Iowa City, IA 52240-4005. (Fax: 319-337-6761)

MUSIC DIVISION 21 Club Rd, Fairfield, New Jersey 07004.

MYSTIC CURIO Leathers, readings, custom jewellery and mystic supplies. 833 Royal St, New Orleans, LA 70116.

NARCISSUS PRESS Box Office 5554, Atlanta, GA 31107.

NATIONAL SELECTED MORTICIANS This is where you write for that career in the funeral business! 5 Revere Drive, Suite 340, Northbrook, IL 60062-8009.

NEVERMORE PRODUCTIONS Gig promotions set up by the band Falling Janus for the bands who want to play New Orleans, as I'd have thought every Goth band would. They even provide somewhere for you to stay. PO Box 55371 Metairie, LA 70055. (Fax (504) 895 4293) (e-mail: cyk01@www.gnofn.org)

NEW ORLEANS HISTORIC VOODOO MUSEUM Charles M. Gandolfo, curator and strangely named man, 724 Dumaine, New Orleans, LA 70116.

NIGHT'S CHILDREN PO Box 5010 Suite #5 P, Salem, MA 01970.

NO PIGEONHOLES Radio Show on KKUP 91.5 FM. PO Box 23952, San Jose, CA 95153.

NOTRE SAGESSE INFORMATION Tatiana De Profundis, PO Box 824, Middlebury, CT 06762.

OLIVER'S RECORDS Music and mags. 107 Marshall St, Syracuse, NY 13210.

PRIESTESS Cindy Sudano, artist. Prints and cards for sale. PO Box 65, Massapequa, NY 11758.

PSYCHIC PATHWAYS INC Metaphysical newsletters. PO Box 48, Woodmere, NY 11598.

PSYCHOTRONIC VIDEO Weird videos. 151 First Avenue, Dept PV, NY, NY10003.

JOHN WILLIAM PYE Rare Egyptian book specialist. 79 Hollis Street, Brockton, Mass 02402

RARE VIDEOS Bela Lugosi and Ed Wood. Rees, 21334 Park Mount, Katy, TX 77450.

REBEL STUDIOS Independent comics publisher, with a wide range but many already incorporating strong Gothic characters and themes. I believe they have even printed a "Gothic Nights" series. 4716 Judy Court, Sacramento, CA 95841.

THE RECORD COLLECTION 568 Stewart Ave, Bethpage, NY 11714.

REPRESSION RECORDS Record shop with list of 200 zines. 2 IRCs. 22 Dorchester Ave, Geneva, NY 14456-2315.

RHINO VIDEO "Totally bizarre video." 2225 Colorado Avenue, Santa Monica, CA 90404.

ROSE OF BLOOD Gothic illustrations as prints and cards by Rhiannon Cotter and P. Morgan Ravenstone. 3220 N. Arnoult #157, Metairie, LA 70002.

SANCTUARY MUSIC SALES Gothic video and books. PO Box 995, Southbury, Connecticut 06488.

SCAREAPHANALIA PO Box 489, Murray Hill Station, New York, NY 10156-0489.

SCREEM JAMS Dark Theatre merchandising and more. Bat ankhs to t-shirts (designed by Chad Savage and Phill White), posters, bandanas, stickers. PO Box 138300, Chicago, Il 60613.

SEE HEAR Tons of underground publications. 59 East 7th Street, New York, NY 10003.

SANDRA SING Designer. Studio Ze, 312-E 9th St, New York, NY 10003.

SHADOWFOX PRODUCTIONS Create the "Voices In The Shadows" series. Michelle Belanger, PO Box 474, Hinckley, OH 44233.

SINISTER CINEMA Video catalogue. PO Box 4369, Medford, OR 97501-0168.

SOLANO BOTANICA Flowers, plants, oils, perfumes, roots herbs, floor wash (?) etc. 1626 Elysian Fields Ave, New Orleans, LA 70117.

SPELLBOUND Books, crystals, incense, tarot. 480 Washington Ave, Belleville, NJ 07109 and 1586 Irving St, Rahway, NJ 07065.

TAPES OF TERROR Classic horror and kitsch. P Riggs, 6226 Darnell, Houston, TX 77074-7416.

TARA GRAPHIX Sinister t-shirts. 5311 Woodlawn Drive, Harrisburg, PA 17109.

TERMINAL FRIGHT Horror/supernatural fiction zine. PO Box 100 Black River, NY 1361-0100.

THEE EXPERIENCE "Tres bizarre objet d'fashion." 4539 University Way NE, Seattle, WA 98105.

TIME TUNNEL Horror books and zine shop. 13 Beechwood Ave, Middlesex, NJ 08846.

THE ULTIMATE BAND LIST http://american.recordings.com/wwwofmusic/ubl/ubl.shtml

UNDERWORLD STUDIO T-shirts, limited edition prints. 107 Howard Street, Pittsfield, MA 01201.

VICTORIAN PAPERS Replica stationery but also toiletries, jewellery and books. 103 West 19th St, Kansas City, MO 64108.

VINYL FETISH Music shop. 7305 Melrose Avenue, LA, CA 90046. (Fax: 213-935-9896)

VINYL SOLUTION Music. 18822 Beach Blvd., Suite 103, Huntingdon Beach, CA 92648

WANDERING DRAGON TRADING POST No Zip code, so no mail order, as I saw this in *Morbid Outlook* zine. Apparently it's full of human bones, morbid Victoriana, ancient clothes and stuffed animals. Sounds like the House Of Lords. 263 E 10th Street, New York.

WE NEVER SLEEP Mail order music, video and literature. PO Box 92, Denver, CO 80201.

WBEN-NECROPHILIAC RELATIONSHIP Radio show. Jason Ledyard, Bennington College, Bennington, VT 05201.

WESTGATE Ostensibly a gallery of Necromantic Art and Literature, this was created by Leilah Wendell, who has spent her life involved with studies and teaching about certain grey areas. A member of the Authors' Guild, she has over 300 published works and is also a publisher and artist herself. The gallery is a museum really, but also has fine art prints, books, posters, cards, sculptures and artefacts for sale. 5219 Magazine Street, New Orleans, LA 70115

THE WILD PLACES 621a Hanover Street, Santa Cruz, CA 95062. (Fax: 408.427.0643)

WILD PLANET Music and publications. 576 East Main Street, Ventura, CA 93001.

WILOCH, THOMAS Poet. 43672 Emrick Drive, Canton, MI 48187.

XKULL Death site. (http://www.interport,net/-spidr/) Or Spider, Box 1798 Canal Street, New York, NY10013.

216 PHOTO: J. LYNN KOSTER

Pagan

CIRCLE NETWORK NEWS Pagan and Craft newspaper. PO Box 219, Mount Horeb, WI 53572.

LANNY CORNETT Produces a Calendar Of Events, which lists gatherings and workshops from across America. 9527 Blake Lane, Apt 102, Fairfax, VA 22031.

EARTH SPIRIT COMMUNITY Organisers of Rites Of Spring festival. PO Box 365, Medford, MA 02155.

MICHAEL HORN Wiccan expert and Witch. PO Box 4538, Sunnyside, New York 11104-4538.

PAGANS IN RECOVERY NEWSLETTER PO Box 22, Palmer Street, Athens, OH 45701.

PAGAN PARENTS NETWORK Nan Kates, PO Box 834, New York, NY 10185.

THE WICCAN/PRESS ALLIANCE PO Box 1382, Mechanicsburg, PA 17055.

WICCA/PAGANISM
http://www.cascade.net/arachne.html

Pagan publications

THE ALEXANDRIAN PO Box 6114, Grand Rapids, MI 49516

CRUCIBLE PO Box 951, Stevens Point, WI 54481-0951.

THE CRYSTAL MOON PO Box 802, Mateson, IL 60443.

DREAMWEAVER PO Box 150692, Ft. Worth, TX 76108.

EIDOLON PO Box 4117, Ann Arbor, MI 48106.

ENCHANTE Pagan/Wiccan/Mythic magazine. 30 Charlton St (Box 6F), New York, NY 10014-4925.

FIREHEART The only 'slick' Wiccan journal. PO Box 462, Maynard, MA 01754.

FOOL'S JOURNEY Patricia Croteau, 1041 Page St., San Francisco, CA 94117

GNOSIS PO Box 14217, San Francisco, CA 9414-0211.

GREEN EGG PO Box 1452, Ukiah, CA 95482-1542.

HIDDEN STARS Mag devoted to Pagan prisoners. PO Box 1510, Ellicott City, MD 21041.

HOLE IN THE STONE 2049 S. Federal #286, Denver, CO 80219.

MERRYMOUNT MESSENGER Box 458, 1016 El Camino Real, Sunnyvale, CA 94087.

THE MIDNIGHT DRIVE PO Box 1392, Mecanicsburg, PA 17055.

MINNESOTA CHURCH OF WICCA Church newsletter. PO Box 58854, Minneapolis, MN 55408.

MOONWEB Mailings of synchronous rituals designed for solitary witches, pagans and groups. Circle Cithaeron, PO Box 15461, Washington, DC 20002.

NEWS FROM MOTHER GROVE PO Box 1483, Highland Park, NJ 08904.

NOTES FROM TAYCHO-PERA Neo-Pagan network. PO Box 8212, Madison, WI 537087.

OF A LIKE MIND SOURCE BOOK Directory of special interest to women. PO Box 6021, Madison, WI 53716.

OPEN WAYS Newsletter of the Nine Houses of Gaia. PO Box 66932, Portland , OR 97290.

PAN AMERICAN INDIAN ASSOCIATION NEWS Indian tabloid newspaper, penpals and spiritual philosophy. PO Box 58, Montezuma, New Mexico 87731.

PANEGYRIA PO Box 57, Index, WA 98256.

PHILANOR NEWS PO Box 53505, Philadelphia, PA 19107.

QUINTESSENCE PO Box 10634, Winston-Salem, NC 27108.

RED GARTERS PO Box 162046, Sacramento, CA 95816.

SACRED HEART PO Box 72, Kenmore, NY 14217-0072.

SHADOWPLAY PO Box 95657, Seattle, WA 98145.

SOLITARY PATH 609 S. Denver, Russelville, AR 72801.

TALKING LEAVES A newspaper which includes information on "the magic and spirit behind non-violent environmental activism"! 1430 Willamette, #367, Eugene, OR 97401.

TALKING RAVEN PO Box 45758, Seattle, WA 98145.

TIDES PO Box 1445, Littleton, MA 02130-9998.

THE WICCAN/PRESS ALLIANCE PO Box 1382, Mechanicsburg, PA 17055.

218

AGRIPPA

Pagan individuals

MELINDA ALLEN & ADRIAN McKEE Fiber arts, magickal tools, stained glass scrying mirrors. Visions, 349 West Felicita Avenue, #197, Escondido, CA 92025.

A.L.M. Illustration, jainting, jewellery, sculptures. PO Box 300116, Escondido, CA 92030-0116.

TODD ALAN Jewellery. PO Box 32, Peninsula, OH 44264.

AMALTHEA Art, mask-making. 7100 East Mississippi, 1-208, Denver, CO 80224.

AMATERASU-OMI Magickal tools. PO Box 060192, Palm Bay, FL 32906-0192.

ARACHNE Jewellery, magickal tools, sculptures. Route 1, Box 102A, Clear Lake, WI 54005.

ARILYAS UNLIMITED Magickal tools. 606 Thornton Court, North Wales, PA 19454.

DAVID ARONSON Art. 3330 Dogwood Drive, Willow Grove, PA 19090.

ARTHA Art, woodburning. PO Box 4414, Rockford, IL 61110-0914.

DEIRDRE & ANDRAS ARTHEN Dance, ritual craft, storytelling. PO Box 502, Medford, MA 02155.

ATHENE AWAKENINGS Art, stained glass. PO Box 25713, Baltimore, MC 21224.

KARIN CLARK Beaded headdresses. PO Box 07437, Milwaukee, WI 53207.

CROW & BEKKI Tattoos, horsefeathers! 22 Palmer Street, Athens, OH 45701.

FINNEGAN Art, magickal tools, leather craft. PO Box 3304, Kansas City, KS 66103.

WAHABA HEARTSUN Scrimshaw. PO Box 1084, Cottage Grove, OR 97424.

JOHN HEINZ Luthier, harpmaker, toolmaker, custom instruments. 5 South Hunter Street, Joliet, IL 60436.

KATHY JACOBSON Candlemaker. 8987 Lavelle Rd, Athens, OH 45701.

ELYNN JENKINS Magickal tools. 204 North Cottage Rd, Sterling, VA 22170.

KAMITA Art, magickal tools. PO Box 8170, Salem, MA 01971.

DEBORAH LEE Art, jewellery, magickal tools. PO Box 4985, Culver City, CA 90230.

JON PAGE Fantasy art, custom photography. 1400 Colorado, Kansas City, MO 64127-2405.

PASHA Jewellery. 537 Jones Street #165, San Francisco, CA 94102-2007.

DINA L. PAXSON Art, ritual craft. 90 El Camino Real, Berkeley, CA 94705.

LISA PESCHEL Author, art, medieval calligraphy. 5445 Babcock Trail #205, Inver Grove Heights, MN 55077.

DONALD RICARDO Jnr. Art, magickal tools. 3244 Appalkchee Church Rd, Auburn, GA 30203.

ELLIE SCHUSTER Art, jewellery. 15 Yorktown Rd,

219

219 HEATHER SPEAR 220 ALTHEA MORIN

Wayne, NJ 07470.

CLARISSA SHARP Art, sculpture. Scorpio Studios, 1149 NW 56th Street, Oklahoma City, OK 73118.

SILVER RAVENWOLF Author, Beadwork, Ceramics. PO Box 1392, Mechanicsburg, PA 17055.

AEONA SILVERSONG Jewellery. PO Box 337, Redwood Valley, CA 95470.

RUSS STANDING-EAGLE Drum-making. PO Box 208, Jamesport, NY 11947-0208.

CINDY M. SUDANO Art, wooden chests burned with 'magickal' designs. PO Box 65, Massapequa, NY 11758.

CARRIE WESTFALL Art, magickal tools, rune sets. 716 North Sheridan Avenue, Second Floor Left, Pittsburgh, PA 15206-2521.

NIGHTWING WHITEHEAD Jewellery. 34 Parkview Place, Staten Island, NY 10310.

Societies

ASSOCIATION OF GRAVEYARD STUDIES Dedicated to preservation of cemeteries and aiding the research of others. 30 Elm Street, Worcester, MA 01609.

BIZARRE Zine covering oddities, be it shops or galleries, writers, artists. PO Box 40371, Phoenix, AZ 85067-0371.

THE CHAMBRE SOCIETY Musical gatherings. Poetry and melancholia guaranteed. Box 30008, Lafayette, LA 70593.

DEAD WHITE COMMUNION PRODUCTIONS Shawn Terry, 16419 Ledge Trail, San Antonio, TX 78232.

FANS AND ASSOCIATES OF NOCTURNAL GHOULS SOCIETY(FANGS) A group of friends and fiends who enjoy the reading of gothic writing. Events include a monthly "Black Tea" for the reading of their work, plus performance and art, the quaintly named "Gothic Literary Tea Series", with lectures and slide shows, historic graveyard tours and their own zine, *The Sconce*, which actively encourages reader participation. "Why have Spring, when you can carry Winter around with you?" they ask, to which I have no answer. Jo Canning, 42 South 14th Street, San Jose, CA 995112.

GHOST TRACKERS NEWSLETTER Official newsletter of the Ghost Research Society. PO Box 205RV, Oak Lawn, IL 60454-0205.

THE GOTHIC SMALL PRESS ALLIANCE National network of editors, writers and distributors of Gothic material. 3023 N. Clark, Suite 777, Chicago 60657.

GLOSSOLALIA Society which holds weekly meetings to celebrate the poetic and literary arts, run by Heather Spear who used to do *The Web* magazine. They have their own *Gibberish* newsletter, did the 'Convergence' festival and there's a pro-active erotic poetry group who go and read to people outdoors, called The Unbearables. Now, read this and weep. At the 'Convergence' festival they had a few bands playing. Lycia, Mephisto Waltz, Arcanta, Machine In The Garden, Trance To The Sun, The Wake, Sunshine Blind, Lestat, Seraphim Gothique (who?) and Garden Of Dreams. Not that we wish we were there or anything. If you live in the area, have a brain and don't join up it's all a contradiction in terms. Parlor House Productions, 3023 N. Clark, Suite 777, Chicago, Illinois 60657.

HEMLOCK SOCIETY Organisation aiming to help

220

PHOTO: MICHELLE TAYLOR

dying people snuff it with dignity. Box 11830, Eugene, OR 97440.

HORROR FANCLUB PO Box 30443, Cleveland, Ohio 44130.

LOS ANGELES UNDEAD POETS SOCIETY PO Box 3092, Burbank, CA 91508-3092.

MISS LUCY WESTERNA SOCIETY OF THE UNDEAD 11141 Tanglewood Drive, Auburn, CA 95603.

PHANTOM COACHES A society for people who like to drive hearses. It does car shows, movie premieres, picnics etc. They have meetings in cemeteries and "anywhere we can go with twenty hearses and not get kicked out". Cecelia Smith - 'Crypt Keeper', 41050 Via Zedro, Muriette, CA 92562.

THE TEMPLE OF LILITH This is run, ostensibly, by Althea Morin, the producer of *Tongue Of The Serpent* zine, and comprises a network of people who regard themselves as outsiders. Membership does not require any specific belief and they are not affiliated with any other group. "Remember," she reminds, "there are no rules. Trust is what you believe. Magick is what works for you. We welcome all ideas for spells, rituals, mantras etc. The most important tenet is state of mind. The force of Will must be part of every Act in life. There is power latent within us and the world. use it." I've just had a thought. What if your name actually was Will? It would make things quite awkward in some societies. You might be forever going "Yes?" at inopportune moments. Eventually you'd get ratty, barking, "You talking to me?" A fracas would ensue. There'd be all sorts of problems. Box 1483, New York, NY 10009-1483.

WOLF HAVEN INTERNATIONAL Animal Rights. 3111 Offut Lake Rd, Tenino, WA 98589.

Vampire

ALLYSON The vampire mate of The Cold. A poet and aspiring writer/gothic novelist. Has worked with The Cold on musical poetry MC 'Pale'. PO Box 1245, Gardner, MA 01440.

BAT CONSERVATION INTERNATIONAL PO Box 162603, Austin, TX 78716-2603.

ELAINE BERGSTROM Vamp novelist, whose previous activities include editing, teaching, advertising writing, business and crime reporting, private criminal defence investigation and teaching. Her novels to date: *Shattered Glass* (89), *Blood Alone* (90), *Blood Rites* (91) *Daughter Of The Night* (92), *Tapestry Of Dark Souls* (93) *Mina* - under the pseudonym Marie Kiraly (94), *Baroness Of Blood* (95). As Marie Kiraly she has also written *The Rose Wallpaper* (95). Once revered, now adored. 2918 S. Wentworth, Milwaukee, WI 53207.

BLOODREAMS Kelly Gunter Atlas, 1312 West 43rd Street, Little Rock, AZ 72118.

BLOODLUST A cassette by Out Of Band Experience with samples of real vampires and authoress C. Page. Box 221, Boston, MA 02123.

BLOOD AND ROSES Fanzine. 336 Otter River Road, Templeton, MA 01468.

BLOOD AND TEARS Vamp zine. PO Box 448, Hoschton, GA 30548.

BOOTSTRAP COMPANY Weird vampirish publishers who will put your name and the names of your friends into their stories, via a stencil format, and send you bound copies! Unusual but nice idea. Cost per story is $10 or 3 for $25! PO Box 184, Manasquan, NJ 08736-0184.

221

THE CAMARILLA Claims to be a "unique vampire organisation" and could well be right. Preferring active member involvement rather than simply providing newsletters and journals, they focus on the vampire as a romantic and tragic figure; not delving into the violent aspects of the character. They run their own group of White Wolf's 'story-telling game', Vampire, The Masquerade. Here you create a persona to join one of the available clans that make up the fictional social structure. There are seven clans in the Camarilla itself and three clans outside of it.

The Seven: Brujah - Commonly rebels and punks similar to The Lost Boys, with a smaller group being intellectual individuals at odds with the society. Gangrel - Solitary, rustic characters able to transform into animal shape. Malkavian - Regarded by others as insane but possessing unique wisdom. Nosferatu - hideous in appearance, they live apart from the others but hold secrets of many of the preternatural inhabitants of the city. Toreador - Artists. Proud, regal, over-excitable and immaculately dressed. Tremere - Tightly-knit, secretive warlocks. Ventrue - The leaders, possibly, with noble aspects and proud of it, considering themselves a cut above the rest.

The Three: Assamites - Middle Eastern mercenaries of The Kindred. Giovanni - members of a single Italian family, practising necromancy. Ravnos - Gypsy clan, masters of illusion and chicanery. So there's your choice, although werewolves, mummies, gargoyles, cat people, Asian vampires and such can be selected. When you join you'll get all the necessary sourcebook, rules, scenarios and details of how to play by mail, etc. To prove you're paying attention there are also tests via correspondence for those who take on organising small groups, which is basically how it's done. Membership is pretty cheap at $18 within the USA and $40 (Airmail) outside.

(Subscribe to: listserve@oracle.wizards.com) 50 South Main Street #25, Suite 8, Salt Lake City, Utah 84144. (Net: camstuff@regency.wizards.com)

CASTLE DRACULA QUARTERLY Box 423, Glastonbury, CT 06033.

CHEEKY DEVIL VAMPIRE RESEARCH PO Box 7633, Abilene, TX 79608-7633.

CIRCLET PRESS Publisher, with some Vamp Erotica and 'Feline Fetishes', "for those who miaow and claw in bed". PO Box 15143, Boston, MA 02215.

COMMUNION Vamp fan pen-pal network. Lament, 628 Woodlawn Rd, Steens, MS 39766.

COUNT DRACULA FAN CLUB Dracula Unlimited Vampire Bookshop at same address. 29 Washington Square West. Penthouse North, NY 10011.

COUNT DRACULA SOCIETY 334 West 54th St, Los Angeles, CA 90037.

COUNT KEN FAN CLUB Ken Gilbert, 18 Palmer Street, Salem, MA 01970.

DAMIANIA Researching vampire stuff. PO Box 448, Houston, CA 30548-0448.

THE DEAD OF SOCIETY For $15 make your own fangs with customising kit! Takes about an hour, apparently. R. Hood, PO Box 8454, Norfolk, VA 23503-0454.

DEAD PENPAL ZINE Contacts in the vampire world. Rt. 13, Box 802, Lake City, FL 32055.

THE DEAD RECORDS FILE Vamp journal. Fact, fiction and art. PO Box 7633, Abilene, Texas 79608-1567.

DoS SUPERNATURALS The Dead of Society, PO Box 8454, Norfolk, Virginia, VA 23503-0454.

DRACULA MUSEUM One Fifth Avenue, New York, NY 10003.

DRACULA MUSEUM ANNEX Penthouse North, 29 Washington Square West, New York, NY 10011.

DRACULINA PO Box 969, Centralia, Il 62801.

DYNAMITE FAN CLUB PO Box 30443, Cleveland, OH 44130.

EUROPIUM Vamp zine with penpal element. PO Box 674, Goshen, NY 10924-0674.

THE FANG GANG PO Box 273895, Tampa, Florida 33688-3895.

FTWS Vampire greeting cards "for all occasions", I kid you not. Also postcards, custom made or their own design. PO Box 3087, Astoria, NY 11103.

FULL MOON PUBLICATIONS PO Box 517, Metairie, LA 70004.

IMMORTAL WINE Vampire fiction. 100 pages! Julie Ghoul, 2926 W. Leland Avenue, Chicago, IL 60625-3716.

INTERNATIONAL SOCIETY OF VAMPIRES PO Box 474, Hinckley, OH 44233.

JOURNAL OF THE DARK Quarterly Vampzine. PO Box 168, Osceola, IN 46561.

JOURNAL OF VAMPIROLOGY Specialises in Vampirism and Hemophilism. PO Box 881631, San Francisco, CA 94188.

DARRON KILSUNN Psychic vampire and composer of odd music under the name of Noise End Rapture. Four tapes available. PO Box 1245, Gardner, MA 01440.

NEFARIOUS Zine. Rosey Lettich, 1804 Academy Street, Sumner, WA 98309.

NIGHTSONGS A collection of poetry by Tony Lestat. PO Box 786, Ft. Huachuca, AZ 85613.

NIGHTMIST PO Box 17006, Rochester, NY 14617-0306.

NOSFERATU SOCIETY PO Box No. 2, McKean, PA 16426.

NOX Zine - death/vamps/occult. PO Box 2467, Grand Central Station, New York, NY 10163-2467.

ON NIGHT'S WING Vamp/horror mag. PO Box 232-E, Kathleen, FL 33849-0232.

ONYX 8075 Sandleford NW, North Canton, OH 44720.

ORDER OF THE VAMPYRE Closed order of the Temple Of Set. Produces two newsletters for its members. PO Box 4507, St Louis, MO 63108.

PERFECT DARKNESS 530 South Flood, Norman, OK 73069.

PRETERNATURAL PRODUCTIONS Fascinating operation, responsible for the annual chapbook of Vampire poetry, *Rouge et Noir - les poems des vampyres*. Run by editor and publisher Meg Thompson, this has existed for six years and is backed up by poetry readings at clubs and Gothic book and record stores. Meg has also produced Vampire art shows at galleries and given teas to celebrate the birthday of Bram Stoker. Some of her own written vampire pieces have taken performance art into another realm by involving Los Angeles musicians in various roles in the performance. P.P. also produces chapbooks of certain Gothic poets. Obviously worth checking out. PO Box 786, Fort Hauachuca, AZ 85613 (bloodnight@aol.com)

PRISONER OF THE NIGHT PO Box 688, Yucca Valley,

222

223

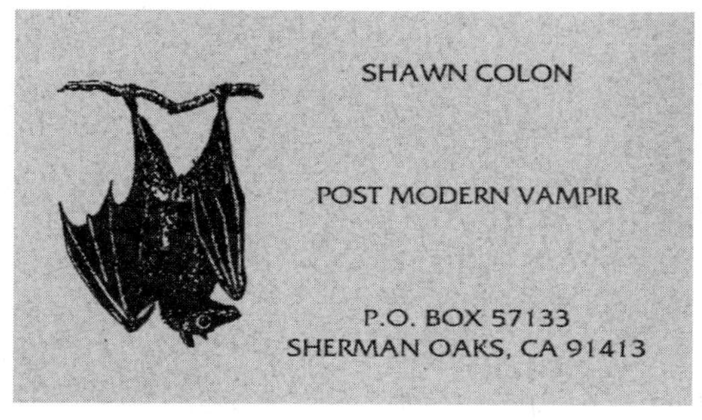

224

CA 92286-0688.

POST MODERN VAMPIR This is, according to creator Shawn Colon, "a raw new line of mature comic books and merchandise for all vampires. Known, unknown and aspiring. The books explores the idea of vampires as a futuristic race hunted and persecuted by mankind and their struggle to be recognised as an ethnicity." A bit X-Factor, then? No, a bit Mister X! PO Box 57133, Sherman Oaks, CA 91413.

ANNE RICE'S VAMPIRE LESTAT FAN CLUB PO Box 58277, New Orleans, LA 70158-8211.

REALM OF THE VAMPIRE "The legion of aficionados dedicated to the preservation of vampires." For $22 one year membership you get two 100 page journals, two large newsletters, extensive lists of vamp-related books and films and a classified catalogue. Also offer book and video search service, forums, meetings and writers group. Ann Hoyt, PO Box 517, Metairie, LA 0004-0517.

R.I.P. Ha! Those sacrilegious folks over at S.O.UND (always raved about by Kev Demant of *V.A.T.*) finally popped their creative clogs and shifted address, to start this - *Red Ink Pages*, "a device for artistic talent to flourish without politics". It's a Goth/Vampire/ Nocturnal magazine coming out quarterly. T.J. Teer, to be played one day - we all pray - by William Shatner - who is head honcho, is also the the Reverend at the head of a church, The Centre Of Triptolemus, but I couldn't quite fathom what he was on about. They also do a few other mags that they can best tell you about when you write but *Pandora's Box* is an in-depth look at female vampires, *The Blynde Eye* about Goddesses, but best of all, *The First Church Of Nick*, devoted to polar bears! 424 West Commonwealth #173, Fullerton, CA 92632.

RUMANIAN GUIDED 'DRAC' TOURS From St Michael's Emporium, although I didn't notice this in their catalogue. Maybe they've stopped? 156 East Second Street, Suite One, New York, NY 10009.

SABRETOOTH Todd Hoyt, 18 First Ave, Raritan, NJ 08869. Custom made fangs, unique contact lenses and other vampiric paraphernalia. (e-mail: vampyre@io.com)

THE SECRET LIFE Newsletter. PO Box 1612, Mt. Vernon, WA 98273.

ANEE STEPHENS Poet. 9 Audrey Rd, Latham, NY 12110

TAL PUBLICATIONS Vamp books. PO Box 1837, Leesburg, VA 22075.

TEMPLE OF THE VAMPIRE Vampire group seeking serious initiates only. I should point out that it may depend on where your preferences lie, as self-proclaimed Satanic band Acheron are involved, although not necessarily in the Society hierachy, as it were, but their CD will apparently revolve around Temple themes and teachings. Anyway, you pays your membership and you receive a copy of *The Vampire Bible*, "a brief tome with but few pages" which hardly sounds a good deal. It includes the following - "the secrets of Vampirism to draw Lifeforce from humans, why vampires never harm humans and are barred from criminal acts, various ancient Magickal rites, the details concerning the Master Plan of the Undead in the coming apocalypse" - which they winningly refer to as The Final Harvest! So that's $25, which shows you're keen. For $50 a piece you can purchase the Vampire Temple Ring or Vampire Ritual Medallion. Both are in mirror-polished sterling silver. The medallion unfortunately looks like something you'd see on your average hells angel but the ring is a real beauty. You buy these

225

222 PRETERNATURAL PRODUCTIONS 225 R.I.P.'S PANDORA

to declare your affiliation. The vampire Creed incidentally starts, "I am a Vampire. I worship my ego and I worship my life, for I am the only God that is", which is cool enough. The Temple itself, legally registered since December 88, has a worldwide membership and, I quote "exists to serve the Undead Gods who rule this earth". Now if each vampire regards himself or herself as the only God that *is*, you can't then serve other gods, as they would technically be Those Who Aren't. So the creed needs a bit of rejigging. PO Box 3582, Lacey, WA 98503.

TRANSFUSION Newsletter of Quincy P. Morris Dracula Society, PO Box 381, Ocean Gate, NJ 08740.

TRANSYLVANIAN SOCIETY OF DRACULA Organising the world's biggest Dracula Centennial Convention in LA, in August 97. They claim affordable digs and top notch entertainment and all British members of the Count Dracula Fan Club will have an opportunity to meet the President and founder, Dr Jeanne Youngson, which sounds just grand. PO Box 91611, Santa Barbara, CA 93190-1611.

VAMPEROTICA "The comic book you can sink your teeth into." Good grief. Brainstorm Comics, Route 3, Box 104, Hope Mills, NC 28348-9803.

VAMPIRE American Mensa group. Terry Cotrell, 5611 Mill Race Circle, Richmond, VA 23234.

VAMPIRE ARCHIVE/GHOUL'S GALLERY Vampire Archives is a "thing" issuing membership cards and four issues per years. *Ghoul's Gallery* is a catalogue of some very strange things indeed. Julie Ghoul, 2926 W. Leland Avenue, Chicago, IL 60625-3716.

VAMPIRES Small Press. PO Box 28324, Jacksonville, FL 32226-8324.

VAMPIRES ANONYMOUS Pagan/vampire/occult journal. PO Box 778, Sexton, PA 19341.

VAMPIRE'S CRYPT Zine - fiction, verse, reviews and interviews with vamp authors. Issues updated Vampire fiction listings. Margaret Carter, 105 Phipps Lane, Annapolis, MD 21403.

VAMPIRE INFORMATION EXCHANGE NETWORK (VIEN) Been going for fifteen years. Lists addresses of new members, reviews fiction, features photos from members and plenty of related adverts.
PO Box 328, Brooklyn, New York, NY 11229 0328.

VAMPIRE JOURNAL PO Box 994, Metairie, LA 70004.

THE VAMPIRE'S JOURNAL PO Box 5685, Stockton, CA 95205.

VAMPIRE JUNCTION Beautiful non-profit zine. 114 NW 13th St, Gainsville, FL 32601.

V.O.A. Vampire video zine! Patty Darrah, PO Box 771321, Wichita, KS 67277.

VAMPIRE QUARTERLY Susan M Garrett, 142 Sunvalley Drive, Toms River, NJ 08753.

VAMPIRE RESEARCH CENTER Academic scholars researching real vampires. PO Box 252, Elmhurst, NY 11373.

VAMPIRE RESEARCH INSTITUTE PO Box 21067, Seattle, WA 98111-3067.

VAMPIRE RESEARCHER Samantha Dixon, 2465 Noble Rd #24, Cleveland Hts., OH 44121

VAMPIRE STUDIES Martin Ricardo, the director of V.S., went public 77, editing *Journal Of Vampirism* for two years. He's had three books published, hosted various vamp forums around the Chicago area.
PO Box 151, Berwyn, Illinois, 60402.

VAMPIRES VAULT Ann M. Hart, Suite 3H, One Fifth Avenue, New York, NY 10003.

VAMPS PO Box 20167, Seattle, WA 98111.

WHITEWOLF GAME STUDIOS Publishers of 'Vampires Of The Masquerade' game. 4598B Stonegate Ind Blvd, Stone Mountain, GA 30083.

"Elvira has left the building..."

"Does that say 'Gothic Bible'?" enquired the despatch rider in a not unfriendly manner, as I signed for a late selection of post biked round from the publisher. It does, I admitted. "Ah, a book about 'Popular Culture'?" he asked, knowingly. "No," I corrected him. "Unpopular culture." My, how we laughed, until I set the dogs on him.

I like to think I had a point, which we'll get to in a minute. As I was digging through tons of old crap in the course of putting this book together I uncovered something I'd written in 94 to someone who was ruthlessly quizzing me about Goth for their thesis, or something similar. This happens fairly regularly and usually I prefer to do it face to face, to avoid confusion. This time it was postal, rather than personal, and I've kept a copy. The following bit actually makes sense.

''It is a scene'', I scribbled, ''and a type of music, which means most to the individual, regardless of how large 'it' becomes. It touches the heart and soothes the emotions, rather than stirring them. Goth sustains people! Goth cannot 'die', because it's an area where people can't quite say, 'it's a state of mind', when they can more accurately announce, 'it's a state of mine'.''

And you thought I was an idiot! The other thing which popped up - oh, the bit about the dogs wasn't true, by the way! - was a phrase from an explanation that Ataraxia sent me, which was presumably intentional - XX Century Music. More than anything it describes the whole thing. Goth is the Past, for obvious reasons, the Present (ditto) and The Future, as it involves a weird amalgam of ideas pulled together, yet always about to be developed into something else. XX Century Music. Perfect! Now, you only to have think what will be happening in two hundred years time. There will be still be a form of Goth relevant to then, because there will always be people involved in some kind of scene where the major influence is the Art, not the music, of the past. And when you use art as an influence you're always talking centuries, rather than decades. And if they are also influenced by horror imagery, they will, by then, be even more enthralled by the pre-60s material we have all seen than we were, because by their era those images will almost be similar to what we regard as Art and History. They will hardly get the same kick from our current cinema, which will surely seem like a cranky, amateur forerunner to what they will have become capable of. The earliest material will be of a totally different 'type'. Black and white horror will be like a dream to them.

So, the truth is out there, for those who look. Does this make our exclusive knowledge that much more special? Something to crow about? Technically, yes, if we're being childish. Most people are unaware of it because there is no media support. If there is another malignant burst of reappraisal it won't last more than a year or so, but it would be helpful because it could no longer be destructive as before. They can't put people off if they're not interested in the first place. All it could do, no matter how hopelessly adrift of the truth it may be, is to draw more in. For you, I hope, there is a mass of contacts here that you will wish to explore. That's the primary goal of the book. But don't trample all over people's feelings. (That's my job.) When you look at what there is to encounter and investigate remember one vital fact that some overlook. Always send IRCs, money or stamps. People aren't going to reply to you otherwise. I haven't listed prices because they're so liable to have changed by the time you get this. If there are catalogues guess at the price, send over the odds, and all but complete misers will doubtless issue a credit note. Do not take advantage of anybody, when you are now in the perfect position to take advantage of everything.

Despite recent years of rampant recidivism and revisionism, Goth somehow still retains its intrinsic sense of beauty and dignity, as well as prevarication, bitchiness and mania. That's as it should be. It's a contrary child. During our time we are going to see the merging of more technology and classical elements and the mating of guitars with thought and direct noise, of different nationalities producing their own distinct strains that will then go on to influence others. Nobody must ever adhere to what they, personally, have experienced as 'the past'. You can never live in a Golden Era. That is up to later generations to decide. If there is anyone reading this who still hankers after the days of The Mission, Sisters or The Nephilim, your determination to keep something dead alive is mad. Would you deliberately save food until three years after its sell-by date for an almighty feast? Do you want a penny-farthing bicycle, or yearn for medical operations without anaesthetic? No, of course not, so why hold on? If you have no wish to actively support Goth society stay indoors. You are barred. Here, we saved you a Meatloaf compilation, you'll enjoy that. Everyone else is looking for what is new, to enjoy it. To participate in it. I think it's called being alive.

I'll leave you with this, written by America's First Lady, the ultra-cool Chaz Matthews, during his tenure of *Machine Gun Etiquette* fanzine, which shows, as did The Cold in our Intro, how sensible, perceptive people, can be driven away by the grotesqueries of behaviour when a scene is working on faulty, facile instructions. When I've needed to buoy myself up, or instill defiance in others, I read this. Now you can.

"You're elitist, pretentious, corrupt, sleazy, money-grubbing, humourless pieces of dung. You worship the trappings of literature without being literary, you involve yourself in clique-ish elitism, and fascist prejudices, while claiming open-mindedness. You use catch-all phrases like 'support the Underground' while kissing ass for money to separate yourselves from the 'underground'. You use the most obvious, stupid, vampire imagery and call it 'gothic', ignoring the intelligence, mystery and genuine thrill of non-vampire horror and goth trappings. You dress only in fashions

approved by *Ghastly* and *Propaganda*, you smoke clove cigarettes, moan about your parents and have sex as cheap as you are. You have no real friends, only kiss-asses and coat-tail riders, people who want to be the elite, the guilty...like you. Aside from a few good bands, 90s Gothic Rock is a vast wasteland of talentless college bands, droning Sisters rip-offs and heavy metal re-runs trying to look bored and immortal. Rozz Williams has become a worthless 90's Goth shit rip-off of his own 80s genius. England's Goth scene is less healthy but much more relevant and real. Ethereal Goth is a shoe gazing bore for pothead college kids depressed over their allowance rate while the homeless die slowly outside. I love all things Goth but I hate *Ghastly* mag and anyone who is desperate enough for acceptance to actually follow their corporate Goth L.A. money-making example. There was a time when Goth and Punk were close cousins and were created for and by the outcast, the misfit. Now Goth is just a new way for the most popular rich kid in class to look down upon the have-nots. Just another MTV generation subculture fad like grunge. Pre-fab all the way. Don't get me wrong, I'll always skulk around in graveyards, I'll always read old ghost stories and love a good blast of camp horror or bloodletting but I'm leaving you with the image you stole from the Batcave scene, even though you're not smart enough to do it right and you certainly don't deserve it. I'll never go into a Goth club or read an Anne Rice novel again. There are much better kicks to be had in this horror house. I can't speak for everyone else here but I no longer consider myself a Goth or consider Goth rock in this day and age to be anything but a bad joke. Take me off your mailing lists, Goth dung of the world. I'm not a Goth, I'm not a punk, I'm not a trash rocker or an Alternite. I gotta be me. And you've got to be kidding, you bunch of junior Lestat sub-morons. I've had it."

Thank you, as Americans like to say, for sharing! Chaz obviously made the right choice under those circumstances but things have changed. If they haven't, in your own local scene, it's now time for you to change them. You can do it easily. Look down upon those who hold themselves aloof, as they once looked down on you. Make it quite clear just what a spineless set of wankers they really are. Situations like that need never happen again. Look to your future kids. It's all we've got.

This is your dead man walking, away. Goodnight everybody.

MICK MERCER (1957 - ?)

R·I·P